HENRY V
by
William Shakespeare

Produced and directed by
Laurence Olivier

Lorrimer Publishing

THE MAKING OF
HENRY V

by Laurence Olivier

It is now possible for a new generation of moviegoers, and
many of those who enjoyed the earlier version of HENRY
V, to set it in a new form. I hope very much that they will
enjoy the latest techniques now used in the projection of
what was, perhaps, the first serious attempt to make a truly
Shakespearian film.

Shakespeare, in a way, "wrote for the films." His
splitting up of the action into a multitude of small scenes is
almost an anticipation of film technique, and more than
one of his plays seems to chafe against the cramping
restrictions of the stage.

"Can this cockpit *(a reference to the shape of the Globe
Theatre)* hold the vasty fields of France?" asks the Chorus
in the Prologue. From the very beginning the play suggests
a film. The seed of it is there: "With winged heels, like
English Mercuries"; the rapid change of scene: "And
thence to France shall we convey you safe, and bring you
back."

There were, however, many difficult things to be done.
Firstly, there was the question of the script. In its long and
chequered career, the play has often been altered
alarmingly. In the Restoration period it was mutilated
almost out of recognition. Kemble cut the text to tatters,
and Fielding wrote scornfully: "Shakespeare is already
good enough for people of taste, but he must be altered to
the palates of those that have none." Remembering this,
we made only a few minute alterations in the text, and the

cuts are even less than those invariably made in a stage production.

The settings were a still greater problem. We decided that the treatment would have to be new, yet in keeping with the period. The middle part of the film especially must have the feeling of the fifteenth century, but we could only achieve this if the settings and composition of the shots caught the spirit of contemporary paintings.

Further unknown factors were the conditions of colour and lighting. Artists of Henry V's day drew attention to certain parts of their pictures by using strong colours and shapes. In translating this technique to the screen, a correct balance had to be struck between the colours and forms of the costumes and those of the background.

Our costume designer, Roger Furse, discovered the correct family arms and accoutrements for the knights and soldiers from an old book. He also designed 100 costumes for the thirty principals. The horses had to be correctly caparisoned, and this, too, called for expert knowledge. We made their saddles of wood on the pattern of Henry V's own saddle. By careful choice of fabrics, we kept the costumes as close as possible to fifteenth century originals, which were principally made of woollen cloth and heavy silk. Our colours had to correspond with the vegetable dyes of the Middles Ages, with due allowance for variations in colour photography.

We had to discover the rules as we went along. But rules alone could never have made Henry V live unless we had been lucky enough to assemble such a magnificent cast.

O for a muse of Fire, that would ascend
The brightest heaven of invention:
A kingdom for a stage, princes to act,
And monarchs to behold the swelling scene!

EDITOR'S NOTE

Although Laurence Olivier was faithful to Shakespeare's text on the whole, he cut whole subplots, such as the treason of Lord Scrope and the Earl of Cambridge and Sir Thomas Grey. He also abridged long-winded scenes, such as the Archbishop of Canterbury's exposition of King Henry V's right to the French throne. Occasionally, lines were transposed in their order in the scene, and also given to other players for the sake of 'character' – some of Canterbury's warlike lines, for instance, were given to the Duke of Exeter.

Generally, however, the screeplay is a model of how to adapt a classic stage play to the needs of the cinema. It was adapted by Olivier himself with Alan Dent.

THE CAST LIST AND THE CREDITS will be found at the end of the screenplay.

Acknowledgements

Lorrimer Publishing wishes to thank Cyril Howard of the Rank Organisation Plc for his kindness in making available the shooting script of *Henry V*, and the British Film Institute for its provision of the script and the photographic stills for this book, which was edited by Andrew Sinclair.

HENRY V
(1945)

We see an aerial view of London, based on Visscher's engraving of 1600. Track back to show the City in long shot, then track in on the Bear Playhouse and then on to the Globe Playhouse, where a flag is being hoisted.

The flag on the Globe Playhouse unfurls and flutters.

At the foot of the flagpole inside the Globe, a man on a small platform tightens the rope and makes it secure. He picks up a trumpet and blows two fanfares. Track down to show the theatre orchestra beginning to play in the gallery beneath. Pan left to show people filling the top gallery, then pan round and down to the second gallery. A girl drops a handkerchief out of shot.

In the third gallery down, a man catches the handkerchief. Pan left to the ground floor entrance where more people are coming in. An Orange Girl steps down into the theatre.

The Orange Girl walks into the theatre offering her wares. Pan with her and track slowly back to reveal an auditorium with the stage in the background. A Prompter gives a signal to the orchestra to play a fanfare.

A low angle shot in the orchestra gallery shows a man blowing his trumpet.

A Boy comes through the curtains on to the stage and holds a board up to the audience.

He swings the board to show the writing on it:

The Chronicle History of
HENRY THE FIFTH
with his battle fought at Agin Court.

Seen from the top gallery with the audience in the foreground, the Boy on the stage swings the board and exits through the curtains. Chorus enters and bows while the audience applauds.

CHORUS: O for a muse of fire . . .

Cut to him as the voices die. He walks around the stage as he speaks. Pan with him.

CHORUS: . . . . That would ascend
The brightest heaven of invention:
A kingdom for a stage, princes to act,
And monarchs to behold the swelling scene.
Then should the warlike Harry, like himself,
Assume the port of Mars, and at his heels,
Leashed in like hounds, should famine, sword, and fire,
Crouch for employment. But pardon, gentles all,
The flat unraisèd spirits that hath dared
On this unworthy scaffold to bring forth
So great an object. Can this cockpit hold
The vasty fields of France? Or may we cram
Within this wooden O the very casques
That did affright the air at Agincourt?

He walks to speak to us in close-up.

CHORUS: On your imaginary forces work.

Track back as music begins to play.

CHORUS: Suppose within the girdle of these walls
Are now confined two mighty monarchies,
Whose high, uprearèd and abutting fronts
The perilous narrow ocean parts asunder.
Piece out our imperfections with your thoughts;
Think, when we talk of horses, that you see them,
Printing their proud hoofs i' th' receiving earth;
For 'tis your thoughts that now must deck our kings,
Carry them here and there, jumping o'er times,
Turning th' accomplishment of many years
Into an hour-glass . . .

The music stops.

CHORUS: . . . . For the which supply
Admit me Chorus to this history,
Who, Prologue-like, your humble patience pray
Gently to hear, kindly to judge, our play.

4

*He bows and pulls the Stage Curtain aside. The music
starts as the* Boy *with a board steps forward and shows his
message to the audience.
Close on the* Boy *with the board which reads:–*

ANTE CHAMBER IN KING HENRY'S PALACE

*Track up to the stage balcony above him. Through
curtains at the back, the* ARCHBISHOP OF CANTERBURY
and the BISHOP OF ELY *enter and bow. The audience
applauds as* CANTERBURY *sits down at a table and
studies a paper. He bangs his first. The music stops.*

CANTERBURY: My lord, I'll tell you. That same bill is urged
Which in th' eleventh year of the last king's reign
Was like, and had indeed against us passed,
But that the scrambling and unquiet time
Did push it out of farther question.

ELY: But how, my lord, shall we resist it now?

CANTERBURY: It must be thought on. If it pass against us,
We lose the better half of our possession:
For all the temporal lands which men devout
By testament have given to the Church
Would they strip from us. Thus runs the bill.

ELY: This would drink deep.

The audience laughs.

CANTERBURY: 'Twould drink the cup and all.

The audience laughs again.

ELY: But what prevention?

CANTERBURY: The King is full of grace and fair regard.

ELY: And a true lover of the holy Church.

CANTERBURY: The courses of his youth promised it not.
Since his addiction was to courses vain,
His companies unlettered, rude and shallow,
His hours filled up with riots, banquets, sports,

5

And never noted in him any study.

ELY: And so the Prince obscured his contemplation
Under the veil of wildness, which, no doubt,
Grew like the summer grass, fastest by night.

The audience laughs.

CANTERBURY: The breath no sooner left his father's body,
But that his wildness, mortified in him,
Seemed to die too. [Sir John Falstaff . . . .

The audience cheers. We see them in a high angle shot.

CANTERBURY: (*off*) . . . . and all
His company along with him . . . .

Return to medium shot of CANTERBURY *and* ELY.

CANTERBURY: . . . . he banished.

The audience groans, seen in a high angle shot.
CANTERBURY *and* ELY *continue talking on stage.*

CANTERBURY: Under pain of death not to come near his
person . . . .

The audience now boos the actors.

CANTERBURY: (*off*) . . . . By ten mile].*

CANTERBURY *now stands up at the table.*

CANTERBURY: . . . . Yea, at that very moment,
Consideration like an angel came
And whipped the offending Adam out of him;
Never was such a sudden scholar made;
Never came reformation in a flood,
As in this king.

ELY *gravely agrees.*

ELY: We are blessèd in the change.

*The lines in square brackets are not from Shakespeare's play of Henry V.

6

The audience jeers as ELY *walks to join* CANTERBURY.

ELY: But, my good lord,
How now for mitigation of this bill
Urged by the Commons? Doth his majesty
Incline to it, or no?

They sit down.

CANTERBURY: He seems indifferent;
Or rather swaying more upon our part.
For I have made an offer to his majesty,
As touching France, to give a greater sum
Than ever at one time the clergy yet
Did to his predecessors part withal.

ELY: How did this offer seem received, my lord?

CANTERBURY: With good acceptance of his majesty,
Save that there was not time enough to hear,
As I perceived his grace would fain have done,
Of his true titles to some certain dukedoms,
And generally to the crown and seat of France,
Derived from Edward, his great grandfather.

ELY: What was th' impediment that broke this off?

CANTERBURY: The French ambassador upon that instant
Craved audience . . . .

The audience chuckles as CANTERBURY *looks off screen.*

CANTERBURY: . . . . and the hour I think is come
To give him hearing. Is it four o'clock?

In his corner, the Prompter gets up from his chair and peers through a grille in the door at the side of the stage. A bell rings three, then four times.
Return to CANTERBURY *and* ELY *on the stage balcony.*

ELY: It is.

CANTERBURY *rises from his chair.*

7

CANTERBURY: Then we go in, to know his embassy:
Which I could with a ready guess declare,
Before the Frenchman speak a word of it.

He goes out, as the music starts.

ELY: I'll wait upon you, and I long to hear it.

The audience titters as ELY *gathers up the documents and follows* CANTERBURY.
CANTERBURY *and* ELY *come down the stairs from the balcony backstage. Track back to reveal the actors getting ready for their entrances. A* Boy *crosses to a fellow youngster to try on a wig.*
The two Boys *try out their headgear. One of them has been shaving prior to playing* MISTRESS QUICKLY.
Backstage, the English Herald *and four soldiers take up their positions before their stage entrance. A fanfare sounds. They exit and actors playing the* EARLS OF SALISBURY *and* WESTMORELAND *exit right to a fanfare. They are followed by* EXETER *and* GLOUCESTER. *The actor playing* KING HENRY V *enters left.*
The music stops. He coughs. The music starts.
Pan with him as he goes through a door on to the stage. The audience applauds in the background.
HENRY V *bows as the music stops.*

KING HENRY: Where is my gracious Lord of Canterbury?

EXETER *enters left.*

EXETER: Not here in presence.

KING HENRY: Send for him, good uncle.

HENRY V *goes off and* EXETER *signals a Herald to fetch the Archbishops. The Herald approaches us.*
Backstage, ELY *is robing for his entrance. He drinks beer with a fellow-actor.*

WESTMORELAND: (*off*) Shall we call in th' ambassador, my liege?

Frontstage, the Herald, seen in close shot, signals to

8

HENRY V, *as* ELY *prepares to go onstage.*

KING HENRY: Not yet, my cousin, We would be resolved,
Before we hear him, of some things of weight
That task our thoughts, concerning us and France.

Backstage, CANTERBURY *comes up and ushers* ELY *into
position. Pan with him as he goes off right with* ELY
following him.
Frontstage, CANTERBURY *enters, his hand raised in
blessing. Pan with him to show* HENRY V *seated on his
throne surrounded by his court. He bows to*
CANTERBURY.

CANTERBURY: God and his angels guard your sacred
throne,
And make you long become it!

KING HENRY: Sure we thank you.

ELY *enters in a flurry and* HENRY V *acknowledges him.
The audience laughs.*

KING HENRY: My learnèd lord, we pray you to proceed,
And justly and religiously unfold
Why the law Salic that they have in France
Or should or should not bar us in our claim.

In medium close shot, HENRY V *rises from his throne and
steps down from it. We track back with him.*

KING HENRY: We charge you in the name of God take
heed
How you awake the sleeping sword of war:
For never two such kingdoms did contend
Without much fall of blood, whose guiltless drops
Do make such waste in brief mortality.

CANTERBURY: Then hear me, gracious sovereign, and you
peers
That owe your selves, your lives, and services
To this imperial throne. There is no bar
To make against your highness' claim to France.

9

But this, which they produce from Pharamond.

CANTERBURY *takes a document from* ELY *and quotes.*
(STILL)

CANTERBURY: *'In terram Salicam mulieres ne succedant':*
'No woman shall succeed in Salic land':
Which 'Salic land' the French unjustly gloss
To be the realm of France.
Yet their own authors faithfully affirm
That the land Salic lies in Germany,
Between the floods of Saala and of Elbe . . . .

ELY *hands him another document. Pan with*
CANTERBURY *as he walks to the left.*

CANTERBURY: Where Charles the Great having subdued
the Saxons,
There left behind and settled certain French
Who, holding in disdain the German women
For some dishonest manners of their life,
Established there this law . . . .

As the audience titters, CANTERBURY *turns and walks*
back to centre stage. Pan with him. He continues walking
to the right to stop at the edge of the stage.

CANTERBURY: . . . . To wit, no female
Should be inheritrix in Salic land:
Which is this day in Germany called Meissen.
Then doth it well appear the Salic Law
Was not devisèd for the realm of France
Nor did the French possess the Salic land,
Until four hundred one-and-twenty years
After defunction of . . . .

He looks at his document and signals ELY *to bring*
another.
ELY *hands another document to* CANTERBURY. *Pan left*
to right with him, as the audience titters.

CANTERBURY: . . . . King Pharamond,
Idly supposed the founder of this law,

10

King Pepin, which deposèd Childeric,
Did as heir general, being descended
Of Blithild . . . .

CANTERBURY *hands the paper back to* ELY. *He slaps*
ELY'S *hand as another document is proffered. Pan right*
to left with CANTERBURY. *He has to return to* ELY *for the*
paper and snatches it from him. ELY *throws the*
remainder of the papers in the air.
The audience titters as CANTERBURY *finds documents*
are falling about his ears.

CANTERBURY: . . . . Which was daughter to . . . .

The audience laughs as ELY *points to the papers on the*
floor. Pan down to the document as CANTERBURY'S
hand comes into the shot.
CANTERBURY *picks up a paper.* HENRY V *is beside him*
and tries to interrupt. CANTERBURY *turns left and we pan*
with him and back again as he walks to the King.

CANTERBURY: . . . . King Clothair,
Make claim and title to the crown of France.
Hugh Capet also, who usurped the crown
Of Charles the Duke of Lorraine, sole heir male
Of the true line and stock of . . . .

CANTERBURY *holds out his hand for another paper.*
The audience titters as ELY *points to the floor. Now the*
audience laughs.
See in close-up, CANTERBURY'S *hand comes into shot,*
but his wrist is seized by HENRY V, *who picks up the next*
paper. Pan up to both of them.

CANTERBURY: . . . . Charles the Great,
Could not keep quiet in his conscience,
Wearing the crown of France, still satisfied
That fair . . . .

ELY *looks for the relevant paper.*

. . . . that fair . . . .

11

The audience roars with laughter.

CANTERBURY: (*off*) . . . . that fair . . . .

EXETER, CANTERBURY *and* HENRY V *are kneeling on the floor, while* ELY *is beside them.* CANTERBURY *has found a paper.* ELY *finds him another.* (*STILL*) HENRY V *and* EXETER *rise to their feet.*

CANTERBURY: . . . . Queen Isabel, his grandmother,
Was lineal of the . . . . the Lady Ermengard,
Daughter to Charles the foresaid Duke of Lorraine:
So that, as clear as is the summer's sun . . . .

The audience laughs.

. . . . all appear
To hold in right and title of the female:
So do the Kings of France unto this day,
Howbeit, they would hold up this Salic Law
To bar your highness claiming from the female.

HENRY V *and* EXETER *help* CANTERBURY *to his feet. Track in on* HENRY V *as he interrupts* CANTERBURY.

KING HENRY: May I with right and conscience make this claim?

CANTERBURY: The sin upon my head, dread sovereign!

ELY *holds up a Bible for* CANTERBURY.

CANTERBURY: For in the Book of Numbers it is writ,
'When the son dies, let the inheritance
Descend unto the daughter.'

EXETER: (*off*) Gracious Lord, stand for your own.

EXETER *is now seen in close-up.*

EXETER: Look back into your mighty ancestors:
Go, my dread lord, to your great-grandsire's tomb,
From whom you claim; invoke his warlike spirit
And your great-uncle's, Edward . . . .

HENRY V *is in close-up.*

12

EXETER: (*off*) . . . . the Black Prince.

SALISBURY: (*off*) Your brother kings and monarchs of . . . .

> *Cut to* SALISBURY *and* WESTMORELAND. *Pan with* SALISBURY *as he walks to the left.*

. . . . the earth
Do all expect that you should rouse yourself
As did the former lions of your blood.

> WESTMORELAND *walks up to join him.*

WESTMORELAND: They know your grace hath cause and means and might;
So hath your highness. Never King of England
Had nobles richer and more loyal subjects,
Whose hearts have left their bodies here in England,
And lie pavilioned in the fields of France.

> *A hand taps him on the shoulder. Pan left to reveal* CANTERBURY.

CANTERBURY: O let their bodies follow my dear liege
With blood and sword and fire, to win your right.
In aid whereof . . . .

> ELY *joins* CANTERBURY.

CANTERBURY: . . . . We of the spirituality
Will raise your highness such a mighty sum
As never did the clergy at one time
Bring in to any of your ancestors.

> HENRY V *is in close-up.*

KING HENRY: Call in the messengers sent from the Dauphin.

> *A fanfare sounds as* CANTERBURY *and* ELY *stand aside.* HENRY V *walks to the throne.*

KING HENRY: Now we are well resolved, and, by God's help,

And yours, the noble sinews of our power,
France being ours, we'll bend it to our awe,
Or lay these bones in an unworthy urn,
Tombless, with no remembrance over them.

The fanfare concludes as the English Herald and the French Herald enter through a door at the side of the stage, followed by the French AMBASSADOR, *the* DUKE OF BERRI, *and two pages carrying a casket. Track back to reveal the stage in long shot.*

KING HENRY: : Now are we well prepared to know the pleasure
Of our fair cousin Dauphin, for we hear
Your greeting is from him, not from the King.

MOUNTJOY, *the French Herald, bows.*

MOUNTJOY: May't please your majesty to give us leave
Freely to render what we have in charge,
Or shall we sparingly show you far off
The Dauphin's meaning and our embassy?

KING HENRY: We are no tyrant, but a Christian king,
Therefore with frank and with uncurbèd plainness
Tell us the Dauphin's mind.

The French AMBASSADOR *bows.*

AMBASSADOR: . . . . Thus then in few . . . .

Seen in medium close shot, the French AMBASSADOR *speaks:*

AMBASSADOR: . . . . Your highness lately sending into France
Did claim some certain dukedoms, in the right
Of your great predecessor, King Edward the Third.
In answer of which claim, the Prince our master
Says that you savour too much of your youth,
He therefore sends you fitter for your study
This tun of treasure . . . .

The two pages carry the casket round to the front of the throne.

14

AMBASSADOR: . . . . and in lieu of this
Desires you let the dukedoms that you claim
Hear no more of you. This the Dauphin speaks.

HENRY V *leans over to* EXETER *on his left.*

KING HENRY: What treasure, uncle?

EXETER *opens the casket and closes it quickly.*

EXETER: Tennis balls, my liege.

There is a nervous giggle from the audience.
HENRY V *is seen in close-up seated on his throne. He
shows no anger.*

KING HENRY: We are glad the Dauphin is so pleasant with
us
His present and your pains we thank you for . . . .

Track back as HENRY V *springs to his feet.*

KING HENRY: When we have matched our rackets to these
balls,
We will in France, by God's grace, play a set
Shall strike his father's crown into the hazard.
Tell him, he hath made a match with such a wrangler
That all the courts of France will be disturbed
With chases . . . .

HENRY V *steps down from the throne. Pan with him as he
walks to the right of the stage.*

KING HENRY: . . . . And we understand him well
How he comes o'er us with our wilder days,
Not measuring what use we made of them.
But tell the Dauphin we will keep our state,
Be like a king, and show our sail of greatness,
When we do rouse us in our throne of France . . . .

He turns. Pan with him as he walks back to centre stage.

KING HENRY: . . . . And tell the pleasant Prince, this
mock of his
Hath turned these balls to gun-stones, and his soul
Shall stand sore-chargèd for the wasteful vengeance

15

That shall fly from them: for many a thousand
widows . . . .

Pan with him as he walks to the left.

KING HENRY: . . . . Shall this his mock mock out of their
dear husbands,
Mock mothers from their sons, mock castles down:
Ay, some are yet ungotten and unborn
That shall have cause to curse the Dauphin's scorn.

*He turns and walks right to stage centre and back to his
throne, turning when he reaches it. Pan with him and
track back to show all the stage.*

KING HENRY: But this lies all within the will of God,
To whom we do appeal, and in whose name
Tell you the Dauphin, we are coming on
To venge us as we may, and to put forth
Our rightful hand in a well-hallowed cause.
So get you hence in peace and tell the Dauphin
His jest will savour but of shallow wit,
When thousands weep more than did laugh at it.
Convey them with safe conduct. Fare you well.

HENRY V *bows to the applause of the audience as the
French* AMBASSADOR *and the Heralds exit on the right.
He goes to sit down on his throne.*
HENRY V *now sits down on his throne with* EXETER
standing on the left.

EXETER: This was a merry message.

HENRY V *rises and takes off his crown. Pan with him as
he walks to the left and pauses in front of the door leading
from the stage.*

KING HENRY: We hope to make the sender blush at it.
Therefore, let our proportions for these wars
Be soon collected, and all things thought upon
That may with reasonable swiftness add
More feathers to our wings: for, God before,
We'll chide this Dauphin at his father's door.

16

HENRY V *bows and goes out through the door. The musicians strike up and the audience applauds.*
CHORUS *comes through the other door and draws the curtain across the inner stage. Pan left to right with him. He turns and walks upstage and throws open his arms as he starts speaking. The music and the applause stop.*

CHORUS: Now all the youth of England are on fire,
And silken dalliance in the wardrobe lies;
Now thrive the armourers, and honour's thought
Reigns solely in the breast of every man:
They sell the pasture now to buy the horse,
Following the mirror of all Christian kings
With wingèd heels, as English Mercuries.

CHORUS *throws up his hands and starts to walk away. Pan left with him until he stands in long shot. He throws up his hands again.*

CHORUS: For now sits expectation in the air
And hides a sword, from hilts unto the point
With crowns imperial, crowns and coronets,
Promised to Harry and his followers.
Linger your patience on, for, if we may,
We'll not offend one stomach with our play.

The audience applauds as CHORUS *bows and goes out through the door behind him. Two stagehands enter with bundles of rough grass. They look skywards. There is a roll of thunder.*
Clouds are covering the sun.
A high angle shot shows the theatre audience. It starts to rain. Some of the audience go home. A BOY *with a billboard appears on the balcony in the foreground. There is the sound of rain and of grumbling people.*
Medium close shot of the BOY *displaying the billboard to the audience: it reads:–*

THE BOAR'S HEAD
He hangs it on a bracket, bows and exits through curtains behind him. Pan with him, then track in to the balcony and curtains. NYM *pokes his head through the curtains*

17

and furtively climbs over the balcony and drops out of shot.
Now NYM *drops into shot.* BARDOLPH *is standing on stage.*

BARDOLPH: Well met, Corporal Nym.

NYM *gets up from the floor of the stage. Pan up to reveal* BARDOLPH *and track back as* BARDOLPH *steps forward.*

NYM: Good morrow, Lieutenant Bardolph.

BARDOLPH: What, are Ensign Pistol and you friends yet?

NYM: For my part, I care not. I say little, but when time shall serve . . . .

NYM *prods* BARDOLPH'S *arm. Pan as* BARDOLPH *walks round* NYM.

BARDOLPH: I will bestow a breakfast to make you friends, and we'll be all three sworn brothers to France. Let it be so, good Corporal Nym.

NYM: Well, I cannot tell.

BARDOLPH: It is certain, Corporal, that he is married to Nell Quickly, and certainly she did you wrong, for you were betrothed to her.

NYM *prods* BARDOLPH's *arm.*

NYM: Things must be as they may. Men may sleep, and they may have their throats about them at that time, and some say knives have edges. Well, I cannot tell.

BARDOLPH *shudders.* NYM *crosses in front of him. The music begins.*

BARDOLPH: Here comes Pistol and his wife. Good corporal, good corporal, be patient here.

BARDOLPH *ushers* NYM *to the side of the stage.*
The audience in the foreground applauds the actors on stage. PISTOL *and* MISTRESS QUICKLY *come through the door in the background. Track in to them as* PISTOL

18

flourishes his hat.
The audience on the edge of the stage applauds ecstatically.
PISTOL *flourishes his hat. Pan with him up to*
BARDOLPH.

BARDOLPH: How now, mine host Pistol?

The music stops as PISTOL *steps back in disgust.*

PISTOL: Base tyke, call'st thou me host?

The audience laughs.

PISTOL: Now by this hand I swear I scorn the title . . . .

He walks over to MISTRESS QUICKLY.

PISTOL: Nor shall my Nell keep lodgers.

The audience laughs as NYM *crosses his legs and rubs his hands smugly.*

MISTRESS QUICKLY: (*off*) No, by my troth, not long.

MISTRESS QUICKLY *and* PISTOL *are seen in a medium close shot.*

MISTRESS QUICKLY: For we cannot lodge and board a dozen or fourteen gentlewomen that live honestly by the prick of their needles, but it will be thought we keep a bawdy house, straight.

PISTOL *leads her by the hand over to* NYM. *Pan right with them, as the audience titters.*

PISTOL: (*slapping Nym on the shoulder*) O hound of Crete, think'st thou my spouse to get? I have and I will hold my honey queen and there's enough. Go to.

NYM: I will prick your guts a little, and that's the truth of it.

The audience laughs.

PISTOL: Ha!

MISTRESS QUICKLY *runs to the lip of the stage.*

MISTRESS QUICKLY: Well-a-day, Lady, we shall see wilful

murder and adultery committed.

BARDOLPH comes into shot as the audience laughs.

BARDOLPH: Good corporal, good lieutenant, offer nothing here.

NYM draws his sword.

NYM: Pish!

PISTOL: Pish for thee, Iceland dog! Thou prick-eared cur of Iceland!

As the audience laughs, MISTRESS QUICKLY walks back to NYM.

MISTRESS QUICKLY: Good corporal Nym, show thy valour, put up thy sword.

She helps him to sheath his sword.

NYM: I will cut thy throat one time or other in fair terms.

PISTOL crows and brandishes his sword. He comes down to the lip of the stage, then back to the group again. Pan with him as the audience laughs.

PISTOL: Ha! I can take! Now Pistol's cock is up, and flashing fire will follow.

BARDOLPH draws his sword.

BARDOLPH: Hear me, hear me what I say. He that strikes the first stroke, I'll run him up to the hilts, as I'm a s-s-s-soldier.

PISTOL walks away from the group. Pan with him as he addresses the audience in the theatre.

PISTOL: An oath of mickle might, and fury shall abate.

The audience laughs as PISTOL turns round.

BOY: (*off*) Mine host Pistol . . . .

The BOY on the balcony is seen in a low angle shot.

BOY: . . . . You must come to Sir John Falstaff.

The music starts as PISTOL *comes into shot with* MISTRESS QUICKLY *on the right, followed by* BARDOLPH.

BOY: . . . And you, hostess. He's very sick and would to bed. Good Bardolph, put thy face between his sheets and do the office of a warming-pan.

BARDOLPH: Away, you rogue!

BOY: Faith, he's very ill.

The BOY *leaves the balcony. Pan down to show the three below.*

MISTRESS QUICKLY: By my troth, the King has killed his heart. Good husband, come home presently.

MISTRESS QUICKLY *goes out. The music stops.* BARDOLPH *takes* PISTOL *by the arm and leads him over to* NYM.

BARDOLPH: Come, shall I make you two friends? We must to France together. Why the devil should we keep knives to cut one another's throats?

PISTOL: Let floods o'erswell, and fiends for food howl on!

The audience giggles.

NYM: You'll pay me the eight shillings I won of you at betting?

PISTOL: Base is the slave that pays.

The audience laughs.

NYM: Now that will I have. That's the humour of it.

PISTOL: *(drawing his sword)* As manhood shall compound. Push home.

The audience laughs, and BARDOLPH *draws his sword. (STILL)*

21

BARDOLPH: By this sword, he that makes the first thrust, I'll kill him. By this s-s-sword I will.

The audience giggles.

PISTOL: Sword is an oath, and oaths must have their course.

The audience laughs, as PISTOL *moves over to the front of the stage to address the audience.*
BARDOLPH *and* NYM *confront each other.*

BARDOLPH: Corporal Nym, an thou wilt be friends, be friends. An thou wilt not, why then, be enemies with me too. Prithee, put up.

BARDOLPH slaps NYM'S *sword with his own.* PISTOL *comes into shot.*
MISTRESS QUICKLY now appears on the balcony.
The music soon begins.

MISTRESS QUICKLY: As ever you come of women, come in quickly to Sir John. He's so shaked of a burning quotidian fever, it's lamentable to behold. Sweet men, come to him.

She beckons to them, then goes through the curtains behind her. Track back to reveal BARDOLPH, PISTOL *and* NYM *looking up at the balcony.*

NYM: The King hath run bad humours on the knight.

PISTOL lays his right hand on NYM'S *shoulder.*

PISTOL: Nym, thou hast spoke the right. His heart is fracted and corroborate.

BARDOLPH: The King is a good King, but it must be as it may. He passes some humours.

PISTOL takes a step forward.

PISTOL: Let us condole the knight. For, lambkins, we will live.

He turns round and places a hand on BARDOLPH'S *and* NYM'S *shoulders, who also turn round. As the audience*

22

applauds, they bow and flourish their hats. Track right back to reveal the theatre. The three actors make their exit through a door, as attendants sweep away the rushes on the floor and CHORUS *pulls across the proscenium arch a curtain depicting Southampton.*
CHORUS *stands in front of the Southampton curtain. He steps forward to address the theatre audience. The music begins.*

CHORUS: Linger your patience on and we'll digest
Th' abuse of distance. Force a play.
The King is set from London, and the scene
Is now transported, gentles, to Southampton.
There is the playhouse now, there must you sit,
And thence to France . . . .

CHORUS *walks back and indicates the curtain. He goes out of shot. Track up to the theatre curtain, and dissolve to:*
A model shot of the City of Southampton in 1415 A.D., exactly as depicted on the curtain. Track on, then pan to reveal the stern of a ship, and Southampton quay. The ARCHBISHOP OF CANTERBURY *is giving benediction to the kneeling* KING HENRY *and his knights.* HENRY V *rises.*

CHORUS: *(off)* . . . shall we convey you safe,
And bring you back charming the narrow seas
To give you gentle pass. And here till then,
Unto Southampton do we shift our scene.

HENRY V *steps down to the deck of the ship. Track with him as he walks to the mast. The music stops.* (STILL)

KING HENRY: Now sits the wind fair.

He turns and walks back to a group of noblemen, including EXETER, WESTMORELAND, GLOUCESTER, *and* SALISBURY.

KING HENRY: Uncle of Exeter,

Set free the man committed yesterday,
That railed against our person. We consider
It was the heat of wine that set him on,
And, on his wiser thought, we pardon him.

EXETER: That's mercy, but too much security.

WESTMORELAND: Let him be punished, sovereign, lest example
Breed, by his sufferance, more of such a kind.

KING HENRY: O let us yet be merciful . . . .

He turns to CANTERBURY *just behind him.*

KING HENRY: . . . . We doubt not now
But every rub is smoothèd on our way.

HENRY V mounts the gangplank.

KING HENRY: Then forth, dear countrymen.

As the soldiers cheer, HENRY V *steps ashore, followed by* CANTERBURY *and the nobles. He walks along the quay to a table.*

KING HENRY: Let us deliver
Our puissance into the hand of God,
Putting it straight in expedition.
Cheerly to sea the signs of war advance . . . .

The soldiers cheer as HENRY V *takes a seal and stamps a paper on the table.*

KING HENRY: No King of England, if not King of France.

He turns and walks away followed by CANTERBURY *and the nobles.*
Music starts as we dissolve to the sign of THE BOAR'S HEAD at night.

CHORUS: *(off)* Still be kind,
And eke out our performance with your mind.

The illusion that we have returned to the Globe Theatre is dissolved with a dissolve to the real upper window of an inn, as it is opened by MISTRESS QUICKLY. *Track up to, and through the window. An old man is lying in bed in the room.* MISTRESS QUICKLY *is by the bed. She goes out through a door on the right.* SIR JOHN FALSTAFF, *the old man, struggles and sits up in bed. He is in delirium.*

FALSTAFF: God save thy Grace – King Hal – my royal Hal,
God save thee my sweet boy:
My King, my Jove, I speak to thee my heart.

Track slowly in on FALSTAFF, *till he is in close-up during* HENRY V'S *speech.*

KING HENRY: *(off and distant)*
I know thee not, old man, fall to thy prayers.
How ill white hairs become a fool and jester!
I have long dreamed of such a kind of man,
So surfeit swelled, so old and so profane,
But being awaked I do despise my dream.
Reply not to me with a foolish jest,
Presume not that I am the thing I was;
For God doth know, so shall the world perceive
That I have turned away my former self
So shall I those that kept me company.*

FALSTAFF sinks back on to the pillow, fumbling convulsively with the sheets.
Now we see a low angle shot of FALSTAFF *in profile with* MISTRESS QUICKLY *at the bedside.* (STILL)
Dissolve to the street outside THE BOAR'S HEAD inn. The street door opens and NYM, *the* BOY, BARDOLPH *and* PISTOL *come out. They are followed out by* MISTRESS QUICKLY *on the balcony.* (STILL) *She comes down to join them sitting on straw. She touches* PISTOL'S *arm. The music stops.*

MISTRESS QUICKLY: Prithee, honey, sweet husband, let me bring thee to Staines.

Track in on the group as PISTOL *rouses himself.*

---

* These lines are taken from Shakespeare's Henry IV, Part Two.

PISTOL: No, for my manly heart doth yearn. Bardolph, be blithe. Nym, rouse thy vaunting veins! Boy, bristle thy courage up. For Falstaff, he is dead. And we must yearn therefore.

BOY: Well, Sir John is gone, God be with him!

MISTRESS QUICKLY *sits down on a stool.* (STILL)

BARDOLPH: Would I were with him wheresome'er he is, either in heaven or in hell.

Track very slowly up to MISTRESS QUICKLY.

MISTRESS QUICKLY: Nay, sure he's not in hell. He's in Arthur's bosom. He made a finer end, and went away an it had been any christom child. He parted e'en just betwixt twelve and one, e'en at the turning o' the tide. For after I saw him fumble with the sheets, and play with flowers, and smile upon his fingers' end, I knew there was no way but one. For his nose was now as sharp as a pen, and he babbled of green fields. 'How now, Sir John?' quoth I: 'What, man? Be o' good cheer!' So he cried out: 'God, God, God!' three or four times. And I, to comfort him, bid him he should not think of God. I hoped there was no need to trouble himself with any such thoughts yet. So he bade me lay more clothes on his feet. I put my hand into the bed and felt them, and they were as cold as any stone. Then I felt to his knees . . .

She touches PISTOL'S *knee. Track slowly back to show the group again.*

MISTRESS QUICKLY: . . . And they were as cold as any stone, and so upwards and upwards, and all was cold as any stone.

NYM *wipes his nose.*

NYM: They say he cried out for sack.

MISTRESS QUICKLY: Ay, that he did.

BARDOLPH: And for women.

MISTRESS QUICKLY: Nay, that he did not.

BARDOLPH: Ay, that he did! And he said they were devils incarnate.

BOY: He said once, the devil would have him about women.

MISTRESS QUICKLY: He did in some sort, indeed, handle women; but then he was rheumatic. He spoke of the Whore of Babylon.

BOY: Do you not remember, he saw a flea stick up on Bardolph's nose, and said it was a black soul burning in hell-fire.

BARDOLPH: Well, the fuel is gone that maintained that fire. That's all the riches I got in his service.

NYM stirs and picks up his helmet.

NYM: Shall we shog? The King will be gone from Southampton.

PISTOL rouses himself, then turns to MISTRESS QUICKLY.

PISTOL: Come, let's away. My love, give me thy lips. Look to my chattels and my moveables. Go, clear thy crystals . . . .

He turns to NYM, BARDOLPH and the BOY.

PISTOL: . . . Yoke-fellows in arms,
Let us to France, like horse-leeches, my boys,
To suck, to suck, the very blood to suck!

He signals to BARDOLPH.

PISTOL: Touch her soft lips and part.

The music starts.

BARDOLPH: Farewell, hostess.

BARDOLPH kisses MISTRESS QUICKLY and goes out, putting on his helmet. NYM moves to go. PISTOL growls at him.

PISTOL: Huh!

NYM turns to say goodbye to MISTRESS QUICKLY. *He kisses his hand to her.*

NYM: I cannot kiss, that's the humour of it, but adieu.

PISTOL embraces his wife.

PISTOL: Let housewifery appear. Keep close, I thee command.

He goes out. The BOY *runs forward to* MISTRESS QUICKLY, *and she kisses his head. The* BOY *runs out. PISTOL and Company are walking along the street away from the inn.* PISTOL *turns and waves his helmet.*

PISTOL: Farewell, farewell, divine Zenocrate –
Is it not passing brave to be a King
And ride in triumph through Persepolis!

As he finishes quoting Marlowe's lines, MISTRESS QUICKLY *comes into the foreground.* PISTOL *turns and continues up the street, and* MISTRESS QUICKLY *looks up to* FALSTAFF'S *window. Pan up with her look to centre on the window. The curtain is drawn across it as the music stops, and we fade out.*
The voice of CHORUS *is heard over a black screen.*

CHORUS: Thus with imagined wing our scene flies swift.
As that of thought . . .

Fade in slowly as the music starts, to show CHORUS *leaning against a dark misty background.*
Track slowly back as he speaks.

CHORUS: . . . Suppose that you have seen
The well-appointed King at Hampton Pier
Embark his royalty, and his brave fleet
Play with your fancies; and in them behold
Upon the hempen tackle ship-boys climbing;
Hear the shrill whistle, which doth order give
To sounds confused; behold the threaden sails,
Born with th' invisible and creeping wind,

Draw the huge vessels through the furrowed sea . . .

He extends his arms, as the mist obscures him.

CHORUS: . . . Breasting the lofty surge. O do but think
You stand upon the shore and thence behold . . .

He swings round, now back to us, and is completely blotted out by mist. A fleet of ships becomes visible through the mist.
Track forward over the model shot of the fleet.

CHORUS: . . . A city on th' inconstant billows dancing,
Holding due course to Harfleur. Follow, follow!
And leave your England as dead midnight still,
Guarded with grandsires, babies, and old women,
For who is he, whose chin is but enriched
With one appearing hair, that will not follow
These culled and choice-drawn cavaliers to France?

Dissolve to a long shot of a model of the Palace of the King of France.
Dissolve to a high angle shot inside the Palace, and slowly track down to ground level where the French KING CHARLES *is seated at the base of a pillar. The room is in the shape of an apse with gothic windows and stone staircases.*

CHORUS: . . . The French, advised by good intelligence
Of this most dreadful preparation,
Shake in their fear, and with pale policy,
Seek to divert the English purposes.

KING CHARLES *looks nervously off screen, then turns back again. The music stops.*

KING CHARLES: Thus comes the English with full power upon us,
And more than carefully it us concerns
To answer royally in our defences.
Therefore, you Dukes of Berri . . .

As KING CHARLES *points left, we cut to the* DUKE OF

BERRI *reading at a lectern. He turns to look right.*

KING CHARLES: *(off)* . . . and of Bourbon . . .

Pan down to show the DUKE OF BOURBON.

KING CHARLES: *(off)* . . . Lord Constable . . .

Pan up and right to show the CONSTABLE *of France.*

KING CHARLES: *(off)* . . . and Orléans shall make forth
. . .

Continue panning right to show the DUKE OF ORLEANS.
Pan with KING CHARLES, *seen in close-up, as he points
to the left and rises and walks across the palace room. The*
DAUPHIN *is standing at a window in the background.*

KING CHARLES: . . . And you, Prince Dauphin, with all
swift despatch,
To line and new-repair our towns of war
With men of courage, and with means defendant.

KING CHARLES *has turned round and goes out right.*

DAUPHIN: My most redoubted father,
It is most meet we arm us 'gainst the foe.

The DAUPHIN *steps down from the window place.*

DAUPHIN: And let us do it with no show of fear,
No, with no more than if we heard that England
Were busied with a Whitsun morris dance.
For, my good liege; she is so idly kinged
By a vain, giddy, shallow, humorous youth,
That fear attends her not.

CONSTABLE: *(off)* O peace, Prince Dauphin!

The DAUPHIN *looks round. The* CONSTABLE *of France
steps down and walks right to the* DAUPHIN. *Pan with
him to leave them standing together. The* CONSTABLE
smiles at ORLEANS *as he walks past.*

CONSTABLE: You are too much mistaken in this King.
Question your grace our late ambassadors

With what great state he heard their embassy,
How well supplied with agèd counsellors,
How terrible in constant resolution.

DAUPHIN: Well, 'tis not so, my Lord Constable,
But though we think it so, it is no matter.
In cases of defence, 'tis best to weigh
The enemy more mighty than he seems.

The CONSTABLE *bows slightly.*

KING CHARLES: *(off)* And he is bred out of . . .

The CONSTABLE *and the* DAUPIN *look right.*
KING CHARLES *is seated on some stone steps.*

KING CHARLES: . . . that bloody strain
That haunted us in our familiar paths,
When Crécy battle fatally was struck,
And all our Princes captured by the hand
Of that black name, Edward, Black Prince of Wales . . .

KING CHARLES *shivers and crosses himself.*

KING CHARLES: . . . This is a stem
Of that victorious stock; and let us fear
The native mightiness and fate of him.

At the sudden sound of a fanfare of trumpets, KING
CHARLES *looks up, startled.*
The Dukes of France are seated about in the middle. A
MESSENGER *dashes in up the staircase on the left of the*
apse.

MESSENGER: Ambassadors from Harry, King of England,
Do crave admittance to your majesty.

KING CHARLES *comes into shot in the foreground, his*
back to us.

KING CHARLES: We'll give them present audience.
Go and bring them.

KING CHARLES *points irritably at the* MESSENGER, *then*
turns and scampers to his throne. Track with his

movements as the music starts. KING CHARLES *sits on the throne and an Attendant proffers the casket containing the Crown Jewels.*
KING CHARLES *takes the crown and puts it on his head. The* DAUPHIN *comes in left. The King impatiently continues to put on his regalia.*

DAUPHIN: Good, my sovereign.
Take up the English short, and let them know
Of what a monarchy you are the head.
Self-love, my liege, is not so vile a sin
As self-neglecting.

KING CHARLES *and the* DAUPHIN *look left on the sound of another fanfare. The English and French Heralds come up the staircase followed by* EXETER *and* ERPINGHAM. *Track back as the Heralds take up position on either side of the throne.* EXETER *turns to address the King. The sound of the trumpet ceases.* (STILL)

KING CHARLES: From our brother England?

EXETER: From him, and thus he greets your majesty:
He wills you, in the name of God Almighty,
That you divest yourself and lay apart
The borrowed glories that by gift of heaven,
By law of nature and of nations, 'longs
To him and to his heirs, namely the crown,
Willing you overlook this pedigree . . .

EXETER *indicates a document. Two Messengers unfurl it and hold it up before the throne.*

EXETER: . . . And when you find him evenly derived
From his most famed of famous ancestors,
Edward the Third, he bids you then resign
Your crown and kingdom, indirectly held . . .

KING CHARLES *fingers his crown.*

EXETER: . . . From him, the native and true challenger.

KING CHARLES *of France is seen in close-up.*

32

KING CHARLES: If not, what follows?

EXETER: Bloody constraint. For if you hide the crown
Even in your hearts, there will he rake for it.
Therefore in fierce tempest is he coming,
In thunder and in earthquake, like a Jove;
That, if requiring fail, he will compel.
This is his claim, his threatening, and my message;
Unless the Dauphin . . .

> *He glances to right and left.*
> KING CHARLES *has the* DAUPHIN *beside him. He edges
> the* DAUPHIN *out of shot on the right.*

EXETER: *(off)* . . . be in presence here,
To whom expressly I bring greeting too.

> KING CHARLES *lays his hand on his breast, then points to
> the left.*

KING CHARLES: For us, we will consider of this further:
Tomorrow shall you bear our full intent
Back to our brother England.

> *The* DAUPHIN *is now seen in medium shot.*

DAUPHIN: For the Dauphin,
I stand here for him. What to him from England?

> EXETER *joins the* DAUPHIN.

EXETER: Scorn and defiance, slight regard, contempt,
And anything that may not misbecome
The mighty sender, doth he prize you at.
Thus says my King; an if your father's highness
Do not, in grant of all demands at large,
Sweeten the bitter mock you sent his Majesty,
He'll make your Paris Louvre shake for it.

> KING CHARLES *now joins them.*

KING CHARLES: Tomorrow shall you know our mind at
full.

EXETER: Dispatch us with all speed, lest that our King

33

Come here himself to question our delay.

KING CHARLES *faints. As the music begins, we dissolve
to:
A stormy sea, then dissolve again to:
English soldiers are storming Harfleur Beach.* (STILL)
*Then dissolve again to:
A few soldiers are hauling a cannon ashore up the beach.*

CHORUS: *(off)*
Work, work your thoughts, and therein see a siege.
Behold the ordnance on their carriages
With fatal mouths gaping on girded Harfleur.

*Track forward as English foot soldiers appear round the
cliff in retreat.* HENRY V *rides round on horseback.*
(STILL)
HENRY V *takes off his helmet.*
The King rides up to his men.

KING HENRY: Once more unto the breach, dear friends,
once more,
Or close the wall up with our English dead.

The music stops as HENRY V *rides into shot from the left,
then from the right.*

KING HENRY: In peace there's nothing so becomes a man
As modest stillness, and humility,
But when the blast of war blows in our ears,
Then imitate the action of the tiger.
Stiffen the sinews, conjure up the blood,
Disguise fair nature with hard-favoured rage.
Then lend the eye a terrible aspect.

Track back slowly until the King is seen in long shot.
(STILL)

KING HENRY: Let it pry through the portage of the head
Like a brass cannon, let the brow o'erwhelm it
As fearfully as doth a gallèd rock
O'erhang and jutty his confounded base,
Swilled with the wild and wasteful ocean.

34

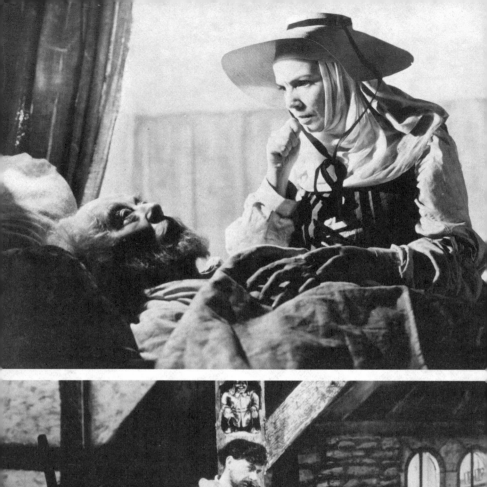

Now set the teeth and stretch the nostril wide,
Hold hard the breath, and bend up every spirit
To his full height. On, on, you noblest English,
Whose blood is fet from fathers of war-proof,
Fathers that like so many Alexanders
Have in these parts from morn till even fought,
And sheathed their swords for lack of argument.
Dishonour not your mothers; now attest
That those whom you called fathers did beget you.
Be copy now to men of grosser blood,
And teach them how to war. And you, good yeomen,
Whose limbs were made in England, show us here
The mettle of your pasture; let us swear
That you are worth your breeding, which I doubt not;
For there is none of you so mean and base
That hath not noble lustre in your eyes.
I see you stand like greyhounds in the slips,
Straining upon the start. The game's afoot.
Follow your spirit, and upon this charge
Cry, 'God for Harry, England and Saint . . .

KING HENRY'S horse rears and he rides away, followed by cheering soldiers.

KING HENRY: . . . George!

The music strikes up as the soldiers chant:

SOLDIERS: God for Harry, England and Saint George!

From a high angle, track down as the soldiers rush up to the breach.
BARDOLPH stands on a rock, waving them on.

BARDOLPH: On! On! On! On to the breach, to the breach!

BARDOLPH drops into shot from the rock and takes refuge beside PISTOL, NYM and the BOY.

NYM : Pray thee, corporal, stay. The knocks are too hot.

Pan with PISTOL as he rises.

PISTOL: Ah, knocks they come and go;

God's vassals drop and die;
And sword and shield
In bloody field
Doth win immortal fame.

He springs back as a horse leaps from the rock.
NYM *and the* BOY *shelter by each other.*

NYM: 'Tis honour, and that's the truth of it.

BOY: Would I were in an alehouse in London. I would give all my fame for a pot of ale, and safety.

FLUELLEN: *(off)* God's plud!

Pan with FLUELLEN *as he pulls* NYM *and the* BOY *to their feet and kicks them up to the breach.*

FLUELLEN: Up to the breach, you dogs! Avaunt, you cullions!

FLUELLEN *sees* PISTOL *hiding behind the rock.*

FLUELLEN: Ah!

PISTOL: Be merciful, great duke, to men of mould. Abate thy rage, abate thy manly rage.

FLUELLEN: On, on!

He slashes at PISTOL *with the flat of his sword.*

PISTOL: Abate thy rage . . .

Dissolve to a close-up of a flaming linstock touching the powder box of a cannon. Track with its recoil from the explosion.

CHORUS: *(off)* . . . And the nimble gunner
With linstock now the devilish cannon touches.

Dissolve to a wall of masonry crashing.

CHORUS: *(off)* And down goes all before them.

Dissolve to a bivouac, outside which Captain GOWER *appears. The music stops.*

GOWER: Captain Fluellen!

Track back to show FLUELLEN *sitting at a table in the bivouac.*

GOWER: Captain Fluellen, you must come presently to the mines. The Duke of Gloucester would speak with you.

FLUELLEN: To the mines? Tell you the Duke, it is not so good to come to the mines! For look you, the mines is not according to the disciplines of war! The concavities of it is not sufficient. For look you, th' athversary, you may discuss unto the Duke, look you, is digt himself, four yards under the countermines. By Cheshu, I think he will plow up all, if there is not better directions.

GOWER: The Duke of Gloucester, to whom the order of the siege is given, is altogether directed by an Irishman, a very valiant gentleman, i' faith.

FLUELLEN: It is Captain MacMorris, is it not?

GOWER: I think it be.

FLUELLEN: By Cheshu, he is an ass, as in the world. I will verify as much in his beard. He has no more directions in the true disciplines of the wars, look you, of the Roman disciplines, than is a puppy dog.

GOWER *looks right and behind him.*

GOWER: Here he comes, and the Scots captain, Captain Jamy, with him.

FLUELLEN: Ah, Captain Jamy is a marvellous falorous gentleman, that is certain, and of great expedition and knowledge in th' ancient wars.

Pan slightly right as CAPTAIN JAMY *and* MACMORRIS *enter.*

JAMY: I say gud day, Captain Fluellen.

FLUELLEN: Gooden to your worship, good Captain James. Captain Jamy is a marvellous falorous gentleman, that is certain.

JAMY *laughs.*

GOWER: How now Captain . . .

MACMORRIS *is seen in close-up.*

GOWER: . . . MacMorris, have you quit the mines? Have the pioneers given o'er?

MACMORRIS: By the Saints, 'tish ill done. The work ish give over, the trumpet sound the retreat. By my hand I swear . . .

Pan left as he walks to FLUELLEN.

MACMORRIS: . . . And by my father's soul, tish ill done. The work ish give over. I would have blowed up the town, so God save me, in an hour! O 'tish ill done, by my hand, 'tish ill done!

Pan right with him as he walks to lean his head against a tree trunk. (STILL)
JAMY *and* FLUELLEN *are sympathetic.*

FLUELLEN: Captain MacMorris, I beseech you now, will you vouchsafe me, look you, a few disputations with you, partly . . .

Seen in close-up, MACMORRIS *leans his head against the tree trunk.*

FLUELLEN: *(off)* . . . to satisfy my opinion, and partly for the satisfaction, look you, of my mind . . . .

JAMY *and* FLUELLEN *watch the sad* MACMORRIS.

FLUELLEN: . . . as touching the direction of the military discipline, that is the point.

JAMY: It shall be very gud, gud faith, gud captains both, and I would fain hear some discourse between you twae!

JAMY *and* FLUELLEN *giggle together.*
Cut to GOWER *with* MACMORRIS *standing behind him.*

MACMORRIS: This is no time to discourse, so God save me!

38

Pan with him as he walks back to FLUELLEN.

MACMORRIS: The day is hot, and the weather and the wars and the King and the Dukes. This is no time to discourse. The town is besieched. An the trumpet call us to the breach, and we talk, and by the Holy do nothing, 'tis a shame for us all. So God sa' me . . .

Pan with him as he walks back to GOWER.

MACMORRIS: . . . 'Tis a shame to stand still, 'tis a shame by my hand. And there is throats to be cut . . .

Pan again as he walks back to the table and flops down on it.

MACMORRIS: . . . And works to be done, and nothing ish done, so help me God!

JAMY *laughs and leans back. Cut to a close-up of him.*

JAMY: By the mess, ere these eyes of mine take themselves to slumber, ay'll de gud service, or ay'll lie i' th' grund for it. Ay, or go to death, and I'll pay't as valorously as I may, that sall I surely do, that is the breff and the long of it.

Track back to show JAMY, FLUELLEN *and* MACMORRIS *around the table.*

FLUELLEN: Captain MacMorris, I think, look you, under your correction, there is not many of your nation –

MACMORRIS: Of my nation? What ish my nation? Ish a villain and a bastard and a knave and a rascal? What ish my nation? Who talks of my nation?

FLUELLEN: Look you, if you take the matter otherwise than is meant, Captain MacMorris, peradventure I shall think you do not use me with that affability as in discretion you ought to use me, look you, being as good a man as . . .

FLUELLEN *jumps up into shot in close-up.*

FLUELLEN: . . . yourself, both in the disciplines of war and the derivation of my birth and other particularities.

39

MACMORRIS'S *head enters the shot.*

MACMORRIS: I do not know you so good a man as myself
. . . so God save me and I will cut off your head.

Track back as GOWER *joins them.*

GOWER: Gentlemen both, you will mistake each other.

JAMY: *(laughs)* That's a foul fault.

He laughs again as a trumpet sounds.

GOWER: The town sounds a parley.

The four Captains cheer and grab their helmets.
Dissolve to a long shot outside the gates of Harfleur.
KING HENRY *at the head of his army addresses the*
GOVERNOR *on the city walls. Track in slowly.*

KING HENRY: How yet resolves the Governor of the town?
This is the latest parley we'll admit.

GOVERNOR OF HARFLEUR: Our expectation hath this day
an end.
The Dauphin, of whom succour we entreated,
Returns us word his powers are yet not ready,
To raise so great a siege. Therefore, dread King,
We yield our town and lives to your soft mercy.
Enter our gates, dispose of us and ours.
For we no longer are defensible.

Seen from a high angle, KING HENRY *commands at the*
gates of Harfleur.

KING HENRY: Open your gates!

GLOUCESTER *stands beside the King.*

KING HENRY: Come, brother Gloucester,
Go you and enter Harfleur. There remain
And fortify it strongly 'gainst the French.
Use mercy to them all. For us, dear brother,
The winter coming on, and sickness growing
Upon our soldiers, we will retire to Calais.

Tonight in Harfleur will we be your guest.
Tomorrow for the march are we addressed.

To the sound of martial music, GLOUCESTER *leads the English Army into Harfleur.* HENRY V *watches them. Pan right as he turns and surveys the country ahead. Dissolve to the model shot of the French Palace. Then dissolve again to the door of the Garden Terrace of the Palace. The door opens.* LADY ALICE *followed by* PRINCESS KATHERINE *comes through. A fanfare sounds.* (STILL) PRINCESS KATHERINE *looks over the balcony.*
From a high angle shot of the Palace Courtyard, we see MOUNTJOY *escorting* EXETER *and his party. They wait for the gates to be opened.*
MOUNTJOY, EXETER *and his party acknowledge the* PRINCESS *on the balcony.*
KATHERINE *watches the party leave. She turns and walks off shot.*
She walks down the terrace into the garden, followed by ALICE.

KATHARINE: Alice, tu as été en Angleterre, et tu bien parles le langage.

ALICE: Un peu, Madame.

KATHARINE: Je te prie, m'enseignez. Il faut que j'apprenne à parler. Comment appelez-vous la main en anglais?

ALICE: La main? Elle est appelée *de hand*.

KATHARINE: *De hand*. Et les doigts?

ALICE: Les doigts? Ma foi, j'oublie les doigts, mais je me souviendrai. Les doigts? Je pense qu'ils sont appelés *de fingres*. Oui, *de fingres*.

KATHARINE: La main, *de hand*, les doigts, *de fingres*. Je pense que je suis le bon écolier; j'ai gagné deux mots d'anglais vitement. Comment appelez-vous les ongles?

41

ALICE: Les ongles? Nous les appelons *de nails*.

KATHARINE: *De nails*. Écoutez; dites-moi si je parle bien: *de hand, de fingres, de nails*.

ALICE: Ah! C'est bien dit, madame. Il est fort bon anglais.

KATHARINE: Dites-moi l'anglais pour le bras.

ALICE: *De arm*, madame.

KATHARINE: Et le coude?

ALICE: *De elbow*.

KATHARINE: *De elbow*. Je m'en fais la répétition de tous les mots que vous m'avez appris dès à présent.

ALICE: Ça c'est trop difficile, madame, comme je pense.

KATHERINE: Excusez-moi, Alice. Ecoutez: *de hand, de fingres, de nails, de arm, de bilbow*.

ALICE: *De elbow*, sauf votre honneur.

KATHERINE: O Seigneur Dieu, je m'en oublie! *De elbow*. Comment appelez-vous le col?

ALICE: *De nick*.

KATHARINE: *De nick*. Et le menton?

ALICE: *De chin*.

KATHARINE: *De sin*. Le col, *de nick*, le menton, *de sin*.

> KATHERINE *has been cutting flowers, and she moves on with* ALICE *following her.*

ALICE: Sauf votre honneur, en vérité, vous prononcez les mots aussi droit que les natifs d'Angleterre.

KATHARINE: Je ne doute point d'apprendre, par la grâce de Dieu, et en peu de temps.

ALICE: N'avez-vous pas déjà oublié ce que je vous ai enseigné?

KATHARINE: Non, je réciterai à vous promptement: *de*

hand, *de fingres, de mails* –

ALICE: *De nails*, madame.

KATHARINE: *De nails, de arm, de bilbow* –

ALICE: Sauf votre honneur, *de elbow.*

KATHARINE: Ainsi dis-je. *De elbow, de nick*, et *de sin.*

KATHARINE *walks right away from* ALICE, *Pan with her.*

KATHARINE: Comment appelez-vous le pied et la robe?

ALICE *speaks after the* PRINCESS.

ALICE: *De foot*, et *de cown!*

ALICE *comes up to the* PRINCESS. *They sit down.* (STILL)

KATHERINE: Oh Seigneur Dieu! Ce sont mots de son mauvais, corruptible, gros, et impudique, et non pour les dames d'honneur d'user. Je ne voudrais pronouncer ces mots devant les seigneurs de France pour tout le monde. Foh! *De foot* et *de cown!* Néanmoins, je réciterai une autre *fois ma leçon ensemble: de hand, de fingres, de nails, de arm, de elbow, de nick, de sin, de foot, de cown.*

ALICE: Oh, Madame, c'est excellent.

KATHARINE: C'est assez pour une fois. Allons-nous à dîner.

The music starts as they rise and walk to the garden gate and go through on to the terrace. Pan with them as they go. A fanfare sounds, and KATHARINE *looks over the balcony.*
Close on KATHERINE *looking over the balcony.*
A high angle shot of the courtyard shows us MOUNTJOY *returning through the gate alone.*
KATHARINE *now looks up to the horizon.*
ESSEX *and his party are riding away in the distance.*
KATHARINE *turns away from the balcony and walks*

43

through a door into the Palace. She is followed by LADY
ALICE.
Inside the French Palace, KATHARINE *and* ALICE
descend the stairs to the floor of the Banqueting Hall.
(STILL) *At a table at the back,* KING CHARLES, QUEEN
ISABEL, *the* DAUPHIN, *the* CONSTABLE, *and the* DUKES
OF BOURBON *and* ORLEANS *are seated.*

KING CHARLES: 'Tis certain he hath passed the river
Somme.

CONSTABLE: And if he be not fought withal, my lord,
Let us not live in France; let us quit all
And give our vineyards to a barbarous people.

> *Track in to feature* BOURBON, KATHARINE *and* ALICE
> *behind him on the stairs.*

BOURBON: Normans, but bastard Normans. Norman
bastards!

> ALICE *screams. The music stops.* BOURBON *looks right.*
> *He looks left.*

BOURBON: Mort de ma vie!

> *He stands up. The music starts.*
> KATHARINE *and* ALICE *walk round and take their places*
> *at table beside the* QUEEN.
> *The* CONSTABLE, ORLEANS *and* BOURBON *sit down.*

BOURBON: If they march along
Unfought withal, then I will sell my dukedom,
To buy a slobbery and dirty farm,
In that nook-shotten isle of Albion.

ORLEANS: Dieu de batailles! Where have they this mettle?
Is not their climate foggy, raw and dull,
On whom as in despite the sun looks pale,
Killing their fruit with frowns?
And shall our quick blood, spirited with wine,
Seem frosty?

BOURBON: By faith and honour,

Our madams mock at us and plainly say
Our mettle is bred out, and they will give
Their bodies to the lust of English youth,
To new-store France with bastard warriers.

> QUEEN ISABEL *screams off. The music stops.*
> *Feature the Queen of France,* KATHARINE, *and* ALICE *at*
> *the table. The* QUEEN *pokes* KING CHARLES *on the arm.*
> KING CHARLES *wakes up.*

KING CHARLES: Where is Mountjoy the Herald? Speed
him hence.
Let him greet England with our sharp defiance.

> *We see* KING CHARLES *and his Court seated at table in*
> *long shot. The King of France rises.*

KING CHARLES: . . . Up, princes, and with spirit of
honour edged . . .

> *The three Dukes get up and come down in front of the*
> *table.*

KING CHARLES: . . . Bar Harry England, that sweeps
through our land
With pennons painted in the blood of Harfleur.
Go down upon him, you have power enough,
And in a captive chariot into Rouen
Bring him our prisoner.

CONSTABLE: This becomes the great.
Sorry am I his numbers are so few,
His soldiers sick and famished in their march,
For I am sure, when he shall see our army,
He'll drop his heart into the sink of fear
And for achievement, offer us his ransom.

KING CHARLES: Therefore, Lord Constable, haste on
Mountjoy.

> *The music starts as the three Dukes walk off left. Pan with*
> KING CHARLES *as he turns and walks over to the*
> DAUPHIN.

KING CHARLES: Prince Dauphin, you shall stay with us in Rouen.

DAUPHIN: Not so, I do beseech your majesty.

KING CHARLES: Be patient, for you shall remain with us.

KING CHARLES turns left.

KING CHARLES: Now forth, Lord Constable and princes all,
And quickly bring us word of England's fall.

KING CHARLES turns back to the DAUPHIN and kisses him.
Dissolve to the fields of Picardy. MOUNTJOY, preceded by two Heralds and followed by his Standard Bearer, rides up. The Heralds sound a fanfare as MOUNTJOY and the Standard Bearer ride off.
KING HENRY V is surrounded by knights. He steps forward as MOUNTJOY and the Standard Bearer ride in. The music stops.

MOUNTJOY: You know me by my habit.

KING HENRY: Well, then, I know thee. What shall I know of thee?

We feature MOUNTJOY and the Standard Bearer with KING HENRY on their left in the foreground.

MOUNTJOY: My master's mind.

KING HENRY: Unfold it.

MOUNTJOY: Thus says my King: 'Say thou to Harry of England: Though we seemed dead, we did but slumber. Tell him we could have rebuked him at Harfleur, but that we thought not good to bruise an injury till it were full ripe. Now we speak upon our cue, and our voice is imperial. England shall repent his folly, see his weakness, and admire our sufferance. Bid him therefore consider of his ransom . . .

KING HENRY is seen in medium close-up with

46

MOUNTJOY *on his right in the foreground..*

MOUNTJOY: . . . Which must proportion the losses we have borne, the subjects we have lost, the disgrace we have digested.

MOUNTJOY *is now in close-up.*

MOUNTJOY: For our losses, his exchequer is too poor; for the effusion of our blood, the muster of his kingdom too faint a number; and for our disgrace, his own person . . .

HENRY V *is now in close-up.*

MOUNTJOY: *(off)* . . . kneeling at our feet, but a weak and worthless satisfaction.

Resume shot of MOUNTJOY *and the Standard Bearer with* KING HENRY *on their left.*

MOUNTJOY: To this add defiance, and tell him for conclusion, he hath betrayed his followers, whose condemnation is pronounced. So far my King and master. So much my office.

KING HENRY: What is thy name? I know thy quality.

MOUNTJOY: Mountjoy.

Resume shot of KING HENRY *with* MOUNTJOY, *on his right.*

HERALD: *(aside to King Henry)* Mountjoy.

KING HENRY: Thou dost thy office fairly. Turn thee back
And tell thy King I do not seek him now,
But could be willing to march on to Calais
Without impeachment . . .

Resume shot of MOUNTJOY *and the Standard Bearer with* KING HENRY *on their left.*

KING HENRY: . . . For, to say the sooth,
My people are with sickness much enfeebled,
My numbers lessened . . .
Go, therefore, tell thy master here I am:

My ransom is this frail and worthless body;
My army, but a weak and sickly guard.

HENRY V is seen in close-up.

KING HENRY: Yet, God before, tell him we will come on,
Though France herself and such another neighbour
Stand in our way . . .
If we may pass, we will; if we be hindered,
We shall your tawny ground with your red blood
Discolour: and so, Mountjoy . . .

*Resume shot of MOUNTJOY and the Standard Bearer
with KING HENRY on their left.*

KING HENRY: . . . Fare you well.
We would not seek a battle as we are,
Nor as we are we say we will not shun it.

HENRY V is seen again in close-up.

KING HENRY: So tell your master.

MOUNTJOY flourishes his hat.

MOUNTJOY: I shall deliver so.

HENRY V takes and throws a purse of money.

KING HENRY: There's for thy labour, Mountjoy.

*MOUNTJOY catches the purse and rides out followed by
his Standard Bearer.*

MOUNTJOY: Thanks to your highness.

*As a fanfare sounds, we feature HENRY V and
GLOUCESTER. The King turns to a knight behind him.*

KING HENRY: March to the bridge!

A drum roll starts.

KING HENRY: It now draws towards night.
Beyond the river we'll encamp ourselves,
And on the morrow bid them march away.

KING HENRY, GLOUCESTER *and the army move off.*
*Dissolve to the English army marching wearily away
along the bank of a river in Picardy.*
*As the drum roll stops, fade out to a black screen, over
which the voice of* CHORUS *is heard, accompanied by
music.*

CHORUS: *(off)* Now entertain conjecture of a time
When creeping murmur and the poring dark
Fills the wide vessel of the universe.

*Fade in on a long shot of the French and the English
camps at night.*

CHORUS: *(off)* From camp to camp through the foul womb
of night,
The hum of either army stilly sounds;
That the fixed sentinels almost receive
The secret whispers of each other's watch.
Fire answers fire, and through their paly flames
Each battle sees the other's umbered face.
Steed threatens steed, in high and boastful neighs
Piercing the night's dull ear, and from the tents
The armourers, accomplishing the knights,
With busy hammers closing rivets up,
Give dreadful note of preparation.

Track in to the French camp.

CHORUS: Proud of their numbers and secure in soul,
The confident and overlusty French
Do the low-rated English play at dice,
And chide the cripple tardy-gaited night,
Who like a foul and ugly witch doth limp
So tediously away.

On the sound of a fanfare, dissolve to a shot of the
CONSTABLE'S *armour inside the tent of the* DUKE OF
ORLEANS. *The music stops.*
On to the CONSTABLE *seated at a dining table.*

CONSTABLE: Tut! I have the best armour of the world.

49

Track back to reveal the DUKES OF ORLEANS *and* BOURBON.

CONSTABLE: Would it were day!

ORLEANS: You have an excellent armour. But let my horse have his due.

CONSTABLE: It is the best horse of Europe.

BOURBON: Will it never be morning?

The DAUPHIN *enters.*

DAUPHIN: My Lord Orléans, my Lord High Constable, you talk of horse and armour?

The DUKES *rise.*

ORLEANS: You are as well provided of both as any prince in the world.

The DAUPHIN *motions them to sit down and they do so.*

DAUPHIN: What a long night is this! I will not change my horse with any that treads on four hooves. Ça, ha! He bounds from the earth.

Track in to feature the DAUPHIN *and the* CONSTABLE.

DAUPHIN: When I bestride him, I soar, I am a hawk; he trots the air, the earth sings when he touches it, he is of the colour of nutmeg. And of the heat of the ginger. He is pure air and fire, and all other jades you may call beasts.

CONSTABLE: It is indeed, my lord, a most absolute and excellent horse.

DAUPHIN: It is the prince of palfreys.

Pan with the DAUPHIN *as he walks behind* ORLEANS *and* BOURBON.

DAUPHIN: His neigh is like the bidding of a monarch, and his countenance enforces homage.

BOURBON: No more, cousin.

DAUPHIN: Nay, cousin, the man hath no wit that cannot from the rising of the lark to the lodging of the lamb vary deserved praise on my palfrey.

Track back to include the whole group as the DAUPHIN *walks round to the front of the table.* (STILL)

DAUPHIN: I once writ a sonnet in his praise. It began thus, 'Wonder of nature' –

BOURBON: I have heard a sonnet begin so to one's mistress.

DAUPHIN: Then did they imitate that which I composed to my courser, for my horse is my mistress.

CONSTABLE: Methought yesterday your mistress shrewdly shook your back.

ORLEANS: My Lord Constable, the armour that I saw in your tent tonight, are those stars or suns upon it?

CONSTABLE: Stars, my lord.

DAUPHIN: Some of them will fall tomorrow, I hope.

CONSTABLE: That may be.

DAUPHIN: *(looking out of the tent)* Will it never be day?

Track back as he turns round.

DAUPHIN: I will trot tomorrow a mile, and my way shall be paved with English faces. Who'll go hazard with me for twenty prisoners?

There is the sound of a fanfare.

BOURBON: 'Tis midnight.

DAUPHIN: I'll go arm myself.

He goes out.

ORLEANS: Ha! The Dauphin longs for morning.

BOURBON *gets up from the table and walks left to the tent opening.*

BOURBON: He longs to eat the English.

CONSTABLE: I think he will eat all he kills.

ORLEANS: He never did harm, that I heard of.

CONSTABLE: Nor will do none tomorrow. He'll keep that good name still.

ORLEANS: I know him to be valiant.

CONSTABLE: I was told that, by one that knows him better than you.

ORLEANS: What's he?

CONSTABLE: Marry, he told me so himself.

ORLEANS *laughs.*

CONSTABLE: And he said he cared not who knew it.

A MESSENGER *enters and bows down to the* CONSTABLE.

MESSENGER: My Lord High Constable . . .

The MESSENGER *and the* CONSTABLE *are seen in close-up.*

MESSENGER: . . . The English lie within fifteen hundred paces of your tents.

CONSTABLE: Who hath measured the ground?

MESSENGER: The Lord Grandpré.

CONSTABLE: A valiant and most expert gentleman.

The MESSENGER *withdraws, leaving the* CONSTABLE *and the Dukes.*

CONSTABLE: *(getting up)* Would it were day!

He turns left to the tent opening. A fanfare sounds as he walks out of the tent.

CONSTABLE: Alas, poor Harry of England. He longs not for the dawning as we do.

The DUKES OF ORLÉANS *and* BOURBON *follow the*

52

CONSTABLE *outside the tent. It is night. They stand overlooking the English camp in the distance. Another fanfare sounds.*

ORLEANS: What a wretched and peevish fellow is this King of England, to mope with his fat-brained followers so far out of his knowledge.

CONSTABLE: If the English had any apprehension, they'd run away.

ORLEANS: That they lack. For if their heads had any intellectual armour, they could never wear such heavy headpieces.

BOURBON: That island of England breeds very valiant creatures. Their mastiffs are of unmatchable courage.

ORLEANS: Foolish curs, that run winking into the mouth of a Russian bear, and have their heads crushed like rotten apples. You may as well say, 'That's a valiant flea, that dare eat his breakfast on the lip of a lion.'

CONSTABLE: Just, just. And the men are like the mastiffs, give them great meals of beef, and iron and steel, they'll eat like wolves and fight like devils.

ORLEANS: Ah, but those English are shrewdly out of beef.

BOURBON: Then shall we find tomorrow, they have only stomachs to eat, and none to fight.

Another fanfare sounds.

CONSTABLE: Now it is time to arm. Come, shall we about it?

They turn and go back into the tent.

ORLEANS: It is now two o'clock. But, let me see – by ten we shall have each a hundred Englishmen.

ORLEANS *drops the tent flap.*
Fade out, then fade in to a long shot of the French camp at night. Then pan slowly left in the direction of the English

camp. Music begins.

CHORUS: *(off)* The country cocks do crow, the clocks do toll
And the third hour of drowsy morning name.
The poor condemnèd English,
Like sacrifices, by their watchful fires
Sit patiently and inly ruminate
The morning's danger; and their gesture sad,
Investing lank lean cheeks and war-worn coats,
Presenteth them unto the gazing moon
So many horrid ghosts.

We hold the English camp in centre frame and track in.

CHORUS: *(off)* O now, who will behold
The royal captain of this ruined band
Walking from watch to watch, from tent to tent,
Let him cry, 'Praise and glory on his head!'

Dissolve to the English camp where we track in slowly to hold an English Soldier warming himself by a brazier.

CHORUS: *(off)* For forth he goes and visits all his host,
Bids them good morrow with a modest smile
And calls them brothers, friends and countrymen.
A largess universal, like the sun,
His liberal eye doth give to everyone,
Thawing cold fear, that mean and gentle all
Behold, as may unworthiness define,
A little touch of Harry in the night.

A shadow falls across the Soldier. KING HENRY, GLOUCESTER, SALISBURY *and their Guard walk away. The music stops.*

KING HENRY: Gloucester!

HENRY V *speaks to his nobles.*

KING HENRY: . . . 'Tis true that we are in great danger,
The greater therefore should our courage be.

ERPINGHAM *comes up from behind.* (STILL)

KING HENRY: Good morrow, old Sir Thomas Erpingham.
A good soft pillow for that good white head
Were better than a churlish turf of France.

ERPINGHAM: Not so, my liege. This lodging suits me better,
Since I may say, 'Now lie I like a king.'

They all laugh.

KING HENRY: Lend me thy cloak, Sir Thomas.
I and my bosom must debate awhile,
And then I would no other company.

HENRY V *takes* ERPINGHAM'S *cloak and puts it on.*

ERPINGHAM: The Lord in heaven bless thee, noble Harry!

The nobles move away.

KING HENRY: God-a-mercy, old heart!

He turns and walks away. Track forward to hold a tent flap from which PISTOL *emerges.*

PISTOL: Qui va là?

HENRY V *swings round.*

KING HENRY: A friend.

PISTOL *draws his sword.*

PISTOL: Discuss unto me: art thou officer, or art thou base, common and popular?

KING HENRY: *(off)* I am a gentleman of a company.

PISTOL: Trail'st thou the puissant pike?

KING HENRY: *(off)* Even so. What are you?

PISTOL: As good a gentleman as the Emperor.

KING HENRY: *(off)* Then you are better than the King.

PISTOL: The King's a bawcock and a heart of gold,
A lad of life, an imp of fame,

Of parents good, of fist most valiant.
I kiss his dirty shoe, and from heart-string
I love the lovely bully.

PISTOL comes closer and peers at us.

PISTOL: What is thy name?

KING HENRY: *(off)* Henry Le Roy.

PISTOL: Le Roy? A Cornish name: are thou of Cornish crew?

KING HENRY: *(off)* No, I'm a Welshman.

PISTOL: Know'st thou Fluellen?

KING HENRY: *(off)* Yes.

PISTOL: Art thou his friend?

KING HENRY: *(off)* I am his kinsman too.

PISTOL: Well, tell him, I'll knock his leek about his head
Upon Saint Davy's day.

KING HENRY: *(off)* Do not wear your dagger in your cap that day,
Lest he knock that about yours.

PISTOL: A fico for thee, then!

PISTOL runs back.

KING HENRY: *(off)* I thank you: God be with you!

PISTOL: My name is Pistol called.

KING HENRY: *(off)* It sorts well with your fierceness.

PISTOL goes out.
HENRY V laughs and walks away. Track with him. He suddenly stops.
A man is scrabbling in the undergrowth. It is FLUELLEN, who stands up and jumps down to a trench.

GOWER: *(off)* Captain Fluellen!

Pan to show GOWER approaching.

56

GOWER: Captain Fluellen!

FLUELLEN jumps up beside him.

FLUELLEN: Sh! Sh! In the name of Beezlebub, speak lower. If you would take the pains but to examine the wars of Pompey the Great, you shall find, I warrant you, there is no tiddle-taddle nor pibble-pabble in Pompey's camp. I warrant you, you shall find the ceremonies of the wars, and the cares of it, and the forms of it, to be otherwise.

GOWER: Why, the enemy is loud. You can hear him all night.

FLUELLEN: If the enemy is an ass and a fool and a prating coxcomb, is it meet, think you, that we should also, look you, be an ass and a fool and a prating coxcomb? In your own conscience, now?

GOWER: I will speak lower.

FLUELLEN: I pray you and do beseech you that you will.

They move off.

KING HENRY: *(off)* Though it appear a little out of fashion There is much care and valour in this Welshman.

Track back and hold three soldiers, COURT, BATES *and* WILLIAMS, *seated round a camp fire.*

COURT: Brother John Bates, is not that the morning which breaks yonder?

BATES: I think it be. But we have no great cause to desire the approach of day.

WILLIAMS: We see yonder the beginning of the day, but I think we shall never see the end of it.

He looks up.

WILLIAMS: Who goes there?

The cloaked KING HENRY *appears.*

KING HENRY: A friend.

WILLIAMS *comes into shot.*

WILLIAMS: Under what captain serve you?

KING HENRY: Under Sir Thomas Erpingham.

WILLIAMS *and* HENRY V *join* COURT *and* BATES *at the camp fire and sit down with them.*

WILLIAMS: A good old commander and a most kind gentleman. I pray you, what thinks he of our estate?

KING HENRY: Even as men wrecked upon a sand that look to be washed off the next tide.

BATES: He hath not told his thought to the King?

KING HENRY: No, nor it is not meet he should. For I think the King is but a man, as I am. The violet smells to him as it doth to me. His ceremonies laid by, in his nakedness he appears but a man. Therefore, when he sees reason of fears, as we do, his fears, without doubt, be of the same relish as ours are. Yet no man should find in him any appearance of fear, lest he, by showing it, should dishearten his army.

WILLIAMS: He may show what outward courage he will, but I believe, as cold a night as 'tis, he could wish himself in Thames up to the neck. So I would he were, and I by him, at all adventures, so we were quit here.

HENRY V *is now seen in close-up.*

KING HENRY: By my troth, I will speak my conscience of the King. I think he would not wish himself anywhere but where he is.

BATES *is seen in close-up.*

BATES: Then I would he were here alone. So should he be sure to be ransomed, and a many poor men's lives saved.

Resume close-up of HENRY V.

KING HENRY: Methinks, I could not die anywhere so contented, as in the King's company, his cause being just and his quarrel honourable.

BATES *and* WILLIAMS *are now seen together.*

WILLIAMS: That's more than we know.

BATES: Ay, or more than we should seek after.
For we know enough, if we know we are the King's
subjects. If his cause be wrong, our obedience to the King
wipes the crime of it out of us.

COURT: *(off)* But if the cause be not good . . .

COURT *is now seen in close-up.*

COURT: . . . the King himself hath a heavy reckoning to
make, when all those legs and arms and heads chopped off
in a battle shall join together at the latter day, and cry all,
'We died at such a place' – some swearing, some crying for
a surgeon, some upon their wives left poor behind them,
some upon the debts they owe, some upon their children
rawly left. I'm afraid there are few die well that die in a
battle, for how can they charitably dispose of anything,
when blood is their argument? Now if these men do not die
well, it will be a black matter for the King that led them to
it.

WILLIAMS: *(off)* Ay!

All four are seen round the fire. COURT *begins to fall
asleep.*

BATES: Ay!

KING HENRY: So, if a son that is by his father sent about
merchandise do sinfully miscarry upon the sea, the
imputation of his wickedness, by your rule, should be
imposed upon his father that sent him. But this is not so.
The King is not bound to answer for the particular endings
of his soldiers, nor the father of his son, for they purpose
not their deaths when they propose their services. Every
subject's duty is the King's, but every subject's soul is his
own.

WILLIAMS: Ay, 'tis certain, every man that dies ill, the ill on his own head. The King's not to answer for it.

BATES: I do not desire he should answer for me, and yet I determine to fight lustily for him.

KING HENRY: I myself heard the King say he would not be ransomed.

WILLIAMS: He said so, to make us fight cheerfully, but when our throats are cut, he may be ransomed, and we ne'er the wiser.

KING HENRY: If ever I live to see it, I'll never trust his word after.

WILLIAMS *laughs in close-up, turning to the others.*

WILLIAMS: That's a perilous shot out of a pop-gun, that a poor and a private displeasure can do against a monarch!

Pan with him as he moves close to HENRY V.

WILLIAMS: You may as well go about to turn the sun to ice with fanning in his face with a peacock's feather. You'll never trust his word after! Come, 'tis a foolish saying.

KING HENRY: Your reproof is something too round. I should be angry with you, if the time were convenient.

There is the sound of a fanfare.

WILLIAMS: Let it be a quarrel between us then, if you live.

BATES: Be . . .

BATES *is seen in close-up.*

BATES: . . . Friends, you English fools . . .

He grabs WILLIAMS *by the arm and they walk away. Track back to leave* HENRY V *sitting alone with the sleeping* COURT.

BATES: . . . Be friends, we have French quarrels enough if you could tell how to reckon.

HENRY V *speaks a soliloquy in close-up.*

KING HENRY: *(off)* Upon the King!
Let us our lives, our souls, our debts, our careful wives,
Our children, and our sins, lay on the King!
We must bear all. What infinite heartsease
Must kings forego that private men enjoy!
And what have kings that privates have not too,
Save ceremony.
And what art thou, thou idol ceremony,
That sufferest more
Of mortal griefs than do thy worshippers?

Track in slowly into a large close-up of HENRY V.

KING HENRY: What drink'st thou oft, instead of homage sweet,
But poisoned flattery? O, be sick, great greatness,
And bid thy ceremony give thee cure.
Canst thou, when thou command'st the beggar's knee,
Command the health of it? No, thou proud dream,
That play'st so subtly with a king's repose;
I am a king that find thee, and I know
'Tis not the orb and sceptre, crown imperial,
The throne he sits on, nor the tide of pomp
That beats upon the high shore of this world;
Not all these, laid in bed majestical,
Can sleep so soundly as the wretched slave . . .

HENRY V *looks down. Track back to show* COURT
asleep at his feet.

KING HENRY: . . . Who with a body filled and vacant mind,
Gets him to rest, crammed with distressful bread;
Never sees horrid night . . .

We still slowly track back as HENRY V *looks at the sunrise
in the night sky.*

KING HENRY: . . . . The child of hell;
But like a lackey from the rise to set

61

Sweats in the eye of Phoebus; and all night
Sleeps in Elysium; next day, after dawn,
Doth rise and help Hyperion to his horse,
And follows so the ever-running year
With profitable labour to his grave.
And, but for ceremony, such a wretch,
Winding up days with toil, and nights with sleep,
Had the forehand and vantage of a king.

> HENRY V *sits back against a tree.* (STILL).
> *Seen in close-up,* HENRY V *hears a voice.*

ERPINGHAM: *(off)* My lord!

> *The King looks up.*
> ERPINGHAM *is now in close shot.*

ERPINGHAM: . . . Your nobles, jealous of your absence,
Seek through your camp to find you.

> HENRY V *stands up and comes into shot.*

KING HENRY: Good old knight.

> HENRY V *turns and walks up to the camp, followed by*
> ERPINGHAM. *Track with them, as we hear prayers being*
> *chanted from a tent.*
> HENRY V *pulls back the tent flap and sees a service in*
> *progress. The chanting has stopped and prayers are being*
> *read. Track with the king as he walks on. An 'AMEN' is*
> *chanted and more prayers are spoken from a second tent.*
> *The King stops and turns to* ERPINGHAM.

KING HENRY: Collect them all together at my tent. I'll be
before thee.

> ERPINGHAM *goes out left. Pan with the King walking on*
> *alone. There is the sound of a fanfare as* HENRY V *turns*
> *round and kneels down.*

KING HENRY: O God of battles, steel my soldiers' hearts,
Possess them not with fear, Take from them now
The sense of reckoning lest the opposèd numbers
Pluck their hearts from them.

GLOUCESTER: *(off)* My lord!

GLOUCESTER comes down the hillside to HENRY V.

GLOUCESTER: My lord, the army stays upon your presence.

There is the sound of a fanfare.

KING HENRY: I know thy errand, I will go with thee.

Again the trumpets sound.

KING HENRY: The day, my friends, and all things stay for me.

As the fanfare sounds for a fourth time, KING HENRY takes GLOUCESTER'S shoulder and they walk away up the hill.
Fade out, then fade in to a fleur-de-lis on a tent flap being swept aside to show the DAUPHIN and the French Dukes arming themselves. The music starts. (STILL)

BOURBON: The sun doth gild our armour! Up, my lords!

DAUPHIN: Monte cheval! My horse! Varlet! Lacquais! Ha!

ORLEANS: O brave spirit!

DAUPHIN: Via les eaux et la terre!

ORLEANS: Rien puis? L'air et le feu!

DAUPHIN: Ciel, cousin Orléans!

The CONSTABLE enters.

CONSTABLE: Hark, how our steeds for present service neigh.

DAUPHIN: Mount them and make incision in their hides,
That their hot blood may spin in English eyes
And quench them with superior courage. Ha!

A MESSENGER comes in.

MESSENGER: The English are embattled, you French peers.

He goes out.

CONSTABLE: A very little little let us do,
And all is done. Then let the trumpets sound
The tucket sonance and the note to mount.

Pan with him as he walks down and goes out.

CONSTABLE: Come, come away!
The sun is high, and we outwear the day.

In the French camp, the CONSTABLE *enters and is
escorted to his horse. Pan to show* BOURBON *and*
ORLEANS *following, and finally the* DAUPHIN *is escorted
to his horse.*
*Dissolve to the Cross of St. George, then pan with it to
reveal the Standard Bearer and a group of English
knights.* GLOUCESTER *enters. It is the English camp.*

GLOUCESTER: Where is the King?

SALISBURY: The King himself is rode to view their battle.

WESTMORELAND: Of fighting men they have full three
score hundred.

EXETER: There's five to one, besides they are all flesh.

GLOUCESTER: God's arm strike with us, 'tis a fearful odds.

SALISBURY *shakes hands with his fellow noble knights.*

SALISBURY: Well, God with you, princes all. I'll to my
charge.
If we no more meet till we meet in heaven,
Then joyfully, my noble Westmoreland,
My dear Lord Gloucester, my good Lord Exeter,
And my kind kinsman, warriors all adieu!

WESTMORELAND: Farewell, good Salisbury.

GLOUCESTER: And good luck go with thee!

EXETER: Farewell, kind lord.

SALISBURY *goes out.*

64

WESTMORELAND: O that we now had here
But one ten thousand of those men in England
That do not work today.

KING HENRY: *(off)* What's he that wishes so?

The music stops as KING HENRY *enters.*

KING HENRY: My cousin Westmoreland? No, my fair
cousin.

Pan with him as he walks to the group of noble knights.

KING HENRY: If we are marked to die, we are enough
To do our country loss; and if to live,
The fewer men, the greater share of honour.
God's will, I pray thee wish not one man more.
Rather proclaim it, Westmoreland, through my host . . .

Pan with the King as he walks away.

KING HENRY: . . . That he which hath no stomach to this
fight,
Let him depart. His passport shall be drawn
And crowns for convoy put into his purse.

He turns round to face us, then walks closer.

KING HENRY: We would not die in that man's company
That fears his fellowship to die with us.
This day is called the Feast of Crispian:
He that outlives this day, and comes safe home,
Will stand a-tiptoe when this day is named
And rouse him at the name of Crispian.

He walks still closer to us.

KING HENRY: He that shall see this day and live t'old age,
Will yearly on the vigil feast his neighbours
And say, 'Tomorrow is Saint Crispian.'
Then will he strip his sleeve and show his scars
And say, 'These wounds I had on Crispian's day.'

Track with him as he turns and walks left.

KING HENRY: Old men forget; yet all shall be forgot,
But he'll remember, with advantages,
What feats he did that day. Then shall our names
Familiar in his mouth as household words –
Harry the King, Bedford and Exeter . . .

He climbs on to a cart. Track slowly back to a long shot to show his army clustered around him. (STILL)

KING HENRY: Warwick and Talbot, Salisbury and Gloucester –
Be in their flowing cups freshly remembered.
This story shall the good man teach his son,
And Crispin Crispian shall ne'er go by
From this day to the ending of the world
But we in it shall be remembered,
We few, we happy few, we band of brothers.
For he today that sheds his blood with me,
Shall be my brother, be he ne'er so base.
And gentlemen in England, now a-bed,
Shall think themselves accursed they were not here,
And hold their manhoods cheap whiles any speaks
That fought with us upon Saint Crispian's day.

The soldiers cheer. SALISBURY *pushes through the soldiers at the side of the cart.*

SALISBURY: My sovereign lord, bestow yourself with speed.
The French are bravely in their battles set
And will with all expedience charge on us.

KING HENRY: All things are ready, if our minds be so.

WESTMORELAND *comes round to the cart.*

WESTMORELAND: Perish the man whose mind is backward now!

HENRY V *is seen in close-up.*

KING HENRY: Thou dost not wish more help from England, coz?

WESTMORELAND *is also seen in close-up.*

WESTMORELAND: God's will, my liege, would you and I alone,
Without more help, could fight this . . .

Resume close-up of HENRY V.

WESTMORELAND: *(off)* . . . battle out!

KING HENRY: You know your places. God be with you all!

Pan with KING HENRY *as he turns and jumps on a horse. The music starts as he rides round close to and then away from us.*
English soldiers are driving in stakes with wooden mallets. (STILL)
An English soldier helps KING HENRY *to put on his chain mail.*
The DAUPHIN *is lowered by pulley on to his horse.* (STILL)
The DAUPHIN *is settled on his horse. Pan with it as it is led round.*
A line of French drummers waits.
ORLEANS, *the* DAUPHIN *and* BOURBON *are being handed cups of wine on horseback.*
The CONSTABLE *and another knight toast the* DAUPHIN *and company.*
The DAUPHIN *and company acknowledge the toast.* (STILL)
Englishmen are banging in stakes.
A line of Englishmen is banging in stakes.
Arrows are being distributed to English archers.
Englishmen are sharpening stakes. There is a fanfare.
The man nearest us looks ahead of him.
MOUNTJOY *and the Standard Bearer, escorted by two Heralds, ride up. The Heralds stop to blow a fanfare. Pan with* MOUNTJOY *and the Standard Bearer as they ride on into the English camp.*
MOUNTJOY *dismounts and is escorted by the English Herald out of shot.*

KING HENRY is in full armour on his horse. MOUNTJOY and the English Herald come in and doff their hats to the King, who smiles at MOUNTJOY.

MOUNTJOY stands by the head of the King's horse. The music stops.

MOUNTJOY: Once more I come to know of thee, King Harry,
If for thy ransom thou wilt now compound
Before thy most assurèd overthrow.

The King's horse shakes its head.
KING HENRY speaks down to MOUNTJOY.

KING HENRY: Who hath sent thee now?

MOUNTJOY: The Constable of France.

Drums sound in the distance.

KING HENRY: I pray thee, bear my former answer back.
Bid them achieve me, and then sell my bones.
Good God, why should they mock poor fellows thus?
The man that once did sell the lion's skin
While the beast lived, was killed with hunting him,
And many of our bodies shall no doubt
Find native graves, upon the which, I trust,
Shall witness live in brass of this day's work
And those that leave their valiant bones in France,
Dying like men, though buried in your dunghills,
They shall be famed. For there the sun shall greet them
And draw their honours reeking up to heaven,
Leaving their earthly parts to choke your clime,
The smell whereof shall breed a plague in France.
Let me speak proudly: tell the Constable
We are but warriors for the working day.
Our gayness and our gilt are all besmirched
With rainy marching in the painful field.
And time hath worn us into slovenry:
But, by the mass, our hearts are in the trim . . .

The English soldiers cheer. Then the music starts.

68

KING HENRY: Come thou no more for ransom, gentle herald,
They shall have none, I swear, but these my bones,
Which if they have as I will leave 'em them,
Shall yield them little. Tell the Constable.

The King rides off.
MOUNTJOY flourishes his hat.

MOUNTJOY: I shall, King Harry. And so fare thee well.

He prepares to mount his horse.
Now MOUNTJOY is on his horse.

MOUNTJOY: Thou never shalt hear herald any more.

To a fanfare, he rides off followed by his Standard Bearer.
KING HENRY rides in from the left.

KING HENRY: Now, soldiers, march away.

The English soldiers cheer him.

KING HENRY: And how thou pleasest, God, dispose the day.

Dissolve to an aerial view of the battlefield.
A fanfare announces a shot of the French army ready for battle. (STILL)
A fanfare announces a reverse shot of the English army, prepared to fight.
A line of French drummers beat their drums.
French crossbowmen move up. (STILL)
French drummers strike their drums.
French cavalry men move up to battle position. The CONSTABLE signals with his sword, and they turn left.
French standards dip and move out of shot.
Pan across the shining mire to show the reflection and then the hoofs of French cavalry.
The French cavalry is in battle order at the walk. (STILL)
A line of English bowmen draw their bows.
KING HENRY bestrides his horse.

The French cavalry break into a trot, then a canter, then a gallop, then a full tilt charge. (STILL)

A line of English archers with bows drawn. (STILL)

A low angle shot of HENRY V *with his sword poised for a signal to the archers. His glance changes from left to right.*

The French cavalry charges at the English stakes in the foreground.

The line of English bowmen wait with bows drawn.

HENRY V *slashes down his sword. The music stops.*

A line of English archers – they fire.

Two lines of English archers – they fire. (STILL)

The French cavalry charge at stake emplacements in the foreground. Arrows sizzle through the air overhead and strike home. The French horses rear.

The music starts as the English archers fire at the French cavalry. (STILL)

Four quick shots show the French cavalry in total confusion.

Two quick shots show French chargers rearing madly.

The English archers keep on firing.

Three quick shots of the confusion of the French horsemen.

Two quick shots of horses neighing hysterically.

English archers run forward and prepare to fire.

A French charger rears.

Four more quick shots of the French cavalry in confusion.

A second wave of French cavalry charges towards us.

The first wave of French cavalry begins to retreat.

French horsemen retreat to the right.

The second wave of French cavalry charge left.

The French cavalry in full retreat.

The second wave of French cavalry charging.

The first wave of French cavalry in retreat clashes with the second wave of advancing French cavalry.

Advancing French cavalry trying to make headway.

The two waves of cavalry enmeshed. (STILL)

English archers firing.

French cavalry enmeshed. Pan to a morass behind them.

English archers fire and run forward.
French infantry men, in support of their cavalry, become entangled in the morass.
French cavalry enmeshed.
The French infantry is struggling in the morass.
The music stops. Dissolve to the French infantry bogged down in the morass. (STILL)
The music starts as we dissolve to the third wave of advancing French cavalry appearing over a hilltop. The horsemen charge towards us. (STILL)
The French cavalry charging. English archers are firing from the fringe of a wood, but they retreat. There is a dissolve.
Seen from above, the French cavalry is charging through the wood. An English infantryman jumps from the branch of a tree onto a French knight.
The infantryman drags the knight from his horse and goes to stab him.
Another infantryman jumps from the branch of tree.
He hits the ground.
Another infantryman jumps from the branch of a tree.
The infantryman lands on the ground among the French knights.
Two more infantrymen jump from the branches.
English and French infantry fighting hand to hand. KING HENRY *with his Standard Bearer leads a flank attack with his knights.* (STILL) *Pan to hold the Standard.*
Dissolve to the battlefield as KING HENRY *rides round from the right. Pan with him.*

KING HENRY: Well have we done, thrice-valiant country-men.
But all's not done. Yet keep the French the field.

He has ridden up and on his last word slashes with his sword.
Dissolve to a close shot of the English Standard, the Cross of St. George. Pan to show HENRY V *and the Standard Bearer riding through the thick of the infantry fighting.*
Dissolve to a close shot of the French Standard. Pan to

71

reveal in long shot French knights and MOUNTJOY
fleeing to a hilltop.
The French knights are distraught on the hilltop.

DAUPHIN: O everlasting shame! Let's stab ourselves.
Be these the wretches that we played at dice for?

ORLEANS: Is this the King we sent to for his ransom?

The CONSTABLE *rides in.*

CONSTABLE: Shame, and eternal shame, nothing but
shame!
Let's die in honour. Once more back again!

The DAUPHIN *and* ORLEANS *look at him.*

ORLEANS: We are enough yet living in the field
To smother up the English in our throngs
If any order might be thought upon.

The CONSTABLE *rides round to the foreground.*

CONSTABLE: The devil take order now! I'll to the throng.
Let life be short, else shame will be too long.

He rides out of shot.
BOURBON *starts to move off after the* CONSTABLE.
The CONSTABLE *and the Standard Bearer ride down the
hill and off.* BOURBON *leads a second party of knights,
who pause to wait for the remaining few, but turn and ride
off.*
The DAUPHIN *and* MOUNTJOY *stay on the hilltop,
looking off.*
MOUNTJOY *looks right and left.*
The DAUPHIN *looks left.*
Dissolve to the English Camp. French knights ride in.
(STILL)
*A French knight rides into the English camp. Pan with
him as he cuts down a tent and kills a Boy.*
*Another camp Boy picks up the dead Boy and looks at
him, then drops him quickly.*
*The second Boy is running hard. A French knight crosses
in front of him.*

*There is a small fire on the ground. A French knight rides
in and picks up a fire brand with his sword. He flings it
into a tent. Another knight rides in. Pan down to the fire,
as this knight spears a fire brand with his sword.*
*Start on a close shot of the fire brand aloft on the sword
point. Pan to reveal the knight preparing to fling it into a
cart. Another French knight crosses the screen as a Boy
runs towards us with a casket in his hand.*
*The Boy runs and stops near a bush with a brazier
alongside.*
The knight flings the fire brand into the cart.
The Boy thrusts the casket under the bush and runs out.
The knight dashes in and overturns the brazier.
The bush catches fire. The music stops.
*We are inside a tent on fire with a dead Boy. Through the
tent opening, French knights are seen to ride away.*
*The music starts as we dissolve to a long shot of the
English camp on fire.*
From the hilltop, the DAUPHIN *looks at the burning
camp. He surveys the scene then rides out.* MOUNTJOY
rides in.
The marauding French knights ride in and join
MOUNTJOY. *In the distance, the* DAUPHIN *is seen in
flight.*
The music stops as we dissolve to FLUELLEN *in the
English Camp with a dead Boy in his arms.*

FLUELLEN: God's plud! Kill the boys and the luggage!

GOWER *walks in with a Monk. Track back to medium
shot.*

FLUELLEN: 'Tis expressly against the law of arms. 'Tis as
arrant a piece of knavery, mark you now, as can be offered.
In your conscience now, is it not?

GOWER: 'Tis certain there's not a boy left alive. And the
cowardly rascals that ran from the battle ha' done this
slaughter.

KING HENRY *on foot, followed by a soldier leading his
horse, enters with his Standard Bearer on another horse.*

MONK: Here comes His Majesty.

Track forward as HENRY V *approaches them.*

KING HENRY: I was not angry since I came to France
Until this instant.

He mounts his horse and rides out. The music starts as
HENRY V *rides full tilt back to the battlefield.* (STILL)
Pan with his ride.
The CONSTABLE *is in the thick of the fighting.* (STILL)
The CONSTABLE *lifts his visor and looks off.*
KING HENRY *followed by his Standard Bearer is riding*
up to meet the CONSTABLE.
The CONSTABLE *slams down his visor.*
The CONSTABLE *rears his horse and rides off.*
KING HENRY *and the* CONSTABLE *clash swords.*
The CONSTABLE *prepares to attack again.*
KING HENRY *swings his horse round and the*
CONSTABLE *rides in. They exchange sword blows.*
(STILL)
The CONSTABLE *striking with his sword.*
The sword crashing on KING HENRY'S *helmet.*
The CONSTABLE'S *horse rearing.*
KING HENRY *rides back. Pan with him as the*
CONSTABLE *rides in.*
The CONSTABLE *swinging his horse round to attack*
again.
KING HENRY *swinging his horse round.*
The CONSTABLE *riding in.*
KING HENRY *and the* CONSTABLE *exchange sword*
blows.
KING HENRY'S *sword knocks the* CONSTABLE'S *sword*
out of his hand.
KING HENRY'S *horse rearing. The* CONSTABLE *rides*
out.
The CONSTABLE *drops his shield. He grabs his mace.*
KING HENRY *rides in. The* CONSTABLE *swings his mace.*
The CONSTABLE'S *mace striking* KING HENRY'S *hand,*
sending the sword flying out of it.

KING HENRY'S sword sticking in the ground.
Low angle shot of the CONSTABLE raising his mace.
KING HENRY looking off.
The CONSTABLE about to strike.
Pan left with KING HENRY as he strikes the CONSTABLE'S chin with his mailed fist.
The CONSTABLE falls off his horse. Pan down to the ground with him.
The CONSTABLE lies on the ground.
Two soldiers leave the circle of English watchers and take the CONSTABLE'S horse. KING HENRY rides to the place where the CONSTABLE fell. He bends down to pick up the CONSTABLE'S sword. Pan with him as he goes.
The CONSTABLE'S body lies with KING HENRY'S sword beside it.
KING HENRY rides down the hill as the English soldiers surge round the body of the CONSTABLE . The King rides up to the English Herald.

KING HENRY: Take a trumpet, Herald.
Ride thou unto the horsemen on yon hill;
If they will fight with us, bid them come down,
Or void the field; they do offend our sight.

KING HENRY rides out, and the Herald rides away toward the French knights on the hill.
KING HENRY rides in to join EXETER and other English knights.

EXETER: Here comes the Herald of the French, my liege.

MOUNTJOY meets the English Herald on the hillside, and they ride down together.
The English knights address their King, as MOUNTJOY approaches.

SALISBURY: His eyes are humbler than they used to be.

KING HENRY: God's will, what mean's this, Herald?
Com'st thou again for ransom?

MOUNTJOY enters and bows. The music stops. (STILL)

75

MOUNTJOY *speaks in close-up.*

MOUNTJOY: No, great king.
I come to thee for charitable licence,
That we may wander o'er this bloody field
To book our dead and then to bury them.
The day is yours.

HENRY V *speaks in close-up.*

KING HENRY: Praisèd be God. and not our strength, for it.

Track back as the King takes off his helmet to show Agincourt Castle in the background. The music starts.

KING HENRY: What is this castle called that stands hard by?

MOUNTJOY: We call it Agincourt.

KING HENRY: Then call we this the field of Agincourt, Fought on the day of Crispin Crispianus.

MOUNTJOY kneels and kisses KING HENRY'S hand. The Standard Bearer steps forward and raises the Cross of St. George.
The Cross of St. George comes into shot with Agincourt Castle in the background.
Dissolve to soldiers lying dead on the Field of the Dead.
Dissolve to the English knights drinking in the English Camp. FLUELLEN ushers the English Herald forward, who walks over to KING HENRY who is surrounded by EXETER and other friends. Track with the Herald as he hands the king a paper.

HERALD: Here is the number of the slaughtered French.

KING HENRY: This note doth tell me of ten thousand French
That in the field lie slain,
Where is the number of our English dead?

The Herald hands him another paper. The music stops.

KING HENRY: Edward, the Duke of York, the Earl of Suffolk,

76

Sir Richard Ketly, Davy Gram Esquire;
And all other men but five-and-twenty score.
O God, thy arm was here!

EXETER: 'Tis wonderful!

KING HENRY: Come, we go in procession to the village.

KING HENRY'S *horse is led in.*

KING HENRY: Let there be sung *Non Nobis* and *Te Deum*.

The chanting begins as the King mounts his horse.

KING HENRY: And then to Calais and to England then . . .

Pan with the King as he leads the procession out of the English camp.

KING HENRY: . . . Where ne'er from France arrived more happier men.

Dissolve to a long shot of the English army walking in procession towards Agincourt village.
Dissolve to the Field of the Dead.
Fade out and cease the chanting in the English army in procession.
The music starts as we fade in to a long shot of Agincourt village under snow.
Dissolve to the gate to the village. Track forward to reveal PISTOL *flirting with village women inside a house. Pan to show three boys singing carols, then track forward again as a couple emerge from a house and go into the church alongside. A man comes out of the church, and pan with him to reveal* FLUELLEN *and* GOWER *sitting on a wall. We track in on them. The music stops.* GOWER *laughs.*

GOWER: Nay, that's right. But why wear you your leek today? Saint Davy's day is past.

FLUELLEN: There is occasions and causes why and wherefore in all things, Captain Gower. I will tell you ass my friend, Captain Gower. The rascally beggarly lousy knave Pistol, which you and yourself and all the world know to be no petter than a fellow, look you, of no merits,

77

he is come to me, and prings me pread and salt yesterday, look you, and bid me eat my leek.

GOWER *laughs.*

FLUELLEN: It was in a place where I could not breed no contention with him. But I will be bold as to wear it in my cap till I see him once again, and then I will tell him a little piece of my desires.

GOWER: Why, 'tis a gull, a fool, a rogue, that now and then goes to the wars, to grace himself at his return into London, under the form of soldier, and what such of the camp can do among foaming bottles, and ale-washed wits, is wonderful to be thought on.

He laughs and points.

GOWER: Here he comes . . .

Pan with PISTOL *as he walks on to bring himself in front of* FLUELLEN *and* GOWER.

GOWER: *(off)* . . . swelling like a turkey-cock.

FLUELLEN: *(off)* 'Tis no matter for his swellings, nor his turkey-cocks.

FLUELLEN *and* GOWER *are now in shot.*

FLUELLEN: God pless you, Pistol! You scurvy lousy knave, God pless you.

PISTOL: Ha! art thou bedlam? Hence! I am qualmish at the smell of leek.

FLUELLEN *jumps off the wall and confronts* PISTOL.

FLUELLEN: I peseech you heartily, scurvy lousy knave, to eat, look you, this leek.

FLUELLEN *snatches the leek from his cap and holds it under* PISTOL'S *nose.*

PISTOL: Not for Cadwallader and all his goats.

PISTOL *walks away. Pan with him, as* FLUELLEN *kicks*

PISTOL'S *backside.*

FLUELLEN: There is one goat for you. Will you be so good, as eat it?

PISTOL *draws his sword.*

PISTOL: Base Trojan, thou shalt die.

FLUELLEN *snatches the sword from* PISTOL *and bangs him on the head with it.* PISTOL *falls to his knees.*

FLUELLEN: You say very true, when God's will is. I will desire you to live in the meantime, and eat your victuals. Come, there is sauce for it.

He hits PISTOL *in the face with the leek.*

FLUELLEN: If you can mock a leek, you can eat a leek. Bite, I pray you.

PISTOL: Must I bite?

FLUELLEN: Out of doubt and out of question too.

PISTOL: By this leek, I will most horribly revenge.

FLUELLEN *threatens him with the sword.* (STILL)

PISTOL: I eat. I eat. I swear.

PISTOL *peels the leek.*

FLUELLEN: Nay, pray you, throw none away. The skin is good for your broken coxcomb. When you take occasions to see leeks hereafter, I pray you mock at 'em, that is all.

PISTOL: Good.

FLUELLEN: Ay, leeks is good.

GOWER *sits on the wall and chuckles.*

FLUELLEN: *(off)* Hold you!

FLUELLEN *and* PISTOL *together.*

FLUELLEN: Here is a penny to heal your hand.

PISTOL: Me, a penny?

FLUELLEN: Yes, verily, and in truth you shall take it, or I have another leek in my pocket, which you shall eat.

PISTOL takes the penny. FLUELLEN *kisses* PISTOL'S *head and goes off.*

FLUELLEN: God be wi' you and keep you and heal your head.

PISTOL gets up and rushes to the gate at the side of the wall. Pan and track with him, as GOWER *comes on.*

PISTOL: All hell shall stir for this.

GOWER: Go, go, you are a counterfeit, cowardly knave.
You thought because he could not speak
English in the native garb, he therefore could not
Handle an English cudgel. You find it
Otherwise, and henceforth let a Welsh
Correction teach you a good English condition.

Pan with GOWER *as he walks away from* PISTOL. *He turns and throws a coin away.*
PISTOL *takes the coin that has fallen into his helmet. He turns and walks straight towards us.*

PISTOL: Doth Fortune play the strumpet with me now?
News have I that my Nell lies dead
I' th' hospital of a malady of France.
And there my rendezvous is quite cut off.
Old do I wax, and from my weary limbs
Honour is cudgelled. Well, bawd I'll turn,
And something lean to cutpurse of quick hand.
To England will I steal, and there I'll steal:
And patches will I get unto these scars,
And swear I got them in these present wars.

The music starts as PISTOL *scurries off and disappears in a barn. Track with him and past the barn.* PISTOL *emerges from the other side of barn with a pig under his arm and a cockerel in his hand. He runs up the hill away*

80

from us and disappears.
Dissolve to a long shot of the French Palace.
Then dissolve again to the great hall of the Palace.
A high angle shot shows a choir in the foreground. We
track forward and down as the DUKE OF BURGUNDY
and attendants take their places, followed by the French
King and KING HENRY V *and their courtiers. The music*
ceases.

KING HENRY: Peace to this meeting, wherefore we are
met.
Unto our brother France and to our sister,
Health and fair time of day. Joy and good wishes
To our most fair and princely cousin Katharine:
And as a branch and member of this royalty,
We do salute you, Duke of Burgundy:
And Princes French, and peers, health to you all!

> KING CHARLES *and* QUEEN ISABEL *of France are*
> *surrounded by their courtiers.*

KING CHARLES: Right joyous are we to behold your face,
Most worthy brother England, fairly met.
So are you, Princes English, every one.

QUEEN ISABEL: So happy be the issue, brother England,
Of this good day, and of this gracious meeting . . .

> KING HENRY *is surrounded by his court.*

QUEEN ISABEL: *(off)* . . . As we are now glad to behold
your eyes . . .

> *Resume shot of* QUEEN ISABEL *and* KING CHARLES.

QUEEN ISABEL: . . . Your eyes which hitherto have borne
in them
Against the French that met them in their bent,
The fatal balls of murdering basilisks.
The venom of such looks we fairly hope
Have lost their quality, and that this day
Shall change all griefs and quarrels into love.

HENRY V *replies in kind.*

KING HENRY: To cry amen to that, thus we appear.

He turns to his right.
KING HENRY *remains in the foreground with* KING
CHARLES, *while the* DUKE OF BURGUNDY *speaks to
them.*

BURGUNDY: My duty to you both, on equal love,
Great Kings of France and England.
Since then my office hath so far prevailed
That face to face and royal eye to eye
You have assembled, let it not disgrace me
If I demand before this royal view,
Why that the naked, poor and mangled peace,
Dear nurse of arts, plenties, and joyful births,
Should not in this best garden of the world,
Our fertile France, put up her lovely visage?

Close shot of BURGUNDY. *The music begins.*

BURGUNDY: Alas, she hath from France too long been
chased . . .

Track with BURGUNDY *as he steps up to a window.*

BURGUNDY: . . . And all her husbandry doth lie in heaps,
Corrupting in its own fertility.
Her vine, the merry cheerer of the heart . . .

*Pan slowly beyond the window out over the fertile
countryside.*

BURGUNDY: *(off)* . . . Unprunèd, dies; her hedges even-
pleached
Put forth disordered twigs; her fallow leas,
The darnel, hemlock, and rank fumitory
Doth root upon, while that the coulter rusts
That should deracinate such savagery.
The even mead, that erst brought sweetly forth
The freckled cowslip, burnet and green clover,
Wanting the scythe, all uncorrected rank,

Conceives by idleness, and nothing teems
But hateful docks, rough thistles, kecksies, burrs,
Losing both beauty and utility.
Even so our houses and ourselves and children . . .

The slow pan holds on two children, then slowly pans up to the French castle.

BURGUNDY: *(off)* Have lost, or do not learn for want of time,
The sciences that should become our country,
But grow like savages, as soldiers will
That nothing do but meditate on blood,
To swearing and stern looks, diffused attire . . .

Now we dissolve to a shot from outside the window with BURGUNDY *standing there.*

BURGUNDY: . . . And everything that seems unnatural
. . .

The music stops as BURGUNDY *turns and steps down from the window.* HENRY V *and his court can be seen in the background. Track forward on them.*

BURGUNDY: Which to reduce into our former favour
You are assembled.

KING HENRY: Then, Duke of Burgundy, you must gain that peace
With full accord to all our just demands.

Resume the shot of KING CHARLES *and* QUEEN ISABEL.

KING CHARLES: I have but with a cursory eye
O'erglanced the articles. Pleaseth your grace
To appoint some of your council presently
To sit with us. We will suddenly
Pass our accept and peremptory answer.

KING HENRY *remains gracious.*

KING HENRY: Brother we shall. Will you, fair sister,
Go with the princes, or stay here with us?

QUEEN ISABEL *still stands at the side of* KING CHARLES.
PRINCESS KATHARINE *is in the background on the left.*
(STILL)

QUEEN ISABEL: Our gracious brother, I will go with them.
Haply a woman's voice may do some good
When articles too nicely urged be stood on.

KING HENRY: *(off)* Yet leave our cousin Katharine here
with us.

QUEEN ISABEL: She hath good leave.

The music starts as QUEEN ISABEL *leads* PRINCESS
KATHARINE *forward. Track back as the French Court
take their leave of* HENRY V, *allowing him to be with*
KATHARINE *alone. He walks over to her. Pan to show*
LADY ALICE *also with them.*

KING HENRY: Fair Katharine and most fair,
Will you vouchsafe to teach a soldier terms
Such as will enter at a lady's ear
And plead his love-suit to her gentle heart?

KATHARINE: Your majesty shall mock at me,
I cannot speak your England.

KING HENRY: O fair Katharine, if you will love me
soundly with your French heart, I will be glad to hear you
confess it brokenly with your English tongue.

HENRY V *is seen in close-up.*

KING HENRY: Do you like me, Kate?

PRINCESS KATHARINE *is also in close-up with* ALICE
behind her.

KATHARINE: *Pardonnez-moi*, I cannot tell vat is 'like me'.

KING HENRY *chuckles. He takes* KATHARINE *by the
hand. She comes into shot followed by* ALICE *as we pan
with them and track back. They are now at a window.*

KING HENRY: An angel is like you, Kate, and you are like
an angel.

The music stops.

KATHARINE: *Que dit-il? Que je suis sembable à les anges?*

ALICE: *Oui, vraiment, sauf votre grâce, ainsi dit-il.*

KATHARINE: *O bon Dieu! Les langues des hommes sont pleines de tromperies.*

KING HENRY: What says she, fair one? That the tongues of men are full of deceits?

ALICE: Oui . . .

ALICE *is now seen in close-up.*

ALICE: . . . dat de tongues of de mans is be full of deceits.

KING HENRY *and* PRINCESS KATHARINE *are at the window. Pan with him walking to* KATHARINE'S *right.*

KING HENRY: I' faith, Kate, I am glad thou canst speak no better English, for if thou couldst, thou wouldst find me such a plain King that thou wouldst think I had sold my farm to buy my crown. I know no ways to mince it in love, but directly to say, 'I love you'. Give me your answer, i' faith do, and so clasp hands and a bargain. How say you, lady?

ALICE *nods encouragingly to* KATHARINE.
KATHARINE *replies to* KING HENRY.

KATHARINE: *Sauf votre honneur*, me understand vell.

KING HENRY: Marry, if you put me to verses, or to dance for your sake, Kate, why you undo me. If I might buffet for my love, or bound my horse for her favours, I could lay on like a butcher, and sit like a jackanapes, never off.

He has stepped down from the window. Track back as he turns his back on us, still talking to KATHARINE.

KING HENRY: But before God, Kate, I cannot look greenly, nor grasp out my eloquence . . .

He walks out of shot. Track slowly in towards KATHARINE.

KING HENRY: *(off)* . . . Nor have I no cunning in protestation. If thou canst love a fellow of this temper, Kate, that never looks in his glass for the love of anything he sees there, whose face is not worth sunburning . . .

He comes into shot in the foreground.

KING HENRY: . . . Take me.

He steps up to the window beside KATHARINE.

KING HENRY: If not, to say to thee that I shall die, is true – but for thy love, by the Lord, no!

KATHARINE *stands up as he sits beside her.*
ALICE *stands up in alarm.*
KATHARINE *confronts* HENRY V.

KING HENRY: Yet I love thee too.

He stands up and KATHARINE *sits down.*

KING HENRY: And while thou livest, dear Kate, take a fellow of plain constancy. For these fellows of infinite tongue, that can rhyme themselves into ladies' favours, they do always reason themselves out again. A speaker is but a prater, a rhyme is but a ballad, a straight back will stoop, a black beard will turn white, a fair face will wither, a full eye will wax hollow, but a good heart, Kate, is the sun and the moon. If thou would have such a one, take me, and take me, take a soldier. Take a soldier, take a King. And what sayest thou then to my love? Speak, my fair, and fairly, I pray thee.

Pan with KATHARINE *as she rises and walks alone to a window.*
KATHARINE *stands at the window.*

KATHARINE: Is it possible dat I sould love de enemy of France?

KING HENRY *steps up to the window beside her.*

KING HENRY: No, Kate. But in loving me, you should love the friend of France, for I love France so well that I will not part with a village of it. And Kate, when France is mine, and I am yours, then yours is France, and you are mine.

KATHARTINE: I cannot tell vat is dat.

KING HENRY: No, Kate? I will tell thee in French, which I am sure will hang upon my tongue like a new-married wife about her husband's neck, hardly to be shook off. *Je quand suis le possesseur de France, et quand vous avez le possession de moi, donc vôtre est France et vous être mienne.*

They both laugh.

KING HENRY: I shall never move thee in French, unless it be to laugh at me.

KATHARINE: *Sauf votre honneur, le français que vous parlez, il est meilleur que l'anglais lequel je parle.*

KING HENRY: No faith, is't not, Kate. Thy speaking of my tongue, and I thine, must needs be granted to be much alike. But, Kate, dost thou understand thus much English? Canst thou love me?

KATHARINE: I cannot tell.

KATHARINE *walks away from the window.*
KING HENRY *stays at the window.*

KING HENRY: Can any of your neighbours tell, Kate? I'll ask them.

Track with him as he steps down from the window and walks past ALICE *over to* KATHARINE.

KING HENRY: Come, I know thou lovest me, and at night, when you are come into your chamber, you will question this gentlewoman about me, and I know, Kate, you will to her dispraise those parts in me that you love with your heart. But, good Kate, mock me mercifully, the rather, gentle Princess, because I love thee cruelly. What sayest thou, my fair flower-de-luce? *La plus belle Katharine du monde, mon très chēr et divin déesse?*

KATHARINE: Your majesty 'ave *fausse* French enough to deceive de most *sage demoiselle* dat is *en France*.

Pan with the King as he laughs and comes round to the right of KATHARINE.

KING HENRY: Now fie upon my false French! But mine honour, in true English, I love thee, Kate. By which honour, though I dare not swear thou lovest me, yet my blood begins to flatter me that thou dost.

Track back a little.

KING HENRY: Put off your maiden blushes, avouch the thoughts of your heart with the looks of an empress, take me by the hand, and say, 'Harry of England, I am thine'. Which word thou shalt no sooner bless mine ear withal, but I will tell thee aloud, 'England is thine, Ireland is thine, France is thine, and Henry Plantagenet is thine'. Therefore, Queen of all, Katharine, break thy mind to me in broken English. Wilt thou have me?

KATHARINE: Dat is as it sall please de *roi mon père*.

KING HENRY: Nay, it will please him well, Kate. It shall please him, Kate.

KATHARINE: Den it sall also content me.

KING HENRY: Upon that I kiss your hand, and I call you my queen.

KING HENRY *kisses her hand. Pan with the shocked* KATHARINE *running to a doorway.* ALICE *joins her.*

KATHARINE: *Laissez, mon seigneur, laissez, laissez! Ma foi, je ne veux point que vous abaissiez votre grandeur en baisant la main de votre indigne serviteur. . .*

HENRY V *is seen in close-up.*

KATHARINE: *(off) Excusez-moi, je vous supplie, mon très-puissant seigneur.*

KING HENRY: Oh, then I will kiss your lips, Kate.

Pan with KATHARINE *and* ALICE *as they shriek and run to stand behind a window.* KING HENRY *stands in the foreground.*

KATHARINE: *Les dames et demoiselles pour être baisées devant leur noces, il n'est pas la coutume de France.*

KING HENRY *walks up to them behind the window. Track to hold on* KING HENRY *and* KATHARINE. *He turns. Pan to hold on him and* ALICE.

KING HENRY: Madame, my interpreter, what says she?

ALICE: Dat is not be de fashion *pour les* ladies of France – I cannot tell vat is *baiser en* Anglish.

KING HENRY: To kiss.

KATHARINE *is seen in close-up.*

ALICE: *(off)* Your majesty *entendre* better *que moi.*

KING HENRY: *(off)* It is not the fashion for the maids in France to kiss before they are married, would she say?

ALICE: *(off) Oui, vraiment.*

KING HENRY: *(off)* O Kate . . .

The music starts as KING HENRY *leads* KATHARINE *from the window and down to us. Pan and track back, then finally move in to a close shot.*

KING HENRY: Nice customs curtsy to great kings. Dear Kate, you and I cannot be confined within the weak list of a country's fashion. We are the makers of manners, Kate. Therefore, patiently and yielding.

He kisses her. (STILL FRONTISPIECE)
In close-up, we see KING HENRY'S *hand clasping* KATHARINE'S. *The heraldry of England and France can be seen on the rings of their fingers.*

KING HENRY: *(off)* You have witchcraft in your lips, Kate.

We begin to track back from them.

BURGUNDY: *(off)* God save your majesty . . .

The music stops, and track back to a long shot showing the French Court assembled behind KING HENRY *and* KATHARINE.

BURGUNDY: . . . My royal cousin, teach you our princess English?

The Court titters.

KING HENRY: I would have her learn, my fair cousin, how perfectly I love her, and that is good English.

The Court applauds.

KING HENRY: Shall Kate be my wife?

KING CHARLES *steps forward and takes the hands of* KING HENRY *and* KATHARINE.

KING CHARLES: Take her, fair son, that the contending kingdoms
Of France and England, whose very shores look pale
With envy of each other's happiness
May cease their hatred; that never war advance
His bleeding sword 'twixt England and fair France.

THE COURT: Amen!

The music starts, and track back as KING HENRY *and* KATHARINE *separate,* HENRY *to the English attendants on the left and* KATHARINE *to the French attendants on the right.*
Now we see a longer shot of the same scene. KING HENRY *and* KATHARINE *are crowned. Joining hands, they walk away to two thrones. Track forward following them. They sit side by side with* CANTERBURY *behind them.* (STILL)
HENRY V *turns round on reaching the throne. He is wearing the crude Globe Theatre make-up.*
Applause is heard as we pan to show a BOY *made-up as* KATHARINE.
Track back from KING HENRY *and the* BOY *playing*

KATHARINE *to reveal the stage of the Globe Theatre.*
CHORUS *enters and pulls the curtain across.*

CHORUS: Thus far, with rough and all-unable pen,
Our bending author hath pursued the story,
In little room confining mighty men,
Mangling by starts the full course of their glory.

    CHORUS *walks towards us and flings out his arms.*

CHORUS: Small time, but in that small most greatly lived
This star of England. Fortune made his sword.
And for his sake . . .

    Shoot down from the top gallery of the theatre past the
    audience towards the stage.

CHORUS: In your fair minds let this acceptance . . .

    CHORUS *is seen in a closer shot.*

CHORUS: . . . take.

He bows. Elizabethan Gallants come onto the stage and
crowd round CHORUS. *Track up to the stage balcony*
where the BISHOP OF ELY *is conducting Choirboys.*
Track in to ELY *as he looks up and nods.*
In the orchestra gallery, the Leader of the orchestra
acknowledges the signal and the orchestra plays louder.
The Leader looks up.
Track up to the platform below the flagpole. A man is
pulling down the Playhouse flag and rolling it up. He
leaves through the door at the back.
Now we see London in 1600 in a long shot with the Globe
Playhouse in the foreground. Track back to a wide shot of
London. A playbill comes fluttering out of the sky and
hits the camera lens. It has the cast and credits on it, which
unroll.

THE CAST
In order of appearance

Chorus	Leslie Banks
Archbishop of Canterbury	Felix Aylmer
Bishop of Ely	Robert Helpmann
The English Herald	Vernon Greeves
Earl of Westmoreland	Gerald Case
Earl of Salisbury	Griffith Jones
Sir Thomas Erpingham	Morland Graham
Duke of Exeter	Nicholas Hannen
Duke of Gloucester	Michael Warre
King Henry V of England	Laurence Olivier
Mountjoy, The French Herald	Ralph Truman
Duke of Berri, French Ambassador	Ernest Thesiger
Corporal Nym	Frederick Cooper
Lieutenant Bardolph	Roy Emerton
Ancient Pistol	Robert Newton
Mistress Quickly	Freda Jackson
Boy	George Cole
Sir John Falstaff	George Robey
King Charles VI of France	Harcourt Williams
Duke of Bourbon	Russell Thorndike
The Constable of France	Leo Genn
Duke of Orléans	Francis Lister
The Dauphin	Max Adrian
The French Messenger	Jonathan Field
Fluellen)	Esmond Knight
Gower) Captains in the	Michael Shepley
Jamy) English Army	John Laurie
MacMorris)	Nial MacGinnis
The Governor of Harfleur	Frank Tickle
Princess Katharine	Renée Ascherson
Alice	Ivy St. Helier
Queen Isabel of France	Janet Burnell
Court)	Brian Nissen
Bates) Soldiers in the	Arthur Hambling
Williams) English Army	Jimmy Hanley
A Priest	Ernest Hare
Duke of Burgundy	Valentine Dyall

Produced and Directed
by
Laurence Olivier

In close association with –

The Editor	Reginald Beck
The Art Director	Paul Sheriff

Assisted by	Carmen Dillon
The Costume Designer	Roger Furse
Assisted by	Margaret Furse
The Associate Producer	Dallas Bower
The Text Editor	Alan Dent
The Director of Photography	Robert Krasker
The Operating Cameraman	Jack Hildyard
The Sound Recorders	John Dennis
	Desmond Dew
Make-up	Tony Sforzini
Hairdressing	Vivienne Walker
Special Effects	Percy Day
Assistant Director	Vincent Permane
Scenic Artist	E. Lindegaard
Continuity	Joan Barry
Chief Electrician	W. Wall
Master of the Horse	John White
Production Unit	Alec Hayes
	P. G. Bangs
	Laurence Evans

and

The music by	William Walton
Conducted by	Muir Mathieson
Played by	The London Symphony Orchestra

Now dissolve to a long shot of London in 1600. The words: THE END: fade in and out of the sky above the city. The music stops.

Counterfeit Gods

Also by Timothy Keller

The Reason for God: Belief in an Age of Scepticism

The Prodigal God

Timothy Keller

Counterfeit Gods

*When the Empty Promises of Love,
Money and Power Let You Down*

HODDER

First published in Great Britain in 2009 by Hodder & Stoughton
An Hachette UK company
This paperback edition first published in 2010

14

A CIP catalogue record for this title is available from the British Library

ISBN 978 0 340 99508 2

Printed and bound in the UK by Clays Ltd, St Ives plc

Hodder & Stoughton policy is to use papers that are natural, renewable
and recyclable products and made from wood grown in sustainable forests.
The logging and manufacturing processes are expected to conform to the
environmental regulations of the country of origin.

Hodder & Stoughton Ltd
338 Euston Road
London NW1 3BH

www.hodderfaith.com

To my sons,
David, Michael, and Jonathan,
who can detect the counterfeit

CONTENTS

[*vii*]

Contents

INTRODUCTION
THE IDOL FACTORY

There are more idols in the world than there are realities.
—Friedrich Nietzsche, *Twilight of the Idols*

A Strange Melancholy

After the global economic crisis began in mid-2008, there followed a tragic string of suicides of formerly wealthy and well-connected individuals. The acting chief financial officer of Freddie Mac, the Federal Home Loan Mortgage Corporation, hanged himself in his basement. The chief executive of Sheldon Good, a leading U.S. real estate auction firm, shot himself in the head behind the wheel of his red Jaguar. A French money manager who invested the wealth of many of Europe's royal and leading families, and who had lost $1.4 billion of his clients' money in Bernard Madoff's Ponzi scheme, slit his wrists and died in his

Madison Avenue office. A Danish senior executive with HSBC Bank hanged himself in the wardrobe of his £500-a-night suite in Knightsbridge, London. When a Bear Stearns executive learned that he would not be hired by JPMorgan Chase, which had bought his collapsed firm, he took a drug overdose and leapt from the twenty-ninth floor of his office building. A friend said, "This Bear Stearns thing . . . broke his spirit."[1] It was grimly reminiscent of the suicides in the wake of the 1929 stock market crash.

In the 1830s, when Alexis de Tocqueville recorded his famous observations on America, he noted a "strange melancholy that haunts the inhabitants . . . in the midst of abundance."[2] Americans believed that prosperity could quench their yearning for happiness, but such a hope was illusory, because, de Tocqueville added, "the incomplete joys of this world will never satisfy [the human] heart."[3] This strange melancholy manifests itself in many ways, but always leads to the same despair of not finding what is sought.

There is a difference between sorrow and despair. Sorrow is pain for which there are sources of consolation. Sorrow comes from losing one good thing among others, so that, if you experience a career reversal, you can find comfort in your family to get you through it. Despair, however, is inconsolable, because it comes from losing an *ultimate* thing. When you lose the ultimate source of your meaning or hope, there are no alternative sources to turn to. It breaks your spirit.

What is the cause of this "strange melancholy" that permeates our society even during boom times of frenetic activity, and which turns to outright despair when prosperity diminishes? De Tocqueville says it comes from taking some "incomplete joy of this world" and building your entire life on it. That is the definition of idolatry.

A Culture Filled with Idols

To contemporary people the word *idolatry* conjures up pictures of primitive people bowing down before statues. The biblical book of Acts in the New Testament contains vivid descriptions of the cultures of the ancient Greco-Roman world. Each city worshipped its favorite deities and built shrines around their images for worship. When Paul went to Athens he saw that it was literally filled with images of these divinities (Acts 17:16). The Parthenon of Athena overshadowed everything, but other deities were represented in every public space. There was Aphrodite, the goddess of beauty; Ares, the god of war; Artemis, the goddess of fertility and wealth; Hephaestus, the god of craftsmanship.

Our contemporary society is not fundamentally different from these ancient ones. Each culture is dominated by its own set of idols. Each has its "priesthoods," its totems and rituals. Each one has its shrines—whether office towers, spas and gyms, studios, or stadiums—where sacrifices must be made in order to procure the blessings of the good life and ward off disaster. What are the gods of beauty, power, money, and achievement but these same things that have assumed mythic proportions in our individual lives and in our society? We may not physically kneel before the statue of Aphrodite, but many young women today are driven into depression and eating disorders by an obsessive concern over their body image. We may not actually burn incense to Artemis, but when money and career are raised to cosmic proportions, we perform a kind of child sacrifice, neglecting family and community to achieve a higher place in business and gain more wealth and prestige.

After New York's governor Eliot Spitzer destroyed his career because of his involvement in a high-priced prostitution ring, David Brooks noted how our culture has produced a class of high achievers with "rank-link imbalances." They have social skills for vertical relationships, for improving their rank with mentors and bosses, but none for genuine bonding in horizontal relationships with spouses, friends, and family. "Countless presidential candidates say they are running on behalf of their families, even though their entire lives have been spent on the campaign trail away from their families." As the years go by they come to the sickening realization that "their grandeur is not enough and that they are lonely."[4] Many of their children and spouses are alienated from them. They seek to heal the hurt. They get into affairs or take other desperate measures to medicate the inner emptiness. Then comes family breakdown or scandal or both.

They had sacrificed everything to the god of success, but it wasn't enough. In ancient times, the deities were bloodthirsty and hard to appease. They still are.

Idols of the Heart

It would have been hard to make this case convincingly during the era of the dot-com boom and of the real estate and stock bubble of the last twenty years. However, the great economic meltdown of 2008–2009 has laid bare what is now being called "the culture of greed." Long ago, Saint Paul wrote that greed was not just bad behavior. "Greed is idolatry," he wrote. (Colossians 3:5) Money, he advised, can take on divine attributes, and our relationship to it then approximates worship and obeisance.

Money can become a spiritual addiction, and like all addictions it hides its true proportions from its victims. We take more and greater risks to get an ever diminishing satisfaction from the thing we crave, until a breakdown occurs. When we begin to recover, we ask, "What were we thinking? How could we have been so blind?" We wake up like people with a hangover who can hardly remember the night before. But why? Why did we act so irrationally? Why did we completely lose sight of what is right?

The Bible's answer is that the human heart is an "idol factory."[5]

When most people think of "idols" they have in mind literal statues—or the next pop star anointed by Simon Cowell. Yet while traditional idol worship still occurs in many places of the world, internal idol worship, within the heart, is universal. In Ezekiel 14:3, God says about elders of Israel, "These men have set up their idols in their *hearts*." Like us, the elders must have responded to this charge, "Idols? What idols? I don't see any idols." God was saying that the human heart takes good things like a successful career, love, material possessions, even family, and turns them into ultimate things. Our hearts deify them as the center of our lives, because, we think, they can give us significance and security, safety and fulfillment, if we attain them.[6]

The central plot device of *The Lord of the Rings* is the Dark Lord Sauron's Ring of Power, which corrupts anyone who tries to use it, however good his or her intentions. The Ring is what Professor Tom Shippey calls "a psychic amplifier," which takes the heart's fondest desires and magnifies them to idolatrous proportions.[7] Some good characters in the book want to liberate slaves, or preserve their people's land, or visit wrongdoers with just punishment. These are all good objectives. But the Ring makes them willing to do *any*thing to achieve them, anything at all. It turns the good thing into an absolute that overturns every other allegiance or value. The wearer of the Ring becomes increasingly enslaved and addicted to it, for an idol is something we cannot live without. We must have it, and therefore it drives us to break rules we once honored, to harm others and even ourselves in order to get it. Idols are spiritual addictions that lead to terrible evil, in Tolkien's novel and real life.

Anything Can Be an Idol

Cultural moments like the one we are in provide us with an opportunity. Many people are now more open to the Bible's warning that money can become much more than money. It can become a powerful life-altering, culture-shaping god, an idol that breaks the hearts of its worshippers. The bad news is that we are so fixated on the problem of greed, which we tend to see in "those rich people over there," that we don't realize the most fundamental truth. Anything can be an idol, and everything has been an idol.

The most famous moral code in the world is the Decalogue, the Ten Commandments. The very first commandment is "I am the Lord your God . . . you shall have no other gods before me" (Exodus 20:3). That leads to the natural question—"What do you mean, 'other gods'?" An answer comes immediately. "You shall not make for yourself an idol in the form of anything in heaven above or on the earth beneath or in the waters below. You shall not bow down to them or worship them. . . ." (Exodus 20:4–5) That includes everything in the world! Most people know you can make a god out of money. Most know you can make god out of sex. However, *any*thing in life can serve as an idol, a God-alternative, a counterfeit god.

I recently heard the account of a field army officer who so exorbitantly pursued physical and military discipline with his troops that he broke their morale. That led to a communication breakdown during combat that resulted in fatalities. I knew a woman who had experienced periods of poverty as she grew up. As an adult she was so eager for financial security that she passed over many good prospective relationships in order to marry a wealthy man she did not really love. This led to an early divorce and to all the economic struggles she feared so much. It appears that some major league baseball players, in a quest to play not just well but at a Hall of Fame level, took steroids and other drugs. As a result, their bodies are more broken and their reputations more sullied than if they had been willing to be good rather than great. The very things upon which these people were building all their happiness turned to dust in their hands *because* they had built all their happiness upon them. In each case, a good thing among many was turned into a supreme thing, so that its demands overrode all competing values.[8] But counterfeit gods always disappoint, and often destructively so.

Is it wrong to want disciplined troops, or financial security, or athletic prowess? Not at all. But these stories point to a common mistake people make when they hear about the biblical concept of idolatry. We think that idols are bad things, but that is almost never the case. The greater the good, the more likely we are to expect that it can satisfy our deepest needs and hopes. Anything can serve as a counterfeit god, especially the very best things in life.

How to Make a God

What is an idol? It is anything more important to you than God, anything that absorbs your heart and imagination more than God, anything you seek to give you what only God can give.[9]

A counterfeit god is anything so central and essential to your life that, should you lose it, your life would feel hardly worth living. An idol has such a controlling position in your heart that you can spend most of your passion and energy, your emotional and financial resources, on it without a second thought. It can be family and children, or career and making money, or achievement and critical acclaim, or saving "face" and social standing. It can be a romantic relationship, peer approval, competence and skill, secure and comfortable circumstances, your beauty or your brains, a great political or social cause, your morality and virtue, or even success in the Christian ministry. When your meaning in life is to fix someone else's life, we may call it "codependency" but it is really idolatry. An idol is whatever you look at and say, in your heart of hearts, "If I have that, then I'll feel my life has meaning, then I'll know I have value, then I'll feel significant and secure." There are many ways to describe that kind of relationship to something, but perhaps the best one is *worship*.

The old pagans were not fanciful when they depicted virtually everything as a god. They had sex gods, work gods, war gods, money gods, nation gods—for the simple fact that anything can be a god that rules and serves as a deity in the heart of a person or in the life of a people. For example, physical beauty is a pleasant thing, but if you "deify" it, if you make it the most important thing in a person's life or a culture's life, then you have Aphrodite, not just beauty. You have people, and an entire culture, constantly agonizing over appearance, spending inordinate amounts of time and money on it, and foolishly evaluating character on the basis of it. If anything becomes more fundamental than God to your happiness, meaning in life, and identity, then it is an idol.

The biblical concept of idolatry is an extremely sophisticated idea, integrating intellectual, psychological, social, cultural, and spiritual categories. There are personal idols, such as romantic love and family; or money, power, and achievement; or access to particular social circles; or the emotional dependence of others on you; or health, fitness, and physical beauty. Many look to these things for the hope, meaning, and fulfillment that only God can provide.

There are cultural idols, such as military power, technological progress, and economic prosperity. The idols of traditional societies include family, hard work, duty, and moral virtue, while those of Western cultures are individual freedom, self-discovery, personal affluence, and fulfillment. All these good things can and do take on disproportionate size and power within a society. They promise us safety, peace, and happiness if only we base our lives on them.

There can also be intellectual idols, often called

ideologies. For example, European intellectuals in the late nineteenth and early twentieth centuries became largely convinced of Rousseau's view of the innate goodness of human nature, that all of our social problems were the result of poor education and socialization. World War II shattered this illusion. Beatrice Webb, whom many consider the architect of Britain's modern welfare state, wrote:

> Somewhere in my diary—1890?—I wrote "I have staked all on the essential goodness of human nature. . . ." [Now thirty-five years later I realize] how permanent are the evil impulses and instincts in man—how little you can count on changing some of these—for instance the appeal of wealth and power—by any change in the [social] machinery. . . . No amount of knowledge or science will be of any avail unless we can curb the bad impulse.[10]

In 1920, in his book *Outline of History,* H. G. Wells praised belief in human progress. In 1933, in *The Shape of Things to Come,* appalled by the selfishness and violence of European nations, Wells believed the only hope was for intellectuals to seize control and run a compulsory educational program stressing peace and justice and equity. In 1945, in *A Mind at the End of Its Tether,* he wrote, "*Homo sapiens,* as he has been pleased to call himself, is . . . played out." What happened to Wells and Webb? They had taken a partial truth and made it into an all-encompassing truth, by which everything could be explained and improved. To "stake everything" on human goodness was to put it in the place of God.

There are also idols, nonnegotiable absolute values, in every vocational field. In the business world, self-expression is suppressed for the ultimate value, profit. In the art world, however, it is the other way around. Everything is sacrificed to self-expression, and it is done in the name of redemption. This, it is thought, is what the human race needs above all. There are idols everywhere.

Love, Trust, and Obey

The Bible uses three basic metaphors to describe how people relate to the idols of their hearts. They *love* idols, *trust* idols, and *obey* idols.[11]

The Bible sometimes speaks of idols using a marital metaphor. God should be our true Spouse, but when we desire and delight in other things more than God we commit spiritual adultery.[12] Romance or success can become "false lovers" that promise to make us feel loved and valued. Idols capture our imagination, and we can locate them by looking at our daydreams. What do we enjoy imagining? What are our fondest dreams? We look to our idols to love us, to provide us with value and a sense of beauty, significance, and worth.

The Bible often speaks of idols using the religious metaphor. God should be our true Savior, but we look to personal achievement or financial prosperity to give us the peace and security we need.[13] Idols give us a sense of being in control, and we can locate them by looking at our nightmares. What do we fear the most? What, if we lost it, would make life not worth living? We make "sacrifices" to appease and please our gods, who we believe will protect us. We look to our idols to provide us with a sense of confidence and safety.

The Bible also speaks of idols using a political metaphor. God should be our only Lord and Master, but whatever we love and trust we also serve. Anything that becomes more important and nonnegotiable to us than God becomes an enslaving idol.[14] In this paradigm, we can locate idols by looking at our most unyielding emotions. What makes us uncontrollably angry, anxious, or despondent? What racks us with a guilt we can't shake? Idols control us, since we feel we must have them or life is meaningless.

Whatever controls us is our lord. The person who seeks power is controlled by power. The person who seeks acceptance is controlled by the people he or she wants to please. We do not control ourselves. We are controlled by the lord of our lives.[15]

What many people call "psychological problems" are simple issues of idolatry. Perfectionism, workaholism, chronic indecisiveness, the need to control the lives of others—all of these stem from making good things into idols that then drive us into the ground as we try to appease them. Idols dominate our lives.

The Opportunity of Disenchantment

As we have seen, there is a big difference between sorrow and despair, since despair is unbearable sorrow. In most cases, the difference between the two is idolatry. A Korean businessman killed himself after losing most of a $370 million investment. "When the nation's stock market index fell below 1,000, he stopped eating and went on a drinking binge for days and finally decided to kill himself," his wife told police.[16] In the midst of the great financial crisis of 2008–2009 I heard a man named Bill recount that three years before he had become a Christian and his ultimate security had shifted from money to his relationship with God through Christ.[17] "If this economic meltdown had happened more than three years ago, well, I don't know how I could have faced it, how I would have even kept going. Today, I can tell you honestly, I've never been happier in my life."

Though we think we live in a secular world, idols, the glittering gods of our age, hold title to the functional trust of our hearts. With the global economy in shambles, many of those idols that we have worshipped for years have come crashing down around us. This is a great opportunity. We are briefly experiencing "disenchantment." In the old stories, that meant that the spell cast by the evil sorcerer was broken and there was the chance to escape. Such times come to us as individuals, when some great enterprise, pursuit, or person on which we have built our hopes fails to deliver what (we thought) was promised. It very rarely comes to an entire society.

The way forward, out of despair, is to discern the idols of our hearts and our culture. But that will not be enough. The only way to free ourselves from the destructive influence of counterfeit gods is to turn back to the true one. The living God, who revealed himself both at Mount Sinai and on the Cross, is the only Lord who, if you find him, can truly fulfill you, and, if you fail him, can truly forgive you.

COUNTERFEIT GODS

ONE

ALL YOU'VE EVER WANTED

The Worst Thing that Can Happen

Most people spend their lives trying to make their heart's fondest dreams come true. Isn't that what life is all about, "the pursuit of happiness"? We search endlessly for ways to acquire the things we desire, and we are willing to sacrifice much to achieve them. We never imagine that getting our heart's deepest desires might be the worst thing that can ever happen to us.

My wife and I once knew a single woman, Anna, who wanted desperately to have children. She eventually married, and contrary to the expectations of her doctors, was able to bear two healthy children despite her age. But her dreams did not come true. Her overpowering drive to give her children a perfect life made it impossible for her to actually enjoy them. Her overprotectiveness, fears and anxieties, and her need to control every detail of her children's lives made the family miserable. Anna's oldest child did poorly in school and showed signs of serious emotional problems. The younger child was filled with anger. There's a good chance her drive to give her children wonderful lives will actually be the thing that ruins them. Getting her heart's deepest desire may end up being the worst thing that ever happened to her.

In the late 1980s, Cynthia Heimel wrote, "The minute a person becomes a celebrity is the same minute he/she becomes a monster," and then gave the names of three well-known Hollywood stars she had known before they became famous. They had been "once perfectly pleasant human beings . . . now they have become supreme beings and their wrath is awful." She went on to say that under the pressure of fame and celebrity all your character flaws and miseries become twice as bad as they were before.[18] You might be curious who these 1980s stars were, but you don't need to know that. Right now, there are any number of "bold-face names" living out the same patterns on the front pages of the newspapers. The names change but the pattern is permanent.

The Inevitability of Idolatry

Why is getting your heart's deepest desire so often a disaster? In the book of Romans, Saint Paul wrote that one of the worst things God can do to someone is to "give them over to the desires of their hearts" (Romans 1:24). Why would the greatest punishment imaginable be to allow someone to achieve their fondest dream? It is because our hearts fashion these desires into idols. In that same chapter, Paul summarized the history of the human race in one sentence: "They worshipped and served created things rather than the Creator" (Romans 1:25). Every human being must live for something. Something must capture our imaginations, our heart's most fundamental allegiance and hope. But, the Bible tells us, without the intervention of the Holy Spirit, that object will never be God himself.

If we look to some created thing to give us the meaning, hope, and happiness that only God himself can give, it will eventually fail to deliver and break our hearts. The woman, Anna, who was ruining her children's lives did not "love her children too much," but rather loved God too little in relationship to them. As a result, her child-gods were crushed under the weight of her expectations.

Two Jewish philosophers who knew the Scriptures intimately concluded: "The central . . . principle of

[*3*]

the Bible [is] the rejection of idolatry."[19] The Bible is therefore filled with story after story depicting the innumerable forms and devastating effects of idol worship. Every counterfeit god a heart can choose—whether love, money, success, or power—has a powerful biblical narrative that explains how that particular kind of idolatry works itself out in our lives.

One of the central figures of the Bible is Abraham. Like most men in ancient times, he longed for a son and heir who would carry on his name. In Abraham's case, however, that desire had become the deepest desire of his heart. Finally, beyond all hope, a son was born to him. He now had all he had ever wanted. Then God asked him to give it all up.

The Call of Abraham

According to the Bible, God came to Abraham and made him a staggering promise. If he would obey him faithfully, God would bless all the nations of the earth through him and his descendents. For this to happen, however, Abraham had to *go*. "Leave your country, your people, and your father's house, and go to the land that I will show you" (Genesis 12:1–3). God called Abraham to leave all that was familiar—his friends, most of his family, and everything that he believed meant safety, prosperity, and peace—and go out into the wilderness, uncertain of his destination. He was asked to give up, for God's sake, nearly all the worldly hopes and things that a human heart desires.

And he did. He was called to "go" and he went, "though he did not know where he was going" (Hebrews 11:8).

However, while God's call had demanded that he give up his other hopes, it had also given him a new one. The prophecy was that the nations of the earth would be blessed through his family, "your offspring" (Genesis 12:7). That meant he had to have children. Sarah, Abraham's wife, had been unable to conceive. Biologically speaking, having children seemed impossible. But God promised that Abraham would have a son.

As the years turned into decades, however, the divine promise became more and more difficult to believe. Finally, after Abraham was over a hundred years old, and Sarah over the age of ninety (Genesis 17:17, 21:5), she gave birth to a son, Isaac. This was clearly divine intervention, and so Isaac's name meant "laughter," a reference to both his parents' joy and to their difficulty in believing that God would ever give them what he had promised.

The years of agonized waiting had taken their toll, as any couple struggling with infertility can attest. The nearly endless delays refined Abraham's faith, which was crucially important. However, the years of infertility had also had another effect. No man had ever longed for a son more than Abraham. He had given up everything else to wait for this. When his son came, he felt, then his community would finally see he hadn't been a fool to give up everything to trust God's word. Then he would finally have an heir, a son in his own likeness, the thing all ancient Middle Eastern patriarchs wanted. He had waited and sacrificed, and finally his wife had a baby and it was a boy!

But the question now was—had he been waiting and sacrificing for God, or for the boy? Was God just a means to an end? To whom was Abraham ultimately giving his heart? Did Abraham have the peace, humility, boldness, and unmovable poise that come to those who trust in God rather than in circumstances, public opinion, or their own competence? Had he learned to trust God *alone*, to love God for himself, not just for what he could get out of God? No, not yet.

The Second Call of Abraham

When our friend Anna, the woman who had longed for children, at last became pregnant, she thought that she would live "happily ever after." Sadly, that did not happen, and it rarely does. Many couples longing for a child believe that having a child will solve all their problems, but that is never the case. Readers of Genesis 12–21 might likewise think that the birth of Isaac would have been the climax and last chapter of Abraham's life. His faith had triumphed. Now he could die a happy man, having fulfilled God's call to him to leave his homeland and wait for a son to be born. But then, to our surprise, Abraham got another call from God. And it could not have been more shocking.

> *Take your son, your only son, Isaac, whom you love, and go to the region of Moriah. Sacrifice him there as a burnt offering on one of the mountains I will tell you about.*
>
> Genesis 22:2

This was the ultimate test. Isaac was now *everything* to Abraham, as God's call makes clear. He does not refer to the boy as "Isaac," but as "your son, your only son, whom you love." Abraham's affection had become adoration. Previously, Abraham's meaning in life had been dependent on God's word. Now it was becoming dependent on Isaac's love and well-being. The center of Abraham's life was shifting. God was not saying you cannot love your son, but that you must not turn a loved one into a counterfeit god. If anyone puts a child in the place of the true God, it creates an idolatrous love that will smother the child and strangle the relationship.

The Horror of the Command

Many readers over the years have had understandable objections to this story. They have interpreted the "moral" of this story as meaning that doing cruel and violent things is fine, as long as you believe it is God's will. No one has spoken more vividly about this than Søren Kierkegaard, whose book *Fear and Trembling* is based on the story of Abraham and Isaac. Kierkegaard ultimately reasons that faith is irrational and absurd. Abraham thought the command made no sense at all, and contradicted everything else God had ever said, yet he followed the command.

Would this command have been totally irrational to Abraham? Kierkegaard's interpretation of the story does not take into consideration the meaning of the firstborn son in Jewish thought and symbolism. Jon Levenson, a Jewish scholar who teaches at Harvard, has written *The Death and Resurrection of the Beloved Son*. In this volume he reminds us that ancient cultures were not as individualistic as ours. People's hopes and dreams were never for their own personal success, prosperity, or prominence. Since everyone was part of a family, and no one lived apart from the family, these things were only sought for the entire clan. We must also remember the ancient law of primogeniture. The oldest son got the majority of the estate and wealth so the family would not lose its place in society.[20]

In an individualistic culture like ours, an adult's identity and sense of worth is often bound up in abilities and achievements, but in ancient times, all the hopes and dreams of a man and his family rested in the firstborn son.[21] The call to give up the firstborn son would be analogous to a surgeon giving up the use of his hands, or of a visual artist losing the use of her eyes.

Levenson argues that we can only understand God's command to Abraham against this cultural background. The Bible repeatedly states that, because of the Israelites' sinfulness, the lives of their firstborn are automatically forfeit, though they might be redeemed through regular sacrifice (Exodus 22:29, 34:20) or through service at the tabernacle among the Levites (Numbers 3:40–41) or through a ransom payment to the tabernacle and priests (Numbers 3:46–48). When God brought judgment on Egypt for enslaving the Israelites, his ultimate punishment was taking the lives of their firstborn. Their firstborns' lives were forfeit, because of the sins of the families and the nation. Why? The firstborn son *was* the family. So when God told the Israelites that the firstborn's life belonged to him unless ransomed, he was saying in the most vivid way possible in those cultures that every family on earth owed a debt to eternal justice—the debt of sin.

All this is crucial for interpreting God's directive to Abraham. If Abraham had heard a voice sounding like God's saying, "Get up and kill Sarah," Abraham would probably never have done it. He would have rightly assumed that he was hallucinating, for God would not ask him to do something that clearly contradicted everything he had ever said about justice and righteousness. But when God stated that his only son's life was forfeit, that was *not* an irrational, contradictory statement to him. Notice, God was not asking him to walk over into Isaac's tent and just murder him. He asked him to make him a burnt offering. He was calling in Abraham's debt. His son was going to die for the sins of the family.

The Walk into the Mountains

Though the command was comprehensible, that did not make it any less terrible. Abraham was faced with the ultimate question: "God is holy. Our sin means that Isaac's life is forfeit. Yet God is also a God of grace. He has said he wants to bless the world through Isaac. How can God be both holy and just and still graciously fulfill his promise of salvation?" Abraham did not know. But he went. He acted in line with another figure in the Old Testament, Job, who was sent countless afflictions with no explanation. Job, however, says about the Lord, "He knows what he is doing with me, and when he has tested me, I will come forth as pure gold" (Job 23:10).[22]

How did Abraham get himself to walk up into the mountains in obedience to God's call? The masterful Hebrew narrative gives us tantalizing hints. He told his servants that "*we* will come back to you" (Genesis 22:5). It is unlikely he had any specific idea of what God would do. But he did not go up the mountain saying, "I *can* do it," filled with willpower and self-talk. Rather, he went up saying, "God will do it . . . but I don't know how." Do what? God would somehow remove the debt on the firstborn and still keep the promise of grace.

Abraham was not just exercising "blind faith." He was not saying, "This is crazy, this is murder, but I'm going to do it anyway." Instead he was saying, "I know God is *both* holy *and* gracious. I don't know how he is going to be both—but I know he will." If he had not believed that he was in debt to a holy God, he would have been too angry to go. But if he had not also believed that God was a God of grace, he would have been too crushed and hopeless to go. He would have just lain down and died. It was only because he knew

God was both holy and loving that he was able to put one foot after another up that mountain.

Finally Abraham and his son could see the sacrifice site.

> When they reached the place God had told him about, Abraham built an altar there and arranged the wood on it. He bound his son Isaac and laid him on the altar on top of the wood. Then he reached out his hand and took the knife to slay his son.
>
> Genesis 22:9–10

But at that very moment, the voice of God came to him from heaven, "Abraham! Abraham!"

"Here I am," he replied from the precipice.

"Do not lay a hand on the boy . . . for now I know that you fear God, because you have not withheld from me your son, your only son" (Verse 12). And at that moment Abraham saw a ram caught by its horns in a thicket. Abraham untied Isaac and sacrificed it in place of his son.

The Danger of the Best Things in the World

What was this incident all about? It was about two things, one that Abraham probably saw fairly well, and one that he could not have understood clearly.

What Abraham was able to see was that this test was about loving God supremely. In the end the Lord said to him, "Now I know you fear God." In the Bible, this does not refer so much to being "afraid" of God as to being wholeheartedly committed to him. In Psalm 130:4, for example, we see that "the fear of God" is increased by an experience of God's grace and forgiveness. What it describes is a loving, joyful awe and wonder before the greatness of God. The Lord is saying, "Now I know that you love me more than anything in the world." That's what "the fear of God" means.

This doesn't mean that God was trying to find out if Abraham loved him. The All-seeing God knows the state of every heart. Rather, God was putting Abraham through the furnace, so his love for God could finally "come forth as pure gold." It is not hard to see why God was using Isaac as the means for this. If God had not intervened, Abraham would have certainly come to love his son more than anything in the world, if he did not already do so. That would have been idolatry, and all idolatry is destructive.

From this perspective we see that God's extremely rough treatment of Abraham was actually merciful. Isaac was a wonderful gift to Abraham, but he was not safe to have and hold until Abraham was willing to put God first. As long as Abraham never had to choose between his son and obedience to God, he could not see that his love was becoming idolatrous. In a similar way, we may not realize how idolatrous our career has become to us, until we are faced with a situation in which telling the truth or acting with integrity would mean a serious blow to our professional advancement. If we are not willing to hurt our career in order to do God's will, our job will become a counterfeit god.

How could the woman we met earlier in this chapter, Anna, have given God what he asked of Abraham? Counselors would tell her she has to stop pushing her children into activities and projects they have no aptitude for. She has to stop punishing them emotionally for bad grades. She would have to give them the freedom to fail. That's all true, but there is an underlying issue that has to be confronted. She must be able to say in her heart, "My desire for completely successful and happy children is selfish. It's all about my need to feel worthwhile and valuable. If I really knew God's love— then I could accept less-than-perfect kids and wouldn't be crushing them. If God's love meant more to me than my children, I could love my children less selfishly and more truly." Anna has to put her "Isaacs" on the altar and give God the central place in her life.

Her overcontrol of her children was not only an unwillingness to let God be God in her own life, but also in their lives. Anna could not imagine that God might have a plan for her children's lives wiser than her own.

She had mapped out a perfect life, without failures or disappointments. But that *is* more of a flawed life-plan than the bumpy ride God inevitably maps out for us. People who have never suffered in life have less empathy for others, little knowledge of their own shortcomings and limitations, no endurance in the face of hardship, and unrealistic expectations for life. As the New Testament book of Hebrews tells us, anyone God loves experiences hardship (Hebrews 12:1–8).

The success and love of Anna's children has been more important to her self-image than the glory and love of God. Though she believes in God with her mind, her heart's deepest satisfaction comes from hearing a child saying, "Oh, Mother, I owe everything to you!" Tragically, she may never hear the words that she longs for most, because her inordinate need for their approval is pushing away the ones she loves most. She must be willing to put God first, to trust God with her children by letting them fail, and to find her peace in his love and will. She needs to follow Abraham up into the mountains.

Abraham took that journey, and only after that could Abraham love Isaac well and wisely. If Isaac had become the main hope and joy of Abraham's life, his father would have either overdisciplined him (because he needed his son to be "perfect") or underdisciplined him (because he couldn't bear his son's displeasure) or both. He would have overindulged him but also become overly angry and cruel, perhaps even violent, when his son disappointed him. Why? Idols enslave. Isaac's love and success would have become Abraham's only identity and joy. He would have become inordinately angry, anxious, and depressed if Isaac ever failed to obey and love him. And fail he would have, since no child can bear the full weight of godhood. Abraham's expectations would have driven him away or twisted and disfigured his spirit.

Abraham's agonizing walk into the mountains was therefore the final stage of a long journey in which God was turning him from an average man into one of the greatest figures in history. The three great monotheistic faiths of the world today, Judaism, Islam, and Christianity, name Abraham as founder. Over one half the people in the human race consider him their spiritual father. That would have never happened unless God had dealt with the idol of Abraham's heart.

The Substitute

This famous incident was also about something that Abraham could not see, or at least not see very well in his time. Why had Isaac not been sacrificed? The sins of Abraham and his family were still there. How could a holy and just God overlook them? Well, a substitute was offered, a ram. But was it the ram's blood that took away the debt of the firstborn? No.

Many years later, in those same mountains,[23] another firstborn son was stretched out on the wood to die. But there on Mount Calvary, when the beloved son of God cried, "My God, my God—why hast thou forsaken me?" there was no voice from heaven announcing deliverance. Instead, God the Father paid the price in silence. Why? The true substitute for Abraham's son was God's only Son, Jesus, who died to bear our punishment. "For Christ died for sin once for all, the just for the unjust, to bring us to God" (1 Peter 3:18). Paul understood the true meaning of Isaac's story when he deliberately applied its language to Jesus: "He who did not spare his own Son, but gave him up for us all—how will he not also, along with him, freely give us all things?" (Romans 8:32)

Here, then, is the practical answer to our own idolatries, to the "Isaacs" in our lives, which are not spiritually safe to have and hold. We need to offer them up. We need to find a way to keep from clutching them too tightly, of being enslaved to them. We will never do so by mouthing abstractions about how great God is. We have to know, to be assured, that God so loves, cherishes, and delights in us that we can rest our hearts in him for our significance and security and handle anything that happens in life.

But how?

God saw Abraham's sacrifice and said, "Now I know that you love me, because you did not withhold your only son from me." But how much more can we look at *his* sacrifice on the Cross, and say to God, "Now, *we* know that you love *us*. For you did not withhold your son, your only son, whom you love, from us." When the magnitude of what he did dawns on us, it makes it possible finally to rest our hearts in him rather than in anything else.

Jesus alone makes sense of this story. The only way that God can be both "just" (demanding payment of our debt of sin) *and* "justifier"[24] (providing salvation and grace) is because years later another Father went up another "mount" called Calvary with his firstborn and offered him there for us all. You will never be as great, as secure in God, as courageous, as Abraham became simply by trying hard, but only by believing in the Savior to whom this event points. Only if Jesus lived and died for us can you have a God of infinite love and holiness at once. Then you can be absolutely sure he loves you.

Your Walk into the Mountains

Think of the many disappointments and troubles that beset us. Look at them more closely, and you will realize that the most agonizing of them have to do with our own "Isaacs." In our lives there are always some things that we invest in to get a level of joy and fulfillment that only God can give. The most painful times in our lives are times in which our Isaacs, our idols, are being threatened or removed. When that happens we can respond in two ways. We can opt for bitterness and despair. We will feel entitled to wallow in those feelings, saying, "I've worked all my life to get to this place in my career, and now it's all gone!" or "I've slaved my whole life to give that girl a good life, and this is how she repays me!" We may feel at liberty to lie, cheat, take revenge, or throw away our principles in order to get some relief. Or we may simply live in a permanent despondency.

Or else, like Abraham, you could take a walk up into the mountains. You could say, "I see that you may be calling me to live my life without something I never thought I could live without. But if I have you, I have the only wealth, health, love, honor, and security I really need and cannot lose." As many have learned and later taught, you don't realize Jesus is all you need until Jesus is all you have.

Many, if not most, of these counterfeit gods can remain in our lives once we have "demoted" them below God. Then they won't control us and bedevil us with anxiety, pride, anger, and drivenness. Nevertheless, we must not make the mistake of thinking that this story means all we have to do is be *willing* to part with our idols rather than actually leave them behind. If Abraham had gone up the mountain thinking, "All I'll have to do is put Isaac on the altar, not really give him up"— he would have failed the test! Something is safe for us to maintain in our lives only if it has really stopped being an idol. That can happen only when we are truly willing to live without it, when we truly say from the heart: "Because I have God, I can live without you."

Sometimes God seems to be killing us when he's actually saving us. Here he was turning Abraham into a great man—but on the outside it looked like God was being cruel. To follow God in such circumstances seems to some to be "blind faith," but actually it is vigorous, grateful faith. The Bible is filled with stories of figures such as Joseph, Moses, and David in which God seemed to have abandoned them, but later it is revealed he was dealing with the destructive idols in their lives and that could only have come to pass through their experience of difficulty.

Like Abraham, Jesus struggled mightily with God's call. In the garden of Gethsemane, he asked the Father if there was any other way, but in the end, he obediently walked up Mount Calvary to the cross. We can't know all the reasons that our Father is allowing bad things to happen to us, but like Jesus did, we can trust

him in those difficult times. As we look at him and rejoice in what he did for us, we will have the joy and
hope necessary—and the freedom from counterfeit
gods—to follow the call of God when times seem at
their darkest and most difficult.

TWO

LOVE IS NOT ALL YOU NEED

The Search for Love

The human longing for true love has always been celebrated in song and story, but in our contemporary culture it has been magnified to an astonishing degree. Musical theater is filled with many sunny love songs, but some reveal the dark side of this modern quest. In "Being Alive" from the musical *Company*, a man falls in love with a woman and sings that she will "need me too much . . . know me too well . . . pull me up short, and put me through hell." He insists, nonetheless, that only romance will "give me support for being alive, make me alive." He must go from one draining relationship to the next, because it is the only way he can feel alive. In the song "Bewitched" a woman admits that the man she's fallen for is a fool, and will let her down, but, she says, "I'm wild again, beguiled again, a simpering, whimpering child again." The singers are overdependent on being in love. Without a romantic relationship of some kind, even the wrong kind, their lives feel meaningless.

In the early days of my pastoral ministry, I met a woman named Sally, who'd had the misfortune of being born beautiful. Even in childhood she saw the power that she could wield with her physical attractiveness. At first she used her beauty to manipulate others, but eventually others used it to manipulate her. She came to feel that she was powerless and invisible unless some man was in love with her. She could not bear to be alone. As a result, she was willing to remain in relationships with men who were abusive.

Why did she endure such treatment? She had come to look to men for the kind of deep affirmation and acceptance that only God can provide. As a result, she became a slave to love. Nowadays we may hear someone say, "Oh, my boss is a slave master," but that is only a loose metaphor. Some bosses can make things hard on you, but real slave masters know no boundaries. They can literally do anything they want to you—beat you, rape you, or even kill you. In the same way, we know a good thing has become a counterfeit god when its demands on you exceed proper boundaries. Making an idol out of work may mean that you work until you ruin your health, or you break the laws in order to get ahead. Making an idol out of love may mean allowing the lover to exploit and abuse you, or it may cause terrible blindness to the pathologies in the relationship. An idolatrous attachment can lead you to break any promise, rationalize any indiscretion, or betray any other allegiance, in order to hold on to it. It may drive you to violate all good and proper boundaries. To practice idolatry is to be a slave.

There is a story in the Bible that illustrates how the quest for love can become a form of slavery. It is the story of Jacob and Leah in Genesis 29, and while very ancient, it has never been more relevant. It has always been possible to make romantic love and marriage into a counterfeit god, but we live in a culture that makes it even easier to mistake love for God, to be swept up by it, and to rest all our hopes for happiness upon it.

The Promise of the Messiah

As we saw in the last chapter, God came to Abraham and promised to redeem the world through his family, through a line of his descendents. Therefore, in every generation one child would be chosen to bear the line, to walk with God as head of the family, and to pass the faith on to the next generation. Then there would be another child that would carry on, and another, until the day when one of Abraham's descendents would be *the* Messiah himself.

Abraham fathered Isaac. Years later Isaac's wife, Rebekah, became pregnant with twins, and God spoke through a prophecy saying, "The elder will serve the younger" (Genesis 25:23). That meant that the second twin born had been chosen to carry on the Messianic line. In spite of the prophecy, Isaac set his heart on the older son, Esau, and favored him over the younger Jacob. Ironically, this was the same tragic mistake that God had saved Abraham from making, when he had called him to offer up his only son. Because of Isaac's favoritism, Esau grew up proud, spoiled, willful, and impulsive, while Jacob grew up cynical and bitter.

The time came for the aged Isaac to give the blessing to the head of the clan, which, in defiance of God's prophecy, he intended to give to Esau. But Jacob dressed up as his older brother, went in to his nearly blind father, and received the blessing from the unsuspecting Isaac. When Esau found out about it, he vowed to kill Jacob, and Jacob had to flee for his life into the wilderness.

Jacob's life was in ruins. He had lost his family and his inheritance. He would never see his mother and his father alive again. Jacob headed to the other side of the Fertile Crescent, where many of the relatives of his mother and his grandfather still lived. There he hoped at least to survive.

Jacob's Longing

Jacob escaped to his mother's family, and they took him in. His uncle Laban hired him as a shepherd of some of his flocks. Once Laban realized that Jacob had real ability as a manager, he offered him a management job. "What can I pay you to be in charge of my flocks?" he asked. Jacob's answer was one word: Rachel.

> *Now Laban had two daughters; the name of the older was Leah, and the name of the younger was Rachel. Leah had weak eyes, but Rachel was lovely in form, and beautiful. Jacob was in love with Rachel and said, "I'll work for you seven years in return for your younger daughter Rachel." Laban said, "It's better that I give her to you than to some other man. Stay here with me." So Jacob served seven years to get Rachel, but they seemed like only a few days to him because of his love for her.*
>
> Genesis 29:16–20

The Hebrew text says, literally, that Rachel had a great figure, and on top of that was beautiful. Jacob was more than smitten with her. Robert Alter, the great Hebrew literature scholar at Berkeley, points out the many signals in the text showing how lovesick and overwhelmed Jacob was with Rachel.[25] Jacob offered seven years' wages for her, which was, in the currency of the time, an enormous price for a bride. "But they seemed like only a few days to him because of his love for her (Verse 20)." "Then Jacob said to Laban, 'Give me my wife. My time is completed, and I want to lie with her. (Verse 21)'" Alter says that the Hebrew phrase is unusually bald, graphic, and sexual for ordinarily reticent ancient discourse. Imagine saying to a father even today, "I can't wait to have sex with your daughter. Give her to me now!" The narrator is showing us a man overwhelmed with emotional and sexual longing for one woman.

Why? Jacob's life was empty. He never had his father's love, he had lost his beloved mother's love, and he certainly had no sense of God's love and care. Then he beheld the most beautiful woman he had ever seen, and he must have said to himself, "If I had her, finally, something would be right in my miserable life. If I had her, it would fix things." All the longings of his heart for meaning and affirmation were fixed on Rachel.

Jacob was unusual for his time. Cultural historians tell us that in ancient times people didn't generally marry for love, they married for status. Nevertheless Jacob would not be rare today. Ernest Becker, who won the Pulitzer Prize for his book *The Denial of Death,* explained the various ways secular people have dealt with the loss of belief in God. Now that we think we are here by accident and not made for any purpose, how do we instill a sense of significance in our lives? One of the main ways is what Becker called "apocalyptic romance." We look to sex and romance to give us the transcendence and sense of meaning we used to get from faith in God. Talking about the modern secular person, he wrote:

> He still needed to feel heroic, to know that his life mattered in the scheme of things. . . . He still had to merge himself with some higher, self-absorbing meaning, in trust and gratitude. . . . If he no longer had God, how was he to do this? One of the first ways that occurred to him, as [Otto] Rank saw, was the "romantic solution." . . . The self-glorification that he needed in his innermost nature he now looked for in the love partner. The love partner becomes the divine ideal within which to fulfill one's life. All spiritual and moral needs now become focused in one individual. . . . In one word, the love object is God. . . . Man reached for a "thou" when the world-view of the great religious community overseen by God died. . . . [26] After all, what is it that we want when we elevate the love partner to the position of God? We want redemption—nothing less.[27]

[28]

That is exactly what Jacob did, and, as Becker points out, that is what millions of others are doing in our culture. The popular music and art of our society calls us to keep on doing it, to load all of the deepest needs of our hearts for significance and transcendence into romance and love. "You're nobody till somebody loves you," went the popular song, and we are an entire culture that has taken it literally. We maintain the fantasy that if we find our one true soul mate, everything wrong with us will be healed. But when our expectations and hopes reach that magnitude, as Becker says, "the love object is God." No lover, no human being, is qualified for that role. No one can live up to that. The inevitable result is bitter disillusionment.

The Power of Love

Some say that Becker's cultural analysis is dated. We now live in "the hookup culture," in which young people have turned sex into something ordinary, casual, and free from commitment. Fewer men and women actually date or have boyfriends and girlfriends. In the interest of gender equality, women have begun to say, "We deserve to have as much fun with our sexuality as guys do." There is growing peer pressure to engage in sex and not get too emotionally involved.[28] Surely, then, our culture is moving away from any hope in "apocalyptic romance." Once we get over our lingering Puritanism, the argument goes, sex will be no big deal.

Don't bet on it.

Laura Sessions Stepp, in her book *Unhooked,* found that hookups left most young women unsatisfied, though they are unwilling to admit this to their peers. And the enormous stress our culture puts on physical and sexual beauty belies any notion that sex is no big deal. In the 1940s, C. S. Lewis heard from many of his peers in the British academy that sex was nothing but an appetite, like that for food. Once we recognized this, they said, and began to simply have sex whenever we wanted it, people would cease to be "driven mad" by desire for love and sex. Lewis doubted this, and proposed a thought experiment.

Suppose you come to a country where you could fill a theatre by simply bringing a covered plate on to the stage and then slowly lifting the cover so as to let every one see, just before the lights went out, that it contained a mutton chop or a bit of bacon, would you not think in that country something had gone wrong with the appetite for food? . . . One critic said that if he found a country in which such strip-tease acts with food were popular, he would conclude that the people of that country were starving.[29]

However, Lewis goes on to argue, we are not starving for sex; there is more sex available than ever before. Yet pornography, the equivalent of striptease acts, is now a trillion-dollar industry. Sex and romantic love are therefore not "just an appetite" like food. They are far more meaningful to us than that. Evolutionary biologists explain that this is hardwired into our brains. Christians explain that our capacity for romantic love stems from our being in the image of God (Genesis 1:27–29; Ephesians 5:25–31). Perhaps it can be said that both are true.

In any case, romantic love is an object of enormous power for the human heart and imagination, and therefore can excessively dominate our lives. Even people who completely avoid romantic love out of bitterness or fear are actually being controlled by its power. I once knew a man who said he had been so disappointed by women that he now engaged only in no-commitment sexual encounters. No longer would he be manipulated by love, he boasted. In response, I argued that if you are so afraid of love that you *cannot* have it, you are just as enslaved as if you *must* have it. The person who can't have it will avoid people who would be wonderful partners. The person who must have it will choose partners who are ill-fitting to them or abusive. If you are too afraid of love *or* too enamored by it, it has assumed godlike power, distorting your perceptions and your life.

The Sting

Jacob's inner emptiness had made him vulnerable to the idolatry of romantic love. When he offered to work seven years for Rachel, nearly four times more than the ordinary price for a bride, the unscrupulous Laban saw how lovesick he was. He decided to take advantage of his condition. When Jacob asked if he could marry Rachel, Laban's response was deliberately vague. He never actually said, "Yes, it's a deal," but rather "It's better that you get her than some other man" (Genesis 29:19). Jacob wanted to hear the answer yes, and so he heard a yes. But it was not a yes. Laban merely said, "I think it is a good idea for you to marry Rachel."

Seven years passed, and Jacob came to Laban and said, "Now give me my wife." As was customary, there was a great wedding feast. In the middle of the celebration Laban brought Jacob's wife to him, heavily veiled. Already inebriated from the festivities, Jacob lay down with her and had sex with her. But "when morning came, there was Leah!" (Genesis 29:25) In the full light of day, Jacob looked and saw that the woman with whom he had consummated his marriage was Leah, the unattractive older sister of Rachel. Trembling with anger, Jacob went to Laban and said, "What is this you have done to me?" Laban replied calmly that he should have known that it was customary in their land for the older girl to be married before the younger girl. If Jacob was committed to work for an additional seven years, he added, he'd be happy to throw Rachel in as part of the deal. Stung and trapped, Jacob submitted to seven more years in order to marry Rachel as well as Leah.[30]

The Devastation of Idolatry

We may wonder how Jacob could have been so gullible, but Jacob's behavior was that of an addict. There are many ways that romantic love can function as a kind of drug to help us escape the reality of our lives. Sally, the beautiful woman who was trapped in abusive relationships, once said to me that "men were my alcohol. Only if I was on a man's arm could I face life and feel good about myself." Another example is the older man who abandons his spouse for a far younger woman, in a desperate effort to hide the reality that he is aging. Then there is the young man who finds a woman desirable only until she sleeps with him a couple of times, after which he loses interest in her. For him, women are simply a necessary commodity to help him feel desirable and powerful. Our fears and inner barrenness make love a narcotic, a way to medicate ourselves, and addicts always make foolish, destructive choices.

That is what had happened to Jacob. Rachel was not

just his wife, but his "savior." He wanted and needed Rachel so profoundly that he heard and saw only the things he wanted to hear and see. That is why he became vulnerable to Laban's deception. Later, Jacob's idolatry of Rachel created decades of misery in his family. He adored and favored Rachel's sons over Leah's, spoiling and embittering the hearts of all his children, and poisoning the family system. We have a phrase to describe someone who has fallen in love: "He worships the ground she walks on." How destructive this can be when it is literally the case.

We see how idolatry ravaged Jacob's life, but perhaps the greatest casualty of all is Leah. Leah is the older daughter, and the narrator gives us but one important detail about her. The text says that she had "weak or poor eyes." Some have assumed it meant she had bad eyesight. But the passage does not say, "Leah had weak eyes, but Rachel could see very well." It says Leah had weak eyes, but Rachel was beautiful. So "weakness" probably meant she was cross-eyed or literally unsightly in some way. The point is clear. Leah was particularly unattractive, and she had to live all of her life in the shadow of her sister, who was absolutely stunning.

As a result, her father, Laban, knew that no man was ever going to marry her or offer any money for her. For years he had wondered how he was going to get rid of her so that Rachel, who would bring a fine price, could be wed. In Jacob, Laban found the solution to his financial problem. He saw his opportunity, and he capitalized on it. But see what this meant for Leah—the daughter whom her father did not want was now a wife whom her husband did not want. "Jacob loved Rachel more than Leah" (Genesis 29:30). She was the girl that nobody wanted. [31]

Leah, then, had a hollow in her heart every bit as big as the hollow in Jacob's heart. And now she began to respond to it the same way Jacob had. She did to Jacob what Jacob had done to Rachel and what Isaac had done to Esau. She set her heart's hope on getting Jacob's love. The last verses here are some of the most plaintive you will find in the Bible.

> When the LORD saw that Leah was not loved, he opened her womb, but Rachel was barren. Leah became pregnant and gave birth to a son. She named him Reuben, for she said, "It is because the LORD has seen my misery. Surely my husband will love me now." She conceived again, and when she gave birth to a son she said, "Because the LORD heard that I am not loved, he gave me this one too." So she named him Simeon. Again she conceived, and when she gave birth to a son she said, "Now at last my husband will become attached to me, because I

have borne him three sons." So he was named Levi.
She conceived again, and when she gave birth to a
son she said, "This time I will praise the LORD."
So she named him Judah. Then she stopped having
children.

Genesis 29:31–35[32]

What was she doing? She was trying to find happiness and an identity through traditional family values. Having sons, especially in those days, was the best way to do that; but it was not working. She had set all of her hopes and dreams on her husband. "If I have babies and sons, then my husband will come to love me, and then finally my unhappy life will be fixed," she thought. But instead, every birth pushed her down deeper into a hell of loneliness. Every single day she was condemned to see the man she most longed for in the arms of the one in whose shadow she had lived all of her life. Every day was like another knife in the heart.

Cosmic Disillusionment

At this point in the story, many contemporary readers will be wondering: "Where are all the spiritual heroes in this story? Whom am I supposed to be emulating? What is the moral of the story?"

The reason for our confusion is that we usually read

the Bible as a series of disconnected stories, each with a "moral" for how we should live our lives. It is not. Rather, it comprises a single story, telling us how the human race got into its present condition, and how God through Jesus Christ has come and will come to put things right. In other words, the Bible doesn't give us a god at the top of a moral ladder saying, "If you try hard to summon up your strength and live right, you can make it up!" Instead, the Bible repeatedly shows us weak people who don't deserve God's grace, don't seek it, and don't appreciate it even after they have received it. If that is the great biblical story arc into which every individual scriptural narrative fits, then what do we learn from this story?

We learn that through all of life there runs a ground note of cosmic disappointment. You are never going to lead a wise life until you understand that. Jacob said, "If I can just get Rachel, everything will be okay." And he goes to bed with the one who he thinks is Rachel, and literally, the Hebrew says, "in the morning, behold, it was Leah" (Genesis 29:25). One commentator noted about this verse, "This is a miniature of our disillusionment, experienced from Eden onwards."[33] What does that mean? With all due respect to this woman (from whom we have much to learn), it means that no matter what we put our hopes in, in the morning, *it is always Leah, never Rachel.*

Nobody has ever said this better than C. S. Lewis in *Mere Christianity*:

> Most people, if they have really learned to look into their own hearts, would know that they do want, and want acutely, something that cannot be had in this world. There are all sorts of things in this world that offer to give it to you, but they never quite keep their promise. The longings which arise in us when we first fall in love, or first think of some foreign country, or first take up some subject that excites us, are longings which no marriage, no travel, no learning, can really satisfy. I am not now speaking of what would be ordinarily called unsuccessful marriages, or holidays, or learned careers. I am speaking of the best possible ones. There was something we have grasped at, in that first moment of longing, which just fades away in the reality. I think everyone knows what I mean. The wife may be a good wife, and the hotels and scenery may have been excellent, and chemistry may be a very interesting job: but something has evaded us.[34]

If you get married as Jacob did, putting the weight of all your deepest hopes and longings on the person you are marrying, you are going to crush him or her with your expectations. It will distort your life and your spouse's life in a hundred ways. No person, not even the best one, can give your soul all it needs. You are going to think you have gone to bed with Rachel, and you will get up and it will always be Leah. This cosmic disappointment and disillusionment is there in all of life, but we especially feel it in the things upon which we most set our hopes.

When you finally realize this, there are four things you can do. You can blame the things that are disappointing you and try to move on to better ones. That's the way of continued idolatry and spiritual addiction. The second thing you can do is blame yourself and beat yourself and say, "I have somehow been a failure. I see everybody else is happy. I don't know why I am not happy. There is something wrong with me." That's the way of self-loathing and shame. Third, you can blame the world. You can say, "Curses on the entire opposite sex," in which case you make yourself hard, cynical, and empty. Lastly, you can, as C. S. Lewis says at the end of his great chapter on hope, reorient the entire focus of your life toward God. He concludes, "If I find in myself a desire which no experience in this world can satisfy, the most probable explanation is that I was made for another world [something supernatural and eternal]."[35]

Male and Female Idolatries

Jacob is after "apocalyptic sex." Leah, the traditionalist, is having babies and trying to find her identity in being a wife. But they are both frustrated. Ernest Becker explains why:

> The failure of romantic love as a solution to human problems is so much a part of modern man's frustration. . . . No human relationship can bear the burden of godhood. . . . However much we may idealize and idolize him [the love partner], he inevitably reflects earthly decay and imperfection. . . . After all, what is it that we want when we elevate the love partner to this position? We want to be rid of our faults, of our feeling of nothingness. We want to be justified, to know our existence has not been in vain. We want redemption—nothing less. Needless to say, human partners cannot give this.[36]

Both the stereotypically male and female idolatries regarding romantic love are dead ends. It is often said that "men use love to get sex, women use sex to get love." As in all stereotypes there is some truth to this, but this story shows that both of these counterfeit gods disappoint. Because Jacob sought to get his life validated from having a physically beautiful wife, he gave his heart to a woman toward whose immaturity and shortcomings he was blind. Leah's counterfeit god was not sex. She obviously had access to her husband's body, but not to his love and commitment. She wanted him to be "attached" to her, to have his soul cleave to her. But he did not. Her life became bound in shallows and miseries.

In our modern culture, there has been a growing awareness that many women are victims of "commitment idolatry." In a *New York Times* review of the movie *He's Just Not That Into You*, Manohla Dargis laments that Hollywood keeps giving us movies about young women "where female desire now largely seems reserved for shoes, wedding bells, and babies." One of the characters goes out on her first date and afterward calls a friend to tell her she thought the evening went well. Meanwhile, the man is home calling up another woman.[37]

The writer is right to point out that women who have made an idol of romance and a big wedding to Prince Charming become enslaved to their own desires. She advises women to abandon their typical love-idolatries and take up the male version. But, as we have seen, *all* idolatries enslave. Male love idolatries make them addicted to being independent, so they can "play the field." Female love idolatries, as the reviewer points out, make them addicted and dependent—vulnerable and easily manipulated. Both are a form of slavery, both blind us so we can't make wise life choices, both distort our lives. So what can we do?

Leah's Breakthrough

Leah is the one person in this sad story to make some spiritual progress, though this happens only at its very end. Look first at what God does in her. One of the things Hebrew scholars notice is that in all of Leah's statements, she was calling on *the LORD*. She used the name *Yahweh*. "*The Lord* [Yahweh] has seen my misery," she says in verse 32. How did she know about Yahweh?

Elohim was the generic Hebrew word for God. All cultures at that time had some general idea of God or gods, but Yahweh was the name of the God who had revealed himself to Abraham, and later to Moses. He was the one who told Abraham that he would bless the earth through his line. The only way Leah could have known about *Yahweh* was if Jacob had told her about the promise to his grandfather. So even though she was struggling and confused, she was nonetheless reaching out to a personal God of grace.

After years of childbearing, however, there's a breakthrough. When Leah gave birth to her last son, Judah, she said, "*This* time, I will praise the LORD." There was a defiance in that claim. It was a different declaration from the ones she had made after the other births. There was no mention of husband or child. It appears that finally, she had taken her heart's deepest hopes off of her husband and her children, and had put them on the Lord. Jacob and Laban had stolen Leah's life, but when she gave her heart finally to the Lord, she got her life back.

The True Bridegroom

We shouldn't just look at what God did in her. We have to also look at what God did *for* her. Leah might have had a sense that there was something special about this last child. She may have had an intuition that God had done something for her. And he had. Certainly, the writer of Genesis knew it. This child was Judah, and in Genesis 49 we are told that it is through him that the true King, the Messiah, will someday come. God had come to the girl that nobody wanted, the unloved, and made *her* the ancestral mother of Jesus. Salvation came into the world, not through beautiful Rachel, but through the unwanted one, the unloved one.

Does God just like to root for underdogs? No, this wonderful gift to Leah meant far more than that. The text says that when the Lord saw that Leah was not loved, *he* loved her. God was saying, "I am the real bridegroom. I am the husband of the husbandless. I am the father of the fatherless." This is the God who saves by grace. The gods of moralistic religions favor the successful and the overachievers. They are the ones who climb the moral ladder up to heaven. But the God of the Bible is the one who comes down into this world to accomplish a salvation and give us a grace we could never attain ourselves. He loves the unwanted, the weak and unloved. He is not just a king and we are the subjects; he is not just a shepherd and we are the sheep. He is a husband and we are his spouse. He is ravished with us—even those of us whom no one else notices.

And here is the power to overcome our idolatries. There are many people in the world who have not found a romantic partner, and they need to hear the Lord say, "I am the true Bridegroom. There is only one set of arms that will give you all your heart's desire, and await you at the end of time, if only you turn to me. And know that I love you now." However, it is not just those without spouses who need to see that God is our ultimate spouse, but those *with* spouses as well. They need this in order to save their marriage from the crushing weight of their divine expectations. If you marry someone expecting them to be like a god, it is only inevitable that they will disappoint you. It's not that you should try to love your spouse less, but rather that you should know and love God more. How can we know God's love so deeply that we release our lovers and spouses from our stifling expectations? By looking at the one to whom Leah's life points.

The Man Nobody Wanted

When God came to earth in Jesus Christ, he was truly the son of Leah. He became the man nobody wanted. He was born in a manger. He had no beauty that we should desire him (Isaiah 53:2). He came to his own and his own received him not (John 1:11). And at the end, everybody abandoned him. Jesus cried out even to his Father: "Why have you forsaken me?"

Why did he become Leah's son? Why did he become the man nobody wanted? For you and for me. He took upon himself our sins and died in our place. If we are deeply moved by the sight of his love for us, it detaches our hearts from other would-be saviors. We stop trying to redeem ourselves through our pursuits and relationships, because we are already redeemed. We stop trying to make others into saviors, because we have a Savior.

The only way to dispossess the heart of an old affection is by the expulsive power of a new one. . . . Thus . . . it is not enough . . . to hold out to the world the mirror of its own imperfections. It is not enough to come forth with a demonstration of the evanescent character of your enjoyments . . . to speak to the conscience . . . of its follies. . . . Rather, try every legitimate method of finding access to your hearts for the love of Him who is greater than the world.[38]

One day Sally told me how she got her life back. She went to a counselor who rightly pointed out that she had been looking to men for her identity, for her "salvation." Instead, the counselor proposed, she should get a career and become financially independent as a way of building up her self-esteem. The woman agreed wholeheartedly that she needed to stand on her own two feet economically, but she resisted the advice about finding self-esteem. "I was being advised to give up a common female idolatry and take on a common male idolatry," she said. "But I didn't want to have my self-worth dependent on career success any more than on men. I wanted to be free."

How did she do it? She came across Colossians 3, where Saint Paul writes: "Your life is hidden with Christ in God . . . and when Christ who is your life appears, you will appear with him in glory" (Colossians 3:1–4). She came to realize that neither men nor career nor anything else should be "her life" or identity. What mattered was not what men thought of her, or career success, but what Christ had done for her and how he loved her. So when she saw a man was interested in her, she would silently say in her heart toward him, "You may turn out to be a great guy, and maybe even my husband, but you cannot ever be *my life*. Only Christ is my life." When she began to do this, like Leah, she got her life back. This spiritual discipline gave her the ability to set boundaries and make good choices, and eventually to love a man for himself, and not simply to use men to bolster her self-image.

She had answered the question that we all must address in order to live our lives the way we should: Who can I turn to who is so beautiful that he will enable me to escape all counterfeit gods? There is only one answer to this question. As the poet George Herbert wrote, looking at Jesus on the Cross: "Thou art my loveliness, my life, my light, Beauty alone to me."[39]

THREE

❧❧❧

MONEY CHANGES EVERYTHING

Naked Greed

In 2005, investment bank Credit Suisse aggressively promoted loans to resorts. These loans offered instant personal proceeds to borrowers and high yields to institutional investors. In response, the founder and largest shareholder of the Yellowstone Club, a private ski resort catering to the very wealthy in the mountains of Montana, took out a $375 million loan. Two hundred nine million immediately went to his personal accounts, as the loan agreement permitted. Credit Suisse did little to appraise the ability of the borrower to repay, since it had no money of its own at risk. The loan was packaged and sold as part of a "collateralized loan obligation," transferring all potential problems to institutional investors such as pension funds who were buying loan products whose risks were vastly underestimated by the sellers. Credit Suisse did about six resort deals like this from 2002 to 2006, totaling close to $3 billion.

By 2007, however, the Yellowstone Club was in serious financial trouble. Routinely poor management was aggravated by the heavy debt service on the Credit Suisse loan. When the recession hit and real estate values declined, the club filed for bankruptcy. Credit Suisse, who had "first lien" rights, proposed an interim funding plan to "mothball" the club, which would have thrown hundreds of employees out of work. The vendors, waitresses, gardeners, and lift operators of the small towns of Montana, who had few other employment options, were about to take a terrible economic hit.

Fortunately, a Montana bankruptcy judge saw through what had happened. He blasted Credit Suisse and the club owner for "naked greed" and a "predatory loan" that had made them rich while laying all the risk and consequences on the backs of the working class people of the area. He stripped Credit Suisse of its first lien position, a rare act in bankruptcy court. The judge's rulings made it possible for another buyer to purchase the club, and so many jobs were saved.[40]

A journalist reporting this story called this a snapshot of the "economic zeitgeist" of the age. The new explosion in executive salaries, the increased emphasis on luxury goods, the rapacious deals that make millions for the deal makers at the expense of thousands of common workers, the lack of concern about steep debt—all of these things represent profound social changes in our society. Paul Krugman writes about these changes in attitudes:

> We should not think of it as a market trend like the rising value of waterfront property, but as something more like the sexual revolution of the 1960s—a relaxation of old strictures, a new permissiveness, but in this case the permissiveness is financial rather than sexual. Sure enough, John Kenneth Galbraith described the honest executive of 1967 as being one who "eschews the lovely, available, and even naked woman by whom he is intimately surrounded. . . . Management does not go out ruthlessly to reward itself. . . ." By the end of the 1990s, the executive motto might as well have been, "If it feels good, do it."[41]

We Can't See Our Own Greed

Ernest Becker wrote that our culture would replace God with sex and romance. Even earlier, Friedrich Nietzsche had a different theory. He wrote that, with the absence of God growing in Western culture, we would replace God with money.

> What induces one man to use false weights, another to set his house on fire after having insured it for more than its value, while three-fourths of our upper classes indulge in legalized fraud . . . what gives rise to all this? It is not real want—for their existence is by no means precarious . . . but they are urged on day and night by a terrible impatience at seeing their wealth pile up so slowly, and by an equally terrible longing and love for these heaps of gold. . . . What once was done "for the love of God" is now done for the love of money, i.e., for the love of that which at present affords us the highest feeling of power and a good conscience.[42]

In short, Nietzsche foretold that money in Western culture would become perhaps its main counterfeit god.

Innumerable writers and thinkers have been pointing out "the culture of greed" that has been eating away at our souls and has brought about economic collapse. Yet no one thinks that change is around the corner. Why? It's because greed and avarice are especially hard to see in ourselves.

Some years ago I was doing a seven-part series of talks on the Seven Deadly Sins at a men's breakfast. My wife, Kathy, told me, "I'll bet that the week you deal with greed you will have your lowest attendance." She was right. People packed it out for "Lust" and "Wrath" and even for "Pride." But nobody thinks they are greedy. As a pastor I've had people come to me to confess that they struggle with almost every kind of sin. Almost. I cannot recall anyone ever coming to me and saying, "I spend too much money on myself. I think my greedy lust for money is harming my family, my soul, and people around me." Greed hides itself from the victim. The money god's modus operandi includes blindness to your own heart.

Why can't anyone in the grip of greed see it? The counterfeit god of money uses powerful sociological and psychological dynamics. Everyone tends to live in a particular socioeconomic bracket. Once you are able to afford to live in a particular neighborhood, send your children to its schools, and participate in its social life, you will find yourself surrounded by quite a number of people who have more money than you. You don't compare yourself to the rest of the world, you compare yourself to those in your bracket. The human heart always wants to justify itself and this is one of the easiest ways. You say, "I don't live as well as him or her or them. My means are modest compared to theirs."

You can reason and think like that no matter how lavishly you are living. As a result, most Americans think of themselves as middle class, and only 2 percent call themselves "upper class."[43] But the rest of the world is not fooled. When people visit here from other parts of the globe, they are staggered to see the level of materialistic comfort that the majority of Americans have come to view as a necessity.

Jesus warns people far more often about greed than about sex, yet almost no one thinks they are guilty of it. Therefore we should all begin with a working hypothesis that "this could easily be a problem for me." If greed hides itself so deeply, no one should be confident that it is not a problem for them. How can we recognize and become free from the power of money to blind us?

The Seductive Power of Money

Jesus entered Jericho and was passing through. A man was there by the name of Zacchaeus; he was a chief tax collector and was wealthy.

Luke 19:1–2

With brief but telling strokes, the gospel of Luke introduces us to Zacchaeus. He was a "tax collector" who was shunned by his community. Even today, people who work for the IRS don't advertise it at parties, but we must understand what this meant at that time and place. Israel was a conquered nation, under military occupation. Their conquerors, the Romans, levied oppressive taxes on each colony as a means for transferring most of the nation's wealth and capital to Rome and its citizens. This left the colonial societies impoverished, which kept them subjugated. The only people who lived in comfort and ease in Israel were the Romans who ruled and their local collaborators, the tax collectors. The tax system depended on officials who were charged with extracting, for their Roman overlords, the tax income from each region targeted for collection. Everyone despised them. The people called Zacchaeus a "sinner" (Verse 7), which meant apostate or outcast. If you want to get a sense of how these functionaries were regarded, think of what people thought of the collaborators who, under the Nazis, oppressed their own people during World War II; think of drug lords who get rich enslaving thousands of the weakest people of the inner city; think of modern-day "robber barons" who buy out and then destroy companies, or sell common people mortgages they cannot afford, while making millions for themselves. Now you can understand the stature of tax collectors at this time.

Why would anyone take such a job as a tax collector? What could seduce a man to betray his family and country and live as a pariah in his own society? The answer was—money. The incentive the Romans offered tax collectors was almost irresistible. Backed by military force, the tax collector was allowed to demand much more money from his fellow Jews than he had contracted to pay the government. Today, we call this extortion. It was extremely lucrative. Tax collectors were the wealthiest people in society, and the most hated.

One of the reasons Luke brought Zacchaeus to our attention was that he was not just a regular tax collector. He was an *architelones* (Verse 2), literally, the *arch*-tax collector. It was not surprising that we find him in Jericho, a major customs center. As a head of the entire system he would have been one of its wealthiest and the most hated members. He lived in a time, unlike ours, when there was a stigma attached to conspicuous consumption and to reveling in wealth. But that didn't matter to him. He had sacrificed everything else in order to get money.

Money as a Master

Paul says greed is a form of idolatry (Colossians 3:5; Ephesians 5:5). Luke is teaching us the same thing in his gospel.[44] In Luke 12:15 Jesus says to listeners: "Watch out! Be on your guard against all kinds of greed, for a man's life does not consist in the abundance of his possessions." What is greed? In the surrounding passages of Luke 11 and 12, Jesus warned people about worrying over their possessions. For Jesus, greed is not only love of money, but excessive anxiety about it. He lays out the reason our emotions are so powerfully controlled by our bank account—"a man's life does not consist in the abundance of his possessions." To "consist" of your possessions is to be defined by what you own and consume. The term describes a personal identity based on money. It refers to people who, if they lose their wealth, do not have a "self" left, for their personal worth is based on their financial worth. Later Jesus comes right out and calls this what it is.

> *"No servant can serve two masters; either he will hate the one and love the other, or he will be devoted to the one and despise the other. You cannot serve both God and money." The Pharisees, who loved money, heard all this and were sneering at Jesus. He said to them, "You are the ones who justify yourselves in the eyes of men, but God knows your hearts. What is highly valued among men is detestable in God's sight."*
>
> Luke 16:13–15

Jesus uses all the basic biblical metaphors for idolatry and applies them to greed and money. According to the Bible, idolaters do three things with their idols.

They love them, trust them, and obey them.[45] "Lovers of money" are those who find themselves daydreaming and fantasizing about new ways to make money, new possessions to buy, and looking with jealousy on those who have more than they do. "Trusters of money" feel they have control of their lives and are safe and secure because of their wealth.

Idolatry also makes us "servants of money." Just as we serve earthly kings and magistrates, so we "sell our souls" to our idols. Because we look to them for our significance (love) and security (trust) we *have* to have them, and therefore we are driven to serve and, essentially, obey them. When Jesus says that we "serve" money, he uses a word that means the solemn, covenantal service rendered to a king. If you live for money you are a slave. If, however, God becomes the center of your life, that dethrones and demotes money. If your identity and security is in God, it can't control you through worry and desire. It is one or the other. You either serve God, or you become open to slavery to Mammon.

Nowhere is this slavery more evident than in the blindness of greedy people to their own materialism. Notice that in Luke 12 Jesus says, "Watch out! Be on your guard against all kinds of greed." That is a remarkable statement. Think of another traditional sin that the Bible warns against—adultery. Jesus doesn't say, "Be careful you aren't committing adultery!" He doesn't have to. When you are in bed with someone else's spouse—you know it. Halfway through you don't say, "Oh, wait a minute! I think this is adultery!" You know it is. Yet, even though it is clear that the world is filled with greed and materialism, almost no one thinks it is true of them. They are in denial.

Can we look at Zacchaeus any longer and ask, "How could he have betrayed and harmed so many people? How could he have been willing to be so hated? How could he have been so blinded by money to do all that and live like that?" Zacchaeus is just one example of what Jesus has been teaching all through the book of Luke. Money is one of the most common counterfeit gods there is. When it takes hold of your heart it blinds you to what is happening, it controls you through your anxieties and lusts, and it brings you to put it ahead of all other things.

The Beginnings of Grace

[Zacchaeus] wanted to see who Jesus was, but being a short man he could not, because of the crowd. So he ran ahead and climbed a sycamore-fig tree to see him, since Jesus was coming that way. When Jesus reached the spot, he looked up and said to him, "Zacchaeus, come down immediately. I must stay

at your house today." So he came down at once and
welcomed him gladly. All the people saw this and
began to mutter, "He has gone to be the guest of a
'sinner.'"

Luke 19:3–7

Zacchaeus was a short man, but why couldn't
a short man stand on the road in front of the taller
people? Obviously, the people would not give way to
him. In response, Zacchaeus did a surprising thing.
He climbed a tree. We must appreciate the significance
of this. In traditional cultures it was not freedom and
rights that mattered but honor and dignity. For any
grown male to climb up into a tree would have invited
enormous ridicule. Surely a person like Zacchaeus, who
was already despised and a short man as well, would be
more careful to act in a way that was fitting to a digni-
fied personage. So why did he do it? Luke tells us, "He
wanted to see who Jesus was." Zacchaeus was eager to
connect to Jesus. *Eager* may be too weak a word. His
willingness to climb a tree signifies something close to
desperation.

Jesus came along and he saw a crowd of mainly
respectable, religious people, all of whom felt superior to prostitutes and tax collectors (Luke 19:7;
Matthew 21:31). Instead of addressing any of them,
he singled out the most notorious "sinner" in the

whole throng. Zacchaeus was the *arch* collector, the worst of all. Yet right in the face of this very moral crowd, he selected this man not only to talk to but to eat with. In that culture, eating with someone meant friendship. Everyone was offended, but Jesus did not care. He said, "Zacchaeus, I don't want to go to their houses, but to yours." And Zacchaeus welcomed him home with joy.

This simple interchange could not have been more instructive for us. Zacchaeus did not approach Jesus with pride but with humility. He did not stand on his dignity and wealth; instead he put aside his station in life and was willing to be ridiculed in order to get a glimpse of Jesus. Ultimately, it was not Zacchaeus who asked Jesus into his life, but Jesus who asked Zacchaeus into his. You can almost hear Jesus laugh as he says it. "Zacchaeus! Yes, you! It's *you* I'm going home with today!" Jesus knew how outrageous his action looked to the crowd, how it contradicted everything they knew about religion, and how startling it was to the little man himself who was up in the tree.

When Zacchaeus saw that Jesus had chosen the least virtuous person in the crowd—himself—for a personal relationship, his whole spiritual understanding began to change. Though it is unlikely that he had a clear, conscious understanding of this, he began to realize that God's salvation was by grace, not through moral achievement or performance. That realization went through him like lightning, and he welcomed Jesus with joy.

Grace and Money

But Zacchaeus stood up and said to the Lord, "Look, Lord! Here and now I give half of my possessions to the poor, and if I have cheated anybody out of anything, I will pay back four times the amount." Jesus said to him, "Today salvation has come to this house, because this man, too, is a son of Abraham. For the Son of Man came to seek and to save what was lost."

Luke 19:8–10

Zacchaeus wanted to follow Jesus, and immediately he realized that, if he was to do that, money was an issue. So he made two remarkable promises.

He promised to give away 50 percent of his income to the poor. This was far beyond the 10 percent giving that the Mosaic law required. Today, to give away even 10 percent of our income to charity seems an enormous sum, though wealthy people could do much more and still live comfortably. Zacchaeus knew that when he made this offer. His heart had been affected. Since he knew salvation was not through the law, but

[*61*]

through grace, he did not aim to live by only fulfilling the letter of the law. He wanted to go beyond it.

There have been times when people have come to me as their pastor, and asked about "tithing," giving away a tenth of their annual income. They notice that in the Old Testament there are many clear commands that believers should give away 10 percent. But in the New Testament, specific, quantitative requirements for giving are less prominent. They often asked me, "You don't think that now, in the New Testament, believers are absolutely required to give away ten percent, do you?" I shake my head no, and they give a sigh of relief. But then I quickly add, "I'll tell you why you don't see the tithing requirement laid out clearly in the New Testament. Think. Have we received more of God's revelation, truth, and grace than the Old Testament believers, or less?" Usually there is uncomfortable silence. "Are we more 'debtors to grace' than they were, or less? Did Jesus 'tithe' his life and blood to save us or did he give it all?" Tithing is a minimum standard for Christian believers. We certainly wouldn't want to be in a position of giving away less of our income than those who had so much less of an understanding of what God did to save them.

Zacchaeus's second promise did not have to do so much with charity and mercy but with justice. He had made a great deal of money by cheating. There were many people from whom he had taken exorbitant revenues. Here again, the Mosaic law made a provision. Leviticus 5:16 and Numbers 5:7 directed that if you had stolen anything, you had to make restitution with interest. You had to give it back with 20 percent interest. However, Zacchaeus wanted to do far more. He would give back "four times the amount" he had stolen. That's 300 percent interest.

In response to these promises, Jesus said, "Salvation has come to this house." Notice, he didn't say, "If you live like this, salvation will come to this house." No, it *has* come. God's salvation does not come in response to a changed life. A changed life comes in response to the salvation, offered as a free gift.

That was the reason for Zacchaeus's new heart and life. If salvation had been something earned through obedience to the moral code, then Zacchaeus's question would have been "How much *must* I give?" However, these promises were responses to lavish, generous grace, so his question was "How much *can* I give?" He realized that while being financially rich, he had been spiritually bankrupt, but Jesus had poured out spiritual riches on him freely. He went from being an oppressor of the poor to being a champion of justice. He went from accruing wealth at the expense of the people around him to serving others at the expense of his wealth. Why? Jesus had replaced money as Zacchaeus's savior, and so money went back to being merely that, just money. It was now a tool for doing good, for serving people. Now that his identity and security were rooted in Christ, he had more money than he needed. The grace of God had transformed his attitude toward his wealth.

Grace and Deep Idols

To understand how Zacchaeus's heart began to change, we should consider that counterfeit gods come in clusters, making the idolatry structure of the heart complex. There are "deep idols" within the heart beneath the more concrete and visible "surface idols" that we serve.[46]

Sin in our hearts affects our basic motivational drives so they become idolatrous, "deep idols." Some people are strongly motivated by a desire for influence and power, while others are more excited by approval and appreciation. Some want emotional and physical comfort more than anything else, while still others want security, the control of their environment. People with the deep idol of power do not mind being unpopular in order to gain influence. People who are most motivated by approval are the opposite—they will gladly lose power and control as long as everyone thinks well of them. Each deep idol—power, approval, comfort, or control—generates a different set of fears and a different set of hopes.

"Surface idols" are things such as money, our spouse, or children, through which our deep idols seek fulfillment. We are often superficial in the analysis of our idol structures. For example, money can be a surface idol that serves to satisfy more foundational impulses. Some people want lots of money as a way to control their world and life. Such people usually don't spend much money and live very modestly. They keep it all safely saved and invested, so they can feel completely secure in the world. Others want money for access to social circles and to make themselves beautiful and attractive. These people *do* spend their money on themselves in lavish ways. Other people want money because it gives them so much power over others. In every case, money functions as an idol and yet, because of various deep idols, it results in very different patterns of behavior.

The person using money to serve a deep idol of control will often feel superior to people using money to attain power or social approval. In every case, however, money-idolatry enslaves and distorts lives. Another pastor at my church once counseled a married couple who had severe conflicts over how they handled money. The wife considered the husband a miser. One day the pastor was speaking one-on-one to the husband who was complaining bitterly about what a spendthrift his spouse was. "She is so selfish, spending so much on clothes and appearance!" He saw clearly how her need to look attractive to others influenced her use of money. The pastor then introduced him to the concept of surface and deep idols. "Do you see that by *not* spending or giving away anything, by socking away every penny, you are being just as selfish? You are 'spending' absolutely everything on your need to feel secure, protected, and in control." Fortunately for the counselor, the man was shocked rather than angered. "I'd never thought of it like that," he said, and things began to change in the marriage.

This is why idols cannot be dealt with by simply eliminating surface idols like money or sex. We can look at them and say, "I need to de-emphasize this in my life. I must not let this drive me. I will stop it." Direct appeals like that won't work, because the deep idols have to be dealt with at the heart level. There is only one way to change at the heart level and that is through faith in the gospel.

The Poverty of Christ

In 2 Corinthians 8 and 9 Paul asks a church to give an offering to the poor. Though he is an apostle with authority, he writes:, "I say this not by way of command" (2 Corinthians 8:8). He means: "I don't want to order you. I don't want this offering to be simply the response to a demand." He doesn't put pressure directly on the will and say, "I'm an apostle, so do what I say." Rather, he wants to see the "genuineness of your love," and then writes these famous words:

> *For you know the grace of our Lord Jesus Christ,*
> *that though he was rich, yet for your sake he became*
> *poor, so that you by his poverty might become rich.*
>
> 2 Corinthians 8:9

Jesus, the God-Man, had infinite wealth, but if he had held on to it, we would have died in our spiritual poverty. That was the choice—if he stayed rich, we would die poor. If he died poor, we could become rich. Our sins would be forgiven, and we would be admitted into the family of God. Paul was not giving this church a mere ethical precept, exhorting them to stop loving money so much and become more generous. Rather, he recapitulated the gospel.

This is what Paul was saying. Jesus gave up all his treasure in heaven, in order to make you his treasure— for you are a treasured people (1 Peter 2:9–10). When you see him dying to make you his treasure, that will make him yours. Money will cease to be the currency of your significance and security, and you will want to bless others with what you have. To the degree that you grasp the gospel, money will have no dominion over you. Think on his costly grace until it changes you into a generous people.

The solution to stinginess is a reorientation to the generosity of Christ in the gospel, how he poured out his wealth for you. Now you don't have to worry about money—the Cross proves God's care for you and gives you the security. Now you don't have to envy anyone else's money. Jesus's love and salvation confers on you a remarkable status—one that money cannot give you. Money cannot save you from tragedy, or give you control in a chaotic world. Only God can do that. What breaks the power of money over us is not just redoubled effort to follow the example of Christ. Rather, it is deepening your understanding of the salvation of Christ, what you have in him, and then living out the changes that that understanding makes in your heart—the seat of your mind, will, and emotions. Faith in the gospel restructures our motivations, our self-understanding and identity, our view of the world. Behavioral compliance to rules without a complete change of heart will be superficial and fleeting.

Man Must Have an Idol

Andrew Carnegie became one of the wealthiest men in the world when his steel company, the forerunner of U.S. Steel, became the most profitable business enterprise in the world. Early on in his success, at only age thirty-three, Carnegie took a ruthless evaluation of his own heart and produced a "note to self" memorandum.

Man must have an idol—The amassing of wealth is one of the worst species of idolatry. No idol more debasing than the worship of money. Whatever I engage in I must push inordinately therefore should I be careful to choose the life which will be the most elevating in character. To continue much longer overwhelmed by business cares and with most of my thoughts wholly upon the way to make more money in the shortest time, must degrade me beyond hope of permanent recovery. I will resign business at Thirty five, but during the ensuing two years, I wish to spend the afternoons in securing instruction, and in reading systematically.[47]

The candor and self-knowledge in this note is remarkable, and one of his biographers, Joseph Frazier, commented, "Neither Rockefeller, nor Ford, nor Morgan could have written this note, nor would they have understood the man who did."[48] Nevertheless, despite his insight into his own heart, Carnegie obviously did not "resign business" two years later, and many of the very character-degrading effects he feared worked themselves out in his life.

> Although Carnegie built 2,059 libraries . . . a steelworker, speaking for many, told an interviewer, "We didn't want him to build a library for us, we would rather have had higher wages." At that time steelworkers worked twelve-hour shifts on floors so hot they had to nail wooden platforms under their shoes. Every two weeks they toiled an inhuman twenty-four-hour shift, and then they got their sole day off. The best housing they could afford was crowded and filthy. Most died in their forties or earlier, from accidents or disease. . . . [49]

Bill, whom we met in the introduction, had lost a great deal of money during financial downturn of 2008–2009, after having become a Christian three years before. "If this had happened to me before I became a Christian, I would have hated myself, it would have driven me back to the bottle, and maybe to suicide," he said. At one time Bill could only feel like a person of worth and value if he was making money. He knew that if he had been in that kind of a spiritual relationship with money during the financial crisis, he would have lost all his sense of significance and meaning.[50] But his identity had shifted. It had ceased to rest in being successful and affluent and had come to be grounded in the grace and love of Jesus Christ. That was why he could say despite his losses, "Today, I can tell you honestly, I've never been happier in my life."

Andrew Carnegie knew that money was an idol in his heart, but he didn't know how to root it out. It can't be removed, only replaced. It must be supplanted by the one who, though rich, became poor, so that we might truly be rich.

FOUR

THE SEDUCTION OF SUCCESS

Fast-Fading Satisfaction

Pop legend Madonna describes the seduction of success in her own words.

I have an iron will, and all of my will has always been to conquer some horrible feeling of inadequacy. . . . I push past one spell of it and discover myself as a special human being and then I get to another stage and think I'm mediocre and uninteresting. . . . Again and again. My drive in life is from this horrible fear of being mediocre. And that's always pushing me, pushing me. Because even though I've become Somebody, I still have to prove that I'm *Somebody*. My struggle has never ended and it probably never will.[51]

The Seduction of Success

For Madonna, success is like drug that gives her a sense of consequence and worth, but the high quickly wears off and she needs a repeat dose. She must prove herself again and again. The driving force behind this is not joy but fear.

In the movie *Chariots of Fire,* one of the main characters is an Olympic sprinter who eloquently articulates the same philosophy. When asked why he runs, he says he does not do it because he loves it. "I'm more of an addict . . . ," he replies. Later, before running the hundred-meter Olympic event, he sighs: "Contentment! I'm twenty-four and I've never known it. I'm forever in pursuit and I don't even know what it is I'm chasing. . . . I'll raise my eyes and look down that corridor, four feet wide, with ten lonely seconds to justify my whole existence . . . but will I?"[52] Not long before film director Sydney Pollack died, there was an article written about his inability to slow down and enjoy his final years with his loved ones. Though he was unwell, and the grueling process of filmmaking was wearing him down, "he couldn't justify his existence if he stopped." He explained, "Every time I finish a picture, I feel like I've done what I'm supposed to do in the sense that I've earned my stay for another year or so."[53] But then he had to start over.

"Achievement is the alcohol of our time," says Mary

[*73*]

Bell, a counselor who works with high-level executives. She goes on:

> These days, the best people don't abuse alcohol. They abuse their lives. . . . You're successful, so good things happen. You complete a project, and you feel dynamite. That feeling doesn't last forever, and you slide back to normal. You think, "I've got to start a new project"—which is still normal. But you love the feeling of euphoria, so you've got to have it again. The problem is, you can't stay on that high. Say you're working on a deal and it doesn't get approved. Your self-esteem is on the line, because you've been gathering your self-worth externally. Eventually, in this cycle, you drop to the pain level more and more often. The highs don't seem quite so high. You may win a deal that's even bigger than the one that got away, but somehow that deal doesn't take you to euphoria. Next time, you don't even get back to normal, because you're so desperate about clinching the next deal. . . . An "achievement addict" is no different from any other kind of addict.[54]

In the end, achievement can't really answer the big questions—Who am I? What am I really worth? How do I face death? It gives the initial illusion of an answer. There is an initial rush of happiness that leads us to believe we have arrived, been included, been accepted, and proved ourselves. However, the satisfaction quickly fades.

The Idolatry of Success

More than other idols, personal success and achievement lead to a sense that we ourselves are god, that our security and value rest in our own wisdom, strength, and performance. To be the very best at what you do, to be at the top of the heap, means no one is like you. You are supreme.

One sign that you have made success an idol is the false sense of security it brings. The poor and the marginalized expect suffering, they know that life on this earth is "nasty, brutish, and short." Successful people are much more shocked and overwhelmed by troubles. As a pastor, I've often heard people from the upper echelons say, "Life isn't supposed to be this way," when they face tragedy. I have never heard such language in my years as a pastor among the working class and the poor. The false sense of security comes from deifying our achievement and expecting it to keep us safe from the troubles of life in a way that only God can.

Another sign that you have made achievement an idol is that it distorts your view of yourself. When your achievements serve as the basis for your very worth as a person, they can lead to an inflated view of your abilities. A journalist once told me that she was at a dinner party with a highly successful and wealthy businessman. He dominated the conversation all evening, but the reporter noticed that almost none of the discussion was about economics and finance, his only field of expertise. When he held forth on interior design or single-sex schools or philosophy he acted as if his opinions were equally well informed and authoritative. If your success is more than just success to you—if it is the measure of your value and worth—then accomplishment in one limited area of life will make you believe you have expertise in all areas. This, of course, leads to all kinds of bad choices and decisions. This distorted view of ourselves is part of the blindness to reality that the Bible says always accompanies idolatry (Psalm 135:15–18; Ezekiel 36:22–36).[55]

The main sign that we are into success idolatry, however, is that we find we cannot maintain our self-confidence in life unless we remain at the top of our chosen field. Chris Evert was a leading tennis player in the 1970s and 1980s. Her career win-loss record was the best of any singles player in history. But as she contemplated retirement, she was petrified. She said to an interviewer:

> I had no idea who I was, or what I could be away from tennis. I was depressed and afraid because so much of my life had been defined by my being a tennis champion. I was completely lost. Winning made me feel like I was somebody. It made me feel pretty. It was like being hooked on a drug. I needed the wins, the applause, in order to have an identity.[56]

A friend of mine had reached the top of his profession, but an addiction to prescription drugs forced him to resign his position and enter a period of rehabilitation for substance abuse. He had become addicted in part because of the expectation that he should always be productive, dynamic, upbeat, and brilliant. But he refused to blame other people's demands for his collapse. "My life was built on two premises," he said. "The first was that I could control your opinion and approval of me through my performance. The second was—*that* was all that mattered in life."

It would be wrong for us to think that this idolatry applies only to individuals. It is also possible for an entire field of professionals to be so enamored of their skills and policies that they treat them as a form of salvation. Do scientists, sociologists, therapists, and politicians admit the limitations of what they can accomplish, or do they make "messianic" claims? There should be a chastened humility about how much any public policy or technological advance can do to solve the problems of the human race.

A Culture of Competition

Our contemporary culture makes us particularly vulnerable to turning success into a counterfeit god. In his book *The Homeless Mind*, Peter Berger points out that in traditional cultures, personal worth is measured in terms of "honor." Honor is given to those who fulfill their assigned role in the community, whether it be as citizen, father, mother, teacher, or ruler. Modern society, however, is individualistic, and bases worth on "dignity." Dignity means the right of every individual to develop his or her own identity and self, free from any socially assigned role or category.[57] Modern society, then, puts great pressure on individuals to prove their worth through personal achievement. It is not enough to be a good citizen or family member. You must win, be on top, to show you are one of the best.

David Brooks's book *On Paradise Drive* describes

what he calls "the professionalization of childhood." From the earliest years, an alliance of parents and schools creates a pressure cooker of competition, designed to produce students who excel in everything. Brooks calls this "a massive organic apparatus . . . a mighty Achievatron." The family is no longer what Christopher Lasch once called a "haven in a heartless world," a counterbalance to the dog-eat-dog areas of life.[58] Instead, the family has become the nursery where the craving for success is first cultivated.

This profound emphasis on high achievement is taking a great toll on young people. In spring of 2009, Nathan Hatch, president of Wake Forest University, admitted what many educators have seen for years, that a disproportionate number of young adults have been trying to cram into the fields of finance, consulting, corporate law, and specialized medicine because of the high salaries and aura of success that these professions now bring. Students were doing so with little reference to the larger questions of meaning and purpose, said Hatch. That is, they choose professions not in answer to the question "What job helps people to flourish?" but "What job will help *me* to flourish?" As a result, there is a high degree of frustration expressed over unfulfilling work. Hatch hoped that the economic downturn of 2008–2009 would force many students to reassess their fundamental way of choosing their careers.[59]

If our entire culture strongly encourages us to adopt this counterfeit god, how can we escape it?

The Successful Dead Man

One of the most successful and powerful men in the world in his time was Naaman, whose story is told in the Bible, in 2 Kings 5. Naaman had what some might call "a designer life." He was commander of the army of Aram, which today we call Syria. He was also the equivalent of the prime minister of the nation, since the king of Syria "leaned on his arm" at formal state occasions (2 Kings 5:18). He was a wealthy man and a valiant soldier, highly decorated and honored. However, all of these great accomplishments and abilities had met their match.

> *Naaman was commander of the army of the king of Aram. He was a great man in the sight of his master and highly regarded, because through him the LORD had given victory to Aram. He was a valiant soldier, but he had leprosy.*
>
> 2 Kings 5:1

Notice how the author of 2 Kings piles up the accolades and accomplishments, and suddenly adds that, despite all of them, he was a dead man walking. *Lep-*

rosy in the Bible encompassed a variety of fatal, wasting skin diseases that slowly crippled, disfigured, and finally killed their victims. The word had the resonance in its day that *cancer* has in ours. Naaman's body was going through a slow-motion explosion. His body would puff up, his skin and bones would crack, and then they would fall off in stages as he died by inches. Naaman had everything—wealth, athletic prowess, popular acclaim—but under it all he was literally falling apart.

One of the main motivations behind the drive for success is the hope of entering the "Inner Ring." C. S. Lewis wrote insightfully about this subject in one of his most famous essays.

> I don't believe the economic motive and the erotic motive account for everything that goes on in the world. It's a lust . . . a longing to be inside, [which] takes many forms. . . . You want . . . the delicious knowledge that just we four or five—we are the people who (really) *know*. . . . As long as you are governed by that desire you will never be satisfied. Until you conquer the fear of being an outsider, an outsider you will remain. . . .

What does Lewis mean—"an outsider you will remain"? Naaman had success and money and power, but he was a leper. Success, wealth, and power are supposed to make you the consummate *in*sider, admitted to the most exclusive social circles and inner rings. However, his contagious skin disease had made him an outsider. All his success was useless, since it could not overcome his social alienation and emotional despair.

In this, the story of Naaman functions as a parable. Many people pursue success as a way to overcome the sense that they are somehow "outsiders." If they attain it, they believe, it will open the doors into the clubs, into the social sets, into relationships with the connected and the influential. Finally, they think, they will be accepted by all the people who really matter. Success promises to do that, but in the end it cannot deliver. Naaman's leprosy represents the reality that success can't deliver the satisfaction we are looking for. Many of the most successful people testify to still feeling like "outsiders" and having doubts about themselves.

Looking in the Wrong Places

Now bands from Aram had gone out and had taken captive a young girl from Israel, and she served Naaman's wife. She said to her mistress, "If only my master would see the prophet who is in Samaria! He would cure him of his leprosy."

2 Kings 5:2–3

Naaman's wife had a slave girl who told him about a great prophet in Israel. Desperate enough to grasp at this straw, Naaman set off to Israel, seeking a cure from Elisha. With him he took "ten talents of silver, six thousand shekels of gold, and ten sets of clothing" as well as a letter of reference from the king of Syria to the king of Israel, which read, "With this letter I am sending my servant Naaman to you so that you may cure him of his leprosy" (2 Kings 5:5–6). He immediately headed to the king of Israel, giving him the letter and offering him the money. He expected that, because of the wealth and the letter, the king of Israel would command the prophet to cure him, and he could go home a healthy man.

Naaman expected to get his cure through letters of high recommendation from one king to another king. He thought he could use his success to deal with his problems. Naaman did not understand that there are some things only God can do. The slave girl had told Naaman to simply "see the prophet in Israel," to go directly to the prophet and ask for a cure. This did not fit Naaman's view of the world. Instead he amassed an enormous payout, brought a letter of recommendation from the highest possible source, and went to the top man in Israel, the king. The king of Israel, however, was not pleased.

As soon as the king of Israel read the letter, he tore his robes and said, "Am I God? Can I kill and bring back to life? Why does this fellow send someone to me to be cured of his leprosy? See how he is trying to pick a quarrel with me!"

2 Kings 5:7

Naaman and the Syrian king believed that religion in Israel functioned the way it worked in virtually all nations at that time, and in many nations today. They believed religion was a form of social control. The operating principle of religion is: If you live a good life, then the gods or God will have to bless you and give you prosperity. It was only natural, then, to assume that the most successful people in a society were those closest to God. They would be the ones who could get whatever they wanted from God. That is why traditional religion always expects that the gods will be working through the successful, not the outsider and the failures. That is why Naaman went directly to the king.

The king of Israel, however, tears his clothes when he reads the letter. He knows that the Syrian king will not understand that Israel's God is different and that he cannot command a healing for Naaman. The God of Israel is not on a leash, he cannot be bought or appeased. The gods of religion can be controlled. If we offer them hard work and devotion, then they are be-holden to us. However, the God of Israel cannot be approached like that. Whatever he gives us is a gift of grace.

When the king of Israel cried out, "Am I God? Can I kill and bring to life?" he was getting at the heart of Naaman's problem. Naaman had made success an idol. He expected that on the basis of his achievement, he could go to others in his "success-class" and get what-ever he needed. But achievement, money, and power cannot "kill and make alive."

The more I have studied this text over the years, the more I admire Naaman. He really was a good and ac-complished person. But that only goes to show that the finest person in the world hasn't the slightest idea how to search for God. Let's not be too hard on him. He pulls strings, drops names, spends a lot of money, and goes to the top. This is the way you deal with all im-portant human beings, so why not deal with God this way? But the God of the Bible is not like that. Naaman is after a tame God, but this is a wild God. Naaman is after a God who can be put into debt, but this is a God of grace, who puts everyone else in his debt. Naaman is after a private God, a God for you and you but not a God for everybody, but this God is the God of every-one, whether we acknowledge it or not.

Some Great Thing

When Elisha the man of God heard that the king of Israel had torn his robes, he sent him this message: "Why have you torn your robes? Have the man come to me and he will know that there is a prophet in Israel." So Naaman went with his horses and chariots and stopped at the door of Elisha's house.

2 Kings 5:8–9

Naaman went to the house of Elisha, and what he saw and heard there shocked him. Apparently insensible of the honor being done him, the prophet did not even come to the door. He merely sent his servant to speak with Naaman. The second shock was the message itself.

[The messenger said,] "Go, wash yourself seven times in the Jordan, and your flesh will be restored and you will be cleansed." But Naaman went away angry and said, "I thought that he would surely come out to me and stand and call on the name of the LORD his God, wave his hand over the spot and cure me of my leprosy. Are not Abana and Pharpar, the rivers of Damascus, better than any of the waters of Israel? Couldn't I wash in them and be cleansed?" So he turned and went off

> *in a rage. Naaman's servants went to him and*
> *said, "My father, if the prophet had told you to do*
> *some great thing, would you not have done it? How*
> *much more, then, when he tells you, 'Wash and be*
> *cleansed'!"*
>
> 2 Kings 5:10–13

Naaman expected that Elisha would take the money and perform some magic ritual. Or, he thought, if Elisha did not take the money, he would at least demand that Naaman do "some great thing" to earn his healing. Instead he was asked to simply go and dip himself seven times in the Jordan River. At this he went off in a rage.

Why? Again, Naaman's entire worldview was being challenged. He had just learned that this God is not an extension of culture, but a transformer of culture, not a controllable but a sovereign Lord. Now he was being confronted with a God who in his dealings with human beings only operates on the basis of grace. These two go together. No one can control the true God because no one can earn, merit, or achieve their own blessing and salvation. Naaman was angry because he thought he was going to be asked to do a mighty thing, as it were; to bring back the broomstick of the Wicked Witch of the West, or to return the Ring of Power to Mount Doom. Those would have been requests in keeping with his self-image and worldview. But Elisha's message was an insult. "Any idiot, any child, anyone can go down and paddle around in the Jordan," he thought to himself. "That takes no ability or attainment *at all!*" Exactly. That is a salvation for anyone, good or bad, weak or strong.

Until Naaman learned that God was a God of grace, whose salvation cannot be earned, only received, he would continue to be enslaved to his idols. He would continue to use them to earn a security and significance that they could not produce. Only if he understood God's grace would he see his successes were ultimately gifts from God. Yes, Naaman had expended much energy to procure them, but only with talents, abilities, and opportunities that God had given to him. He had been dependent on God's grace all his life, but he didn't see it.

"Just wash yourself," then, was a command that was hard because it was so easy. To do it, Naaman had to admit he was helpless and weak and had to receive his salvation as a free gift. If you want God's grace, all you need is need, all you need is nothing. But that kind of spiritual humility is hard to muster. We come to God saying, "Look at all I've done," or maybe "Look at all I've suffered." God, however, wants us to look to him—to just wash.

Naaman needed to learn how to "lay his deadly doing down." That phrase comes from an old hymn:

> *Lay your deadly "doing" down*
> *Down at Jesus' feet.*
> *Stand in him, in him alone,*
> *Gloriously complete.*

The Little Suffering Servant

At every point in the Bible, the writers are at pains to stress that God's grace and forgiveness, while free to the recipient, are always costly for the giver. From the earliest parts of the Bible, it was understood that God could not forgive without sacrifice. No one who is seriously wronged can "just forgive" the perpetrator. If you have been robbed of money, opportunity, or happiness, you can either make the wrongdoer pay it back or you can forgive. But when you forgive, that means *you* absorb the loss and the debt. You bear it yourself. All forgiveness, then, is costly.[60]

It is remarkable how often the biblical narratives make reference to this basic principle. In this story, too, someone had to bear her suffering with patience and love, in order for Naaman to receive his blessing. I'm referring to a character in the narrative who entered and exited so quickly that she is hardly noticed. Yet she was in some ways the most important character in the story. Who was she? The slave girl of Naaman's wife was captured by raiding bands of Syrians. At best that meant her family was taken captive and all sold off. At worst, it meant they had been killed before her eyes. When we meet her in the story, she's at the bottom of the bottom of Syria's social structure. She's a racial outsider, a slave, a woman—and a young one, probably aged twelve to fourteen. In short, her life has been ruined utterly. And who is responsible? Field Marshal Naaman, the supreme military commander. Yet how does she respond when she learns that her nemesis has been struck down with leprosy?

If we set our hearts on getting to the top, but instead find ourselves on the bottom rung of the ladder, it will usually lead to great cynicism and bitterness. We will desperately look around for people to blame for our failures. We might even indulge in fantasies of revenge. However, the little slave girl did not fall into that trap. Did she say, "Ha! Leprosy! I saw another finger fall off today! Oh, I will dance on his grave!" No, not at all. Look at her words—"If only my master would see the prophet!" There is sympathy and concern in those words. She must have really wanted to relieve his suffering and save him. There was no other reason to tell him about the prophet. Think of it. He was now in her hands. What she knew could save him, and by withholding it she could make him suffer horribly. She could have made him pay for his sins. She could have made *him* bear the cost for what he had done to her. He had abused her, and now she could abuse him.

However, she did not do that. This unsung heroine of the Bible refused to relieve her own suffering by making him pay. She did what the entire Bible tells us to do. She did not seek revenge, she trusted God to be the judge of all. She forgave him and became the vehicle for his healing and salvation. She trusted God and bore her suffering with patience. As the British preacher Dick Lucas once said about her, "She paid the price of usefulness." She suffered and forgave not knowing how much God would use her sacrifice.[61]

The Great Suffering Servant

This biblical theme, that forgiveness always requires a suffering servant, finds its climax in Jesus, who fulfills the prophecies of a Suffering Servant who will come to save the world (Isaiah 53). Though he had lived in joy and glory with his father, he lost it all. He became a human being, a servant, and was subject to beatings, capture, and death. As he looked down from the

Cross at his so-called friends, with some of them denying, some betraying, and all forsaking him, he paid the price. He forgave them and died on the Cross for them. On the Cross we see God doing at the cosmic level what we all have to do when we forgive. There God absorbed the punishment and debt for sin himself. He paid it so we did not have to.

We will not escape our idolatry of success simply by berating ourselves over it. At the end of the 1990s, just before the dot-com crash and September 11, 2001, the excessive emphasis on success and materialism was exposed in an article by Helen Rubin in the magazine *Fast Company.*

> Of all the subjects we obsess about . . . success is the one we lie about the most—that success and its cousin money will make us secure, that success and its cousin power will make us important, that success and its cousin fame will make us happy. It's time to tell the truth: Why are our generation's smartest, most talented, most successful people flirting with disaster in record numbers? People are using all their means to get money, power, and glory—and then self-destructing. Maybe they didn't want it in the first place! Or didn't like what they saw when they finally achieved it.[62]

The Seduction of Success

Not long after this article was written, in light of the mild recession of 2000–2001, there were many similar jeremiads about how our culture had become addicted to success. When would we learn that we have made success and its "cousins" into the gods of our society? Then the attacks of September 11, 2001, occurred and the media announced the "end of irony." Now, it was said, we would go back to more traditional values of hard work, modest expectations, and delayed gratification. Nothing like that happened. In 2008–2009, when the global economy crashed, it became clear that our culture had gone back to its addiction.

The idol of success cannot be just expelled, it must be replaced. The human heart's desire for a particular valuable object may be conquered, but its need to have *some* such object is unconquerable.[63] How can we break our heart's fixation on doing "some great thing" in order to heal ourselves of our sense of inadequacy, in order to give our lives meaning? Only when we see what Jesus, our great Suffering Servant, has done for us will we finally understand why God's salvation does not require us to do "some great thing." We don't have to do it, because Jesus has. That's why we can "just wash." Jesus did it all for us, and he loves us—that is how we know our existence is justified. When we believe in what he accomplished for us with our minds, and when we are moved by what he did for us in our hearts, it begins to kill off the addiction, the need for success at all costs.

The End of Idolatry

Naaman humbled himself and went to the Jordan. The results were astonishing.

> So he went down and dipped himself in the Jordan seven times, as the man of God had told him, and his flesh was restored and became clean like that of a young boy. Then Naaman and all his attendants went back to the man of God. He stood before him and said, "Now I know that there is no God in all the world except in Israel. Please accept now a gift from your servant." The prophet answered, "As surely as the LORD lives, whom I serve, I will not accept a thing." And even though Naaman urged him, he refused.
>
> 2 Kings 5:14–16

The biblical story of salvation assaults our worship of success at every point. Naaman, to be cured, had to accept a word through a servant girl, and later through a servant of Elisha, and finally other servants of his own. In those days such people were treated as no more important than a pet or a beast of burden by the high and mighty. Yet God sent his message of salvation through them. The answer came not from the palace, but from the slave quarters! The ultimate example of this theme, of course, is Jesus Christ himself. He came not to Rome or Alexandria or to China, but to a backwater colony. He was born not in the palace, but in a manger, in a stable.

> *Seek not in courts nor palaces*
> *Nor royal curtains draw—*
> *But search the stable, see your God*
> *Extended on the straw.*
>
> —William Billings

All during his ministry, the disciples continually asked Jesus, "When are you going to take power? When are you going to stop fraternizing with simple people? When are you going to start networking and raising money? When will you run for office? When's the first primary? When's our first TV special?" Instead, Jesus served humbly and then was tortured and killed. Even when Jesus rose from the dead he first appeared to women, the people who then had no status. Jesus's salvation is received not through strength but through the admission of weakness and need. And Jesus's salvation was achieved not through strength but through surrender, service, sacrifice, and death. This is one of the great messages of the Bible: God chooses the weak things of the world to shame the strong, the foolish and despised things to shame the wise, even the things that are not, to bring to nothing the things that are (1 Corinthians 1:29-31). That's how God does it.

FIVE

THE POWER AND THE GLORY

A World Possessed

Just before Europe plunged into World War II, Dutch historian Johan Huizinga wrote, "We live in a world possessed. And we know it."[64] The Nazis claimed to promote deep love of country and people. But somehow as they pursued this thing, "love of country," their patriotism became demonic and destructive. In the end, Nazism accomplished the very opposite of what it sought—endless shame rather than national honor.

In 1794, Maximilien Robespierre, the leader of the French Revolution, said to the National Convention, "What is the goal towards which we are heading? The peaceful enjoyment of liberty and equality. . . . The Terror is nothing other than prompt, severe, inflexible justice."[65] However, his "Reign of Terror" was so horrendously *un*just that Robespierre himself was made a scapegoat and guillotined without any trial. "Liberty and equality" are obviously great goods, but again, something went horribly wrong. A noble principle became "possessed," went insane, and ultimately accomplished the very opposite of the justice the revolutionaries sought.

What happened? Idolatry. When love of one's people becomes an absolute, it turns into racism. When love of equality turns into a supreme thing, it can result in hatred and violence toward anyone who has led a privileged life. It is the settled tendency of human societies to turn good political causes into counterfeit gods. As we have mentioned, Ernest Becker wrote that in a society that has lost the reality of God, many people will look to romantic love to give them the fulfillment they once found in religious experience. Nietzsche, however, believed it would be money that would replace God. But there is another candidate to fill this spiritual vacuum. We can also look to politics. We can look upon our political leaders as "messiahs," our political policies as saving doctrine, and turn our political activism into a kind of religion.

The Signs of Political Idolatry

One of the signs that an object is functioning as an idol is that fear becomes one of the chief characteristics of life. When we center our lives on the idol, we become dependent on it. If our counterfeit god is threatened in any way, our response is complete panic. We do not say, "What a shame, how difficult," but rather "This is the end! There's no hope!"

This may be a reason why so many people now respond to U.S. political trends in such an extreme way. When either party wins an election, a certain percentage of the losing side talks openly about leaving the country. They become agitated and fearful for the future. They have put the kind of hope in their political leaders and policies that once was reserved for God and the work of the gospel. When their political leaders are out of power, they experience a death. They believe that if *their* policies and people are not in power, everything will fall apart. They refuse to admit how much agreement they actually have with the other party, and instead focus on the points of disagreement. The points of contention overshadow everything else, and a poisonous environment is created.

Another sign of idolatry in our politics is that opponents are not considered to be simply mistaken, but to be evil. After the last presidential election, my eighty-four-year-old mother observed, "It used to be that whoever was elected as your president, even if he wasn't the one you voted for, he was still your president. That doesn't seem to be the case any longer." After each election, there is now a significant number of people who see the incoming president lacking moral legitimacy. The increasing political polarization and bitterness we see in U.S. politics today is a sign that we have made political activism into a form of religion. How does idolatry produce fear and demonization?

Dutch-Canadian philosopher Al Wolters taught that in the biblical view of things, the main problem in life is sin, and the only solution is God and his grace. The alternative to this view is to identify something besides sin as the main problem with the world and something besides God as the main remedy. That demonizes something that is not completely bad, and makes an idol out of something that cannot be the ultimate good. Wolters writes:

> The great danger is to single out some aspect or phenomenon of God's good creation and identify it, rather than the alien intrusion of sin, as the villain in the drama of human life. . . . This "something" has been variously identified as . . . the body and its passions (Plato and much of Greek philosophy), culture in distinction from nature (Rousseau and Romanticism), institutional authority, especially in the state and the family (much of depth psychology), technology and management techniques (Heidegger and Ellul). . . . The Bible is unique in its uncompromising rejection

of all attempts to . . . identify part of creation as either the villain or the savior.[66]

This accounts for the constant political cycles of overblown hopes and disillusionment, for the increasingly poisonous political discourse, and for the disproportionate fear and despair when one's political party loses power. But *why* do we deify and demonize political causes and ideas? Reinhold Niebuhr answered that, in political idolatry, we make a god out of having power.

The Idolatry of Power

Reinhold Niebuhr was a prominent American theologian of the mid-twentieth century. He believed all humans struggle with a sense of being dependent and powerless. The original temptation in the Garden of Eden was to resent the limits God had put on us ("You shall not eat of the tree. . . ."; Genesis 2:17) and to seek to be "as God" by taking power over our own destiny. We gave in to this temptation and now it is part of our nature. Rather than accept our finitude and dependence on God, we desperately seek ways to assure ourselves that we still have power over our own lives. But this is an illusion. Niebuhr believed this cosmic insecurity creates a "will to power" that dominates our social and political relationships.[67] He observed two ways this works itself out.

First, said Niebuhr, pride in one's people is a good thing, but when the power and prosperity of the nation become unconditioned absolutes that veto all other concerns, then violence and injustice can be perpetrated without question.[68] When this happens, Dutch scholar Bob Goudzwaard writes:

> . . . the end indiscriminately justifies every means. . . . Thus a nation's goal of material prosperity becomes an idol when we use it to justify the destruction of the natural environment or allow the abuse of individuals or classes of people. A nation's goal of military security becomes an idol when we use it to justify the removal of rights to free speech and judicial process, or the abuse of an ethnic minority.[69]

Niebuhr believed that entire nations had corporate "egos," and just as individuals, national cultures could have both superiority and inferiority complexes. An example of the former would be how America's proud self-image as "the land of the free" blinded most people to their hypocritical racism toward African-Americans. A society can also develop a sense of inferiority and become aggressive and belligerent. Writing his book in 1941, it was easy for Niebuhr to identify Nazi Germany as an example of this form of power idolatry. Germany's humiliation after World War I left the whole society eager to prove its power and superiority to the world.[70]

It is not easy to draw an exact line between ascribing value to something and assigning it absolute value. There is likewise no precise way to define when patriotism has crossed over into racism, oppression, and imperialism. Yet no one denies that nations have often slid down that slippery slope. It is no solution to laugh at all expressions of patriotism, as if it were an evil thing in itself. As we have seen all along, idols are good and necessary things that are turned into gods. C. S. Lewis wrote wisely about this:

> It is a mistake to think that some of our impulses—say mother love or patriotism—are good, and others, like sex or the fighting instinct, are bad. . . . There are situations in which it is the duty of a married man to encourage his sexual impulse and of a soldier to encourage the fighting instinct. There are also occasions on which a mother's love for her own children or a man's love for his own country have to be suppressed or they will lead to unfairness towards other people's children or countries.[71]

Turning a Philosophy into an Idol

Niebuhr recognized another form of the "will to power." You make not your people, but your political philosophy into a saving faith. This happens when politics becomes "ideological."

Ideology can be used to refer to any coherent set of ideas about a subject, but it can also have a negative connotation closer to its cousin word, *idolatry*. An ideology, like an idol, is a limited, partial account of reality that is raised to the level of the final word on things. Ideologues believe that their school or party has the real and complete answer to society's problems. Above all, ideologies hide from their adherents their dependence on God.[72]

The most recent example of a major ideology that failed is communism. For nearly a hundred years, large numbers of Western thinkers had high hopes for what once was called "scientific socialism." But from the end of World War II to the fall of the Berlin Wall in 1989, those beliefs came crashing down. C. E. M. Joad was a leading British agnostic philosopher who turned back to Christianity after World War II. In his book *The Recovery of Belief* he wrote:

> The view of evil implied by Marxism, expressed by Shaw and maintained by modern psychother-

apy, a view which regards evil as the by-product of circumstances, which circumstances can, therefore, alter and even eliminate, has come to seem [in light of World War II and atrocities by both Nazis and Stalinists] intolerably shallow. . . . It was because we rejected the doctrine of original sin that we on the Left were always being disappointed, disappointed . . . by the failure of true socialism to arrive, by the behavior of nations and politicians . . . above all, by the recurrent fact of war.[73]

One of the key volumes that came out of this time was a book by several disillusioned communists and socialists, including Arthur Koestler and André Gide, entitled *The God that Failed*.[74] The title says it all, describing how a political ideology can make absolute promises and demand total life commitment.

In the wake of the collapse of socialism, the pendulum swung toward an embrace of free market capitalism as the best solution for dealing with the recurrent problems of poverty and injustice. Many would say today that this is the new reigning ideology. Indeed, one of the source documents of modern capitalism, Adam Smith's *The Wealth of Nations,* seemed to deify the free market when it argued that the market is an "invisible hand" that, when given free rein, automatically drives human behavior toward that which is most beneficial for society, apart from any dependence on God or a moral code.[75] It is too early to be sure, but it may be that in light of the massive financial crisis of 2008–2009, the same disaffection with capitalism may occur that happened to socialism a generation before. A wave of books revealing the ideological nature of recent market capitalism, both popular[76] and scholarly,[77] both secular[78] and religious,[79] is appearing. Some even have variants on the title "the god that failed," since free markets have been ascribed a godlike power to make us happy and free.[80]

Niebuhr argued that human thinking always elevates *some* finite value or object to be The Answer.[81] That way we feel that we are the people who can fix things, that everyone opposing us is a fool or evil. But as with all idolatries, this too blinds us. In Marxism the powerful State becomes the savior and capitalists are demonized. In conservative economic thought, free markets and competition will solve our problems, and therefore liberals and government are the obstacles to a happy society.

The reality is much less simplistic. Highly progressive tax structures can produce a kind of injustice where people who have worked hard go unrewarded and are penalized by the high taxes. A society of low taxes and few benefits, however, produces a different kind of injustice, where the children of families who can afford good health care and elite education have vastly better opportunities than those who cannot. In short, ideologues cannot admit that there are always significant negative side-effects to *any* political program. They cannot grant that their opponents have good ideas too.

In any culture in which God is largely absent, sex, money, and politics will fill the vacuum for different people. This is the reason that our political discourse is increasingly ideological and polarized. Many describe the current poisonous public discourse as a lack of bipartisanship, but the roots go much deeper than that. As Niebuhr taught, they go back to the beginning of the world, to our alienation from God, and to our frantic efforts to compensate for our feelings of cosmic nakedness and powerlessness. The only way to deal with all these things is to heal our relationship with God.

The Bible gives us a dramatic example of such a healing. It is the story of a man whose will to dominance drove him to become the most powerful man in the world.

The Insecure King

In the sixth century before Christ, the Babylonian empire rose to displace Assyria and Egypt as the dominant world power. Soon it invaded Judah and captured Jerusalem, exiling Israel's professional class, including military officers, artists, and scholars, to Babylon. Eventually most of the known world was under the sway of Babylon's king and general, Nebuchadnezzar. In the biblical book of Daniel, chapter 2, however, we learn that the most powerful man on earth slept uneasily.

> *In the second year of his reign, Nebuchadnezzar had dreams; his mind was troubled and he could not sleep. So the king summoned the magicians, enchanters, sorcerers and astrologers to tell him what he had dreamed. When they came in and stood before the king, he said to them, "I have had a dream that troubles me and I want to know what it means."*
>
> Daniel 2:1–3

Nebuchadnezzar was deeply troubled by the dream. His dream had been about a towering figure, and it may be that this is the vision he wanted the world to have of him—"an impregnable giant, towering over the world. . . ."[82] However, the statue had "feet of clay" and came crashing down. He woke up in a sweat. Did this mean his empire would fail? Or that someone would come and exploit hidden weaknesses?

Many people with a great drive for power are very anxious and fearful. Niebuhr believed that fear and anxiety are the reason that many seek political power.[83] However, even if fear is not a reason for seeking power, it almost always comes with having it. Those in power know that they are the object of jealousy and stand in the crosshairs of their competitors. The higher a person climbs the greater the possibility of a terrible fall, for there is now so much to lose. When Bernard Madoff was sentenced to 150 years in prison for running a $65 billion Ponzi scheme, he publicly blamed his pride. At some time in the past he had faced a year in which he should have reported significant losses, but he could not "admit his failures as a money manager."[84] He could not accept the loss of power and reputation that such an admission would bring. Once he began to hide his weaknesses through the Ponzi scheme, he then "couldn't admit his error in judgment while the scheme grew," always thinking he could "work his way out."[85]

Power, then, is often born of fear and in turn gives birth to more fear. The dream was forcing Nebuchadnezzer's insecurity to the surface, and it was exceedingly uncomfortable. Powerful people do not like to admit how weak they really feel.

The Fear of Powerlessness

Nebuchadnezzar is a classic case study of what Niebuhr says about sin, politics, and power in *The Nature and Destiny of Man.* In the chapter "Man as Sinner" Niebuhr argues that "man is insecure, and . . . he seeks to overcome his insecurity by a will-to-power. . . . He pretends he is not limited."[86] Human beings have very little real power over their lives. Ninety-five percent of what sets the course of their lives is completely outside their control. This includes the century and place they are born in, who their parents and family are, their childhood environment, physical stature, genetically hardwired talents, and most of the circumstances that they find themselves in. In short, all we are and have is given to us by God. We are not infinite Creators, but finite, dependent creatures.

The British poet W. E. Henley had a leg amputated as a teenager. Yet he went on to have a career as a critic and author. As a young man Henley defiantly penned the famous "Invictus," Latin for "unconquered."

> *It matters not how strait the gate,*
> *How charged with punishments the scroll,*
> *I am the master of my fate:*
> *I am the captain of my soul.*

As Niebuhr points out, this is an enormous exaggeration, a view of reality distorted and "infected with the sin of pride."[87] No one wants to minimize the importance of learning to overcome obstacles in one's life, but Henley's success would have been impossible had he been born without literary talent, with below-average IQ, or with different parents and social connections. And, somewhat like Nebuchadnezzar, he was forced to face his own powerlessness when his five-year-old daughter died, a blow from which he never recovered. He was a finite and limited man in a world of indomitable forces.

If Niebuhr is right, and human beings have a deep fear of powerlessness stemming from their alienation from God, then there must be many ways that they deal with it, not just through politics and government. Power idols are a "deep idols" that can express themselves through a great variety of other "surface" idols.[88]

During my college years I knew a man who, before professing faith in Christ, was a notorious womanizer. James's pattern was to seduce a woman and, once he had sex with her, lose interest and move on. When he embraced Christianity he quickly renounced his sexual escapades. He became active in Christian ministry. However, his deep idol did not change. In every class or study, James was argumentative and dominating. In every meeting he had to be the leader, even if he was not designated to be so. He was abrasive and harsh with skeptics when talking to them about his new-found faith. Eventually it became clear that his meaning and value had not shifted to Christ, but was still based in having power over others. That is what made him feel alive. The reason James wanted to have sex with those women was not because he was attracted to them, but because he was seeking the power of knowing he could sleep with them if he wanted to. Once he achieved that power, he lost interest in them. The reason he wanted to be in Christian ministry was not because he was attracted to serving God and others, but to the power of knowing he was right, that he had the truth. His power idol took a sexual form, and then a religious one. It hid itself well.

Idols of power, then, are not only for the powerful. You can pursue power in small, petty ways, by becoming a local neighborhood bully or a low-level bureaucrat who bosses around the few people in his field of authority. Power idolatry is all around us. What is the cure?

The Chastened King

Nebuchadnezzar's wise men could not interpret his dream for him. Finally, a court official who was one of the Jewish exiles, named Daniel, came forward. By God's power he was able to tell the king the content of his dream, even though Nebuchadnezzar had yet to reveal it. Then he went on to interpret it.

"You looked, O king, and there before you stood a large statue—an enormous, dazzling statue, awesome in appearance. The head of the statue was made of pure gold, its chest and arms of silver, its belly and thighs of bronze, its legs of iron, its feet partly of iron and partly of baked clay. While you watched, a rock was cut out, but not by human hands. It struck the statue on its feet of iron and clay and smashed them. Then the iron, the clay, the bronze, the silver and the gold were broken to pieces at the same time and became like chaff on a threshing floor in the summer. The wind swept them away without leaving a trace. But the rock that struck the statue became a huge mountain and filled the whole earth."

Daniel 2:31–35

The statue represented the kingdoms of the earth. It appeared as a giant idol, and represented the idolization of human power and achievement. It was human civilization—commerce and culture, rule and power, all exercised by human beings to glorify themselves. What smashed the idol was a stone. In contrast to the rest of the materials in the statue it was "cut out, not by human hands." It was from God. Though the stone was less valuable than any of the metals in the statue, it was ultimately the most powerful component. It was, as Daniel says, God's kingdom (Verse 44) that would someday be set up on the earth.

The dream was a call to humility. Though circumstances often appear to favor tyrants, God will eventually bring them down, whether gradually or dramatically.[89] Those in power should see that they have not achieved power but have only been given it by God, and that all human power crumbles in the end.

Nebuchadnezzar was being asked to change his conception of God. As a pagan, he would have believed in pluralism, that there are many gods and supernatural forces in the world. He had not believed, however, that there was one preeminent, all-powerful lawgiver to whom everyone was accountable, including him. He was being told that there was one supreme God, who was sovereign and judge, and to whom he was responsible for his use of power.

Nebuchadnezzar accepted the message.

Then King Nebuchadnezzar fell prostrate before Daniel and paid him honor and ordered that an offering and incense be presented to him. The king said to Daniel, "Surely your God is the God of gods and the Lord of kings and a revealer of mysteries, for you were able to reveal this mystery."

Daniel 2:46–47

The king confessed that God is "Lord of kings," and the most powerful man in the world prostrated himself—an act of humility quite out of accord with Nebuchadnezzar's accustomed pride.

The Illusion that We Are in Control

What we learn here is that theology matters, that much of our addiction to power and control is due to false conceptions of God. Gods of our own making may allow us to be "masters of our fate." Sociologist Christian Smith gave the name "moralistic, therapeutic deism" to the dominant understanding of God he discovered among younger Americans. In his book *Soul Searching: The Religious and Spiritual Lives of American Teenagers,* he describes this set of beliefs. God blesses and takes to heaven those who try to live good and decent lives (the "moralistic" belief). The central goal of life is not to sacrifice, or to deny oneself, but to be happy and feel good about yourself (the "therapeutic" belief). Though God exists and created the world, he does not need to be particularly involved in our lives except when there is a problem (that is "deism").[90]

This view of God literally makes you master of your fate and captain of your soul. Salvation and happiness is up to you. Some have pointed out that "moralistic, therapeutic deism" could only develop in a comfortable, prosperous society among privileged people. People "at the top" are eager to attribute their position to their own intellect, savvy, and hard work. The reality is much more complicated. Personal connections, family environment, and what appears to be plain luck determine how successful a person is. We are the product of three things—genetics, environment, and our personal choices—but two of these three factors we have no power over. We are not nearly as responsible for our success as our popular views of God and reality lead us to think.

Popular culture often tells young people, "You can be *any*thing you set your mind to." But it is cruel to say that to a five-foot-four-inch eighteen-year-old boy who yearns, more than anything else, to be an NFL linebacker. To use an extreme example, if you had been born in a yurt in Outer Mongolia, instead of where you were, it wouldn't have mattered how hard you worked or used your talents—you would have ended up poor and powerless. To come closer to home, think of the impact of your family background on you. You may spend your younger years telling yourself that you will *not* be like your parents, you will be your own person. However, somewhere around the middle of your life, it will become clearer how indelibly your family has shaped you.

The Power and the Glory

Malcolm Gladwell's book *Outliers* is filled with case studies that demonstrate how our success is largely the product of our environment. He gives an example of a number of Jewish New York City lawyers, all born about 1930. An "accident of time" gave them many advantages. They went to underpopulated schools where they received more attention from teachers. Extremely high-quality yet inexpensive college and legal educations were open to them at the time. Because of anti-Semitic attitudes, they were excluded from white-shoe law firms, which forced them to go into specializations such as proxy fights that established lawyers would not touch. But it turned out that this gave them enormous competitive advantage in the seventies and eighties when hostile takeovers began. They all made enormous amounts of money.[91] Although, unlike Gladwell, I would grant equal importance to the three factors of heredity, environment, and personal choice, his book makes a strong case that we are not as personally responsible for our success as we would like to think. Most of the forces that make us who we are lie in the hand of God. We should not "take pride in one man over against another," wrote the Apostle Paul. "For who makes you different from anyone else? What do you have that you did not receive? And if you did receive it, why do you boast as though you did not?" (1 Corinthians 4:6–7)

Nebuchadnezzar had taken personal credit for his rise to prominence. Now he began to be humbled, and his false views of God began to change, but the changes didn't go very deep. More intervention by God would be necessary.

The Mad King

In chapter 4 Nebuchadnezzar describes himself as being at home in his palace, contented and prosperous, when he suffered another dream, this one not merely troubling but terrifying. It was a dream about an enormous tree: "Its top touched the sky, it was visible to the ends of the earth. . . . From it every creature was fed" (Daniel 4:11–12). But then a voice was heard, calling to "cut down the tree." And the voice began to talk about the tree, calling it "he," saying, "Let the stump and its roots . . . remain in the ground. . . . Let his mind be changed from that of a man and let him be given the mind of an animal, till seven times pass by for him."

With fear and trembling, the king called for Daniel, who heard the dream and blanched. After standing silent for a time, he gave the interpretation.

This is the interpretation, O king, and this is the decree the Most High has issued against my lord the king: You will be driven away from people and will

live with the wild animals; you will eat grass like
cattle and be drenched with the dew of heaven. Seven
times will pass by for you until you acknowledge that
the Most High is sovereign over the kingdoms of men
and gives them to anyone he wishes. The command
to leave the stump of the tree with its roots means
that your kingdom will be restored to you when you
acknowledge that Heaven rules. Therefore, O king,
be pleased to accept my advice: Renounce your sins
by doing what is right, and your wickedness by being
kind to the oppressed. It may be that then your pros-
perity will continue.

Daniel 4:24–27

The first dream had been, in a sense, an academic
lesson. It spoke in general terms about the character
of God, and the character of human power. This time,
God was getting personal. The academic lessons had
not helped. He was still a tyrant. He still oppressed
particular races, classes, and the poor (Verse 27). Now
God was going to teach him what he needed to learn.
But there was hope. The tree would be cut down, but
the stump would be left in the ground to grow back.
God was not after retribution, vengeance, or destruction. This was discipline—pain inflicted with the motive of correction and redemption.

What was, then, the lesson that God wanted to drive

into Nebuchadnezzar's heart? It was this: "The Most High is sovereign over the kingdoms of men and gives them to anyone he wishes and sets over them the lowliest of men." This means that anyone who is successful is simply a recipient of God's unmerited favor. Even the people at the top of the world's hierarchy of power, wealth, and influence are really "lowliest"—they are no better than anyone else. This is a rudimentary form of the gospel—that what we have is the result of grace, not of our "works" or efforts.

God was saying something like this: "King Nebuchadnezzar—you must understand that your power has been given to you by grace from God. If you knew that, you would be both more relaxed and secure *and* more humble and just. If you think you earned your position through your own merit and works, you will continue to be both scared and cruel."

Twelve months later, as the king was walking on the roof of the royal palace of Babylon, he said, "Is not this the great Babylon I have built as the royal residence, by my mighty power and for the glory of my majesty?"

Daniel 4:29–30

The king looked over his realm and as he did so the pride of his heart asserted itself. At that moment, a voice from heaven said: "You will be driven away from people and will live with the wild animals; you will eat grass like cattle . . . until you acknowledge that the Most High is sovereign over the kingdoms of men and gives them to anyone he wishes" (Daniel 4:31–32). Immediately, Nebuchadnezzar fell into what apparently was a period of severe mental illness, in which he was too deranged to live inside the palace but lived on palace grounds among the animals.

A Resurrection from the Death of Pride

What happened? One of the great ironies of sin is that when human beings try to become more than human beings, to be as gods, they fall to become lower than human beings. To be your own God and live for your own glory and power leads to the most bestial and cruel kind of behavior. Pride makes you a predator, not a person.[92] That is what happened to the king.

In C. S. Lewis's children's book *The Voyage of the Dawn Treader,* one of the main characters is a young boy named Eustace Scrubb. Eustace clearly had a lust for power, but he expressed it in the mean, petty ways that only a schoolboy could, in teasing, torturing animals, tattling, and ingratiating adult authorities. He was a Nebuchadnezzar-in-training.

One night Eustace found an enormous pile of treasure in a cave. He was elated and began to imagine the life of ease and power he would now have. When he woke, however, to his horror, he had turned into a hideous dragon. "Sleeping on a dragon's hoard with greedy, dragonish thoughts in his heart, he had become a dragon himself."[93]

Becoming a dragon was a "cosmic natural consequence." Because he thought like a dragon, he had become a dragon. When we set our hearts on power, we become hardened predators. We become like what we worship.[94]

Eustace was now an enormously powerful being, far more powerful than he had ever dreamed, but he was also fearful, hideous, and completely lonely. This, of course, is what power for its own sake does to us. The shock of his transformation humbled Eustace and he longed to be a normal boy again. As his pride faded, the idolatry in his heart began to be healed.

One night Eustace the dragon met a mysterious lion. The lion challenged him to "undress," to try to take off his dragon skin. He managed to peel off a layer, but found he was still a dragon underneath. He tried repeatedly but made no further progress. The lion finally said:

> "You will have to let me undress you." I was afraid of his claws, I can tell you, but I was pretty nearly

desperate now. So I just lay flat down on my back to let him do it. The very first tear he made was so deep that I thought it had gone right into my heart. And when he began pulling the skin off, it hurt worse than anything I've ever felt. . . . Well, he peeled the beastly stuff right off—just as I thought I'd done it myself the other three times, only they hadn't hurt—and there it was lying on the grass: only ever so much thicker, and darker, and more knobbly-looking than the others had been. And there was I as smooth and soft as a peeled switch and smaller than I had been. . . . I'd turned into a boy again.[95]

The lion of the fairy tale, Aslan, represents Christ, and the story bears witness to what all Christians have discovered, that pride leads to death, to breakdown, to a loss of humanity. But if you let it humble you rather than embitter you, and turn to God instead of living for your own glory, then the death of your pride can lead to a resurrection. You can emerge, finally, fully human, with a tender heart instead of a hard heart.

Something like this happened to Nebuchadnezzar. In the words of his own testimony:

At the end of that time, I, Nebuchadnezzar, raised my eyes toward heaven, and my sanity was restored.

Then I praised the Most High; I honored and glorified him who lives forever. His dominion is an eternal dominion; his kingdom endures from generation to generation. . . . At the same time that my sanity was restored, my honor and splendor were returned to me for the glory of my kingdom. My advisers and nobles sought me out, and I was restored to my throne and became even greater than before.

Daniel 4:34, 36

When he "raised his eyes toward heaven," to look to God, the result was more than the restoration of his sanity. He had become "greater than before" (Verse 36). This is a deep pattern of grace, which we see supremely in Jesus. Our hearts say, "I will ascend, I will be as the Most High for my own sake," but Jesus said, "I will descend, I will go low, for their sakes." He became human and went to the Cross to die for our sins (Philippians 2:4–10). Jesus *lost* all power and served, in order to save us. He died, but that led to redemption and resurrection. So if like Eustace, Nebuchadnezzar, and Jesus you fall into great weakness, but say, "Father, into your hands, I commit my spirit" (Luke 23:46), there will be growth, a change, and a resurrection.

Jesus's example and grace heals our will to power. The normal response to our sense of powerlessness is to deny it, to find people to dominate and control in order to live in that denial. But Jesus shows us another way. By giving up his power and serving, he became the most influential man who ever lived. Jesus is not only an example, however, he is a Savior. Only by admitting our sin, need, and powerlessness, and by casting ourselves on his mercy, will we finally become secure in his love, and therefore empowered in a way that does not lead us to oppress others. The insecurity is gone, the lust for power is cut at the root. As a preacher once said, "The way up is to go down; the way down is to go up."

SIX

THE HIDDEN IDOLS IN OUR LIVES

So far we have looked at personal idols, such as romantic love, financial prosperity, or political success. These counterfeit gods are not so hard to spot. There are others, however, that influence us but are more hidden. They are not the idols of our heart, but of our culture and society.

The God of Profit

A writer in the *New York Times* Sunday Opinion section recently wrote about a friend named Melissa, a twenty-nine-year-old who was a vice president at J. P. Morgan until recently being laid off. While "just about everyone is still angry at Wall Street . . . Melissa doesn't exactly fit the villainous cliché of the greedy trader who's collecting millions in bonus money while her company burns." She was well-paid but was very generous with her money toward friends and charitable nonprofits. However, her specialty was securitizing subprime mortgages, student loans, and credit card debt. "That all this debt she was putting together like a puzzle and selling to investors would play such a sinister role in the downfall of the economy didn't occur to her—although it probably should have."[96] Why didn't it occur to her? As Nathan Hatch said in Chapter Four, our culture does not equip students to ask those kinds of questions about a job. Usually the only question is—what does it pay?

In an unofficial ceremony the day before they graduated, nearly half of the 2009 class of Harvard Business School promised to "act with the utmost integrity," resist "decisions and behavior that advance my own narrow ambitions," and work in a manner that "enhances the value my enterprise can create for society over the long term."[97] In coverage of this "MBA Oath," *The Economist* evoked Milton Friedman's claim that business managers have one and only one goal—to maximize shareholder value.[98] That, goes the traditional argument, is the only way that a business promotes the common good, by creating jobs and generating new products. The market itself rewards integrity and punishes dishonesty; if you lie or cheat, it will catch up with you and you will lose money. The only goal of business, then, is to maximize profits. All other talk of ethical management or socially conscious business, it was said, is unnecessary.

The signers of the oath begged to differ. Managers in pursuit of profit can do things to run up share price quickly at the expense of the company's long-term health, and also at the expense of the good of its workers, its customers, and the environment. Then they can cash out and leave everyone else poorer. While some argue that paying employees more and giving them a good working environment pays off in greater profits in the long run, that is not self-evident. It should be done because it is a good and right thing to do in and of itself, not only as a means to the end of higher profits.

Also, it is not true to say that honesty and integrity always make for good business. In certain situations doing the honest thing would be financially ruinous, and therefore, according to strict cost-benefit analysis, the risk of getting caught in a lie is clearly worth taking. Things like honesty and commitment to one's workers and environment must be embraced as goods in themselves—equally important as profit—or integrity will not be maintained.

The signers, then, were arguing that profit had become a counterfeit god—a good thing turned into an absolute value. The result has been moral and social breakdown. Their oath was an effort to take on a cultural idol that has had a broad, systemic influence on how society is ordered.

Idols in Our Culture

In his book *The Real American Dream: A Meditation on Hope,* Andrew Delbanco wrote, "I will use the word *culture* to mean the stories and symbols by which we try to hold back the melancholy suspicion that we live in a world without meaning."[99] At the heart of every culture is its main "Hope," what it tells its members that life is all about. Delbanco traces three phases of American civilization by looking at the fundamental hope of each era, which he names in sequence "God, Nation, and Self." In the first era "hope was chiefly expressed through a Christian story that gave meaning to suffering and pleasure alike and promised deliverance from death." In the second phase, "the Enlightenment removed a personal God . . . and substituted . . . the idea of a deified nation."[100] This second phase, which Delbanco says only began to pass away during the 1960s, transferred older ideas of sacredness to America itself, so that it came to see itself as the "Redeemer nation" whose system of government and way of life was the hope for the whole world.

Today the need for transcendence and meaning has detached itself from anything more important than the individual self and its freedom to be what it chooses. Among younger people, the older flag-waving "America first" mind-set is out. Now life is about creating a self through the maximization of individual freedom from the constraints of community.

Delbanco's cultural analysis is essentially an idol analysis. The age of "Self" explains why the maximization of profit has taken on the power that it has. Now we see the complexity of what shapes and drives us. Any dominant cultural "Hope" that is not God himself is a counterfeit god. Idols, then, do not only take individual form, but can be corporate and systemic. When we are completely immersed in a society of people who consider a particular idolatrous attachment normal, it becomes almost impossible to discern it for what it is.

We should not think that one culture is less idolatrous than the next. Traditional societies tend to make the family unit and the clan into an absolute, ultimate thing. This can lead to honor killings, the treatment of women as chattel, and violence toward gay people. Western, secular cultures make an idol out of individual freedom, and this leads to the breakdown of the family, rampant materialism, careerism, and the idolization of romantic love, physical beauty, and profit.

How can we be less enslaved by our cultural idols? Delbanco points out that in the beginning of our history society was built around God and religion. The answer to our cultural problem must be more religion, right? Not necessarily. Idolatry is so pervasive that it dominates this area as well.

Idols in Our Religion

An idol is something that we look to for things that only God can give. Idolatry functions widely inside religious communities when doctrinal truth is elevated to the position of a false god. This occurs when people rely on the rightness of their doctrine for their standing with God rather than on God himself and his grace. It is a subtle but deadly mistake. The sign that you have slipped into this form of self-justification is that you become what the book of Proverbs calls a "scoffer."[101] Scoffers always show contempt and disdain for opponents rather than graciousness. This is a sign that they do not see themselves as sinners saved by grace. Instead, their trust in the rightness of their views makes them feel superior.[102]

Another form of idolatry within religious communities turns spiritual gifts and ministry success into a counterfeit god. Spiritual gifts (talent, ability, performance, growth) are often mistaken for what the Bible calls spiritual "fruit" (love, joy, patience, humility, courage, gentleness).[103] Even ministers who believe with the mind that "I am only saved by grace" can come to feel in their heart that their standing with God depends largely on how many lives they are changing.

Another kind of religious idolatry has to do with moral living itself. As I have argued at length elsewhere,[104] the default mode of the human heart is to seek to control God and others through our moral performance. Because we have lived virtuous lives we feel that God (and the people we meet) owe us respect and support. Though we may give lip service to Jesus as our example and inspiration, we are still looking to ourselves and our own moral striving for salvation.

Delbanco explains how the great cultural shift known as the Enlightenment abandoned religious orthodoxy and put in God's place things like the American system or individual self-fulfillment. The results have not been good. Putting Nation in place of God leads to cultural imperialism, and putting Self in the place of God leads to many of the dysfunctional dynamics we have discussed throughout this book.[105] Why did our culture largely abandon God as its Hope? I believe it was because our religious communities have been and continue to be filled with these false gods. Making an idol out of doctrinal accuracy, ministry success, or moral rectitude leads to constant internal conflict, arrogance and self-righteousness, and oppression of those whose views differ. These toxic effects of religious idolatry have led to widespread disaffection with religion in general and Christianity in particular. Thinking we have tried God, we have turned to other Hopes, with devastating consequences.

The Mission of Jonah

We do not have only idols of the heart to confront. Corporate gods of the culture and religion can supercharge personal idols and create a poisonous mix. A poor young man who personally feels powerless can be easily swept up by social movements that fan racial and religious hatred. A young woman unloved by her family, and raised in a consumer culture of image and glamour, can become afflicted with an eating disorder. The idols that drive us are complex, many-layered, and largely hidden from us.

Perhaps the best example of this in the Bible is found in the famous story of Jonah. Most people think of it as a children's Sunday school lesson about a man swallowed by a big fish. On the contrary, it is a subtly crafted narrative about the idols that drive our actions on many levels and pull us farther from God even when we think we are doing his will. What is truly shocking about the story comes only at the very end, long after Jonah has left the fish far behind. The first, skillful sentence of the book introduces a plot full of dramatic tension.

The word of the LORD came to Jonah the son of Amittai, "Arise, go to Nineveh, that great city, and proclaim against her, for their evil has come up before my face."

Jonah 1:1–2[106]

From 2 Kings 14:25 we know that Jonah had called Israel's King Jeroboam to pursue an expansionist military policy to extend the nation's boundaries. His contemporaries, Amos and Hosea, were against the corruption of the royal administrations. Jonah, however, appears to have deliberately ignored the king's wrongdoing in his nationalistic zeal to build up his country's power and influence.[107] Such a prophet would have been stunned by God's command that he go to the city of Nineveh and preach to it.

Nineveh was the most powerful city in the world, the seat of the Assyrian Empire whose military threatened to overrun Israel and its neighbors. Doing anything that in any way benefited Assyria would have been seen as suicidal for Israel. Although the mission was only to "preach against" the city for its wickedness, there would have been no reason to send a warning unless there was a chance of judgment being averted, as Jonah knew full well (Jonah 4:1–2).

God was reaching out in mercy to the great enemy of his people—no more counterintuitive mission could have been imagined. God was sending a patriotic Jewish prophet to do this—no more unlikely emissary could have been chosen. God was asking him to do what he must have considered unconscionable. But that was the mission, and he was the missionary.

The Man on the Run

But Jonah arose to flee to Tarshish from the face of the LORD. He went down to Joppa and, finding a ship bound for Tarshish, he paid the fare and went down into it, to go with them to Tarshish, away from the face of the LORD.

Jonah 1:3

In deliberate contradiction of the charge to go east to Ninevah, Jonah arose and instead went to Tarshish, a town on the western rim of the known world. He did the very opposite of what God wanted him to do. Why? Jonah's internal motives are not fully revealed until chapter 4, but at this point, the text gives us several clues as to why he would so flagrantly disobey a direct divine command.

Jonah would have been afraid of failure. God was summoning a lone Hebrew prophet to walk into the most powerful city in the world and call it to get down on its knees before his God. The only possible outcome seemed to be mockery or death, with the second as likely as the first. Preachers want to go where they will be persuasive.

He would have been just as afraid, however, of the possibility of the mission's success, small as that might have been. Assyria was a cruel and violent empire. The empire was already demanding tribute from Israel, a kind of international protection money. Jonah was being called to warn Nineveh of God's wrath, to give them a chance to survive and continue to be a threat to Israel. As a patriotic Israelite, Jonah wanted no part of such a mission.

So why did he run? The answer is, again, idolatry, but of a very complex kind. Jonah had a personal idol. He wanted ministry success more than he wanted to obey God. Also, Jonah was shaped by a cultural idol. He put the national interests of Israel over obedience to God and the spiritual good of the Ninevites. Finally, Jonah had a religious idol, simple moral self-righteousness. He felt superior to the wicked, pagan Ninevites. He didn't want to see them saved. Jonah's cultural and personal idols had melded into a toxic compound that was completely hidden from him. It led him to rebel against the very God he was so proud of serving.

Jonah in the Deep

Jonah got on a boat in order to flee from God and his mission. But God sent a ferocious storm that threatened to sink the boat (Jonah 1:4–6). The sailors in the boat sensed that the storm was unusually violent, so they cast lots to see who had brought this calamity upon them. The lot fell on Jonah.

> *The men were seized by a great fear and—after he admitted that he was fleeing from the face of the Lord—they said to him: "How could you have done this!" Then they said to him, "What must we do to you, that the sea may become quiet for us, for the sea is more and more tempestuous?" He said to them, "Lift me up and hurl me into the sea; then the sea will become quiet for you, for I declare it is on my account that this great storm has come upon you."*
>
> Jonah 1:10–12

Afraid for their lives, the sailors did what Jonah asked. They threw him into the sea, and God provided a fish to save Jonah by swallowing him. The fish was God's provision for Jonah. It gave Jonah a chance to recover and repent. Inside the fish, Jonah offered a prayer to God.

Then Jonah prayed to the LORD his God from the belly of the fish, saying, "I call out to the LORD, out of my distress, and he answers me; I said, 'I am driven away from your sight; Nevertheless, I continue to gaze toward your holy temple.' . . . Those obeying empty idols forsake their own covenantal love. But I, with the voice of thanksgiving, will sacrifice to you; what I have vowed I will fulfill. Salvation comes only from the LORD!" And the LORD spoke to the fish, and it vomited Jonah out upon the dry land.

Jonah 1:17–2:1, 4, 8–10

He spoke of "those obeying empty idols. . . ." Idol worshippers were the people God had called Jonah to go to in Nineveh. But then he said something remarkable about them, that idolaters "forsake their own *chesedh.*" *Chesedh* is the Hebrew word for God's covenantal love, his redeeming, unconditional grace. This term had been used to describe God's relationship with Israel, his people. Now Jonah says that idol worshippers forsake "their *own* grace." It came to him like a thunderbolt that God's grace was as much theirs as it was his. Why? Because grace is grace. If it is truly grace, then no one was worthy of it at all, and that made all equal. And with that realization, he added, "Salvation comes only from the Lord!" It doesn't belong to any race or class of people, nor do religious people deserve it more than the irreligious. It does not come from any quality or merit in us at all. Salvation is only from the Lord.

There is an intriguing hint of self-insight in this prayer. What, according to Jonah, blocks the coming of grace into one's life? It is clinging to idols. Why, then, had Jonah himself so badly missed in his understanding of God's will and heart? The answer is—*his* idolatry. His fear of personal failure, his pride in his religion, and his fierce love of his country had coalesced into a deadly idolatrous compound that spiritually blinded him to the grace of God. As a result he did not want to extend that grace to an entire city that needed it. He wanted to see them all dead.

Race and Grace

Racial pride and cultural narrowness cannot coexist with the gospel of grace. They are mutually exclusive. One forces the other out. Because of the self-justifying nature of the human heart, it is natural to see our own culture or class characteristics as superior to everyone else's. But this natural tendency is arrested by the gospel.

We see this in Paul's confrontation with Peter in Galatians 2. Peter, as a Jewish apostle, had been raised to see Gentiles as spiritually "unclean," people with whom he should not eat. In ancient cultures, eating with someone symbolized openness and acceptance. When Paul saw Peter refusing to eat with Gentile Christians he confronted him about his racism. But how? Paul did not say, "You are breaking the rule against racism," but rather that Peter was "not acting in line with the gospel" (Galatians 2:14). Racial prejudice, Paul argued, was a denial of the very principle of grace salvation. He argued, "Peter, if we are all saved by grace alone—how can you feel superior to anyone? How can you continue to be racially and nationally exclusive? Use the gospel on your heart!" Peter, of course, did know the gospel at one level, but at a deeper level he wasn't fully shaped by it. He wasn't "walking in line" with it.

Those who are not secure in Christ cast about for spiritual life preservers with which to support their confidence, and in their frantic search they cling not only to the shreds of ability and righteousness they find in themselves, but they fix upon their race, their membership in a party, their familiar social and ecclesiastical patterns, and their culture as means of self-recommendation. The culture is put on as though it were armor against self-doubt, but it becomes a mental straitjacket which cleaves to the flesh and can never be removed except through comprehensive faith in the saving work of Christ.[108]

In the belly of the fish Jonah began to grasp what he had been missing, and why he had been so antagonistic to God's original call. Jonah had been called to go and preach grace to the greatest city in the world, but he hadn't understood that grace himself. Battered and humbled, he began to realize the truth. Salvation was by grace, and therefore it was available to anyone at all. His cultural idols seem to have been removed as all this dawned on him. And at that, the fish vomited him out. Jonah the prophet had another chance.

The Shocking Ending

Then the word of the LORD came to Jonah the second time, saying, "Arise, go to Nineveh, that great city, and proclaim to her the message that I tell you." So Jonah arose and set out for Nineveh, according to the word of the LORD. Now Nineveh was a very large city—three days' journey in breadth—and one important to God. Jonah went a day's journey into the city and then called out, "In forty days, Nineveh shall be overthrown!" And the people of Nineveh believed God. They called for a fast and put on sackcloth, from the greatest of them to the least. . . . When God examined their deeds, how they forsook their evil way, he renounced the disaster he had said he

would do to them, and he did not carry it out. But
what God did was so terrible in Jonah's eyes, that he
burned with anger.

Jonah 3:1–5, 10; 4:1

Now comes the part of the story that is almost universally ignored. God again gave Jonah the call to go to Nineveh, and this time he obeyed. There he began to preach, and to Jonah's surprise and ours, the people of the city responded. They began to repent as some said, "Who knows? God may yet relent and with compassion turn from his fierce anger so we may not perish" (Verse 9). The result was that the city turned from "its evil ways," which Verse 8 describes as "their violence." The nation of Assyria was indeed exceedingly violent but here, at least temporarily, they showed remorse and willingness to reform.

God had mercy on them. There was no indication that the Ninevites became Jews or converted to full service of the God of Israel. Nothing like that happened, and yet God refrained from punishment, so predominant is his will to save rather than to punish.

Anyone reading this story would have expected the book to end on this wonderful note. Beyond hope, Jonah had returned from the dead and had fulfilled his mission, the Ninevites had repented and shown promise of turning from their violence and imperialism, and

God had shown how merciful and loving he is toward all peoples. All it would take now to complete the story would be a final verse, Jonah 3:11—"And Jonah returned to his own land rejoicing!"

But that is *not* what happened. The real shock of the story comes at the moment of what should have been Jonah's greatest triumph. He had preached to the most powerful city in the world and had brought it literally to its knees. Yet Nineveh's positive response to Jonah's preaching so infuriated him that he charged God with evil and asked God to kill him on the spot!

> *And he prayed to the LORD and said, "O LORD, is this not what I spoke of when I was still in my homeland? That is why I fled with haste to Tarshish; for I knew that you are a gracious and compassionate God, very patient, and abounding in steadfast love, and who also renounces plans for bringing disaster. Therefore now, O LORD, please take my life from me, for to me death is better than life."*

> Jonah 4:1–3

The motives of Jonah's heart are finally revealed fully. "I knew it!" he says. "I knew you were a compassionate God, so quick to forgive, so eager to save, so unceasingly patient! I *knew* I couldn't trust you! That's the reason I ran away to begin with! I was afraid that if I got a God like you near these people and they made even a gesture in the direction of repentance you would forgive them. I've had it with you! I resign! Just take away my life!" There is no more astonishing speech in the Bible, or perhaps in all of ancient literature. Finally Jonah's idol was laid bare, revealing his abhorrence of this race and nation.

Jonah so loathed the Assyrian race that he saw God's forgiveness of them to be the worst thing that could have happened. He was willing to confront and denounce the Ninevites, but he could not love them. He didn't want them saved; he didn't want them to receive God's mercy.[109]

What happened? In the belly of the fish, Jonah had begun to grasp the idea that all human beings are equally unworthy of God's love and that therefore all human beings have equal access to God's grace. But Jonah's idolatries had reasserted themselves with a vengeance. His apprehension of God's grace in chapter 2 had been mainly intellectual. It had not penetrated his heart. Jonah stands as a warning that human hearts never change quickly or easily, even when a person is being mentored directly by God. Just as Paul had to confront Peter about how he had failed to use the gospel on his racism, so God's work with Jonah is incomplete.

Someone once said that if you want to know if there

are rats in your basement, you shouldn't walk down the steps slowly, making a lot of noise. Then you will look around and not see anything. If you want to know what is really down there, you have to surprise it by running and leaping down the steps quickly. Then you will see a bunch of little tails scurrying away. And so it is under stress, in real life experience, that the true nature of our hearts is revealed. For example, all Christians say and believe that Christ is their Savior, not their career or their wealth. What Christ thinks of us is what matters, not human approval. That is what we *say*. But while Jesus is our Savior in principle, other things still maintain functional title to our hearts. Jonah shows us that it is one thing to believe the gospel with our minds, and another to work it deep into our hearts so it affects everything we think, feel, and do. He is still being largely controlled by idolatry.

Idols, Thinking, and Feeling

Idolatry has distorted Jonah's thinking. [110] He goes on a tirade that most people would think insane. How could Jonah be furious that God is a God of compassion, love, and patience?! For the same reason that lovesick Jacob could be so easily duped and greedy Zacchaeus could betray his country and everyone around him. They were all blinded by their idols.

When an idol gets a grip on your heart, it spins out a whole set of false definitions of success and failure and happiness and sadness. It redefines reality in terms of itself. Nearly everyone thinks that an all-powerful God of love, patience, and compassion is a good thing. But if, because of your idol, your ultimate good is the power and status of your people, then anything that gets in the way of it is, by definition, bad. When God's love prevented him from smashing Israel's enemy, Jonah, because of his idol, was forced to see God's love as a bad thing. In the end idols can make it possible to call evil good and good evil.[111]

Idols distort not only our thinking, but also our feelings.

And the LORD said, "Is it good for you to burn with such anger?" Jonah then left the city and sat down just east of it and made a shelter for himself there. He sat under it in the shade, waiting to see what would happen to the city. To deliver him from his dejection, the LORD God appointed a qiqayon plant that grew rapidly up over Jonah, to be a shade over his head. And Jonah was delighted and glad for the plant. But at the break of dawn the next day, God appointed a worm that attacked the qiqayon plant, so that it withered. And when the sun rose higher, God appointed a cutting east wind, and the

> *sun beat down on the head of Jonah so that he was*
> *faint and weak. And he longed to die, thinking, "It*
> *is better for me to die than to live." But God said to*
> *Jonah, "Is it good for you to be so angry and dejected*
> *over the plant?" And he said, "Yes, it is. I am angry*
> *and dejected enough to die."*
>
> Jonah 4:4–9

Jonah left the city he despised and made himself a shelter from the sun. He was still hoping that God might relent from his relenting and smite Nineveh. But God's concern was now with Jonah. He allowed a *"gigayon plant,"* a fast-growing vine, to grow up and make his shelter cool and shady. The greenery and the comfort were a consolation for the despondent prophet. But then God brought a new, though small-scale, disappointment into his life, by having the plant die. Jonah's emotions were so raw that this new discouragement pushed him back to the edge. Again he was too angry to live. This time, when God asked him whether his anger was warranted, Jonah retorted that it was, that he was "angry enough to die."

God confronted him about this. God did not say that anger is wrong, since he himself regularly speaks about his own "fierce anger" against injustice and evil. However, Jonah's anger was unwarranted and disproportionate.

Idolatry distorts our feelings. Just as idols are good things turned into ultimate things, so the desires they generate become paralyzing and overwhelming. Idols generate false beliefs such as "if I cannot achieve X, then my life won't be valid" or "since I have lost or failed Y, now I can never be happy or forgiven again." These beliefs magnify ordinary disappointments and failures into life-shattering experiences.

A young woman named Mary was an accomplished musician who once attended my church. For many years she had battled mental illness and had checked in and out of psychiatric institutions. She gave me permission as her pastor to speak to her therapist so my pastoral guidance to her could be well-informed. "Mary virtually worships her parents' approval of her," her counselor told me, "and they always wanted her to be a world-class artist. She is quite good, but she's never reached the top of her profession, and she cannot live with the idea that she has disappointed her parents." Medications helped to manage her depression, but they could not get to the root of it. Her problem was a false belief, driven by an idol. She told herself, "If I cannot be a well-known violinist, I have let down my parents and my life is a failure." She was distressed and guilty enough to die. When Mary began to believe the gospel, that she was saved by grace, not by musicianship, and that, "though my father and mother forsake me, the Lord shall take me in" (Psalm 27:10), she began to get relief from her idolatrous need for her parents' approval. In time her depression and anxiety began to lift, and she was able to reenter her life and musical career.

There is legitimate guilt that is removed through repentance and restitution, and then there is irremediable guilt. When people say, "I know God forgives me, but I can't forgive myself," they mean that they have failed an idol, whose approval is more important to them than God's. Idols function like gods in our lives, and so if we make career or parental approval our god and we fail it, then the idol curses us in our hearts for the rest of our lives. We can't shake the sense of failure.

When idolatry is mapped onto the future—when our idols are threatened—it leads to paralyzing fear and anxiety. When it is mapped onto the past—when we fail our idols—it leads to irremediable guilt. When idolatry is mapped onto the present life—when our idols are blocked or removed by circumstances—it roils us with anger and despair.[112]

All that was happening in Jonah's heart. Why had Jonah lost the will to live? You don't lose your desire to live unless you have lost your meaning in life. His meaning in life was the freedom of his nation. That is a good thing to want, but it had become a supreme thing. Therefore, the Assyrians filled him with deep hate and anger because they were an obstacle to obtaining the idol. Now it was God and his mercy that filled Jonah with anger and despair, because the Lord was an omnipotent roadblock to the future for Israel that Jonah wanted.

The True Jonah

And the LORD said, "You grieved over the gigayon plant, which you did not plant, you did not make grow, and which came into being and perished in one night. And should I not have compassion for Nineveh, that great city, in which there are more than 120,000 persons who do not know their right hand from their left, and so much livestock?"

Jonah 4:10–11

God confronted Jonah with the fact that he was more upset about his sunburn than he was about thousands of people who "did not know their right hand from their left." His idolatrous love for his own country and his moral self-righteousness had removed Jonah's compassion for the great cities and nations of the world. All he cared about was his own country.

God was different. He ended his instruction to Jonah by drawing a deliberate contrast between Jonah and himself. He had asked Jonah to leave his comfort zone and his safety, and to go in love to minister to a people who might harm him. At first, Jonah didn't go at all, and then he went, but without compassion. God responded: "You did not have compassion on this city, but I will." God implied that he would love the wicked, violent city in a way Jonah had refused to do.

What did that mean? How did God do what Jonah did not?

Centuries later, someone came who said to his astonished listeners that he was the ultimate Jonah (Matthew 12:39–41). When Jesus Christ came to earth, he was leaving the ultimate comfort zone, in order to come and minister not just to a people who *might* harm him, but to people who would. And to save them, he would have to do much more than preach, he would have to die for them. While the original Jonah was merely thought to be dead, Jesus actually died and rose again. It was what Jesus called the sign of Jonah (Matthew 12:31).

Consider another way in which Jesus was the ultimate Jonah. In Mark 4 we have an account from Jesus's life that deliberately evoked the Old Testament story. There was a terrible storm and, like Jonah, Jesus was asleep in the midst of it. Like the sailors, Jesus's disciples were terrified and woke him up to say that they were going to perish. In both cases the storm was miraculously calmed and those in the boat were saved by the power of God.

But here is the great difference. Jonah was thrown only into a storm of wind and water. Jesus on the Cross, however, was thrown into the ultimate storm—of all the divine justice and punishment that we deserve for our wrongdoing. When I struggle with my idols, I think of Jesus, voluntarily bowing his head into that ultimate storm, taking it on frontally, for me. He sank in that storm of terror so I would not fear any other storm in my life. If he did that for me, then I know my value, confidence, and mission in life all rest in him. Storms here on earth can take away many things, even my physical life, but not my Life.

God hinted to Jonah that he would love the great, lost cities of the earth in a way that Jonah would not. In the gospel of Jesus Christ, the true Jonah, that commitment was fulfilled.

Jonah and Us

The book of Jonah ends with a question. God asks Jonah: "Shouldn't your love be like mine? Will you come out of your self-absorption and idolatry and begin to live for me and for others?" We wait for an answer, and it never comes! Because the book ends.

The ending is brilliant and satisfying. It's satisfying because we don't need to wonder whether Jonah repented and saw the light. He must have. How do we know? Well, how else would we know this story, unless Jonah told it to someone? And who would *ever* tell a story in which he is seen as an evil fool on every page, except a man in whom God's grace had reached the center of his heart?

Why, though, are we not shown Jonah's response in the book? It is as if God aimed an arrow of loving rebuke at Jonah's heart, set it a-fly, and suddenly Jonah vanishes, leaving us in its path. The question is coming right at us, because you are Jonah and I am Jonah. We are so enslaved to our idols that we don't care about people who are Different, who live in the big cities, or who are just in our own families but very hard to love. Are we, like Jonah, willing to change? If we are, then we must look to the Ultimate Jonah, and to his sign, the death and resurrection of Jesus Christ.

SEVEN

THE END OF COUNTERFEIT GODS

Nothing Is More Common

The seventeenth-century English minister David Clarkson preached one of the most comprehensive and searching sermons on counterfeit gods ever written.[113] About idolatry he said, "Though few will own it, nothing is more common." If we think of our soul as a house, he said, "idols are set up in every room, in every faculty." We prefer our own wisdom to God's wisdom, our own desires to God's will, and our own reputation to God's honor. Clarkson looked at human relationships and showed how we have a tendency to make them more influential and important to us than God. In fact, he showed that "many make even their enemies their god . . . when they are more troubled, disquieted, and perplexed at apprehensions of danger to their liberty, estates, and lives from men" than they are concerned about God's dis-

[154]

pleasure.[114] The human heart is indeed a factory that mass-produces idols.

Is there any hope? Yes, if we begin to realize that idols cannot simply be removed. They must be replaced. If you only try to uproot them, they grow back; but they can be supplanted. By what? By God himself, of course. But by *God* we do not mean a general belief in his existence. Most people have that, yet their souls are riddled with idols. What we need is a living encounter with God.

Jacob, whom we met in Chapter Two, certainly believed in God, but he needed something more to defeat the counterfeit gods that enslaved him. In Genesis 32 he found it. This is one of the most powerful and dramatic narratives in the Bible. It is also one of the most mysterious, but it clearly stands as the centerpiece of Jacob's life.

The Returning Brother

Jacob had fled to a far country and despite many struggles had prospered there. Yet his uncle Laban and his cousins were resentful and jealous of Jacob (Genesis 31:1–2). He realized that he had to leave or face strife, perhaps even violent conflict. At last he decided to return to his homeland with his large family, his two wives, Leah and Rachel, and all their servants, flocks, and herds.

The author of Genesis recounted a short but significant subplot about Jacob's wife Rachel, who, as she left, stole her father Laban's household idols (Genesis 31:19). Why did she do it? It may have been a kind of spiritual insurance policy. Maybe, thought Rachel, the Lord would help her the next time she was in trouble, as he seemed to help Leah, but if not, she would call on the old gods. However, the Lord cannot be added to a life as one more hedge against failure. He is not one more resource to use to help us achieve our agenda. He *is* a whole new agenda. Rachel had not learned this. The family that was to bring the salvation of the Lord into the future was deeply flawed and in need of grace.

Jacob set out for his homeland with his entire family and estate. As he drew near he received some alarming news. "We went to your brother Esau, and now he is coming to meet you and four hundred men are with him." (Genesis 32:6) Jacob's worst fears seemed to be realized. Why else would Esau be coming with a small army except to attack him? He sprang into action. First he prayed to God for help. Then he sent an enormous gift of livestock to Esau with some servants. After that he divided his family and company in half, thinking that if Esau attacked one half of his people the other half would have time to escape (Genesis 32:7–8). After all the preparations had been made, and both halves of his company had been sent on ahead, Jacob sat down to spend the night alone.

The Struggle for Blessing

In Jacob's mind, the next day would be the climax of his life. All his life he had been wrestling with Esau. In their mother's womb, the twins Esau and Jacob had been unusually active, "striving with each other" (Genesis 25:22). As they grew up, Jacob contended with Esau for the favor and love of their father and for the honor and leadership of their family. Their father constantly favored Esau over Jacob, and there are few things more wounding to a son. Finally the day came that Isaac was to give Esau the ritual blessing that went with his birthright, the lion's share of the family estate. Jacob, however, disguised himself as Esau and fooled his nearly blind father just long enough to get him to pronounce the blessing. Then he ran. When Esau discovered what had happened he vowed to kill Jacob. So Jacob had fled for his life into exile.

Why did Jacob steal Esau's blessing? Modern readers find his motives difficult to understand. Surely Jacob knew his ruse would be discovered quickly, and that Isaac would never have actually given Jacob the majority of the family's wealth. All Jacob got was the ceremonial affirmation. Why did he lose so much to gain so little? I believe it was because Jacob, even under false pretenses, longed to hear his father say, "I delight in you more than anyone else in the world!" Every human being, then, needs blessing. We all need assurance of our unique value from some outside source. The love and admiration of those you most love and admire is above all rewards. We are all looking for this deep admiration, looking for it from our parents, our spouse, and our peers.

Jacob's life had been one long wrestling match to get blessing. He had wrestled with Esau to hear it from his father's lips. He had wrestled with Laban to find it in Rachel's face. But it hadn't worked. He was still needy and empty inside. The relationships within his own family were stormy. His idolatry of Rachel and her children had poisoned the lives of Leah and her children, and it would bear bitter fruit in the future.

And now Esau was on his way, the man who had kept him from his father's love, from his inheritance, from his destiny, from happiness. He was coming with an army. Tomorrow would be the last battle. It was not surprising that Jacob wanted to spend this last night alone to prepare for the day of reckoning. But that night, in the deep darkness, he was unexpectedly attacked by a lone figure, and they wrestled for hours.

The Mysterious Stranger

The dramatic story is depicted with great economy.

> *So Jacob was left alone, and a man wrestled with him till daybreak. When the man saw that he could not overpower him, he touched the socket of Jacob's hip so that his hip was wrenched as he wrestled with the man. Then the man said, "Let me go, for it is daybreak." But Jacob replied, "I will not let you go unless you bless me." The man asked him, "What is your name?" "Jacob," he answered. Then the man said, "Your name will no longer be Jacob, but Israel, because you have struggled with God and with men and have overcome." Jacob said, "Please tell me your name." But he replied, "Why do you ask my name?" Then he blessed him there. So Jacob called the place Peniel, saying, "It is because I saw God face to face, and yet my life was spared." The sun rose above him as he passed Peniel, and he was limping because of his hip.*

> Genesis 32:24–31

Who was this mysterious figure? The narrator deliberately obscures his identity to the reader, but leaves a few clues. First, there was the powerful "touch" (Verse 28). The Hebrew word translated "touch" literally meant the lightest contact or tap. The wrestler merely touched Jacob's hip with his finger and it was instantly ripped out of its socket, permanently disabling him. It was now clear that the wrestler had been holding back so as not to kill Jacob. He had enormous, superhuman power.

Also, the figure insisted he must leave as dawn neared. Why? Jacob knew that no one could look upon God's face and live (Exodus 33:20). Afterward, Jacob realized that this was the reason the wrestler had wanted to leave before the sun came up. It was for Jacob's own protection, for, as Jacob said, he "saw God's face and lived." This may mean that in the first grayness of incipient dawn he was able to make out the lines on the face of the divine wrestler just before he vanished. Had he seen God's face in the clear light of day, he would have perished.

Winning through Weakness

Jacob recognized who he was wrestling with—God himself! When he realized this, and saw the sun coming up, Jacob did the most astonishing thing he had ever done. He did not do the rational thing, which would have been to cry out, "Let me go! Let me go! I don't want to die!" Instead he did the very opposite. He held on tight, and said, "I will not let you go until you bless me!"

Jacob was saying something like this.

What an idiot I've been! Here is what I've been looking for all my life. The blessing of God! I looked for it in the approval of my father. I looked for it in the beauty of Rachel. But it was in you. Now I won't let you go until you bless me. Nothing else matters. I don't care if I die in the process, because if I don't have God's blessing, I've got nothing. Nothing else will do.

As a result, we read, God "blessed him there." Wonderful, mysterious words. A blessing in the Bible is always verbal, so God must have spoken words into Jacob's heart. What were they? We are not told. Was it anything like the voice of blessing that was spoken from heaven over the great descendent of Jacob—"You are my son, whom I love, with you I am well pleased"? (Mark 1:11) We don't know the exact words, but there is nothing greater than the blessing of God. And Jacob walked away as the very picture of one who has believed the gospel, for he had been permanently lamed, yet permanently fulfilled. He had been humbled, yet emboldened—all at the same time.

So Jacob won! God said, "You have struggled with God . . . and overcome." He was victorious because, once he realized the divinity of this mysterious wrestler, he did not flee but rather held on. Jacob finally got the blessing that he had longed for all his life. Soon afterward, Jacob met Esau and his band of men, and to his relief he learned that Esau was coming to greet him in peace and welcome him home. So that feud was ended.

The Weakness of God

The reader of the life of Jacob might be perplexed at this point. In no episode throughout the life of Jacob does he ever emerge as the hero. He never behaved as a moral paragon; instead he continually acted in foolish, devious, or even vicious ways. He didn't seem to deserve any blessing from God at all. Why, if God is holy and just, was he so gracious to Jacob? Why would God feign weakness to keep from killing him, then give him clues as to who he was, then bless him for no better reason than that he held on desperately?

The answer to our question comes later in the Bible, when the Lord again appeared as a man. In the darkness with Jacob, God feigned weakness in order to save Jacob's life. But in the darkness of Calvary, the Lord appeared as a man and became truly weak to save us. Jacob held on in obedience at the risk of his life, in order to gain blessing for himself. But when facing the Cross, though he could have turned aside, Jesus held on in obedience at the cost of his life, in order to gain the blessing, not for himself, but for us.

> *Christ redeemed us from the curse of the law by becoming a curse for us. . . . He redeemed us in order that the blessing given to Abraham might come to the Gentiles through Christ Jesus, so that by faith we might receive the promise of the Spirit.*
>
> Galatians 3:13–14

Why could Jacob come so close to God and still live? It was because Jesus came in weakness and died on the Cross to pay the penalty for our sin. The blessing of God, promised to Abraham, "comes . . . through Christ Jesus, so that by faith we might receive the promise of the Spirit." What was that "promise of the Spirit"? Later in Galatians, Paul writes that "God sent the Spirit of his Son into our hearts who cries out, 'Abba, Father'" (Galatians 4:6). *Abba* was the Aramaic diminutive word for "father," roughly to be translated "papa." It is a term of trusting confidence that a little child has in a parent's love. Paul is saying that, if you believe the gospel, the Spirit will make God's love and blessing an existential reality in your heart.

Have you heard God's blessing in your inmost being? Are the words *"You are my beloved child, in whom I delight"* an endless source of joy and strength?

Have you sensed, through the Holy Spirit, God speaking them to you? That blessing—the blessing through the Spirit that is ours through Christ—is what Jacob received, and it is the only remedy against idolatry. Only that blessing makes idols unnecessary. As with Jacob, we usually discover this only after a life of "looking for blessing in all the wrong places." It often takes an experience of crippling weakness for us to finally discover it. That is why so many of the most God-blessed people limp as they dance for joy.

> *For the foolishness of God is wiser than man's wisdom, and the weakness of God is stronger than man's strength.*

> 1 Corinthians 1:25

EPILOGUE:
FINDING AND REPLACING
YOUR IDOLS

The Importance of Discerning Idols

It is impossible to understand your heart or your culture if you do not discern the counterfeit gods that influence them. In Romans 1:21–25 Saint Paul shows that idolatry is not only one sin among many, but what is fundamentally wrong with the human heart:

> For although they knew God, they neither glorified
> him as God nor gave thanks to him. . . . They ex-
> changed the truth of God for a lie, and worshipped
> and served created things rather than the Creator.
>
> Romans 1:21, 25

Paul goes on to make a long list of sins that create misery and evil in the world, but they all find their roots in this soil, the inexorable human drive for "god-making." [115] In other words, *idolatry is always the reason we ever do anything wrong.* No one grasped this better than Martin Luther. In his *Large Catechism* (1529) and in his *Treatise on Good Works* he wrote that the Ten Commandments begin with a commandment against idolatry. Why does this come first? Because, he argued, the fundamental motivation behind lawbreaking is idolatry. [116] We never break the other commandments without breaking the first one. Why do we fail to love or keep promises or live unselfishly? Of course, the general answer is "because we are weak and sinful," but the specific answer in any actual circumstance is that there is something you feel you *must* have to be happy, something that is more important to your heart than God himself. We would not lie unless we first had made something—human approval, reputation, power over others, financial advantage—more important and valuable to our hearts than the grace and favor of God. The secret to change is to identify and dismantle the counterfeit gods of your heart. [117]

It is impossible to understand a culture without discerning its idols. The Jewish philosophers Halbertal and Margalit make it clear that idolatry is not simply a form of ritual worship, but a whole sensibility and pattern of life based on finite values and making created things into godlike absolutes. In the Bible, therefore, turning from idols always includes a rejection of the culture that the idols produce. God tells Israel that they must not only reject the other nations' gods, but "you shall not follow their practices" (Exodus 23:24). There is no way to challenge idols without doing cultural criticism, and there is no way to do cultural criticism without discerning and challenging idols.[118] A good example of this is the preaching of Saint Paul in Athens (Acts 17) and Ephesus (Acts 19). Paul challenged the gods of the city of Ephesus (Acts 19:26), which led to such an alteration in the spending patterns of new converts that it changed the local economy. That in turn touched off a riot led by local merchants. Contemporary observers have often noted that modern Christians are just as materialistic as everyone else in our culture. Could this be because our preaching of the gospel does not, like Saint Paul's, include the exposure of our culture's counterfeit gods?

Identifying Idols

I am not asking whether or not you have rival gods. I assume that we all do; they are hidden in every one of us.[119] The question is: What do we do about them? How can we become increasingly clear-sighted rather than remaining in their power? How can we be freed from our idols so we can make sound decisions and wise choices that are best for us and those around us? How can we discern our idols?

One way requires that we look at our imagination. Archbishop William Temple once said, "Your religion is what you do with your solitude."[120] In other words, the true god of your heart is what your thoughts effortlessly go to when there is nothing else demanding your attention. What do you enjoy daydreaming about? What occupies your mind when you have nothing else to think about? Do you develop potential scenarios about career advancement? Or material goods such as a dream home? Or a relationship with a particular person? One or two daydreams are no an indication of idolatry. Ask rather, what do you habitually think about to get joy and comfort in the privacy of your heart?

Another way to discern your heart's true love is to look at how you spend your money. Jesus said, "Where your treasure is, there is your heart also" (Matthew 6:21). Your money flows most effortlessly toward your heart's greatest love. In fact, the mark of an idol is that you spend too much money on it, and you must try to exercise self-control constantly. As Saint Paul has written, if God and his grace is the thing in the world you love most, you will give your money away to ministry, charity, and the poor in astonishing amounts (2 Corinthians 8:7–9). Most of us, however, tend to overspend on clothing, or on our children, or on status symbols such as homes and cars. Our patterns of spending reveal our idols.

A third way to discern idols works best for those who have professed a faith in God. You may regularly go to a place of worship. You may have a full, devout set of doctrinal beliefs. You may be trying very hard to believe and obey God. However, what is your real, daily functional salvation? What are you really living for, what is your real—not your professed—god? A good way to discern this is how you respond to unanswered prayers and frustrated hopes. If you ask for something that you don't get, you may become sad and disappointed. Then you go on. Hey, life's not over. Those are not your functional masters. But when you pray and work for something and you don't get it and you respond with explosive anger or deep despair, then you may have found your real god. Like Jonah, you become angry enough to die.

A final test works for everyone. Look at your most uncontrollable emotions.[121] Just as a fisherman looking for fish knows to go where the water is roiling, look for your idols at the bottom of your most painful emotions, especially those that never seem to lift and that drive you to do things you know are wrong. If you are angry, ask, "Is there something here too important to me, something I must have at all costs?" Do the same thing with strong fear or despair and guilt. Ask yourself, "Am I so scared, because something in my life is being threatened that I think is a necessity when it is not?

Am I so down on myself because I have lost or failed at something that I think is a necessity when it is not?" If you are overworking, driving yourself into the ground with frantic activity, ask yourself, "Do I feel that I *must* have this thing to be fulfilled and significant?" When you ask questions like that, when you "pull your emotions up by the roots," as it were, you will often find your idols clinging to them.

David Powlison writes:

> . . . that most basic question which God poses to each human heart: "Has something or someone besides Jesus the Christ taken title to your heart's functional trust, preoccupation, loyalty, service, fear and delight? Questions . . . bring some of people's idol systems to the surface. 'To who or what do you look for life-sustaining stability, security and acceptance? . . . What do you really want and expect [out of life]? What would [really] make you happy? What would make you an acceptable person? Where do you look for power and success?' These questions or similar ones tease out whether we serve God or idols, whether we look for salvation from Christ or from false saviors."[122]

Replacing Idols

In Paul's letter to the Colossians he exhorted them to "put to death" the evil desires of the heart, including "greed, which is idolatry" (Colossians 3:5). But how? Paul laid out the way in the preceding verses.

Since, then, you have been raised with Christ, set your hearts on things above, where Christ is seated at the right hand of God. Set your minds on things above, not on earthly things. For you died, and your life is now hidden with Christ in God. When Christ, who is your life, appears, then you also will appear with him in glory. Put to death, therefore, whatever belongs to your earthly nature: sexual immorality, impurity, lust, evil desires and greed, which is idolatry.

Colossians 3:1–5

Idolatry is not just a failure to obey God, it is a setting of the whole heart on something besides God. This cannot be remedied only by repenting that you have an idol, or using willpower to try to live differently. Turning from idols is not less than those two things, but it is also far more. "Setting the mind and heart on things above" where "your life is hid with Christ in God" (Colossians 3:1–3) means appreciation, rejoicing, and resting in what Jesus has done for you. It entails joyful worship, a sense of God's reality in prayer. Jesus must become more beautiful to your imagination, more attractive to your heart, than your idol. That is what will replace your counterfeit gods. If you uproot the idol and fail to "plant" the love of Christ in its place, the idol will grow back.

Rejoicing and repentance must go together. Repentance without rejoicing will lead to despair. Rejoicing without repentance is shallow and will only provide passing inspiration instead of deep change. Indeed, it is when we rejoice over Jesus's sacrificial love for us most fully that, paradoxically, we are most truly convicted of our sin. When we repent out of fear of consequences, we are not really sorry for the sin, but for ourselves. Fear-based repentance ("I'd better change or God will get me") is really self-pity. In fear-based repentance, we don't learn to hate the sin for itself, and it doesn't lose its attractive power. We learn only to refrain from it for our own sake. But when we rejoice over God's sacrificial, suffering love for us—seeing what it cost him to save us from sin—we learn to hate the sin for what it is. We see what the sin cost God. What most assures us of God's unconditional love (Jesus's costly death) is what that most convicts us of the evil of sin. Fear-based repentance makes us hate ourselves. Joy-based repentance makes us hate the sin.

Rejoicing in Christ is also crucial because idols are almost always *good* things. If we have made idols out of work and family, we do not want to stop loving our work and our family. Rather, we want to love Christ so much *more* that we are not enslaved by our attachments. "Rejoicing" in the Bible is much deeper than simply being happy about something. Paul directed that we should "rejoice in the Lord always" (Philippians 4:4), but this cannot mean "always feel happy," since no one can command someone to always have a particular emotion. To rejoice is to treasure a thing, to assess its value to you, to reflect on its beauty and importance until your heart rests in it and tastes the sweetness of it. "Rejoicing" is a way of praising God until the heart is sweetened and rested, and until it relaxes its grip on anything else it thinks that it needs.

Putting the Gospel on Video

Henry and Kevin had both lost their jobs because of an unfair action by their bosses, and they came to see me for counseling within a year of each other. Henry forgave his boss and moved on and was doing very well, while Kevin could not move past it; he stayed bitter and cynical, and it affected his future career path. Some people tried to help him by working on his emotions. The more sympathy people showed Kevin, the more he felt justified in his anger and the more his self-pity grew. Other people tried to work directly on his will ("get past it and move on"). That did not work either. The gospel works in a different way. It does not work directly on the emotions or the will. The gospel asks, *What is operating in the place of Jesus Christ as your real, functional salvation and Savior?* What are you looking to in order to justify yourself? Whatever it is, is a counterfeit god, and to make a change in your life, you must identify it and reject it as such.

Kevin was looking to his career to prove himself, and when something went wrong, he felt condemned. He was paralyzed because the very foundations of his identity were falling apart. He made no progress until he saw that he had made his career his self-salvation. It was not just that he had to forgive his boss; his real problem was that something besides Jesus Christ was functioning as his Savior. There is always something underneath your inordinate and out-of-control problems, desires, patterns, attitudes, and emotions. Until you find out what it is you cannot have life and peace.

Kevin came to see that though he technically believed he was loved with God's costly grace, it wasn't an absorbing truth that had captured his heart and imagination. What his boss said to him was more real and affecting to his heart than what the King of the universe had said. It is possible to listen to an audio recording while doing other things around the house, but to watch and listen to a visual presentation is much more absorbing. It fills your vision. In the same way, you may know about the love of Christ with your head but not with your heart, as in Kevin's case. How can that be remedied? How can we put the gospel truths "on video" in our lives so that they shape all we feel and do?

This takes what are called "the spiritual disciplines," such as private prayer, corporate worship, and meditation.[123] The disciplines take cognitive knowledge and make it a life-shaping reality in our hearts and imaginations. Spiritual disciplines are basically forms of *worship*, and it is worship that is the final way to replace the idols of your heart. You cannot get relief simply by figuring out your idols intellectually. You have to actually get the peace that Jesus gives, and that only comes as you worship. Analysis can help you discover truths, but then you need to "pray them in" to your heart. That takes time. It is a process about which there is much to say, but we cannot take it up in this book.

Be Patient

I believe that this process will take our entire lives. In the 1960s and '70s Interstate 79 was being built in western Pennsylvania. My wife, Kathy, often drove this route from her home in Pittsburgh to her college in Meadville, Pennsylvania, and to the family vacation spot on Lake Erie. For years the highway remained uncompleted at one spot, where there was a particularly nasty swamp. On at least one occasion, construction workers parked a bulldozer overnight on what seemed to be solid ground. However, by morning they discovered that it had sunk. Often when they put down pilings in the attempt to find bedrock, the pilings disappeared.

Our hearts are like that. We think we've learned about grace, set our idols aside, and reached a place where we're serving God not for what we're going to get from him but for who he is. There's a certain sense in which we spend our entire lives thinking we've reached the bottom of our hearts and finding it is a false bottom. Mature Christians are not people who have completely hit the bedrock. I do not believe that is possible in this life. Rather, they are people who know how to keep drilling and are getting closer and closer.

The great pastor and hymn-writer John Newton once wrote about this struggle:

If I may speak my own experience, I find that to keep my eye simply on Christ, as my peace and my life, is by far the hardest part of my calling. . . . It seems easier to deny self in a thousand instances of outward conduct, than in its ceaseless endeavors to act as a principle of righteousness and power.[124]

The man or woman who knows the difference that Newton refers to—the difference between obeying rules of outward conduct rather than setting your heart on Christ as your peace and your life—is on the road to freedom from the counterfeit gods that control us.

NOTES

INTRODUCTION—The Idol Factory

1. All of these suicides occurred between May 2008 and April 2009. They were compiled on a blog post at http://copy cateffect.blogspot.com/2009/04/recess-x.html

2. Alexis de Tocqueville, *Democracy in America*, trans. George Lawrence (New York, Harper, 1988), p. 296, quoted in Andrew Delbanco, *The Real American Dream: A Meditation on Hope* (Cambridge, Mass.: Harvard University Press, 1999), p. 3.

3. *Ibid.*

4. David Brooks, "The Rank-Link Imbalance," *New York Times,* March 14, 2008.

5. The use of idolatry as a major category for psychological and sociocultural analysis has been gaining steam again in the last fifteen years in the academic world. First there was the heyday of Feuerbach, Marx, and Nietzsche, who used the vocabulary of "idolatry" to critique religion and Christianity

itself, saying the church had created God in its own image, to further its own interests. See Merold Westphal, *Suspicion and Faith: The Religious Uses of Modern Atheism* (The Bronx: Fordham, 1999). After neglect, the concept has been given groundbreaking, serious academic treatment by two prominent Jewish philosophers, Moshe Halbertal and Avishai Margalit, in *Idolatry* (Cambridge, Mass.: Harvard University Press, 1992). Building on this work, there has been a recent wave of serious scholarship on the subject. For example, see Stephen C. Barton, ed., *Idolatry: False Worship in the Bible, Early Judaism, and Christianity* (London and New York: T and T Clark, 2007), G. K. Beale, *We Become What We Worship: A Biblical Theology of Idolatry* (Downers Grove, Ill.: InterVarsity Press, 2008), Edward P. Meadors, *Idolatry and the Hardening of the Heart: A Study in Biblical Theology* (London and New York: T and T Clark, 2006), Brian S. Rosner, *Greed as Idolatry: The Origin and Meaning of a Pauline Metaphor* (Grand Rapids, Mich.: Eerdmans, 2007).

6. In the Bible, idolatry includes, of course, the ritual worship of gods other than the true God of Israel. It means to bow down or to "kiss the hand" or make sacrifices to the gods of other religions and nations (Exodus 20:3; 23:13; Job 31:26–28; Psalms 44:20–21). Anyone who does so forfeits God's salvation (Jonah 2:8). But the Bible makes it clear that we cannot confine idolatry to literal bowing down before the images of false gods. It can be done internally in the soul and heart without being done externally and literally (Ezekiel 14:3ff). It is substituting some cre-

ated thing for God in the heart, in the center of the life. For example, the prophet Habakkuk speaks of the Babylonians, "whose own strength is their god" (Habakkuk 1:11) and of their military power, to which they "sacrifice . . . and burn incense" (Habakkuk 1:16). In Ezekiel 16 and Jeremiah 2–3, the prophets charge Israel with idolatry because they entered into protective treaties with Egypt and Assyria. These treaties offered the payment of high taxes and political subjugation in exchange for military protection. The prophets considered this idolatry because Israel was relying on Egypt and Assyria to give them the security that only God could give them (Halbertal and Margalit, *Idolatry*. pp. 5–6). When King Saul disobeyed the word of the Lord from Samuel and began to conduct business and foreign policy in a way typical of imperialistic powers, the prophet Samuel told him that arrogant disobedience to the Lord *was* idolatry (I Sam 15:23). In the Bible, then, idolatry is looking to your own wisdom and competence, or to some other created thing, to provide the power, approval, comfort, and security that only God can provide. One of the classic Protestant expositions of idolatry is found in the Puritan David Clarkson's sermon "Soul Idolatry Excludes Men Out of Heaven" (*The Works of David Clarkson* [Edinburgh: James Nichols, 1864], vol. 2). Clarkson distinguishes between "External" idolatry, which consists in literal bowing down to a physical image, and "Internal" idolatry, which consists of an act of the soul. "When the mind is most taken up with an object and the heart and affections most set upon it, this is *soul* worship; and this is . . . the honor due only to the Lord, to have the first, the highest place, both in our minds and hearts and endeavors" (p. 300).

7. Tom Shippey, *J. R. R. Tolkien: Author of the Century* (New York: Houghton Mifflin, 2000), p. 36.

8. Near the end of the magisterial book *Idolatry* by Moshe Halbertal and Avishai Margalit, they summarize the nature of idolatry this way. "Granting something ultimate value does not necessarily mean attributing a set of metaphysical divine attributes; the act of granting ultimate value involves a life of full devotion and ultimate commitment to something or someone. Absolute value can be conferred upon many things. . . . In this *extension* of worship, religious attitude is perceived not as part of metaphysics or as an expression of customary rituals, but as a form of absolute devotion, an attitude that makes something into a godlike being. What makes something into an absolute is that it is both overriding and demanding. It claims to stand superior to any competing claim. . . . Any nonabsolute value that is made absolute and demands to be the center of dedicated life is idolatry." From *Idolatry* (Cambridge, Mass.: Harvard University Press, 1992), pp. 245–246.

9. "When a finite value . . . [becomes] a *center of value* by which other values are judged . . . [and] has been elevated to centrality and imagined as a final source of meaning, then one has chosen what Jews and Christians call a *god*. . . . To be worshipped as a god, something must be sufficiently good to be plausibly regarded as the rightful center of one's valuing. . . . One has a god when a finite value is worshipped

Notes

and adored and viewed as that without which one cannot receive life joyfully." Thomas C. Oden, *Two Worlds: Notes on the Death of Modernity in America and Russia* (Downers Grove, Ill: InterVarsity Press, 1992), p. 95.

10. Margaret I. Cole, ed. *Beatrice Webb's Diaries, 1924–1932* (London: Longmans, Green, and Co., 1956), p. 65.

11. Brian Rosner does the best job of showing the basis for each of these three models in Biblical exegesis and the history of interpretation. See especially pp. 43–46 and Chapter 10 in Brian S. Rosner, *Greed as Idolatry: The Origin and Meaning of a Pauline Metaphor* (Grand Rapids, Mich.: Eerdmans, 2007). He bases much of his analysis on the work of Moshe Halbertal and Avishai Margalit, *Idolatry* (Cambridge, Mass.: Harvard University Press, 1992). Most books on idolatry tend to stress only one of the three models.

12. Biblical texts that spell out idolatry as adultery toward God as our true Spouse: Jeremiah 2:1–4:4; Ezekiel 16:1–63; Hosea 1–4; Isaiah 54:5–8; 62:5. See also Chapter 1, "Idolatry and Betrayal," in Halbertal and Margalit, *Idolatry*.

13. Biblical texts that spell out idolatry as self-salvation, rejecting God as our true Savior, include those in which God asks his people: *"Where are the gods you have made for yourselves? Let them come and save you when you are in trouble"* (Jeremiah 2:28). Cf. also Judges 10:13–14, Isaiah 45:20, Deuteronomy 32:37–38. Also see 1 Samuel 15:23, where arrogant self-sufficiency is considered idolatry.

14. Biblical texts that spell out idolatry as spiritual treason, betraying our true King: 1 Samuel 8:6–8, 12:12; Judges 8:23. Romans 1:25–26 teaches that whatever we worship

and center our lives on we must "serve" and obey (Verse 25). Verse 26 goes on to say this means that the heart falls into the grip of overwhelming, inordinate drives and desires. In the rest of the New Testament, these idolatrous, enslaving desires (Greek *epithumia*) are mentioned whenever the need for personal change is addressed. See Galatians 5:16ff; Ephesians 2:3, 4:22; 1 Peter 2:11, 4:2; 1 John 2:16; James 1:14ff. See also Chapter 8, "Idolatry and Political Authority," in Halbertal and Margalit, *Idolatry*.

15. Rebecca Pippert, *Out of the Saltshaker* (Downers Grove, Ill.: InterVarsity Press, 1979), p. 53.

16. The suicide was described in the blog post cited earlier at http://copycateffect.blogspot.com/2009/04/recess-x.html.

17. I have changed his name and the names of others throughout the book whose lives I use as examples of the principles we are treating.

ONE—All You've Ever Wanted

18. Cynthia Heimel, *If You Can't Live Without Me, Why Aren't You Dead Yet?* (New York: Grove Press, 2002), p. 13. This quote originally appeared in *The Village Voice*.

19. Halbertal and Margalit, *Idolatry*, p. 10.

20. Ishmael, though older, was born not of Abraham's wife, but of his wife's servant woman. Had Isaac not been born to Sarah, Ishmael would have been Abraham's heir.

21. Jon Levenson, *The Death and Resurrection of the Beloved Son: The Transformation of Child Sacrifice in Judaism and Christianity* (New Haven: Yale University Press, 1995).

22. For this rendering of Job 23:10, see Francis I. Anderson, *Job: An Introduction and Commentary* (Downers Grove, Ill.: InterVarsity Press, 1976), p. 230.

23. See 2 Chronicles 3:15. "Moriah" is a name given to the mountains and hills surrounding Jerusalem. On one of these hills, Jesus Christ was put to death.

24. Romans 3:26.

TWO—Love Is Not All You Need

25. Robert Alter, *Genesis: Translation and Commentary* (New York: W. W. Norton, 1996), pp. 151–157.

26. Ernest Becker, *The Denial of Death* (New York: Free Press, 1973), p. 160.

27. Ernest Becker, *The Denial of Death*, p. 167.

28. There has been a wave of articles and books on this minor cultural shift. See the article by Barbara F. Meltz, "Hooking Up Is the Rage, but Is It Healthy?" in *The Boston Globe*, February 13, 2007. Also see Laura Sessions Stepp, *Unhooked: How Young Women Pursue Sex, Delay Love, and Lose at Both* (New York: Riverhead, 2007).

29. *Mere Christianity,* Book II, Chapter 5, "Sexual Morality."

30. Why didn't Jacob simply refuse to go along with this bold, obvious swindle? Again, Robert Alter's insights are invaluable. When Jacob asks, "Why have you *deceived* me?" the Hebrew word is the same one used in chapter 27 to describe what Jacob did to Isaac. Alter then quotes an ancient rabbinical commentator who imagines the conversation the next day between Jacob and Leah. Jacob says to

Leah: "I called out 'Rachel' in the dark and you answered. Why did you do that to me?" And Leah says to him, "Your father called out 'Esau' in the dark and you answered. Why did you do that to him?" His fury dies on his lips. He sees what it is like to be manipulated and deceived, and he meekly complies with Laban's offer.

31. It is likely that, since most marriages were arranged in this way, many women felt unwanted by their husbands, and so this story would have had direct resonance to many readers in ancient times. If a modern reader finds offensive the whole account of women being bought and sold by men, it would be important to keep in mind that the overall thrust of the Genesis narrative is to undermine the practice by describing it so negatively. Robert Alter, in *The Art of Biblical Narrative,* says that if you read the book of Genesis and think it is condoning primogeniture, polygamy, and bride purchase, you are misunderstanding it. Throughout the book polygamy always wreaks devastation. It never works out. All you ever see is the misery the patriarchal institutions cause in families. Alter concludes that all the stories in Genesis are *subversive* to those ancient patriarchal practices.

32. Most English translations provide footnotes to tell you what the names mean. Leah gave birth to her first child, a boy, and she named him Reuben. Reuben meant "to see," for she thought, "Now maybe my husband will see me; I won't be invisible to him anymore." It did not happen. She then had a second son, and she named him Simeon, which had to do with hearing: "Now maybe my husband

will finally listen to me." Again he did not. She then had a third son and named him Levi, which meant "to be attached," and she said, "Finally, now that I've borne him *three* sons, my husband's heart will be attached to me."

33. Derek Kidner, *Genesis: An Introduction and Commentary* (Downers Grove, Ill.: InterVarsity Press, 1967), p.160.

34. C. S. Lewis, *Mere Christianity* (various editions), Book III, Chapter 10, "Hope."

35. C. S. Lewis, *Mere Christianity*, "Hope."

36. Ernest Becker, *The Denial of Death*, pp. 166–67.

37. Whatever happened, Dargis asks, to *Thelma and Louise*, the 1991 movie in which women "wore old blue jeans and confidently put the moves on men . . . and no marriage plans?" Manohla Dargis, "Young Women Forever Stuck at Square One in the Dating Game," *New York Times*, February 6, 2009.

38. Thomas Chalmers, "The Expulsive Power of a New Affection." This is a classic sermon by a nineteenth-century Scottish Presbyterian minister and statesman. The sermon is available many places on the Internet.

39. George Herbert, "Dulness" in *The Complete English Poems* ed. James Tobin (London: Penguin, 1991), p. 107.

THREE—**Money Changes Everything**

40. This account is taken from Jonathan Weber, "Greed, Bankruptcy, and the Super Rich" on the *Atlantic Monthly*'s Web site "Atlantic Unbound." Accessed May 30, 2009 at http://www.theatlantic.com/doc/200905u/yellowstone-club

Notes

41. Paul Krugman, "For Richer," *New York Times Magazine,* October 20, 2002. Krugman quotes John Kenneth Galbraith's 1967 book, *The New Industrial State:* "Management does not go out ruthlessly to reward itself—a sound management is expected to exercise restraint. . . . With the power of decision goes opportunity for making money. . . . Were everyone to seek to do so . . . the corporation would be a chaos of competitive avarice. But these are not the sort of thing that a good company man does; a remarkably effective code bans such behavior. Group decision-making insures, moreover, that almost everyone's actions and even thoughts are known to others. This acts to enforce the code and, more than incidentally, a high standard of personal honesty as well."

42. Friedrich Nietzsche, *The Dawn of Day,* trans. J. M. Kennedy (London: Allen and Unwin, 1911), pp. 209–210.

43. See the 2008 study from the Pew Research Center. Twenty-five percent of people called themselves "Lower" or "Lower-middle" class, 72 percent called themselves "Middle" or "Upper-Middle" class, and only 2 percent named themselves members of the "Upper Class." The report was accessed at http://pewresearch.org/pubs/793/inside-the-middle-class on July 1, 2009.

44. There is far more material in Luke-Acts about the relationship of the gospel to greed and idolatry than we can treat here. According to Luke, acquisitiveness is a sign of those who reject the call to follow Jesus, whether it is Judas (Acts 1:17–20), Ananias and Sapphira (5:1–11), or Simon the Sorcerer (8:18–24). Most telling of all, there are two

riots against Christians described in the Book of Acts, and in both cases, opposition to the gospel was motivated by greed (Acts 16:19–24; 19:23–41). The riot in Ephesus in Acts 19 is particularly instructive. Christianity was spreading and causing people to turn from idols. That affected the economy, since the banking system and the idol makers and shrines were all intertwined. Christianity changed the way people spent and used their money, and that threatened the cultural status quo.

45. See especially Chapters 9 and 10 in Brian S. Rosner, *Greed As Idolatry: The Origin and Meaning of a Biblical Metaphor* (Grand Rapids, Mich.: Eerdmans, 2007).

46. Richard Keyes speaks of "near" and "far" idols in "The Idol Factory," in *No God but God: Breaking with the Idols of Our Age* (Chicago: Moody, 1992), pp. 29ff. Here I sketch out a similar concept, but he defines "far idols" more as cognitive false belief systems, and in this chapter I speak of "deep idols" as motivational drives.

47. Joseph Frazier Wall, *Andrew Carnegie* (Pittsburgh: University of Pittsburgh Press, 1989), pp. 224–225. Quoted in the chapter "Andrew Carnegie," *The Wise Art of Giving: Private Generosity and the Good Society* (Maclean, Va: Trinity Forum, 1996), pp. 5–25.

48. "Andrew Carnegie," *The Wise Art of Giving*, pp. 5–26.

49. Annie Dillard, *An American Childhood,* quoted in *The Wise Art of Giving,* pp. 3–48.

50. The Bible sees idols not only as false lovers and pseudo-saviors, but as slave masters. The Bible understands all relationships with rulers, both divine and human, to be

covenantal in nature. People enter into a covenant or contract with their ruler and with their God. Both they and their ruler are bound by oath to fulfill the duties outlined in the covenant. To each covenant, blessings and curses are attached (see the end of the book of Deuteronomy). The covenant keeper gets specified blessings, while the covenant breaker receives the curses. If, then, a man centers his life on making a lot of money he has (unwittingly) entered into an idol covenant with moneymaking. This means money becomes his slave master. It will drive him to overwork, and to cut corners ethically in order to make money. And if his career falters he will find himself with a deep sense of failure and guilt that he cannot remedy. The reason is that his idol is "cursing" him. Since he has failed his ultimate "Lord," he cannot escape a sense of complete worthlessness. Unless he gets a new center for his life and a new "lord," he cannot escape the sense of being cursed.

FOUR—The Seduction of Success

51. Lynn Hirshberg, "The Misfit," *Vanity Fair,* April 1991, Volume 54, Issue 4, pp. 160–169, 196–202.

52. The actor Ben Cross, playing the 1924 Gold Medalist Harold Abrahams, speaks these words in the film. It would not be fair to attribute these motives to Harold Abrahams himself. But the writer of the screenplay has perfectly depicted the interior life of many success-oriented, ambitious people.

Notes

53. Article accessed on March 28, 2009, at http://www.contact music.com/new/xmlfeed.nsf/mndwebpages/pollack moviesjustifymyexistence.

54. From "Success and Excess" by Harriet Rubin. This is the online edition that can be accessed at http://www.fast company.com/node/35583/print on March 28, 2009.

55. See the book-length study on this subject. Edward P. Meadors, *Idolatry and the Hardening of the Heart* (London and New York: T and T Clark, 2006).

56. *Good Housekeeping,* October 1990, pp. 87–88.

57. Peter L. Berger, Brigitte Berger, Hansfield Kellner, *The Homeless Mind: Modernization and Consciousness* (New York: Penguin, 1974), p. 89.

58. The David Brooks and Christopher Lasch quotes are taken from Nathan O. Hatch, "Renewing the Wellsprings of Responsibility," an address to the Council of Independent Colleges in Indianapolis, March 12, 2009.

59. Nathan O. Hatch, "Renewing the Wellsprings of Responsibility."

60. For more development of this argument see Timothy Keller, *The Reason for God* (New York: Dutton, 2007), the chapter on "The Cross."

61. We should not infer from this story of a slave girl forgiving her master that we should submit passively to oppression and injustice. The Bible's call to forgive *and* to seek justice are not mutually exclusive but complementary. Miroslave Volf, in his volumes *Exclusion and Embrace* (Nashville: Abingdon, 1996) and *The End of Memory: Remembering Rightly in a Violent World* (Grand Rapids, Mich.: Eerd-

mans, 2006) makes a strong case that it is necessary to forgive oppressors in order to truly seek justice. If you cannot do the interior work of forgiveness, you will seek excessive personal revenge rather than true justice, and so, ironically, you will remain oppressed. You will be drawn into the endless cycle of violent repayments yourself. Even in relationships that are not physically violent, but just unfair, you will not do a good job at confronting and correcting wrongdoers unless you first forgive them in your heart. If you don't forgive the perpetrator, you will overreach in your confrontation. You will be seeking not justice or change but only to inflict pain. Your demands will be excessive and your attitude abusive. The wrongdoer will see the confrontation as intended simply to cause hurt. A cycle of retaliation will begin. Only when you have lost the inner need to see the other person hurt will you have any chance of actually bringing about justice, change, and healing.

62. This is from the opening paragraph of "Success Excess" by Harriet Rubin. This is from the newsstand edition of *Fast Company,* October 1998. Current versions of this article now online have been revised.

63. This is a summary of a paragraph from the famous sermon by nineteenth-century Scottish minister Thomas Chalmers, "The Expulsive Power of New Affection" (available many places on the Internet). The paragraph itself reads: "It is thus that the boy ceases, at length, to be the slave of his appetite; but it is because a manlier taste has now brought it into subordination, and that the youth ceases to idolize

pleasure, but it is because the idol of wealth has become the stronger and gotten the ascendancy, and that even the love of money ceases to have the mastery over the heart of many a thriving citizen; but it is because, drawn into the whirl of city polities, another affection has been wrought into his moral system, and he is now lorded over by the love of power. There is not one of these transformations in which the heart is left without an object. Its desire for one particular object may be conquered; but as to its desire for having some one object or other, this is unconquerable."

FIVE—The Power and the Glory

64. Quoted in Bob Goudzwaard, *Idols of our Time* (Downers Grove, Ill: InterVarsity Press, 1984), p. 9.

65. From Robespierre's full speech quoted in Richard Bienvenu, *The Ninth of Thermidor* (Oxford: Oxford University Press, 1970), pp. 32–49.

66. Al Wolters, Michael Goheen, *Creation Regained: Basics for a Reformational Worldview,* second edition (Grand Rapids, Mich.: Eerdmans, 2005), p. 61.

67. "The lust for power is prompted by a darkly conscious realization of its insecurity." Reinhold Niebuhr, *The Nature and Destiny of Man: Volume I, Human Nature* (New York: Scribner, 1964), p. 189.

68. "The most obvious forms of idolatry are those in which the world of meaning is organized around a center . . . such as the life of a tribe or nation, which is patently contingent and not ultimate." Niebuhr, p. 165.

Notes

69. Goudzwaard, p. 23.

70. "Her [Germany's] boundless contemporary self-assertion which literally transgresses all bounds previously known in religion, culture, and law, is a very accentuated form of the power impulse. . . ." Niebuhr, p.189n.

71. C. S. Lewis, *Mere Christianity* (New York: HarperCollins, 2001), p. 11.

72. ". . . the effort is made to comprehend the meaning of the world through the principle of natural causation alone . . . [this] implies the deification of reason. That such an identification represents idolatry and that the laws of reason and logic are incapable of fully comprehending the total meaning of the world, is attested by the fact that life and history are full of contradictions which cannot be resolved in terms of rational principles." Niebuhr, p. 165.

73. C. E. M. Joad, *The Recovery of Belief* (London: Faber and Faber, 1952), pp. 62–63.

74. Richard Crossman, ed., *The God that Failed* (New York: Harper, 1949).

75. See the interesting study by Steward Davenport, *Friends of the Unrighteous Mammon: Northern Christians and Market Capitalism 1815–1860* (Chicago: University of Chicago, 2008). Davenport tries to discover why some Christian leaders embraced Adam Smith's version of capitalism, when it was clearly "ideological," asserting that if a government's only concerns were economic ones, morality and community would flourish naturally.

76. One thoughtful voice that has exposed the ideological nature of modern capitalism has been Wendell Berry, who

calls Americans to "waste less, spend less, use less, want less, need less." See his *Sex, Economy, Freedom, and Community: Eight Essays* (New York: Pantheon, 1994). Berry is not really liberal, since he is against big government, nor conservative or libertarian, since he balances individual rights against the common good more than conservatives would do. This makes his thought a good hedge against the development of modern ideologies.

77. Stephen Marglin, *The Dismal Science: How Thinking Like an Economist Undermines Community* (Cambridge: Harvard University Press, 2008). Marglin's point is that modern economics have become ideological, conceiving human beings as interest-maximizing individuals who don't need human community, who define themselves in terms of how much they can afford to consume, not their roles in a complex of human relationships. Over the last four centuries, this economic ideology has become the dominant ideology in much of the world.

78. Richard A. Posner, *A Failure of Capitalism: The Crisis of '08 and the Descent into Depression* (Cambridge: Harvard University Press, 2009). Posner makes the case against a major part of capitalist dogma, namely, that markets are self-correcting.

79. See William T. Cavanaugh, *Being Consumed: Economics and Christian Desire* (Grand Rapids, Mich.: Eerdmans, 2008). Cavanaugh discusses the temptation for Christians to seal off their private from their public lives in a society dominated by market capitalism. Traditionally, greed is one of the Seven Deadly Sins, and somehow we are supposed to avoid

it in our private life while pursuing it in our public, business life. Also, in our society we are called to define ourselves by what we consume, but in Christianity we are called to define ourselves by what we love. The logic and values of the market, Cavanaugh says, are spreading over into every area of life. This is because modern capitalism is "ideological."

80. Larry Elliott and Dan Atkinson, *The Gods that Failed: How Blind Faith in Markets Has Cost Us Our Future* (New York: Nation Books, 2009).

81. Niebuhr defined idolatry as raising some finite and relative thing to being "the final and ultimate value." Niebuhr, p. 225.

82. Roy Clements, *Faithful Living in an Unfaithful World* (Downers Grove, Ill: InterVarsity Press, 1998), p.153.

83. Reinhold Niebuhr, *The Nature and Destiny of Man: Volume I Human Nature* (New York: Scribner, 1964), p. 189.

84. Diana R. Henriques, "Madoff, Apologizing, Is Given 150 Years," *New York Times*, June 30, 2009.

85. "Bernard Madoff Gets 150 Years in Jail for Epic Fraud," Bloomberg News, June 29, 2009, http://www.bloomberg .com/apps/news?pid=20601087&sid=aHSYu2UPYrfo

86. Niebuhr, pp. 179–180.

87. *Ibid*.

88. What I am describing in this paragraph is how "surface idols"—sex, religion, money—can serve the "deep idol" of power. Compare this with what was said about deep and surface idols in Chapter Three.

89. Over the years many interpreters have worked to identify

every part of the idol as a historical kingdom. Since Nebuchadnezzar is said to be "the head" (Verses 36–39), it has been reasoned that each of the other metal parts of the idol must be the next dominant world power. But the dream probably cannot be interpreted so specifically. Notice that in Verse 35 we are told that the stone (the kingdom of God) breaks the whole idol to pieces *"at the same time."* If the kingdoms are centuries apart, how could the stone smash them all at the same time? I think that therefore the statue represents the world kingdoms in general, with all their might, and ways, and power. The dream is not giving us a specific sequence of specific kingdoms, nor is it emphasizing specific time frames. It is telling us that God is sovereign despite the rising of injustice and tyranny, and that all human power will be judged in the end. For a commentary that lays out this interpretive approach, see Tremper Longman, *The NIV Application Commentary: Daniel* (Grand Rapids, Mich.: Zondervan, 1999), pp. 79–93.

90. Christian Smith, *Soul Searching: The Religious and Spiritual Lives of American Teenagers* (Oxford: Oxford University Press, 2005), pp. 162–170.

91. Malcolm Gladwell, *Outliers* (New York: Little, Brown and Company: 2008), pp.125–128, 132–133, 156–158. Gladwell acknowledges that talent (heredity) and hard work are important to success, but he argues that environment is the biggest factor: including timing, family background, and culture.

92. For a book-length treatment on this theme, see Edward P. Meadors, *Idolatry and the Hardening of the Heart: A*

Study in Biblical Theology (London and New York: T and T Clark, 2006.)

93. C. S. Lewis, *The Chronicles of Narnia: The Voyage of the Dawn Treader* (New York: Harper Trophy, 2000), p. 91.

94. For a book-length treatment on this theme, see G. K. Beale, *We Become What We Worship: A Biblical Theology of Idolatry* (Downers Grove, Ill: InterVarsity Press, 2008).

95. Lewis, pp. 108–110.

SIX—The Hidden Idols in our Lives

96. Sheelah Kolhatkar, "Trading Down," *New York Times*, July 5, 2009.

97. The oath could be found online on June 10, 2009, at mbaoath.org/take-the-oath

98. "Forswearing Greed," in *The Economist*, June 6, 2009, p. 66. See also Leslie Wayne, "A Promise to Be Ethical in an Era of Immorality," in the *New York Times*, May 29, 2009.

99. Andrew Delbanco, *The Real American Dream: A Meditation on Hope* (Cambridge, Mass.: Harvard University Press, 1999), pp. 3, 23.

100. Delbanco, p. 5.

101. The "scoffer" (Hebrew *les*) is often translated "mocker" or "scorner." This figure appears fourteen times in the book of Proverbs. His problem is pride and arrogance (14:6, 21:24). See Bruce Waltke, *The Book of Proverbs: Chapters 1–15* (Grand Rapids, Mich.: Eerdmans, 2004), p. 114.

102. Among orthodox Christians, there are many people and churches that issue warnings against unbelief and error.

Indeed this often needs to be done, and Proverbs 26:28 says that a "flattering tongue," unwilling to criticize those in power, is destructive to the church. But many believers, even when they flag teaching and practices that should be flagged, do it with the characteristics of the scoffer in the book of Proverbs. In response to this charge, some of them point out that some biblical speakers and writers used sarcasm. That is true—you can see it in Elijah's debate with the prophets of Baal in 1 Kings 18, or especially in Paul's critique of his critics in 2 Corinthians 10–13. Sarcasm and irony can be effective ways to drive a point home, but derision and contempt cannot be the settled, main way that sinners talk to other sinners.

103. "Gifts of the Spirit are excellent things, but . . . they are not things which are inherent in the nature, as true grace and holiness are . . . gifts of the Spirit are, as it were, precious jewels, which a man carries about him. But true grace in the heart is, as it were, the preciousness of the heart, by which . . .the soul itself becomes a precious jewel. . . . The Spirit of God may produce effects on many things to which he does not communicate himself. So the Spirit of God moved on the face of the waters, but not so as to impart himself to the waters. But when the Spirit by his ordinary influences bestows saving grace, he therein imparts himself to the soul. . . . Yea, grace is as it were the holy nature of the Spirit of God imparted to the soul." From Jonathan Edwards, "Charity and Its Fruits, Sermon Two," in Paul Ramsey, ed., *Ethical Writings,* Volume 8 of *Works of Jonathan Edwards* (New Haven: Yale University Press, 1989), pp. 152–173.

104. See Timothy Keller, *The Prodigal God* (New York: Dutton, 2008).

105. Kenneth Gergen lists more than twenty psychological problems that have appeared only in the twentieth century with its new emphasis on self-fulfillment—anorexia, bulimia, stress, low self-esteem. See Kenneth Gergen, *The Saturated Self: Dilemmas of Identity in Contemporary Life* (Basic Books, 1991) p. 13.

106. The Bible passages quoted in this book are ordinarily taken from the New International Version. But in this chapter, I will rely on my own translation of the book of Jonah. (In this translation I depended most often on the insights of Jack Sasson, *Jonah: A New Translation with Introduction, Commentary, and Interpretation;* The Anchor Bible (New York: Doubleday, 1990); Phyllis Trible, *Rhetorical Criticism: Context, Method, and the Book of Jonah* (Minneapolis: Augsburg Fortress, 1994); and *Young's Literal Translation of the Bible*).

107. Leslie C. Allen posits that the memory of Jonah's blind nationalism would have been similar to the way we remember Hitler's assertion of the need for *Lebensraum*. Allen, *The Books of Joel, Obadiah, Jonah, and Micah* (Grand Rapids, Mich.: Eerdmans, 1976), p. 202. cf. Rosemary Nixon, *The Message of Jonah* (Downers Grove, Ill.: InterVarsity Press, 2003,), pp. 56–58). Both Nixon and Allen believe listeners would have remembered Jonah as a partisan and jingoist, and therefore would have been shocked to hear that he had been called to preach and spiritually warn people in the Assyrian capital of Nineveh.

108. Richard Lovelace, *The Dynamics of Spiritual Life* (Downers Grove, Ill.: InterVarsity Press, 1982), pp. 198, 212.

109. Jonathan Edwards in his work of moral philosophy, *The Nature of True Virtue*, argues that if you love your country more than God, you will be belligerent toward other nations and races. He points out that the Romans considered love of country to be the highest of all virtues, yet this priority "was employed as it were for the destruction of the rest of mankind." P. Ramsey, ed. *Ethical Writings*, in vol. 8 of *Works of Jonathan Edwards.*

110. Halbertal and Margalit give substantial treatment to this dynamic—namely, that idolatry stems from error and illusion in the mind, and erroroneous beliefs lead in turn to idolatry. See chapters "Idolatry and Representation," "Idolatry as Error," "The Wrong God," and "The Ethics of Belief" in *Idolatry* (Cambridge: Harvard University Press, 1992).

111. Biblically, idolatry and mental error go hand in hand, and this helps us understand the relationship between the first commandment, "Have no other gods before me," and the second commandment, "Make no graven images." Not only are we forbidden to worship false gods, but we are not to try to make a visual image of the true God. Why would this be? Halbertal and Margalit explore this question at length and conclude that anyone who tries to produce images of God will lead him- or herself into distortions and reductions. For example, a picture might show God to be quite majestic but could it at the same time depict his great love? In the end, anyone trying to produce an image

of deity will create a distortion and therefore a false God, even if the intention is to worship the true God. One of the great areas of idolatry, then, is doctrinal or theological error. If a person believes in a God of love but not justice, or of holiness and not mercy, that person's understanding falls short of the biblical God and so he or she is actually an idolater, worshipping a false god. See Margalit and Halbertal, Chapters 2, 4, 5, and 6. The New Testament answer to the question why God forbids us making a physical likeness of him (Exodus 33:20) is that he himself has given us an image of himself—Jesus Christ, who is (literally) the *icon* of the invisible God (Colossians 1:15).

112. This paragraph summarizes Thomas Oden's *Two Worlds*, Chapter 6.

SEVEN—The End of Counterfeit Gods

113. David Clarkson, "Soul Idolatry Excludes Men from Heaven," in *The Practical Works of David Clarkson*, Volume II (Edinburgh: James Nichol, 1865), pp. 299ff.

114. Clarkson, p. 311.

EPILOGUE—Finding and Replacing Your Idols

115. On Romans 1:21–25, commentator Douglas Moo writes: "In . . . paradigmatic fashion, [Paul] describes the terrible proclivity of all people to corrupt the knowledge of God they possess by making gods of their own. The tragic process of 'god-making' continues apace in our own day. . . .

Thus, as verses 24–31 show, the whole dreadful panoply of sins that plague humanity has it roots in the soil of this idolatry." Douglas J. Moo, *The Epistle to the Romans* (Grand Rapids, Mich.: Eerdmans, 1996), p. 110.

116. "All those who do not at all times trust God and do not in all their works or sufferings, life and death, trust in His favor, grace and good-will, but seek His favor in other things or in themselves, do not keep this [First] Commandment, and practice real idolatry, even if they were to do the works of all the other Commandments, and in addition had all the prayers, obedience, patience, and chastity of all the saints combined. For the chief work is not present, without which all the others are nothing but mere sham, show, and pretense, with nothing back of them. . . . If we doubt or do not believe that God is gracious to us and is pleased with us, or if we presumptuously expect to please Him only through and after our works, then it is all pure deception, outwardly honoring God, but inwardly setting up self as a false [savior]. . . ." Excerpts from Martin Luther, *Treatise Concerning Good Works* (1520), Parts X, XI.

117. Luther was not the only great theologian to see that idolatry lay behind all sin. Saint Augustine wrote, "Sins are committed when, out of an immoderate litany for . . . the least goods, we desert the best and highest goods which are you, O Lord our God, and your truth and law." John K. Ryan, ed., *The Confessions of St. Augustine* (Doubleday, 1960) p. 71. See also John Calvin, *Institutes of the Christian Religion*, ed. J. T. McNeil (Westminster, 1961) I. II. 8 and 3.3.12. Also, Jonathan Edwards' great work on ethics, *The*

Nature of True Virtue, assumes that idolatry, a failure to love God supremely, is at the root of human failure to live virtuous lives.

118. M. Halbertal and A. Margalit, *Idolatry* (Cambridge, Mass.: Harvard, 1992), p. 6: "[Communally] shared values, derived from the association of fixed visual perceptions, create a certain shared sensibility in people. . . . The commandment 'You shall not follow their practices,' which is meant as a rejection of the lifestyle of the idolatrous culture, reflects a complex weave of lifestyle, ritual, and faith. . . . the category of idolatry includes a criticism of the culture in which idolatry developed."

119. Here is a brief list of idol categories. The list may help us see the broad scope of idolatry in order to better recognize our own:

Theological idols—Doctrinal errors that produce such distorted views of God that we end up worshipping a false god.

Sexual idols—Addictions such as pornography and fetishisms that promise but don't deliver a sense of intimacy and acceptance; ideals of physical beauty in yourself and/or your partner; romantic idealism.

Magic/ritual idols—Witchcraft and the occult. All idolatry is in the end a form of magic that seeks to rebel against the order of transcendent reality rather than submitting to it in love and wisdom.

Political/economic idols—Ideologies of the left, right, and libertarian that absolutize some aspect of political order and make it *the* solution. Deifying or demonizing free markets, for example.

Racial/national idols—Racism, militarism, nationalism, or ethnic pride that turns bitter or oppressive.

Relational idols—Dysfunctional family systems of codependency; "fatal attractions"; living your life through your children.

Religious idols—Moralism and legalism; idolatry of success and gifts; religion as a pretext for abuse of power.

Philosophical idols—Systems of thought that make some created thing the problem with life (instead of sin) and some human product or enterprise the solution to our problems (instead of God's grace).

Cultural idols—Radical individualism, as in the West, that makes an idol out of individual happiness at the expense of community; shame cultures that make an idol out of family and clan at the expense of individual rights.

Deep idols—Motivational drives and temperaments made into absolutes: a. Power idolatry: "Life only has meaning /I only have worth if—I have power and influence over others." b. Approval idolatry: "Life only has meaning /I only have worth if—I am loved and respected by _____." c. Comfort idolatry: "Life only has meaning /I only have worth if—I have this kind of pleasure experience, a particular quality of life." d. Control idolatry: "Life only has meaning /I only have worth if—I am able to get mastery over my life in the area of _____."

120. This saying is widely attributed to the archbishop, but I

have not been able to confirm it or identify a source. It may be a paraphrase.

121. According to the Bible, all idol worshippers look to counterfeit gods in order to get more freedom and control, but in the end the result is less freedom and control, a form of slavery. We think that by pursuing sex, money, and power rather than the true God we are striking a blow for liberation, but ultimately we become enslaved to these things. Using the marital metaphor for idolatry, Jeremiah 2 and Ezekiel 16 show that when we leave our True Spouse for other lovers, we fall into a kind of spiritual sexual addiction. "You said, 'It's no use! I love foreign gods, and I must run after them!'" (Jeremiah 2:25) "Indeed, on every high hill and under ever spreading tree you lay down as a prostitute" (Jeremiah 2:20).

122. David Powlison, "Idols of the Heart and Vanity Fair," *The Journal of Biblical Counseling,* Volume 13, Number 2 (Winter 1995).

123. A good place to begin would be Kenneth Boa, *Conformed to His Image* (Grand Rapids, Mich.: Zondervan, 2001). An important book to read as an introduction to spiritual disciplines is Edmund P. Clowney, *CM: Christian Meditation* (Vancouver, B.C.: Regent, 1979). Clowney makes important distinctions between the meditation techniques of Eastern mysticism and those of orthodox Christianity.

124. John Newton, *Works of John Newton,* Volume VI (Edinburgh, UK, and Carlisle, Pa.: Banner of Truth reprint), p. 45.

BIBLIOGRAPHY

Barton, Stephen C., ed. *Idolatry: False Worship in the Bible, Early Judaism, and Christianity*. London and New York: T and T Clark, 2007.

Beale, G. K. *We Become What We Worship: A Biblical Theology of Idolatry*. Downers Grove, Ill.: InterVarsity Press, 2008.

Benson, Bruce Ellis. *Graven Ideologies: Nietzsche, Derrida, and Marion on Modern Idolatry*. Downers Grove, Ill.: InterVarsity Press, 2002.

Bobick, Michael W. *From Slavery to Sonship: A Biblical Psychology for Pastoral Counseling*. Unpublished D. Min. dissertation, Westminster Theological Seminary, 1989.

Clarkson, David. "Soul Idolatry Excludes Men from Heaven," in *The Practical Works of David Clarkson*, Volume II. Edinburgh: James Nichol, 1865, pp. 299ff.

Goudzwaard, Bob. *Idols of Our Time*. Sioux City, Iowa.: Dordt College Press, 1989.

Halbertal, Moshe and Avishai Margalit, *Idolatry*. Cambridge, Mass.: Harvard University Press, 1992.

Bibliography

Keyes, Richard. "The Idol Factory," in Os Guinness and John Seel, eds., *No God But God: Breaking with the Idols of Our Age*. Chicago: Moody Press, 1992.

Lints, Richard. "Imaging and Idolatry: The Sociality of Personhood in the Canon," in Lints, Michael Horton, and Mark Talbot, eds., *Personal Identity in Theological Perspective*. Grand Rapids, Mich.: Eerdmans, 2006.

Luther, Martin. *Larger Catechism* with study questions by F. Samuel Janzow. Saint Louis: Concordia, 1978.

Meadors, Edward P. *Idolatry and the Hardening of the Heart: A Study in Biblical Theology*. London and New York: T and T Clark, 2006.

Niebuhr, Reinhold. "Man as Sinner," in *The Nature and Destiny of Man*, Volume 1, Human Nature. New York: Scribner, 1964.

Nietzsche, Friedrich. *The Twilight of the Idols* and *The Anti-Christ*, translated by R. J. Hollingdale. New York: Penguin, 1990.

Oden, Thomas C. *Two Worlds: Notes on the Death of Modernity in America and Russia*. Downers Grove, Ill.: InterVarsity Press, 1992.

Oden, Thomas C. "No Other Gods" in Carl Braaten, Christopher Seitz, eds., *I Am The Lord Your God: Christian Reflections on the Ten Commandments*. Grand Rapids, Mich.: Eerdmans, 2005.

Powlison, David. "Idols of the Heart and Vanity Fair." *The Journal of Biblical Counseling*, Volume 13, Number 2, Winter 1995.

Bibliography

This article has been in circulation for over two decades and has been seminal for my thinking. It is also online at http://www.ccef.org/idols-heart-and-vanity-fair.

Ramachandra, Vinoth. *Gods That Fail: Modern Idolatry and Christian Mission.* Downers Grove, Ill.: InterVarsity Press, 1996.

Rosner, Brian S. *Greed as Idolatry: The Origin and Meaning of a Pauline Metaphor.* Grand Rapids, Mich.: Eerdmans, 2007.

Westphal, Merold. *Suspicion and Faith: The Religious Uses of Modern Atheism.* The Bronx, N.Y.: Fordham University Press, 1999.

ACKNOWLEDGMENTS

Again I thank Jill Lamar, David McCormick, and Brian Tart, my literary dream team that keeps stimulating and encouraging me in my writing. Also, thanks to Janice Worth and Lynn Land, who help me get away to write each summer.

This book is about our culture, and at my age people often lose their sympathy for it, and therefore their understanding of it. I have been fortunate in my sons—David, Michael, and Jonathan—in more ways than I can number. The one that bears most directly on this book is their wise, clear-eyed observation of the idols of their worlds, and their willingness to talk to me about them, long and intensely. Guys, thanks for the walks, dinners, and just hanging out. I respect how you've grown up loving the city and have become men of integrity.

I want to thank Kathy, who labored with me over

the book for months and over the ideas behind the book for years. I must say to Kathy what John Newton wrote to his wife Polly, namely, it is no wonder if so many years, so many endearments, so many obligations have produced such an uncommon effect, that by long habit, it is almost impossible for me to draw a breath, in which you are not involved.

About the Author

TIMOTHY KELLER was born and raised in Pennsylvania, and educated at Bucknell University, Gordon-Conwell Theological Seminary, and Westminster Theological Seminary. He was first a pastor in Hopewell, Virginia. In 1989 he started Redeemer Presbyterian Church in Manhattan, with his wife, Kathy, and their three sons. Today Redeemer has more than 5,000 regular Sunday attendees, plus the members of more than 100 new churches around the world. Also the author of *The Prodigal God* and the *New York Times* bestseller *The Reason for God*, he lives in New York with his family.

CROOKED

LAKE

First paperback edition October 2022

ISBN Paperback: 9798849498959

Book design by Nuno Moreira, NM DESIGN

CROOKED LAKE

P.M. BERK

For Nancy, my best friend

CHAPTER ONE

She laid there, still and bleeding profusely. Roy stood motionless, frozen for a moment by the sudden change in the normal progression of events. He knelt beside Allison and placed two fingers at the side of her neck. He felt a faint pulse. The gash on the side of her head appeared so deep he thought it must have cracked through her skull. She was alive, but barely and likely not for long.

Two days earlier

He knew he was playing with dynamite—still she was gorgeous and so accessible to him. He buzzed his secretary.

"Jen, see if you can locate Allison and ask her to come to my office."

Impressed by her smarts and physical beauty, as well as the fact that her grandfather was the recently retired senator from Ohio, Roy Dennison had persuaded his partner at Rogers and Dennison to offer employment to Allison Jameson three years ago. He opted to have her work under his supervision.

During the first year they had a model employer-employee relationship. He frequently complimented her on her work and attitude and she enjoyed providing him competent work.

Things started to change with his frustrations related to his wife's progressing third pregnancy. Clara had always been a satisfying partner for him. There were times during her other pregnancies, even other times, when he was tempted. Those were passing fancies, easy to dismiss in favor of being faithful to the wife he loved.

This was different. Allison's beautiful face and provocative body were there every day. He looked forward to leaving the pressures at home to be greeted by Allison's bright, shining personality. He would call her into the office, just to watch her as she left, with those lovely legs and hips that swayed with each step.

He started by having her work overtime a couple of days a week, even when it wasn't really necessary. That led to invitations to join him for dinner, always careful to not let it sound like a power play. He told her things he thought might engender sympathy for him. He told her he was upset with Clara for allowing herself to become pregnant for the third time, when she knew he didn't want to have any more children. He suggested that things at home were not really that great—that he and Clara had problems. One evening, after dinner and two cognacs, he drove her home. While parked in front of her building, he said, "You must know I'm very fond of you—I have feelings for you." Allison replied, "And I have feelings for you." He kissed her, and that was how it began.

"I was just packing my stuff up to leave for the day," Allison said.

"I just want to get the logistics right for our trip."

"I'm not sure I should go. The girls may be getting suspicious about your calling me in here so often."

"No way. Everyone knows you're working on two projects for

me. Here's the deal. I'll meet you at Palwaukee Airport tomorrow at 6:00 p.m. You can cab out there. Same routine as last spring. Jerry, I think that's his name, the tower guy at Eagle River, is lending us his jeep for the weekend. We'll fish with Cal on Friday, Saturday and Sunday, and fly back Sunday night. I've been looking forward to this trip with you ever since last spring."

"We'll both be gone from the office on Friday. Maybe I shouldn't go?"

"You'll call in sick and Jen knows my trip north has been planned for weeks. Try not to worry. We'll be fine."

Roy Dennison, one of the founders of Rogers and Dennison, a forty-two lawyer general corporate firm with offices in Chicago and Philadelphia, peered out one of the large windows of his seventeenth-floor corner office in the Chicago Title and Trust building, gazing at the famous yet peculiar Picasso bird hovering over the Civic Center Plaza. His walk and jog two miles four or five times a week had held back development of the usual middle-age paunch. Grand success had come easily to this slender six-footer. Thoughts of the coming weekend brought on a smile. He believed Clara's depression following the birth of their third child Jessica fifteen months ago, and the loss of libido she suffered, justified his taking up with Allison. This was a diversion he felt entitled to. After all, he had provided his wife and his children with a grand life. The country club was full of men who continually had affairs, one-nighters and more. He was not some chronically unfaithful husband. Never before Allison.

Before leaving the office Thursday afternoon, Dennison

chatted with his partner, Dan Rogers.

"I'm taking off for walleye country tonight. Spending the weekend fishing the Upper Peninsula."

"You going to run your big fish fry party for the firm again this Labor Day?"

"Clara really enjoys hosting it. That's why she sends me off to bring back the fish. Does my bachelor partner have anything interesting planned for the weekend?"

"Working on Saturday and Sunday to keep the firm afloat while my partner goes playing with minnows and worms."

"Eighteen years with me as your partner and you still haven't learned how to treat yourself to a good time."

They started the firm when Dennison was a twenty-six-year-old Harvard Law School graduate and Rogers a thirty-five-year-old assistant professor at Harvard. Through their Harvard Law School graduate friends, many of whom had been students of Rogers in years gone by, they had access to management of numerous major corporations. The skill and personality power of Roy Dennison in board rooms and on the golf course was magical. He could ooze charm, often exhibiting a sense of humor with sparkle in his eyes that would always produce laughter They were like magnets from the get-go, attracting important clients as the firm grew like wildfire.

Their social and philanthropic activities gave Roy's parents limited time for him. An only child, one go-round being enough for his mother, his early years, at least until fifth grade, were managed mainly by a live-in nanny. His only crisis as a youth was being clipped by a swing in a playground, leaving him with a quite prominent two-inch scar below his right eye over his cheek bone. His mother fretted over the tragedy of scarring such a beautiful face. In adulthood, the scar proved to be an asset, giving Roy a hint of macho toughness. Their posh Lake Forest home featured a swimming pool, used only in July and August, and a putting green, used by his father to help maintain his twelve-handicap at the country club. Many of Roy's teenage friends were from high school, but the coolest were from the country club. Golf, tennis and the pool made for busy summers. He was popular with the boys and the girls. Roy had his own car at age sixteen. He wanted for nothing. Spoiled was an under-statement. He excelled academically in high school with limited effort and was able to gain acceptance to Harvard on merit, without pulling strings.

The absence of any struggle or failure in his young adulthood gave Roy a sense of invincibility. He was inundated with self-confidence and flaming self-esteem. You could see it in his eyes and in his walk.

The Dennisons lived in a massive residence in upscale suburban Winnetka, near the shore of Lake Michigan. Roy acquired the double lot bearing a sixty-year-old Tudor Revival home after his first son was born. He then had the old house demolished and constructed the present 6,000 square foot sprawling U- shaped ranch home. The house was ideal for entertaining. The large great room with multiple French doors leading to an extensive, magnificently tiled patio surrounded by a variety of flowering plants and miniature trees. Clara loved to entertain and show off her home to friends and clients.

Dennison had already loaded his clothes, rain gear and

fishing equipment in his jeep, located between Clara's Acura and his Alfa Romeo in the three-car garage. He said his goodbyes to the children in the reception room of the house, crouching to eye level with Rob, his oldest at age eight. Rob was Roy's first and secretly his favorite. As he'd gotten older, he took on a striking resemblance to his father.

"You be good now, and be nice to your brother and sister while I'm away."

"When do I get to go fishing?"

"Your day is coming, Rob. Might even be next summer. Give me a hug and wish me good luck."

"Good luck Daddy. Catch some big ones."

Ben was sprawled on the reception floor, intrigued by a battery-operated tiger pacing back and forth as Roy lifted him up, kissed him on the cheek and said good-bye. Clara, carrying Jessica, walked with Roy down the driveway. Roy kissed Jessica on the top of her head, gave a quick kiss on the lips to Clara, and entered the jeep.

"I expect you to bring home the bacon, sweetheart," said Clara, bending toward the open jeep window.

"You can count on it. Sweet walleye fillets for everyone. Mobil cell phone probably won't work in the UP. It didn't last spring. If we don't talk, I'll be home Sunday night."

"Have fun and fly safe."

After the birth of Jessica and the onset of her depression, Clara consented to Roy's urging to have a second live-in help to administer to the care and needs of the children, while Lily continued to maintain the house and kitchen. Eventually, she renewed her philanthropic activities with fulfilling memberships on the boards of the Civic Opera and Chicago Public Library. She carried herself with elegance—a popular figure in the life of the city of Chicago with her name appearing frequently in gossip columns, but always favorably and with respect.

Born in Odessa, Ukraine, Clara, her older sister and her parents immigrated to America in 1990, one year before Ukraine declared itself an independent country. Her mother was a strict disciplinarian, common to Russian parenting. She also took commitment very seriously. At age twelve, much to her mother's joy, Clara showed an interest in ballet. Her mother signed her up for a year of study with a Russian teacher. After the first month Clara lost interest in ballet and wanted to try out for the volleyball team at the grade school. Her mother would have none of that. She committed to a year of ballet, and that was that.

"Commitment, my darling, is a sign of character. When you commit, you complete. You *will* finish the year of ballet."

Clara had a magnificent Slavic face. Her hazel eyes, dark brownish hair and eyebrows contrasted stunningly with her pale skin. She had typically full lips, always lip-sticked bright red. She used a good deal of makeup, although she was equally attractive without.

* * *

Allison had been raised by her maternal grandfather, the Senator, as an observant Catholic girl. Roy was her first serious relationship. She had, indeed, fallen in love with him. She gave up her virginity for him. Having had very little father in her life, his strength and maturity, as well as good looks, filled a void. He was her leader, her lover, her everything. She truly believed he loved her and there was a future for them to be together.

In the bathroom of her apartment that night, she was about to perform a test. She missed her last period and feared she may have become pregnant. Allison prayed it would not be so. Roy would be furious if she had allowed that to happen. She could not imagine explaining such a situation to her grandfather. The three-test packet explained that the result of each test would be reported as PREGNANT or NOT PREGNANT. Test one reported PREGNANT, test two the same, and test three, still PREGNANT.

* * *

Roy arrived at the airport at 5:30 p.m., giving him adequate time to load his Piper Cherokee PA-28 before Allison showed up. He acquired the four-seater two years ago, after concluding that driving seven hours up to and then back from the UP was too much for just three-day visits. It took him only four months of once-a-week lessons to become a certified private pilot. He could make it to the Eagle River airport in less than three hours without pushing it too hard. It was a beautiful early evening for flying. They had an extra-long view of the sunset from 2500 feet and arrived in Eagle River in the dark.

CHAPTER TWO

There were no street lights on the drive to Crooked Lake. The only things visible were the stars sprinkled in the dark, moonless sky and the painted line separating the two lanes of Route 45. Roy held his speed under sixty mph, keeping a vigilant lookout for the reflection of his headlights in the eyes of deer that might be ready to pounce into his path.

He turned right onto Crooked Lake Road. After three miles he turned another right onto a narrow dirt and sand road marked by a sign which read *Dennison's Den*. The road, captured by thick forest, was plagued by ruts and grooves resulting from the harsh winter followed by the spring thaw, making it a bumpy ride the 300 yards to the destination, which looked in the dark to be a log cabin but was, in fact, a large log home on a bluff high above Crooked Lake.

There was a chill in the evening air, the remnants of ice and snow still appearing in spots. After unloading the jeep and putting their things in the master suite on the second floor, they returned to the great room. The wall of the great room facing the lake was eighty per cent windowed extending to the high ceiling. Roy poured brandy into two large snifters at the well-stocked wet bar. He started a fire in the great stone fireplace. They sat on the oversized furniture facing the fire, sipping their brandy. A ten-point deer mounted above the fireplace looked down at them. For a time neither spoke as they watched the embers and listened to the crackle and snap of the fire. Allison put down her glass and sat at Roy's feet on the thick shag rug in front of the fireplace.

"I wish I could stay here forever," Allison said.

"You belong here." He smoothed his hand lovingly down her blonde hair. Responding to his touch, she turned her head to look at him. He said, "My God, you are beautiful."

"Is this what it'll be like after you leave Clara?"

Roy had been willing to exaggerate and tell half-truths to overcome her Catholic resistance to his early approaches. He was careful, however, not to let Allison think their relationship could be a permanent one. One night in the office, after hours, in the midst of a moment of passion, his ardor got the best of him.

"Allie, I think I'm in love with you. I could see being with you for the rest of my life." Oops! The whispered words "I love you", said so easily in the breathless peak of passion. A mistake, an unintended hint that helped pave the way to a full sexual relationship. It worked. That assertion, apparently taken by Allison to be a promise, was enough to overcome her religious resistance. Bringing up the subject now caused him to wince. He wondered why, all of a sudden, she wanted to put him on the spot?

"Let's save that conversation for another time. It's very complicated."

"But you did mean what you said, that you want to be with me for the rest of your life?"

"You know I'm crazy about you. I'm going to make things right. You just have to be patient."

"I'm afraid you didn't mean it. If you didn't mean it, I don't belong here."

Of course he didn't mean it, but this was no time for that confession.

"Come here." He held her close as she nestled her head under his chin. "Don't ever doubt how much I love you."

CHAPTER THREE

Cal and Emma Cooley had been married for twenty-six years and had been empty nesters the past three. Their two boys struck out on their own after each completed two years of junior college. Their daughter, Meg, twenty-five, was living in Madison while attending her final year of nursing school. There wasn't much to do in Watersmeet, a town of 1200. Most folks stayed at home most of the time.

Cal's father, Jeb Cooley, was a legend among the fishing guides of the UP. In his thirty years on the lakes he guided catches of six of the ten largest muskies pulled out of the Cisco Chain. At age sixty he suffered a stroke and was thereafter confined to a wheelchair. He and his wife moved to a small town in Kentucky, where some distant relatives lived, to get away from the harsh UP winters.

"Dennison is flying up with his girl tonight for three days of fishing. He missed the May 13th opener by three days," Cal said.

"Jesus. How does a married man with three young kids get away with that?" asked Emma.

"Power and money. Simple as that."

"What's that simple?"

"Power and money."

"If you ever pulled that shit, I'd have your balls hanging from the mouth of that lunker walleye on the wall."

"No fear. I got no money and no power. Besides, I never seen anything around here that would compare to Dennison's sweet girl—present company excluded."

"You going to fish Crooked with them?"

"You bet. No better way to get walleye limits and I plan to get 'em every day. Going to keep you busy next few days cleaning all them fish."

"That's OK, so long as you don't mind eating leftovers for a while." Emma had a way of always getting the last word in her conversations with Cal.

The rim of the sun was just peeking above the horizon when Cal Cooley, black coffee in hand, climbed into his old Ford pick-up and trailered his fifteen-foot fishing boat from his white, wood-framed house on Catalpa Street to head west onto Main Street. It was quiet, the café being the only Main Street business open at this hour. He stopped at the end of town at Bert Clinton's bait stand.

Bert opened his makeshift outdoor shop with a worn wooden over-hang at 6:00 a.m. every morning, except from November until the ice went out on the lakes. He furnished bait for most of the guides and many of the vacationers in the area. The inventory included minnows of many varieties and sizes, nightcrawlers, red worms and leeches. Suckers were the biggest swimmers, meant only for musky fishermen or those looking for giant northern pike. Cal's choice was always the hardy river mud minnow because of its long life, able to survive a dozen casts or a lengthy troll—an effective and economic choice for those in the guiding business.

Cooley fished mainly the Cisco Chain, which included his favorite, Crooked Lake, just an eight-mile drive from Watersmeet. Located near the south edge of the Upper Peninsula in Michigan, the lake was a short distance above the Wisconsin State Line. He had a reputation, built over twenty-five years of guiding, of regularly providing his customers with limits of bass and walleye pike. Sure, there were times when he couldn't find the fish or he found them but they weren't willing to make that existential mistake. Those times were few and far between for Cal Cooley.

"Howdy Bert. I'll take four dozen of them medium muds." Cal set his minnow bucket alongside the water pressured tank holding the muds. Bert poured two dip nets of muds into the bucket without counting.

"There, that oughtta do it. Did you hear about the nigger coming into town? Checked into Mandy's last night."

Cal winced at eighty-year-old Bert's casual bigotry, but he loved the old guy and was not about to take him up on it.

"No. Hadn't heard. What do you think he's up to?"

"Ain't got no idea. Didn't have no fishin' equipment with him neither. Maybe just passing through or maybe looking for a place to stay permanent."

"Now, wouldn't that be something. Does Jesse know about it?"

"Don't think so. He and Deputy Luke are over at Iron Mountain at some kind of seminar. Won't be back until later today."

"Gotta get going to pick up my customer. Going to hit Crooked today. I kinda like that southwest breeze we're getting. Jesse will figure out how to handle it."

"Any more news on the water level at Crooked?" Bert asked.

"It's up two or three feet but hasn't hurt the fishing none."

"OK Cal. Go get 'em. Have a good luck day."

CHAPTER FOUR

Watersmeet Township was under the supervision of Jesse Wickerham, an undersheriff of Gogebic County. An honorable mention all-state defensive tackle on the Eagle River High football team, he recently celebrated his ten-year anniversary of joining the Sheriff's Department. Jesse was definitely the man to deal with any trouble brewing in the Watersmeet area, either with persuasion or muscle, as the circumstances might require.

Early Friday morning he was knocking on the door of unit nine of Mandy's Motel.

"Who's there?" said a man's voice inside.

"Deputy Wickerham of the Sheriff's Department."

"It's 7:00 a.m. Too early. What's this about?"

"I've been working the township since 6:00 a.m. Come on out here so we can have a talk."

"Give me a couple of minutes to put some clothes on." Opening the door, the man saw the deputy resting against the fender of his Sheriff's Department car. A tall formidable sight, with his weapon holstered to his side, a big Sheriff's Deputy badge on his chest and dark wrap-around sunglasses lifted to his forehead.

"What's the problem officer?"

"What's your name?"

"Marvell Jackson. Is there a problem?"

"We'll see about that. For now, what are you doing here in the UP?"

"I'm up for the weekend to check on cabins to rent for a summer vacation with my wife on Crooked Lake."

"Where you from?"

"Chicago."

"Why the hell would you want to come all the way up here for a few days vacation when there are so many lakes and cabins in Wisconsin?"

"I'm not sure that's any of your business, but I've stayed on Crooked Lake before and loved it and don't mind the drive up to this beautiful part of the country."

"Don't get snotty with me. I'm just asking what brought you here in the first place."

"Are you familiar with Roy Dennison's home on the lake?"

"Of course I am. Everyone around here knows who Roy is."

"I'm a junior partner in his law firm. I spent a few days at his house on the Lake with some other lawyers from the firm last summer. Roy put us there so we could hammer out our strategy for an important litigation without being interrupted by other distractions. I even had a chance to fish the lake a little bit. That's when I fell in love with the area."

"Fell in love, did you? Maybe you didn't realize it, but there aren't any of your people living in Watersmeet Township or on the Cisco Chain. Might be a few working in the mills in Ironwood and Iron Mountain. Still, that's far away from here—like in a different world."

"This is a free country, isn't it?"

"It is, but it's also a free country for the folks who live up here. I think you'll find it difficult to find a cabin owner who'll rent to you. If you do, you won't likely have a peaceful summer vacation. That's just how it is." Jesse walked around to his driver's door and looked back at Marvell. "As long as you're here, enjoy the weekend."

Marvell wasn't surprised to find racial bigots in the UP that wanted to keep the woods white. Different brand of prejudice in the UP from the South. Up here, they just wanted to keep blacks out. In the South, they just wanted to keep them out of power. He was determined to follow through with his weekend plan.

CHAPTER FIVE

Cooley pulled into the Crooked Lake public launch and did his final preparations. He wiped the boat seats dry and covered the backs with life preserver vests. This wasn't going to be a day for cooking up a shore lunch, so he brought sandwiches and a thermos of hot coffee. The launch was a ten-minute boat ride to Dennison's dock. Cal donned his hooded rain poncho for the ride through the drizzle.

Crooked Lake was a remnant of the post glacial Lake Nipissing. Its 2300 acres were separated almost equally by a wide channel winding its way between the west and east portions of the lake. There was very little development of the east portion which was bordered in large part by marsh and wetlands. The west, where the launch was located, was mostly flat, buildable shoreline, except for a stretch of bluffs where Dennison's Den was located. The shoreline was developed with magnificent homes, some individual cabins and three fishing lodges. The west lake contained several islands and reached depths of sixty-five feet.

They could hear Cooley coming even before they saw him rounding the island that was some 300 yards directly opposite where they stood. There was barely any breeze and the lake was still, except for the pockmarks where the rain drops landed. They greeted Cal and started loading tackle on the boat. Cal helped them aboard, complimenting them on their bright yellow matching rain outfits with tops and bottoms.

Roy gave Cal a strong handshake and pulled him close for a half hug. They started fishing together nine years ago and hadn't missed a year of spring fishing. The first seven years they fished alone. Just the two of them. Spending three or four days on a boat with Cal in the northland was just the change of pace Dennison needed to recharge his competitive batteries. Cal was not the typical fishing guide. He was fun to be with. Full of conversation and knowledge of the woods and waters. He would call attention to various sounds of nature and to water disturbances indicating the presence of fish. He could tell you whether leavings on the shore were deposited by a beaver, racoon or a white tail.

Cal enjoyed joking with his customers. Last summer, with his back to Allison, after securing her best catch with a pin through its lip on the chain stringer, a three-pound walleye, he pretended to lose control of the fish and flipped it overboard. "Oh! Sorry Allison, there goes your fish!" Allison let out a wailing "Oh, no!" then joined in the laughter after realizing she'd been had.

"Good to see you again, old friend," said Dennison.

"Sorry you missed the opener this year. It was a great day. Everyone caught fish. Howdy, Miss Allison. You lookin' pretty as ever."

"You can congratulate Allison. She made junior partner three weeks ago."

"Well, congratulations indeed. That sounds very important."

"Hello, again, Cal. This is the first time you arranged wet weather for us."

"Don't you mind, ma'am. The next two days are going to be mostly sunny. Good shore lunch weather."

As they started motoring, Cal told them when he came around the island he saw some bait fish breaking surface about twenty yards off shore. They would stop to check it out on their way to his prime fishing spots. Roy smiled. He was never sure if Cal was being truthful with some of his observations or just trying to inject some excitement into the outing.

*　*　*

Marvell Jackson dropped into the café at 9:00 a.m. The breakfast crowd had thinned out. The few customers still there were on their second cups of coffee. By the time his food came he was the only customer in the café. The waitress, Molly, set down his ham and eggs and offered some cautionary words.

"You may not know it, but your walking in here was not popular with the customers. I just moved up here from Milwaukee last March and I have no problem serving you, but you are really out of place. I don't know what your business is or where you're going. I can tell you it would be best if you were just passing through. If the owner were here, she'd raise a stink with me for just talking to you."

"I appreciate the caution. I'm just here for the weekend. The deputy gave me the same kind of advice."

"If that was Wickerham, you better pay attention."

"Is he liable to cause me trouble?"

"Wickerham causes trouble most everywhere he goes. Keep

your eyes out for him."

Marvell opened a copy of the weekly *Watersmeet News* to the want ad section. His mobile phone was not connecting. Molly let him use the café's phone to make an 11:00 a.m. appointment to see a cabin on Crooked Lake.

He had time to take a drive around the area, including a stop at Dennison's Den. He assumed the old jeep parked near the front door with Wisconsin plates was either a caretaker or a repair person. There was a pause in the rain, so he walked around to the lakeside of the house. It was a magnificent scene. A massive screened porch was set on a bluff some seventy-five feet above the lake with wooden steps leading steeply to the dock. The Dennisons' fleet of a small Chris- Craft speed boat and luxury pontoon party boat were still in dry dock. Marvell remembered the cruise around the lake in the party boat last summer. Upon returning to the house he had called Louanna to tell her they had to think about spending their summer vacations on Crooked Lake.

Marvell arrived at the cabin a little early. With the windshield wipers working on slow, he admired the small log construction cabin. It was advertised at $800 a week in season. He thought this might really work. The contact person arrived and groaned as he watched Marvell exit his car.

"Man, you don't want to rent no cabin up here. Better be on your way," he said out his open window.

"Sorry, sir. I'm a lawyer and can tell you that under the state of Michigan Constitution and the US Constitution you have no right to decline a renter on racial grounds. Now let's take a look inside the cabin."

The lessor rushed out of his car to catch up to Marvell, who was approaching the front porch of the cabin.

"This ain't right for you, boy. Best be on your way."

"Let's take a look inside."

Louanna would, for sure, love this log cabin. Marvell was prepared to rent it for two weeks in mid-July. The lessor told him he could have it for $1500 a week.

"Bullshit. Your ad says $800 a week."

"Yeah, but renting to you brings a whole new level of risk for me. I gotta be paid for taking that risk. Take it or leave it."

The $800 price was less than they had budgeted. He didn't think he'd find anything better than this cabin. Fifteen hundred dollars was well over market, but he decided to take it. The lessor wrote out a short agreement with a carbon paper copy. Marvell gave him a $300 deposit by check to hold those two weeks for them and headed back to the café for lunch.

At 1:30 p.m. only two tables were occupied in the café. One of them was taken by Wickerham and another deputy. Jackson took a seat at a table for two. Wickerham picked up his coffee and walked over to Jackson's table.

"Mind if I join you for a minute?"

"Not at all. Take a seat," Marvell said.

"What you been up to today?"

"I booked a cabin for our July vacation."

"Is that right. Who'd you book it from?"

"Rather not say."

"Why's that?"

"Just think that's my business."

"Well, I'll find out soon enough. Did you know that your boss is up here this weekend with a girlfriend?"

"Are you talking about Roy Dennison?"

"Yes sir. He's fishing with Cal Cooley. Does he know that you're up here?"

"Probably not. We didn't talk about it."

"You better think twice about coming back up here in July?"

"Are you threatening me?"

"Man, I don't threaten. I just do."

CHAPTER SIX

Cooley put the fish in a tub of water and shoved the tub into the bottom shelf of the extra fridge in the garage. He entered the kitchen from the garage where he found Emma busy preparing a beef stew dinner.

"There's some work for you in the fridge when you get 'round to it."

"How'd the day go? Get your limit?"

"Started out wet. Sun came out in the afternoon. Roy's girl, Allison, was in some kind of a funky mood. Didn't talk much and didn't even want to fish much. I had to take out my rod and help make their limit."

"Maybe she was feeling guilty for her part in breaking up that happy family?"

"Maybe. She's usually the life of the party on the boat. I think the weather got her down. The rain wasn't heavy, but steady for four or five hours. She perked up after the rain stopped."

"Wash up and come sit down. Your stew is ready."

Emma had always been a bit slow, accentuated by her progressive hearing loss, only marginally improved by the hearing aids Cal bought for her at the general store. She was alone most of the time, with Cal rising at 5:30 a.m. and not returning until dinnertime. Last year, to avoid sitting on the couch all day, waiting until it was time to start preparing dinner, she started riding her bicycle to the Indian Casino at the outskirts of Watersmeet. She'd sit at a penny or nickel slot machine for hours. When it got to the point where she was losing $20 to $25 a day, which was about what she could make in her fish cleaning business, Cal put his foot down.

"You got to stop pissing away all this money at the casino."

"What else I got to do? I can go crazy sitting alone all day."

"Well, you could read a book and get yourself educated on something."

"I could what?"

"Read a book, take up knitting. There's better things you can do than just sit on the damn couch."

"You just better watch your words, Mr. Cooley."

The one activity common to most permanent residents of Watersmeet, especially in the winter months, was drinking. The bar on Main Street serviced regulars from 6:00 p.m. to midnight closing most every night. Cal didn't drink. He learned as a teenager that alcohol did not set well with him. His early drinking adventures were followed by facial swelling and severe itching all over his body.

The town doc explained to Cal and his mother that he had an alcohol allergy, and these reactions could lead to anaphylaxis which is serious and could be fatal. He never touched alcohol again. That allergy could be a curse or a blessing, depending on how one looked at it.

In view of the allergy, Cal never had any beer or liquor in the house. After he barred Emma from the casino, he learned that she helped pass the time of day by keeping her own stash of cheap whiskey in her bedroom closet, available for a swig or two whenever needed.

"I hope you don't think you're fooling me with the booze you've got hidden in the closet."

"Shit, I don't care if I'm fooling you or not. It makes me feel good and it's something I do now."

"Well, don't come 'round looking for no kisses from me while you've got that crap swirling around in your mouth."

"Who's lookin' for kisses?"

While Emma was busy in the kitchen Cal took his usual position on his frayed, brown recliner and started scanning the *Watersmeet News*. Emma drifted off to the bedroom for a couple of swigs to relax herself before bedtime.

Returning to the living room, she found Cal asleep with his weather beaten hands still holding the *News* on his lap. She leaned in to make sure he was breathing. Cal never snored, so Emma was frequently checking him for signs of life during his after-supper naps and throughout the nighttime. She would lie in bed facing him and periodically open an eye to see if his chest was moving. She had a constant dread of losing him, even though at forty-six he was three years her junior.

Emma did not believe she could survive losing Cal.

CHAPTER SEVEN

Having dined on frozen dinners, they were back breathing in the warmth of the fireplace. The damp wood was making its comforting, crackling sounds as Roy turned the burning logs with his poker, causing a brief shower of embers.

"You've been quiet all day, honey. Is something troubling you? Are you feeling OK?"

"I'm fine. I'm OK."

"Allie, come on. Are you alright?"

"I'm fine, but I'm afraid you'll be angry with me." She turned her face away from his gaze.

"Come, sit on my lap and tell me about it." Allison moved to his lap. He put his arm around her, resting his hand on her breast.

"Don't, Roy, please."

"Whatever it is, it sure got you on edge."

They spoke early in their relationship about the need to protect against pregnancy. He had selfishly placed that responsibility on her, insisting that she take a pill or use a diaphragm. She accepted his direction and assiduously used a diaphragm—that is, until about two months ago. After a quiet dinner at one of their favorite cafes, they continued drinking at her apartment until both were inebriated—particularly Allison, to the point where she forgot about the diaphragm.

Allison was desperately trying to control her emotions. She felt close to tears and was fighting to hold them back. It was not so much the fact of being pregnant as it was the fear of how Roy would react to that news. He had never displayed a temper toward her during their time together, but she knew he had one. She'd seen it numerous times in the office.

Roy was losing patience with Allison's mood and her refusal to speak up.

"We're not going to bed tonight until you tell me what's bugging you. You can't say there's something wrong and then refuse to tell me what it is."

She turned her back to Roy and while walking toward the windowed wall, said, "I'm pregnant."

"How the hell did that happen?"

"I have no idea. You know how careful I am about that."

"Are you sure?"

"I checked it twice, no, three times. No doubt about it. I'm going to make an appointment to see a doctor next week." She turned back to Roy with a new hold on herself since he did not appear to be angry.

"I'll help arrange to take care of the pregnancy."

"If you're talking about abortion, count me out."

"That's impossible. I can't have you walking around the office all blown up. People will think it's mine."

"It is yours, asshole. I will not abort. That would violate everything I believe in. Maybe this is the best time for you to leave Clara and start the rest of your life with me."

Oh my God, she really thinks that is a solution. What am I going to do with her?

After a lengthy pause while pacing around the great room, Dennison proposed a solution.

"You'll take a leave of absence from the firm. I'll find you a place in southern Wisconsin or northern Indiana and I'll pay all your expenses until the baby is born, and I'll visit you whenever I can. After a while you'll come back to the office. Either that or you can go live with your folks and have the baby there."

"What folks?"

"What do you mean?"

"You've never asked me about my parents. They're not a subject I like to bring up. My mother was in an abusive relationship with my father. He was a drunkard and a mean bastard. I witnessed much of his physical and emotional abuse. She killed herself when I was a child. My father was on one of his binges and didn't come home that night. I was the one who found her in the morning, dead on the floor of her bedroom. She died of some kind of pill overdose. As soon as that happened, my father took off and I haven't heard from him since. I was nine years old at the time." A rush of tears came as she muttered, "Oh dear God."

Roy sat next to her and held her close in his arms.

"Why didn't you tell me?"

"You never asked."

"Where did you go then?"

"I went to live with my maternal grandparents. My grandfather was a congressman and later became a US Senator. They raised me to be a devout Catholic. Where does that leave us?"

Dennison rose and stated what he believed to be the only possible options.

"Either you need to get an abortion or take a leave of absence and return to your grandparents until the baby is born."

"My grandmother is deceased and my grandfather is in no condition to handle this. What happened to this great love you have for me? I'm not going anywhere. Either you figure out a way you're going to live with me or you fire me—then we'll see what happens."

"Look, Allie, this just isn't the right time for us. There has to be preparations and they take time. You're so young and just starting a promising career in law. The last thing you need is to be saddled with a child you didn't plan for. God will understand this was a mistake. You won't be punished for doing what is best."

"No, no, no. No abortion."

"Let's sleep on it and talk again tomorrow evening. We can discuss it again tomorrow night. I'm going to stay down here for a while and get the rods and reels ready for tomorrow." Allison left without the usual kiss goodnight.

Dennison poured himself a brandy and sat by the fire, contemplating the situation. His plan for an orgiastic weekend had evaporated. He didn't want to have anything to do with her at this point. Amazing, how suddenly passion can disappear. He would try once again tomorrow night to reason with her.

CHAPTER EIGHT

Mandy's Motel, while on the outskirts of town, was still only a three block walk to the café on Main Street. Marvell picked up two hamburgers from the cafe for dinner and enjoyed them with soda pop while sitting on his bed watching the news on television.

Marvell was contemplating Wickerham's reference to Dennison and a girlfriend. He was aware of a rumor going around the office that Roy Dennison was having an affair with one of the young lawyers. He wondered whether that was the girl Wickerham was talking about. The likely suspect in the office was Allison Jameson. She had been working with Roy closely on two projects, and she was a beautiful gal. He learned from his mother years ago that rumors are often wrong and can cause undeserved damage. It's just something that some of the girls had been whispering about.

While Marvell's business was done, he decided he would stick to the plan of driving home on Sunday. On Saturday he'd drive out to Ironwood and then along Lake Superior to Porcupine Mountain. He had never seen that lake and heard the water was as blue as the Gulf Stream. Tiring of the café's fare, he might even stop for dinner in Ironwood.

* * *

Saturday was a much better-looking day, sixty degrees, partly sunny and fishermen's favorite westerly breeze. Morning fishing was good enough to support a shore lunch of walleye and canned corn. Cal pulled up to one of the islands with a clearing containing a campfire site surrounded by several large boulders. He gave Roy and Allison the task of collecting wood as well as branches for tinder as he scaled and cleaned three of the smaller fish. He constructed a tripod of strong branches on which he hung an open can of corn over the fire and he began frying the fish in his oversized iron skillet. He started with some bacon that sizzled and provided the fat which cooked the fish and browned them in short order. His black, grimy looking coffee pot sat on the edge of the fire. This was the routine he had done hundreds of times. Often, his customers would take photos of the process, but Roy and Allison just sat and watched the master at work while they picked away at the crisp bacon.

Sitting on the boulders, each enjoying two small walleye fillets, the fishermen engaged in no conversation. Cal finally broke the silence.

"You two haven't said a word to each other since we hit this island. In fact, I don't remember hearing much from either one of you all morning, except maybe 'I got one' or 'that one got away'. What's going on with you two?"

"We're just struggling with a personal issue. One that takes more thinking than talking at this stage," Roy said.

Allison looked at Roy and then turned her glance to Cal, nodding agreement.

"I'm sure glad it's nothing I said or done," Cal said with a smile and a grunt.

Cal dropped them off at the dock at about 5:00 p.m. and headed home to Emma with a nice mess of fish for her to clean. He was proud of having produced another days' limit of good eating walleyes for Dennison. He was, after all, Cal's favorite customer. Roy always ended the trip with a $500 gratuity on top of the $660 for three days of guiding. None of his other customers came anywhere close to that.

He hoped they would solve their personal issue so that tomorrow would be a fun last day of fishing for everyone.

CHAPTER NINE

While Allison was taking her turn in the shower, Roy got the BBQ grill going, preparing for the two rib eyes almost totally defrosted in the fridge. He set a table in the breakfast room, opened a bottle of Cabernet and poured two glasses. Allison came down in her white terry-cloth robe with her hair drying in a wrapped towel and took a seat at the table. She emptied her wine before the steaks were done and poured herself another portion. There had been little conversation since Cal dropped them off.

"Is medium rare good for you?" Roy asked.

"Sure."

"Well, then, here they come."

"Steak sauce?" Roy asked.

"No, thank you."

Midway through the steaks, Allison emptied the Cabernet bottle into her glass. Roy started a Pinot Noir. Still no conversation until Roy opened up.

"Look, Allie, we have to talk about this. We need to agree to a solution."

Allison stood up and walked unsteadily and silently to the great room. Dennison followed her.

"If you persist in having the baby, you should confide in your grandfather and go live with him until the baby is born. We can

45

then decide what the next step will be."

"What the next step will be? That's a laugh. The next step will be fuck off, Allison."

She swung around suddenly to face him, causing the towel to fall from her hair. Her eyes were on fire as she started screaming.

"You son-of-a-bitch, you never intended to leave her for me. There's been nothing but bullshit from you. Now that you've knocked me up, you're done with me."

Allison had totally lost it, screaming profanities and sobbing at the same time. Roy grabbed her upper arms and tried to shake her back to sanity. She pulled away from him, turning toward the fire and tripped on the shag rug. She fell toward the fireplace and struck the right side of her head full force on the corner of the stone and marble ledge bordering the fireplace. She lied there, still and bleeding profusely.

Dennison felt faint, took a deep breath and sat down. Looking at Allison, still seeping blood with eyes half open, he assumed she might already be dead. He checked a second time for a pulse and there was none. He now had a graver issue than the pregnancy to deal with.

Assessing risk/benefit ratios had been one of his strengths as a corporate lawyer. Considering whether the suggested synergies were sufficient to justify a client's proposed acquisition or whether it was wise for a client to prosecute a patent infringement litigation were moments when Dennison excelled. Those kinds of decisions were made in calm atmosphere after hours of thought and consultation. The atmosphere in the great room of Dennison's Den was desperate, not calm. There could be no hours of thought and no one to consult with.

As if in a trance, he sat there staring at Allison's dead body. He began sweating from his forehead and neck as a wave of nausea started in his throat and passed down to his core. Feeling he was going to vomit, he went to the powder room and splashed cold water on his face. He returned to look again at Allison. His mind was racing and raised a question he feared to answer.

Did I cause her to fall? Were my hands still on her when she started to go down? Oh my God. Poor Allison.

What were his options. *No matter what I do, my infidelity will be known to Clara, the office and the whole city. I will just have to deal with that. If I report an accident and call for an ambulance, there would be an investigation into whether her death was an accident or a homicide. When the autopsy established she was pregnant, I would be suspected. What would be my chances on trial for murder before a UP jury? This rich Chicago lawyer who impregnated this innocent girl, twenty years his junior, disrespecting his wife and three children. Guilty! Guilty! Guilty! If I don't report this and don't call for an ambulance, I will have to dispose of her body. That would at least spare Clara the humiliation of knowing I had impregnated the poor girl. I could make it appear that she died or disappeared elsewhere, totally unrelated to me. That's the option I prefer, but I will need help.*

He called his caretaker, Frank Wallensky, said he needed his help and asked him to come to the house as soon as possible. He was not happy with his choice of Frank as an accomplice, but there was no one else. Wallensky lived alone and was a bit too simple minded to ever hold down a regular job. He was recommended to Dennison by his building contractor when Dennison's Den was being constructed. Wallensky, he told Dennison, had some basic carpentry and plumbing skills and was fully capable of maintaining landscaping and periodically checking on the security of the house. Most importantly, Wallensky was loyal to a fault.

Ten minutes passed and Frank was at the front door. An imposing muscular figure at six foot three and 235 pounds, he was led into the great room.

"Oh, oh. You got a mess here," Frank said.

"It was an accident. She tripped on the rug, fell and hit her head. She's dead. I need your help to get her out of here. I'll do the clean-up. We need to make it look like she left the Den and disappeared, and make sure her body is never discovered. You're going to help me stay out of trouble, because if I get into trouble, that will be the end of your job here. Do you follow me?"

"Yes, Mr. Dennison. I understand."

"When this is over there will be a big bonus coming to you. After you do everything by my instructions, you'll forget you ever came here tonight or anything about this poor girl. If anyone ever asks, you know absolutely nothing about it. You got that? I'm counting on you, Frank."

"Yes sir, Mr. Dennison. I got it. I know nothing about it."

After wrapping Allison's blood-soaked wound and hair in the bath towel she had been using and rolling her up in one of the extra blankets, Wallensky took the body to the garage. Dennison assisted him in the gruesome task of pressing her fingers to the steering wheel of the jeep, establishing fingerprints. Frank was to return at 1:00 a.m. with a shovel and take Allison in his truck at least ten miles deep into the woods, dig a grave at least four feet deep, and bury her there.

"Find a spot where people are unlikely to ever be. Nowhere alongside any road—deep into the woods. You understand what I'm saying?"

"I understand—deep into the woods."

While Frank was occupied with his ghoulish chore, Roy was busy with his clean-up. He used Clorax to clean blood off the stone ledge of the fireplace and wherever he found blood splatter. He used landscaper shears to cut off about fifteen inches of the blood-stained rug that ran along the stone ledge. More than that length of rug extended under the furniture so that the cut end could be pulled to its' former position adjacent to the ledge, restoring the rug to its normal dimensions. He then repeated the bleach cleaning.

When Frank returned, Dennison asked, "Is it done?"

"It's done."

"Where did you go?"

"North about ten miles, then deep in the woods, just like you asked."

"Thank you. Sorry to get you mixed up with this. I thought it was the best solution for both of us. I'm going to take the jeep and park it on the side of the road on the way into town, on Route 45. You leave ten minutes after I do and pick me up. You understand? Don't just nod your head. Tell me you understand."

"I understand."

"Tell me what you're going to do after I leave?"

"I wait ten minutes and then pick you up on 45."

"Perfect."

At 3:15 a.m. there wasn't a soul awake in Watersmeet Township. Roy wore gloves to avoid leaving prints on the door handle or any other parts. He held the steering wheel by its interior spokes so as not to disturb Allison's prints. He saw no vehicles going either direction as he cruised down Route 45, pulling to the shoulder about a half mile north of Mandy's Motel. He then hammered a large nail into one of the jeep's rear tires, causing it to slowly flatten. Right on schedule came Wallensky. He dropped Roy off at the house and waved goodbye. For one last reminder of silence, Roy put his index finger vertically to his lips as Wallensky drove off.

As he was washing his hands in the kitchen sink, he began thinking. *Can I trust Frank with my life? Could he withstand any kind of questioning? Nobody would miss him if he was gone. Jesus, what are you thinking? What's happening to me? Am I fucked?*

CHAPTER TEN

From 5:00 a.m. to 7:00 a.m. Roy dozed on and off in his chair in the great room. At 7:00 a.m. he called the Sheriff's office to report Allison's failure to return after she left last night to pick up some beauty supplies she needed from the general store, which stayed open until nine. He spoke to Wickerham who asked, "Why'd you wait so long to call?"

"She left around 8:00 p.m. last night. I had so much wine I fell asleep on the couch at around 9:00 p.m. and woke up about a half hour ago. I checked the bedroom. No Allison. The jeep isn't here either."

"What's her full name?"

"Allison Jameson."

"I'll get on it right away. What color is the jeep and what are the plates?"

Roy furnished the information and pleaded with Wickerham to get back to him as soon as he learned anything. His heart was pounding, as he wondered whether his first statement of lies would ring true and be accepted as fact. As he went to the kitchen and started making himself a cup of coffee, his phone rang.

"It's 7:40 a.m. and I'm here at the dock waiting for you guys."

"Of course. I'll be right down." He totally forgot about Cal.

As he hurried down the steps to the dock, he was thinking

how much he should tell Cal.

"Sorry, my friend. My girl is missing and I've been beside myself all morning, calling in to the Sheriff. I forgot about our appointment but of course I'll pay you for the day. Please forgive me for not catching you before you left home." Cooley stepped out of his boat onto the dock.

"That's awful. When did you last see her?"

"About 8:00 p.m. last night. She took the jeep and was going to the general store for some stuff. I overdid the wine and conked out around 9:00 p.m., sleeping until 6:00 a.m. when I started going crazy about her not being back."

Dennison was purposefully repeating his story to ingrain the details in his mind. He knew he would have to repeat them again and again in the future. Frank would only have to remember that he knew nothing, if he was ever asked.

"Did she drive that jeep before? Maybe she had some trouble with it and she's stuck somewhere," Cal said.

"I let her drive a little coming up from Eagle River. She knew how to handle it. I hope you're right and she turns up in one piece. I got to tell you, I'm worried sick about her."

"I don't know how I could help, but please, Roy, if there's anything I can do…"

* * *

Jackson, packed and ready to leave town, stopped at the café for breakfast at about 9:30 a.m. The place was empty. Molly let him use the phone to call his wife as long as he determined the charges and paid for it.

"I heard that Dennison was up here this weekend with a girlfriend. If the office gossip is correct, it might be Allison Jameson," Marvell said.

"This Allison, was she in the same junior partner class with you?" Louanna asked.

"Yes, that's Allison, and Dennison wasted no time getting her involved in some of his major projects. That's what started the rumors."

After breakfast, Jackson started his seven-hour drive to Chicago.

* * *

Emma was surprised to see Cal pulling into the driveway so early in the morning. She went to the back door and called out.

"What are you doing back here on such a beautiful day?"

"Day was canceled 'cause that young Allison is missing. Disappeared last night."

"Oh, dear God!" Emma said, thinking, *please, Lord, not again.*

Cal walked up the stoop and peered through the screen door.

"I know what you're thinking, but good news may yet come. Plenty of time to suffer if the news is bad."

"I know, sweetie, I know. Poor Mr. Dennison. He must be a fright."

"He sure didn't look good when I saw him this morning. He must have really been drunk last night to let that girl go out with the jeep by herself."

"Is that what happened?"

"Yep. She never came back."

CHAPTER ELEVEN

Wickerham was at the front door with a lady pulling court reporter equipment. Dennison came to the door with a somber face.

"I've got some information for you, and it's not good," Wickerham said.

Dennison covered his face in his hands and turned away. They moved into the great room and sat in the oversized chairs, facing the scene of last night's horror, while the steno set up her equipment.

"Did you find her?" Dennison asked in a whisper.

"No, but we found the jeep. It was parked on the shoulder of Route 45, about a half mile north of Mandy's. It had a flat right rear tire which had picked up a nail. The keys were still in it, but no sign or evidence of the girl. We're in the process of trucking the jeep to Marquette, where they have the capacity to do a forensic workup on it. When we're done here, you can come back to town with me and I'll get you a car to use until we drive you back to the airport. Meanwhile, I'm here to get a recorded statement from you as a base line for starting our investigation."

"What do you make of all that?" Dennison asked

"I'm afraid it looks like she was distressed with a flat tire and someone offering help picked her up. Not hearing from her after that is not good."

"Jesus Christ! I can't believe this is happening."

The questioning started with Roy repeating the circumstances leading up to Allison leaving and his falling asleep.

"What was she wearing when she left?"

"The last I remember, she had her white bathrobe on. She obviously threw something on after that, but I have no recollection of seeing what she was wearing when she left the house. I consumed half a bottle of Cabernet and then the whole bottle of another red. I shouldn't have let her go."

"How much did she have to drink before she went out?"

"One or two glasses of wine, I think, with her steak dinner."

"Have you communicated with her parents or anyone else about the situation?"

"No. No one. She has no living parents, just a grandfather in Columbus, Ohio, but I don't know how to reach him."

"By the way, do you know Marvell Jackson?"

"Of course. He's a lawyer in my firm. Why do you ask?"

"Did you know he was up here this weekend, staying at Mandy's?"

"No, I didn't know he was coming up this weekend."

"I take it Marvell knew Allison. Are you aware of any issues they had between them?"

"Not really. Nothing other than the competition associates normally have to progress in the firm."

"What kind of competition is that?"

"Just trying to get an edge to become junior partner. Actually, they both became junior partners together about three weeks ago."

"OK Give me a description of Allison. Hair, height, weight, anything else."

"I would estimate five foot six, 120 pounds. Hair somewhere between light brown and blonde, a very pretty young woman. Is there any hope of finding her—alive?"

"Sure there is, if we can find her in the next forty-eight hours. That's all I need for now. When were you expecting to return to Chicago?"

"I was scheduled for tonight, but I'll stay on for the next forty-eight hours, at least. I want to be as helpful as possible. You will do your best to find her, won't you, Jesse?"

"You can count on me, Mr. Dennison. Let's get going now and get you a car."

As he walked Wickerham to the door, Dennison thought, *Marvel picked a bad time to be up here. Jesse's already got him as a suspect.*

CHAPTER TWELVE

Wickerham was beset with a sense of dread as he left Dennison's Den. He had gone through this once before, six years ago. He took the lead role in the investigation of the missing Margie Leonard, a University of Wisconsin coed, who was spending her summer helping her aunt in the kitchen of her uncle's fishing lodge on Crooked Lake. Almost every day in the late afternoon she'd walk and jog two miles along Crooked Lake Road, returning in time to shower and set the tables for the evening meal. One day she didn't return.

There were no clues to follow. He checked the three motels in the township. No strangers had checked into any of them during the two or three days before and after the disappearance. The only guests were several fishermen, regulars every year, and family members visiting the permanent residents of the area. The same was true of the fishing lodges. His interviews of dozens of those male visitors, including those staying in the trailer park, produced nothing. Several days later her body was found on the west shore of Crooked Lake. Wickerham viewed her half-nude body at that location. He was haunted for weeks with the vision of her gray face and eyes without pupils, her twisted legs and weeds of some kind protruding from her mouth. Later it turned out she had been raped as well as strangled. His reporting the finding of her body to her aunt and uncle and to her parents was the most difficult thing he ever had to do as a member of the Sheriff's Department.

It was generally concluded that no local was involved, that the responsible person was passing through and could be anywhere in the country. After six years, it continued to be a cold case. Reports of the missing Miss Allison were bound to reawaken fears in the community that were rampant for weeks after Margie's body was found. Wickerham was anxious to get started. The two things that distinguished Allison's case from Margie's clueless murder, making it a case more likely to be solved, were the existence of the vehicle and the presence of a stranger in town.

Gathering a crew to search the woods for a missing person had, in the past, been successful when the person was missing from a campsite or other specific location, suggesting the person had lost their way. In this case, as in the Margie Leonard case, where there was no starting point, a foot search of the endless woods surrounding Watersmeet on all sides would be impractical. Even a helicopter search, which would be available if indicated, would be useless. The ninety per cent evergreen woods of the UP were so thick that very little ground could be inspected from the air.

Wickerham chose to create a missing person pamphlet to be distributed throughout the township, including all businesses, motels, lodges, schools, public launching sites and public posting areas. The pamphlet described Allison, "last seen wearing a white terry-cloth bathrobe, but likely was in street clothes". It concluded, ominously, with "Be on the lookout for articles of clothing or recently disturbed ground in the woods or shorelines."

After fixing Roy up with one of the two unidentified vehicles owned by the department, Wickerham headed over to Mandy's. Widow Mandy Oberman owned, managed, cleaned and maintained the ten-unit motel all by herself, except for her sixteen-year-old niece who came in when needed to help with laundry. The vacancy sign was up year-round, except for the three big holiday weekends.

Mandy had put on quite a bit of weight since her husband, fifteen years her senior, passed away from a stroke four years ago. Her increasing weight matched the growing difficulty she had in running the business. The *For Sale* sign had been up for two years without a single inquiry. Selling a business in Watersmeet was about as promising an undertaking as selling bathing suits in Antarctica. One tried and tried, and finally just closed shop and walked away. It's a familiar story. Folks who love the outdoors, fishing, hunting, the woods and waters move north, buying into motels, cafes, bait shops, small resorts, etc. After a few years of hard work, harsh winters and little time to enjoy fishing and hunting, they want out. There is no out, no buyers. They suffer until they walk away with nothing to show for it.

Wickerham stepped into the office and found Mandy seated on her stool behind the counter, eating strawberry ice cream out of a quart container.

"Morning, Mandy. Kind of early for ice cream."

"Never too early for me, Jesse. What are you up to today?"

"I'm looking for Jackson. I see his car is gone. Did he check out?"

"He checked out this morning. Said he was going to stop at the café for breakfast. Might still be there."

"OK, I'll try the café. Save some of that ice cream for desert tonight."

Five minutes later, Wickerham walked into the empty café.

"Hi, Molly. That black guy been in here this morning?"

"He just left here not even ten minutes ago. Said he was going to gas up at Shell before heading back to Chicago. He's probably still there."

The deputy hurried to the Shell station and found Jackson replacing his tank cap.

"Glad I caught you. Your associate, Allison Jameson, was up here for the weekend with Mr. Dennison, and she's missing."

"What do you mean, 'she's missing'?

"Just that. Drove herself to town last night and never came back. I'm sure you want to help us find her, so I need you to hang around. Your boss is staying on for the same reason."

"I didn't even know Allison was here. I'd like to help, but I don't know how I can."

"Well, there's no one here that knows anything about her, except for Dennison. You might be able to fill in on stuff he knows nothing about. It's important that you stay."

CHAPTER THIRTEEN

Back in his great room, Dennison was trying to summon the courage to make the difficult phone calls to Clara and his partner.

"Hello Clara, darling. Don't speak, just listen. I'm in a rush to get to the Sheriff's office. I brought a young junior partner with me on this trip to spend some time working on a pending merger. She's missing up here. An investigation is underway and I'll have to stay around and be as helpful as possible for the next few days. You'll never know how sorry I am. I love you."

Silence—then "She...? I...don't know what to say. Hope *she* turns up." With that, she abruptly hung up.

At least she didn't ask any more difficult questions. That'll come later, he thought. Next, an equally difficult call to his partner.

"Hello, Roy. How's fishing, buddy?"

"Goddamn it, Dan, I really screwed up. I came up here with one of our juniors, Allison Jameson. We've been having a bit of a thing going on. Please forgive me for being so stupid."

Dan interrupts, "That is pretty stupid, I agree."

"You didn't let me finish. Allison is missing. She left the house to drive into town to get some things she needed last night—and never returned."

"What! Jesus Christ. What the hell happened to her? Are the police involved?"

"They found the jeep she was driving on the side of the road with a flat tire. The deputy thinks someone must have stopped and picked her up. No word from her since."

"That doesn't sound good."

"Can you locate her grandfather in Columbus, Ohio and let him know what's going on? It's a lousy job to ask you to do, I know. He's a retired Senator Jameson and shouldn't be hard to find."

"I'll cover it."

"Thanks, Dan. I'm so sorry about all this. I don't know how long I'll be here, but I'll keep in touch."

"Do you need any help there? Do you want me to have Clyde Fuller call you?"

"No. I don't see any need for a lawyer at this point."

CHAPTER FOURTEEN

It was rare for Emma Cooley to have her husband at home on a sunny Sunday in May. She made the most of it by preparing a Sunday brunch of chicken and dumplings. While partaking of the meal at the kitchen table, Emma could no longer contain her fear and emotions.

"Oh God, Cal, do you think the same thing happened to this Allison girl as with Margie?"

"It doesn't look good. If she doesn't turn up today or tomorrow, we better prepare for the worst." He put his spoon down and reached across the table to pat Emma's hand.

When Margie Leonard was first missing the general assumption in the community, not shared by her aunt and uncle, was that she returned to school early or got lost in the woods. Foul play was not even considered. That kind of thing didn't happen in Watersmeet Township. After her body was found, fear gripped the township. Women didn't go out alone, day or night. It happened early in July, the beginning of the summer resort season. There were numerous reservation cancelations due to the highly publicized unsolved crime. The killing of Margie Leonard seriously affected the psyche of the community as well as its economic health.

"Dennison, alone in that house, he must be agonizing about

the girl and how he's going to deal with all of this at home. Isn't there anything we can do for him?" Emma asked.

"You're right. I guess he knows me better than anyone else up here. Maybe we should invite him for dinner or something like that?"

"That's a grand idea. Why don't you call him? I've got plenty of time to cook up something nice for the three of us tonight."

*   *   *

Waiting for Marvell's return, Wickerham sat at the counter and engaged Molly in conversation.

"Did the black guy seem nervous to you this morning?"

"Not especially, I don't think. Want a coffee?"

"No thanks. Did you have any conversation with him?"

"Nothin', other than getting his order."

"Did he make any phone calls? I think I will take a coffee, black."

"He did make a call—to his wife, I think."

"Did you hear any of it?"

"I couldn't make out what he was saying, yet I did hear him mention a name."

"What was that?" Jesse folded his arms on the counter and leaned forward.

"He mentioned the name 'Allison'."

The door opened and Marvell entered. Wickerham walked toward a table and motioned Marvell to join him.

"I can't believe that Allison is up here—and missing!"

"What did you do last night?" Jesse lit a cigarette and offered one to Marvell, who declined.

"Why is that important?"

"I'll explain that in a moment, but first answer the question."

"I spent most of the day and evening up at Lake Superior. Went to Porcupine Mountain and then to Ironwood where I had dinner. Got back to Mandy's at 10:00 p.m., or a little before."

"Did you see any car parked on the shoulder of 45 as you were returning to Mandy's?"

"Don't remember seeing anything?"

"What's the name of the place where you ate dinner in Ironwood?"

"Are you suspecting me of something?" Marvell was growing uncomfortable with this third degree.

"No, not necessarily. Just being a good cop and covering all the bases."

"I think it was called Rusty's BBQ."

"Did you see Mandy when you came in?"

"No. I went direct to my unit."

"I'd like you to stay in town for a couple of nights, just like your boss is doing. I want to meet with you some time tomorrow to get more information about Allison. Is that all right with you?"

"Of course. I'll stay if you think I can be helpful."

CHAPTER FIFTEEN

Roy came in with a bottle of red wine which he handed to Cal, saying "This is for Emma and me." He didn't remember ever seeing Cal without his crumbling black leather cap on his head. The sight was eye-popping. He had a wide ring of stark white skin between his black wetted down hair line and the rest of his dark, weather-beaten face.

"Emma!" Cal shouted toward the kitchen, "Roy's here. Come out and say hello."

In all the years Roy fished with Cal, he had only met Emma once. She was sitting on the porch in her rocking chair when Roy came by to pay Cal for his guiding. Tonight was the first time he had ever been inside their home.

"Good evening Mr. Dennison. Welcome to our home. Have a seat while I put the wine in the fridge to give it just a little chill."

"Good to see you, Emma. Not too much of a chill on the red wine. Please call me Roy."

He sat in a worn but comfortable pillowed chair while Cal sat on the flower- patterned couch at a right angle to him. The room was small and the furniture somewhat tattered and scratched, probably as old as the house itself.

"Those are a couple of nice walleyes you have on the wall," Roy said.

"I caught those the first year I was guiding, when I thought mounting fish was a good idea. They been up there over twenty years. Never mounted another fish after that. Big waste of money."

Emma walked in with the wine and a coke for Cal and took a seat next to her husband on the couch.

"Has there been any news about the young lady today?" she asked.

"No, nothing. We're waiting to get a report from Marquette on their examination of the jeep. Hope they find some clues."

"I want to be honest with you Mr. Dennison... Roy, I never approved of your bringing the young lady with you on these trips. Not that it's for me to approve or disapprove—it's just the way I feel about those things. Cal knows how I feel, and he always tells me to mind my own business, and he's right, that's exactly what I should do. But honestly, my heart goes out to you."

"OK Emma. You've had your say," Cal said dismissively as he turned to Roy and shook his head.

Roy looked crestfallen, his shoulders drooped and his head turned down.

"I'll never forgive myself for this mistake. For all I know, it may have cost Allison her life, and may have cost me my family."

"Oh my," Emma said, getting teary eyed as she rose from the couch and headed for the kitchen to check the dinner.

They dined in the small dining room, at the table that seated six. Emma set out sautéed walleyes covered with flaked almonds, mashed potatoes and green beans, all family style.

"How long you planning on staying at the lake?" Cal asked.

"As long as the authorities think I can be helpful. I got a call today from one of the lawyers in my firm who happens to be staying in Watersmeet this weekend. I didn't know he was coming up. He's here looking for a vacation cabin on the lake for him and his wife this summer. He knows Allison quite well and Deputy Wickerham has asked him to stay around for a couple of days."

"Is he staying at Mandy's?"

"Yes. Why do you ask?"

"Cause I heard there was a black guy came into town and was staying there."

"That's him, Marvell Jackson. He's a junior partner in my firm."

"Well, I got to tell you Watersmeet Township is not a friendly place for black folks to be visiting. Don't get me wrong. I don't feel prejudice towards them. They coming up here doesn't cause me any concern. But the deputy you mentioned, Wickerham, has a different idea about that. I'd bet he conveyed that attitude to your man already. Jesse is a good cop, but sometimes he can get a little heavy handed."

"He didn't say anything to me about that. I'm meeting Marvell for breakfast at the café in the morning. I'll ask him about it."

As Roy prepared to leave after dinner, Emma said, "I want you to know I will be praying for Allison's safe return and praying for you to find peace." She shook her head and dabbed a hankie at her eyes.

Walking to the front door with Cal, he pulled a wad of money from his pocket, peeled off eleven $100 bills, and handed them to Cal.

"Maybe we'll do this again next year—or maybe we won't."

.

CHAPTER SIXTEEN

Dennison slept only in little spurts during the night. He couldn't stop thinking of his stupidity in making the rash decision to remove and hide Allison's body. *Staking my life on half-witted Frank Wallensky. Who is the greater imbecile?* He finally gave up on sleep at 6:00 a.m. He did his usual stretching exercises, then took a thirty-minute walk up and back on Crooked Lake Road. Walking the shoulder on his way out, he came across a fresh, bloody deer road kill. The scavenger birds scattered as he approached. He shuddered as the bloody image of Allison filled his mind. He returned on the other side of the road to avoid another encounter with death.

After a shower and shave, he made himself a cup of coffee. His appointment with Marvell was at 9:30 a.m. At 8:00 a.m. his phone rang. It was his partner.

"Good morning. We need to talk. There's a short piece on page four of the *Trib* this morning about a young female Chicago lawyer reportedly missing in the Upper Peninsula. For some reason neither her name nor yours was mentioned, but I have to handle this some way in the office this morning, and I want your input on how to go about it," Rogers said.

"Let me think about it and I'll call you right back."

Dennison cautioned himself to think rationally. He didn't

want to get this wrong. When he was ready, he called Rogers back.

"First of all, just send the memo to all the juniors and their staff. Doesn't have to go to the whole office. Send a copy of the memo to the managing partner in Philly and let him decide how to handle it there. As far as the memo is concerned, Allison came with me to the UP for some concentrated work on the United Supply Corporation merger. Allison is missing since she went to town on her own. Marvell Jackson is also in the area. He and Mr. Dennison are staying on as long as they can be helpful. End it with saying the firm will keep you informed of developments, and we all pray for Allison's safe return."

"Got it. Anything new on Allison?"

"I haven't talked to anyone yet this morning. I'm meeting Marvell for breakfast in about an hour. I didn't know he was up here. Let me know the reaction to the memo."

* * *

The few eyes left in the café all turned to Marvell, as he entered. He smiled returning glances and took a seat at a table for two. His self-consciousness dissolved as he rose to greet Dennison.

"I had no idea you were going to be up here this weekend," Roy said.

"I didn't know you were either. This Allison business is just awful. Anything new since yesterday?"

"Afraid not. She came up here with me to work on the United Supply Corporation merger. We were behind schedule and needed to really get our heads down." Dennison focused on Marvell's eyes and expression to see if there was an iota of believability to that story. He saw no clue.

"I understand. I know she was worried about meeting some deadlines on that deal. She's such a good kid. I hope this ends well."

"Has Deputy Wickerham been in touch with you?"

"I've had three conversations with him and none of them have been pleasant. First of all, he's as racist as they come. Second, I feel like he suspects me of having done something wrong."

"Why do you say that?"

"Just the kind of questions he was asking me yesterday. I had started for home and he called me back and wants me to stay around, just like you."

"Have you talked to the office yet?" Dennison asked.

"No, I haven't. I spoke to Louanna yesterday. She knows I'm going to be here a bit longer. Should I be worried about this guy, Wickerham?"

"Nothing, other than his racist attitude, which could lead to some trouble if you stay around too long."

"I just put a $300 deposit on a cabin for two weeks this summer. You've got me thinking I should cancel that plan and stop payment on that check."

"If you're worried how safe it would be, you're better off canceling. Worrying about safety is no way to spend a vacation. Why don't you check out of Mandy's and come stay at the house? It's a lot more comfortable and the price is right."

"That's a nice idea. Thank you. I'll do it. I'll come by the Den around 2:00 p.m. OK?"

"I'll be looking out for you."

As a young man in Atlanta, Marvell was inspired by the deeds and philosophy of congressman John Lewis. He met Lewis when he was seventeen years old and Lewis was serving as an Atlanta City Councilman. The meeting occurred in 1985 when Lewis visited a community organizing committee where Jackson was volunteering after school. The mantra he acquired from that man was to stand up for what is right and not be silent in the face of wrong.

Marvell attended night classes at Emory University School of Law in Atlanta. During his final year he met Dennison, who had come to Atlanta on a mission to recruit a black lawyer for his firm. Dennison, a strong advocate for more diversity in his law office, had recently welcomed several women associates, but there were no blacks on the roster. Dennison had published an invitation to graduating students in the three major Atlanta area law schools having predominantly black students, to appear for recruiting interviews.

The invitation was limited to those who would consider acquiring an Illinois license and move to Chicago. Marvell was ready to leave Atlanta. He aced the interview and accepted the invitation. Passing up the Georgia bar, he moved to Chicago, studied for and passed the Illinois Bar exam on the first try. On April 30, 1993, the same day World No.1 tennis player Monica Seles was stabbed in Hamburg, Marvell Jackson became an associate of Rogers and Dennison.

CHAPTER SEVENTEEN

The memo was distributed at 11:00 a.m. At 11:45 a.m., junior partner Cathy Riley buzzed Mr. Rogers' secretary on the intercom and requested to see Rogers before going to lunch.

Sitting up straight in a client chair with hands clasped and resting in her lap, thin and tidy Miss Riley addressed the senior partner.

"Mr. Rogers, sir, after reading your memo this morning I felt compelled to come and talk to you. Allison Jameson is my very best friend. We have been close since we both started here about three years ago."

"All right, Miss Riley, get to the point."

"We confide in each other and she has confided in me. I would never say anything about it, but now with this terrible news about her being missing, I feel I must…"

"And?"

"There may have been a business component to this trip, but it was far more than that. She went away with him on the same trip last spring. They were having an affair. She told me all about it and was very ambivalent about their relationship, him being married with a family and all. With her missing, I thought it was important that the truth be known."

This didn't sound good to Rogers, still maybe not so serious.

Miss Riley actually knew what was going on here, while everyone else would probably be presuming the same thing.

"You did right to come and tell me this. For now, for the benefit of Miss Jameson and the firm, it would be best not to discuss this with anyone else. Let's wait to see how events develop. Best result would be for Allison to be found and she can then participate on deciding how to handle the situation. Do you agree with me on that?"

"Yes, of course I do. Thank you for hearing me out. I won't discuss the matter with anyone in the office."

* * *

Wickerham called Marvell at the motel to schedule an afternoon meeting. Marvell said he was moving into Dennison's house and they could meet there at 3:00 p.m. The deputy said, "He wants you to move in? That's pretty strange."

"Nothing strange about it. Strange is the comment you just made."

"Well, never you mind. See you at three."

Wickerham showed up with his court reporter. They sat on the porch overlooking the lake. Dennison, playing host, walked out with lemonades for them. Did Wickerham mind if he sat in on the meeting?

"Why not? Maybe you can help with some of the info. This is Deputy Jesse Wickerham questioning Marvell Jackson on May 19, 1997. Now, Marvell, let's talk about Allison. How long have you known her?"

"About three years. I was already with the firm for a year when she joined three years ago."

"So, you've been in competition with her for three years?"

"What are you talking about?"

"Mr. Dennison told me that you guys had a competition going."

"I was referring to the general competition among associates trying to rise to junior partners," Dennison said.

"Oh, sure. There was a bunch of us doing our best to impress the partners and in that sense we were competing."

"You and Allison became junior partners at the same time?"

"Yes. Three or four weeks ago. There are now seventeen juniors."

"Has there been any specific competition between the two of you during that time?"

"I wouldn't say so. All the juniors are under the supervision of one of the seniors. I would have preferred Mr. Dennison to Mr. Rogers, only because I was more interested in his area of expertise. Allison got Dennison and I got Rogers, but I never had any problem with that."

"When I spoke to you on the phone after you left for Chicago, you told me you didn't know Allison was here."

"That's right."

"The waitress at the café, Molly, told me a short time before, that you were on the phone in the café and she heard you mention the name 'Allison'. Tell me about that phone call."

"That was to my wife, telling her I was on my way home. I told her I had heard that Mr. Dennison was up here with a young woman. As a matter of fact, I heard that from you. I mentioned to my wife that the young girl might be Allison, because of rumors in the office that she might be having an affair with Mr. Dennison. Sorry, Mr. Dennison, but that's the truth."

"That's all right. You tell the truth and you'll have nothing to be concerned about," Dennison said.

"We'll see about that. What time did you finish your dinner at Rusty's BBQ?"

"About 8:00 p.m. or a little after."

"What did you do between 8:00 p.m. and the time you got back to Mandy's at about 10:00 p.m.?"

"Nothing, just made the drive. It's over fifty miles. Took about an hour and a half. I keep the speed down in the dark."

"Didn't make any stops?"

"No, sir."

"I ask you again, did you see Dennison's jeep on the shoulder of 45 as you got close to Mandy's?"

"Same answer. No, sir."

Dennison was becoming impatient with the tone of Wickerham's questioning. He stood, pushed his open palms forward as if stopping traffic.

"Jesus, Jesse. Sounds like you're trying to make some kind of case against Marvell. That's ridiculous. I'm not Marvell's lawyer, but as a friend I'm telling him to terminate any further conversations with you. I've heard you're not too fond of blacks setting foot in Watersmeet Township. I hope that has nothing to do with your picking on Marvell. We all want to get to the bottom of this, but Marvell is not your answer."

"I expect you ought to just let me do my job the way I see

fit. I'm done here today. You gentlemen will stick around for a couple more days?" They both nodded affirmatively. "Good," Wickerham said as he and the court reporter packed up and left.

CHAPTER EIGHTEEN

In 1947, six men returning from service in World War Two, including the bait man Bert Clinton, wanted to start a VFW Post in Watersmeet Township. Their application to the national organization was declined, based on the size of the community and the limited number of potential members. Undaunted, they proceeded to establish their own unofficial VFW Club. They rented an old abandoned house on Oak Street and eventually managed to get a beer and wine license from the county. You didn't have to be a vet to be a member. Only requirements were you had to be male, over twenty-one and willing to pay dues. They reached their peak membership of nineteen by the mid-eighties. By 1997, the club's roster had shrunk to twelve.

The twelve included Bert Clinton and Cal Cooley. Clinton was a marine who served in the South Pacific. In late 1942, while fighting on Guadalcanal in the Solomon Islands, he had two toes on his right foot shot off by a Japanese sniper. He had been on the island for thirty days in constant fear of being picked off by a Jap in a tree. He was in face-to-face combat at least three times. He'd seen many men he knew die and had caused the death of many others he didn't know. His three months in the hospital were not so much for his toes, but mainly for what was then called shell shock or nervous breakdown, more commonly referred to now as PTSD.

Cal Cooley never served in the military. His father saw some action in the Korean War and thereafter became an active member of the VFW Post in Eagle River. After he passed away from a heart attack in1985, Bert Clinton persuaded Cal to join the club in Watersmeet. It gave Cal something to do on Monday nights when Emma was dedicated to watching double feature movies on television. This was Monday night and Cal was off to the VFW Club.

It was a quiet night at the club. Just a half dozen men smoking cigars, drinking beer and watching a rerun of a Packer game on television. Cal and Bert sat together, as they usually did. Bert with his bottle of Schlitz and Cal with his coke.

"Did you hear any more about the nigger in town?" Bert asked.

"He's a lawyer in Dennison's law firm. Came up to rent a cabin for summer."

"No shit. What a fucking stupid thing is that. First of all, what asshole would have the balls to rent him a cabin?"

"I'm the asshole," interjected Rudy Schmidt, having overheard the conversation. "I rented him my log cabin on Crooked Lake."

"You better be ready to explain yourself to Wickerham when he hears about it," Bert said.

"I refused at first. Then he started citing all kinds of laws to me, so I thought I better do something. I quoted him a price that was double the market and, by God, he took it. Gave me a $300 deposit to hold it."

"That's not going to hold any water with Wickerham. You wait and see," Bert said.

"I don't see why you're in such an uproar about this guy. He must be a very high-class black man to be a lawyer in Dennison's firm. So, he's up here for two weeks in the summer. What's the big deal?" Cal said.

It was a big deal to Bert Clinton. Born to a poor white family eighty years ago in a small town in Mississippi, he grew up in the anti-black culture that dominated life in the redneck Deep South. Nothing about his marine corps experience modified his deeply ingrained prejudice. He took all that baggage with him to the Upper Peninsula.

"Come on, Cal, you know better than that. Give 'em an inch and they'll take a fucking mile. Just because they walk around in a goddamn suit and tie don't mean they're not ready to spread some nasty trouble. I wouldn't be surprised if the nigger didn't have something to do with that girl being missing."

"Calm down now, and don't you go spreading rumors like that. And no offense, but I wish you could find some other way to describe blacks. It's just not a word to be used these days."

"Sorry, Cal. I don't know no other way to describe 'em."

CHAPTER NINETEEN

It was late Tuesday morning when the fax machine in the Sheriff's office started spitting out the four-page forensic report on the jeep. Most aspects of the inspection were negative. There were no suspicious contents, no recent physical damage, a flat tire caused by a nail, and all operating functions of the vehicle, including lights, were in good working condition.

There were some interesting findings with respect to fingerprints. The rain during the day had washed away any exterior prints that may have been present before Allison entered the jeep at about 8:00 p.m. Prints were found in the interior. There were two distinct sets of prints on the steering wheel. Neither print could be matched to anyone in the national database.

The interior prints likely belonged to Allison and Dennison, but Wickerham needed samples to confirm the identification. He called Dennison.

"The report came in on the jeep. Nothing important except for the fingerprints on the steering wheel. Two sets, probably yours and Allison's. I need samples to confirm."

"You can come and get mine, but I don't know about Allison's."

"Maybe there's a glass or a plate or a utensil she handled that hasn't been cleaned yet."

"I'll look around and see what I can find. You want to come by and take mine later today?"

"Yeah. Maybe around 4:00 p.m."

Knowing it was important to establish Allison's prints on the steering wheel, Dennison began a search for a likely source. He found two wine glasses standing in the kitchen sink, where he had placed them earlier, still showing some wine residue.

Wickerham arrived early with a technician. They moved into the kitchen where the technician set up at the counter. Marvell joined them to watch the process. Taking Dennison's prints was a simple procedure. Lifting prints from the glasses was more complicated. The technician handled them by their stems and placed them on the counter. He then dusted the glasses thoroughly with a white powder, causing prints to became visible on both glasses.

Watching the prints appear, Dennison had a vision of Allison in a robe with her hair wrapped in a towel, holding the glass of wine. His knees buckled and he sat in one of the metallic kitchen chairs. The technician continued spreading see-through tape on the clearest and most complete prints he could see. He then lifted the tapes and transferred the prints to contrasting paper, thereby creating a permanent record.

"As long as you're here," Wickerham addressed Marvell, "why don't we take your prints?"

"You don't have to do that if you don't want to," Dennison said.

"No, that's OK. I don't mind being fingerprinted."

"Anything else new in the investigation?" Dennison asked.

"Nothing yet. Deputies are checking the motels and lodges and interviewing a lot of individuals. We are past the forty-eight-hour point without a word from her and no lead on where she might be. That's not good. We're in the process of getting out missing person pamphlets. I'd like you two to stay over until Thursday morning. If nothing breaks by then, you can head on home."

*   *   *

Gogebic County derived its name from the Chippewa Native American word "Agogebic". The most popular translation being "Where the trout make rings upon the water." The county was sprawling, a good fifty-five miles from Watersmeet to the county seat, Bessemer, where the County Prosecutor's offices were located, and another twenty-five miles from Watersmeet to the east border of the county. The County Prosecutor and his First Assistant, Otto Lehman, regularly traveled around the county, holding meetings with law enforcement officials to discuss pending investigations and potential charges.

Lehman was in the Town of Marenisco, thirty miles from Watersmeet, on Wednesday. Deputy Wickerham had a 3:00 p.m. appointment to meet him there regarding the Allison Jameson case. Marenisco was formerly a center for logging and lumber mills. They met in an office in the visitors' center, which occupied the station for the now abandoned railway.

"I hope you're making some progress on the Jameson case. My boss is getting a lot of pressure from the Governor who, I guess, is hearing it from Illinois," Lehman said.

"The only suspect we have is this black guy who's a lawyer in

Roy Dennison's firm."

"What do you have on him?"

"He had the opportunity and I think he lied about not knowing she was up here this weekend. Also, he was in some kind of law competition with her in Chicago. Then there's the fact that Saturday, the day before she disappeared, he wrote a check for $300 as a deposit on a cabin for the summer, stopped payment and canceled the deal on Monday or Tuesday. I know it's not much, but I haven't pushed him very hard yet."

"I read the forensic report on the vehicle. What did you make of that?" Otto asked.

"I got a report on the prints just before I left to meet you. They both, Dennison and Allison, had their prints on the steering wheel."

"Doesn't it strike you as kind of strange there was no print on the outside driver's door handle? It rained for hours that day, which would have wiped the handle clean. It was dry for many hours before 8:00 p.m. You'd think she'd have left some print or partial print on the door handle."

"Maybe she was wearing gloves?"

"It was sixty-three degrees at 8:00 p.m. on Saturday night. Not likely she was wearing gloves. You're going to need some hard evidence or a confession from this black man before we can consider charging."

"One other thing. The jeep was parked on the shoulder facing town, between town and Dennison's place. That would mean she was picked up before she even got to town. I confirmed that with the folks at the general store. They have no recollection of her being in there that night. The black guy insists that he didn't see any vehicle on the side of the road as he approached Mandy's at 10:00 p.m.—yet it must have been there," Wickerham said.

"Keep your mind open to what the hell happened here. There may be other possible explanations to be explored. I'll be in Watersmeet on Monday. Dig in, Jesse—this is our-number one priority."

With that, he called Marvell and asked him to meet at his office so they could have one more conversation before he started back for Chicago in the morning.

"Thanks for coming in. Would you like some water or a coke?" Jesse asked.

"No thanks. I just want to get this over with so I can be on my way."

"I was wondering, how come you canceled your reservation of the cabin for the summer?"

"To tell the truth, I decided not to expose my wife to the hatefulness you expressed in our conversations."

"It was nothing personal. Just thought you ought to know how it is up here. About this Allison business, I got the feeling you're not telling me everything you know about it."

"That, Mr. Deputy, is a misguided feeling. I know nothing about this Allison business."

"It's possible you never intended to rent a cabin up here and only used it as an excuse to be here when you knew Allison was going to be here."

"That's nonsense."

"There are things I know that you don't, so you might as well make it easy on yourself and tell me what happened when you saw that vehicle stopped on the shoulder of 45."

"There's nothing you know that implicates me in any way, and you know it."

"Goddamn it, Marvell, you aren't going to have a moments peace the rest of your life if you don't fess up to what you did with Allison."

Marvell rose, glared at Wickerham and headed toward the door. "I'm leaving for home in the morning. If you need any more information from me, just give me a call."

CHAPTER TWENTY

While Marvell was in town with Wickerham, Dennison was sitting by his fire, reliving the horrifying events that would change his life forever. His ruminations were interrupted by a call from Rogers.

"Hello. Roy…Roy, are you there?"

"Sorry, Dan, lost in some thoughts about Allison. How are things in the office?"

"I have quite a bit to report. The memo went out. No feedback, except for Cathy Riley. Allison told her about the affair and last summer's trip. She thought it was important for me to know."

"Oh shit, that's not good."

"She promised she wouldn't talk about the affair in the office, but nobody's going to believe the business trip story anyhow. That's not the end of it. I spoke to the grandfather in Columbus and told him about her going missing on this business trip. He was devastated, of course. Talked about coming to Chicago or the UP. I persuaded him to sit tight and wait for more information to develop, that I would keep in touch and he could contact the Sheriff in Watersmeet for updates."

"Thanks for doing that."

"Wait, there's more. I received a call today from a lawyer representing the grandfather. Apparently, Cathy called him and told him the story about a business trip was not true. Told him about the affair. He wasted no time retaining counsel."

"Oh God, what a mess. What's your advice, Dan, what should I do?"

"I'm afraid there's nothing until we find out what happened to Allison. The lawyer, by the way, is one of the top civil trial lawyers in the state of Ohio."

"Also, I'm sorry to tell you there's another article in the paper today naming you and Allison and it refers to, and get this, a 'supposed business trip.'"

"I can see Clara's face as she reads that article."

After hanging up, he felt the need for some fresh air. Walking down the steps to the dock, he realized the futility of the business trip story. The *Tribune* had already figured it out. Sitting on the bench at the end of the dock, he was overcome by a feeling of loneliness. He longed to see his family but, at the same time, dreaded returning to Chicago. He thought about some of the tough spots he had been in during the herculean growth of his law firm. He invariably came out of them unscathed. That record was about to come to an end.

* * *

On Thursday morning they packed all their stuff in Marvell's car and set out for breakfast at the café before dropping Dennison at the Eagle River airport. On the way, Dennison asked Marvell to make a stop at Cal's place. There, he told Emma to keep the walleyes for themselves. He didn't think it likely he would have the fish fry this year.

They got to the café around 9:00 a.m. There were just a few customers, and sitting alone in a corner near the bathrooms was Frank Wallensky. Molly served them coffee and took orders. Roy excused himself to go to the men's room. When he came out, he sat down at Frank's table.

"I'm leaving town today and want to make sure you take good care of the house while I'm gone." Also, in a low whispered voice, "You were never at the Den last weekend and you know nothing about the girl or anything. Very important. You know nothing. Right?"

"Yes, Mr. Dennison. I remember that. I know nothing."

"Who was that?" Marvell asked.

"My caretaker. He watches the place for me year-round."

At the airport they shook hands, exchanged hopes and prayers for Allison's safe return and then, after a mournful stare into each other's eyes, embraced in a semi-hug and said goodbye.

Jerry assisted Dennison in bringing his gear to his plane.

"I heard about your companion and didn't want to bother you about the jeep. What's the status of all that?"

"Nothing new on the girl. They took the jeep to Marquette as evidence. I have no idea when it will be released. Could be unavailable for a long time. Check with Wickerham at the Sheriff's office. Meanwhile, find yourself another jeep and call me with the price. I'll send you a check to cover, immediately."

"That sounds fair enough. Have a good flight, Mr. Dennison."

It was a great day for flying. The sparse clouds were high enough that he was able to stay just below them for most of the flight. It was the freest he had felt the entire time in the UP. He was floating above all his problems left below. He was, after all, a good man, a good husband, father, provider, partner, a man of stellar reputation. Could all of that be lost from one mistake?

He was a father. He had been so occupied anticipating Clara's reaction he had given little thought to his children. Jessica was too young to worry about—but Rob and Ben. What had they heard, what did they know, what had Clara told them? He couldn't stand the thought of those boys being disappointed in him. Talk about feet of clay.

Driving to Winnetka, he tried to plan how he would deal with Clara. *Should I admit to the affair? I have no choice. It's definitely coming out. Don't expect any credit for being truthful. Say you're sorry. Beg for forgiveness. It meant nothing. You love only her. She may never forgive me. It may never be the same.*

As he entered the front door, Clara said to the children "Go say hello to your father and then go upstairs to your rooms."

Dennison set down his bags and hugged his three kids, who were wildly happy to see him. This was the first time he had returned from one of these trips without some kind of present for the kids and for Clara. He went to the den and began to mix himself a drink, waiting for Clara to come into the room.

"Clara…I…"

"Save your breath. Do you realize that girl is probably dead, and it's all your fucking fault!"

She was beyond angry. Profanity was not her style. Best for him to say nothing at this point.

"You can stay here for now, but not in my bedroom. Take the

guest room and try to stay out of my sight."

Roy took his travel bag to the guest room, tossed it on the bed, closed the door and sat on the floral-patterned chair he and Clara had selected on one of their shopping sprees with their interior decorator. He stared at his image in the full-length mirror on the back of the guest room door. Not so special anymore. For a fleeting moment he thought he'd be better off dead, but suicide was not in his DNA.

Somehow, he would have to see this through to the end, whatever that might be.

CHAPTER TWENTY-ONE

Deputy Wickerham sat at his desk reviewing the notes he took at the meeting with Otto Lehman. *Keep my mind open to what happened here. Other possible explanations. Lehman was right, it was strange there wasn't any print on the door handle.*

Marvell didn't notice any vehicle parked on the side of the road as he was returning to the motel at about ten. *That doesn't mean it wasn't there. But what if it wasn't there? What if Allison wasn't there with the jeep at all?*

That would explain the absence of her prints on the door handle. Her prints on the steering wheel could have been made at another time. He was getting nowhere with the theory that she was kidnapped at the site of the disabled jeep. Maybe he could develop this other idea further so he would have something new for Lehman when they met on Monday. His next step would be some further questions for Dennison. He placed a call.

"Hello, Mr. Dennison, this is Wickerham. I have a few more questions for you, if you don't mind."

"Actually, Jesse, I just got home. I'm sure you understand I'm in the middle of a lot of explaining. I really can't talk to you now."

"Well, I got a meeting with the prosecutor on Monday, so I need to talk with you before then. Will tomorrow be OK?"

"Sure. I'll be in my office all day tomorrow. You can get me on my cell phone. What's the meeting about on Monday?"

"About a couple of cases we've got going, but mostly about Allison Jameson. I guess the Governor's pushing for some results."

"Are you making any headway on the case?"

"Not really. I've still got my eye on that Jackson fellow, but nothing very concrete. Talk to you tomorrow. Good luck with the explaining."

Roy wished they'd close the investigation and let it become an unsolved cold case. He believed his cover-up would succeed as long as her body was not discovered. *I should have gone with Frank to be sure he picked an undiscoverable location.*

Their time spent together the past few days created a new relationship between Roy and Marvell. No longer just employer-employee, but bonded in the sadness and mystery of the missing Allison. Unfortunate that Marvell was exposed to Wickerham's racism, but his suspicion of Marvell would lead nowhere.

*   *   *

This different approach excited Wickerham. With renewed motivation, he decided not to wait until tomorrow's conversation with Dennison. At 6:30 p.m. he phoned Cal Cooley, interrupted his dinner and said they needed to talk in person. They agreed to meet at the VFW Club at 8:00 p.m.

"I'm trying every way possible to solve this Allison mystery. Damn it, I don't want to draw a blank like I did with poor Margie Leonard."

"I'm here, ain't I? How can I help?"

"You had them out fishing on Friday and Saturday?"

"Sure did."

"What did you notice about them? How were they getting along?"

"They got along fine on Friday. Weather wasn't great. Rained for four or five hours. Allison was uncomfortable and was kind of grouchy about it, but she was a trooper. Rain stopped around 2:00 or 3:00 p.m. and she was her usual upbeat self the rest of the day. You could tell that Roy was really smitten with her."

"What about Saturday?"

"Saturday was a different story. They weren't talking to each other hardly at all. I asked them what was wrong."

"And?" Jesse quickly reached for a note pad and pencil in his shirt pocket.

"Roy said it was something about a personal issue. She agreed."

"Anything else said?"

"No. They were just quiet the rest of the day. I'll tell you—it was not the most comfortable day I've had on the boat."

"How'd you hear she was missing?"

"I came to the dock Sunday morning. They didn't show, so I called Roy and he came right down and told me she was missing—hadn't returned from a trip to town. Where you going with this thing, Jesse?"

"I'm not sure yet, but you've been very helpful. Thanks for coming out."

Wickerham left and went directly home to his cottage on Marion Lake, a few miles from town. He had lived there alone ever since his wife died seven years ago in a high-speed collision with a deer. That tragedy occurred less than two years after they married. Jesse became unsociable after recovering from a bout of depression and focused his life almost entirely on his duties as a deputy sheriff.

Sitting on his porch with a beer, looking out at the hundred-acre Marion Lake, with only two dock lights flickering on the opposite shore, he contemplated what he had heard from Cal Cooley. *Holy Jesus, could Dennison be involved in some way?*

CHAPTER TWENTY-TWO

Jessica was on her knees at the breakfast table playing with some cold cereal when Dennison walked in, dressed for his day at the office. The boys were sleeping late because it was teachers' conference day at the grade school. He offered a "good morning" to Clara, who was busy at the sink. She ignored him. After pouring himself a cup of coffee, he asked "Should I come home for dinner?"

"Let's make this look as normal as possible for the kids until we figure this out, so yes."

Dennison kissed Jessica on the top of her head. As he walked toward the front door, he turned and said goodbye to Clara, avoiding any move suggestive of the usual morning kiss.

Going up the elevator to the seventeenth floor, he had a surge of uneasiness as to how he would be received in the office. *Will anyone believe I am returning from a business trip?*

The receptionist greeted him. "Hi, Mr. Dennison." He nodded, smiled and proceeded toward his corner office at the end of a long corridor, passing numerous secretary cubicles on the left, only three of which were occupied and closed-door lawyer offices on the right. The secretaries acknowledged him with "Good morning Mr. Dennison" as he passed, but only one with eye contact. That was Jennifer, who followed him into his office.

"Good morning boss. Any news on Allison?"

"Not yet. I expect a call from the Sheriff today. Please get my supplemental file on the United Supply Corporation merger and ask Dan if he can pop in to see me. Are things a little bit tense around here?"

"What do you think? Everyone is heartsick about Allison. We had a staff meeting yesterday where we joined in a prayer for her safe return."

"Anything said at the meeting about my trip with her?"

'Of course not. I'll look for Dan."

Roy walked over to his floor-to-ceiling windows and looked down on the plaza. He thought about the call he was expecting from Wickerham. What more could he want to ask him? *Maybe he's looking for more ways to nail Marvell for Allison's disappearance. Could he suspect me of anything? I better be cautious to avoid conflicts with previous statements.* Dan entered the room.

"I'm glad you're back," Dan said.

"I hope you still love me, partner."

"You're making it tough, but I'm trying. Anything new about Allison?"

"Not that I've heard. Sheriff's deputy is calling me today with more questions. I'm hoping he'll have some good news. Heard any more from the Ohio lawyer?"

"No, but I've done some research on him. His name is Ben Greenblatt."

"Jewish guy?"

"Sounds like it. He's had half a dozen multi-million-dollar verdicts and settlements in things like airplane crashes and product liability cases, especially against major pharma companies. He's said to be smart, tenacious and effective with juries."

"Where do we send the check?"

"Very funny."

Jennifer entered, placed a file folder on Dennison's desk, and left. Roy held the folder up, showing Dan it related to the United Supply Corporation matter.

"This was Allison's baby. I'm going to fall behind without her. Do you mind if I borrow Marvell Jackson for the balance of this week to work on the documentation for the merger?"

"I'll check with him this afternoon to see if he's clear of anything pressing this week and get back to you."

Later that day, Jackson came to Roy's office.

"Here's a list of the terms of the merger that Allison put together, another outline of how the common shares will be apportioned and my rough draft regarding projections and synergy. You can use the documents in the Transcon merger as a guide. That was a similar deal," Dennison said.

"Feels kind of weird taking over Allison's work when we don't know if she's alive or dead."

"I know what you mean. I keep thinking about the Senator in Columbus. He lost his daughter, his wife, and now maybe his only grandchild. Hard to concentrate on the law business, but we have a responsibility to our clients to get the work done."

"I'll get on it right away."

On the intercom, Jennifer announced she had Deputy Wickerham on hold.

"Excuse me, Marvell, I need to take this call." Marvell left the office.

"Hello Jesse. Any new developments?"

"Afraid not, Mr. Dennison, but I'm still plugging away at it. I won't take up much of your time. Just a few questions and I'll be gone."

"Hope I can be helpful."

"Well, let's see now…Did Allison ever drive that jeep at any time before she went out that Saturday night?"

"I'm trying to think. She might have."

"You and her fished with Cooley on Friday and Saturday?"

"Yes, we did."

"What was she like, what was her mood on the boat? Let's start with Friday."

"She was fine. Wasn't happy she was getting wet, but then neither was I. We had a great time with Cal and caught a lot of fish."

"What about Saturday?"

"Where are you going with this, Jesse?"

"Trying to figure what was going on in her mind. Maybe she wasn't kidnapped. Maybe she just ran out and made it look like she was taken. That is a possibility. So, what about Saturday?"

Dennison knew he had to be careful here. He tried to remember precisely what he said to Cooley about the silence between them.

"She was in a different mood on Saturday. Very quiet, not talking and maybe a little depressed."

"Did you ask her if anything was wrong or what was bothering her?"

"Actually, I didn't. Her mood caused me to be quiet as well. There was very little conversation the whole day."

"Cal said you and her had some kind of personal issue. What was that about?"

"Something that came up from time to time. Her feeling guilty about being with a married man. We were fine by dinnertime."

"Why did you say she went to town?"

"She was going to the general store."

"What for?"

"Something she needed she forgot to bring from home. I don't recall what it was."

"Do you mind if we inspect the Den?" Dennison was feeling the heat.

"What are you looking for?"

"Any of her belongings that might give us a clue. Inspection of the living premises is always part of this kind of investigation."

"That's fine. Go at it."

"Who's your caretaker up here? We'll have him open it up for us."

"Frank Wallensky. He lives on Crooked Lake Road."

"I know Frank. Well, that's it for now. Thanks for your cooperation."

As soon as Wickerham hung up, Dennison called Wallensky.

"Deputy Wickerham is going to call you to let him in the house. Do what he says, and stay there until he leaves. Remember, you haven't been at the house since I got there. You haven't even seen me in the past couple of weeks. You don't know anything about any girl who is missing. You just don't know anything about it. If he asks if I talked to you, just tell him I told you to let him in and nothing more. Frank, you understand what I'm saying?"

"Yes, Mr. Dennison, I understand."

Dennison didn't like this at all.

CHAPTER TWENTY-THREE

On Saturday morning, Wickerham, Deputy Luke and Frank Wallensky arrived at Dennison's Den. Wickerham had been there three times already, but not for inspection of the premises and its' contents. For that, it was necessary to have a witness, Deputy Luke, who was equipped with a camera and evidence bags.

They started in the great room, kitchen and other areas of the first floor. Wickerham had prepped Luke to look for any personal property that likely belonged to a woman, and especially keep an eye out for a white bathrobe. The first-floor inspection produced nothing other than a woman's wind beater jacket hanging in the reception room closet. They proceeded upstairs, leaving Wallensky sitting on the stone ledge of the inactive fireplace.

Wickerham took the master bedroom and bath, while Luke checked the other three bedrooms and two bathrooms on the second floor. One side of the huge walk-in closet contained a large collection of summer and fall female clothing, probably belonging to Mrs. Dennison. On the men's side there was a section cleared on the lower bar for a small collection of women's things—two pairs of jeans, two pairs of other slacks, a sweatshirt, a sweater and three blouses. An open suitcase rested on the bench in the center of the closet, containing two bras, other feminine underclothing, stockings and miscellaneous travel items. Below the bench were two pair of shoes, casual loafers and canvas boat shoes.

As directed by Wickerham, Luke started photographing each item of women's things on the lower bar, with the size label showing, as well as the shoes and the open suitcase. Meanwhile, Wickerham checked the master bath. No white bathrobe anywhere in the master suite. He then went to the dresser. As he opened the top drawer and gazed in, "Oh, I'll be damned!" Luke rushed from the closet. "What happened?"

"Look at this." Wickerham pointed to an open lady's purse showing a pink wallet inside.

"What's the big deal?" Luke said.

"What lady goes to town to buy something without her purse and wallet? Photograph the purse and wallet and bag them."

Before leaving, Wickerham asked Frank if he had been to the Den since Mr. Dennison came up with a young lady. Frank answered, "No,sir."

Wallensky locked up and Wickerham returned to his office to write a report on his computer. He placed the purse and wallet in the locked evidence closet. When he finished, he e-mailed the report to Lehman in Bessemer, and then leaned back in his desk chair to ponder the meaning of what he had found. *It's possible she had clothes and shoes other than what I found in the closet, but who would need any more than that for a three-day trip to go fishing? What happened to the white bathrobe? Then there's the purse. She could have taken some cash out of her wallet, but she didn't take her driver's license. Is that the way women normally conduct their business? Is Dennison hiding what the personal issue was between them or was it really only about her feelings of guilt?*

Was there enough there to make Dennison a suspect of some

wrongdoing? At the very least, there were more questions to be answered by him. He looked forward to bringing these facts to Otto Lehman's attention at the Monday meeting.

CHAPTER TWENTY-FOUR

All five members of the Dennison family were seated at the table as dinner was served by Lily. The conversation was dominated by Rob, by far the most loquacious member of the family. He started with how he beat his neighbor friend in two games of pinners, then how he beat his six-year-old brother, Ben, in a race to the corner and back, and what a funny movie he saw on the Disney Channel. Clara finally cut him off.

"OK, Rob, time to stop talking and start eating."

After dinner, per Clara's instructions, Martha, the other live-in, took the children downstairs to the family room for television and games. She and Roy sat at opposite ends of the dining room table.

"Do you want to tell me the truth about your weekend?" Clara asked.

Between Cathy Riley, Senator Jameson and the Ohio lawyer, it's all going to come out, so there's little point in my trying to continue the lie.

"I made a terrible mistake and was having a thing with this lawyer in the office. I'm so sorry, Clara. It had nothing to do with love, just a surge of lust."

"What about your trip last spring? Did you go alone or did you have someone with you?"

Oh, boy, here we go. I'm in too deep now.

"She was with me on the trip last spring."

"The same woman?"

"Yes."

"So, this 'thing', as you describe it, has been going on since last spring?"

"Not constant, but on and off."

"How long before last spring's trip?"

"Maybe about a month. It was stupid. She means nothing to me. I can't explain how I let it happen. It won't happen again, ever."

"Of course it won't happen again, because she's probably dead. My God, Roy, how could you—how could you have destroyed this family? I can't believe how little your commitment to me and our family meant to you. You can stay in the guest room tonight, but I want you out of this house tomorrow while the boys are at school. I'll explain that you're away on a business trip for the time being."

Clara's eyes were red and tearing as she rose from her seat and left the room.

There was no point in going after her. There were no words to comfort her or ease the pain he had caused. He sensed this may well be the end of life as he had known and enjoyed it. He would leave in the morning and hope the separation and passage of time would lead a brighter light to shine.

CHAPTER TWENTY-FIVE

Otto Lehman had been Assistant Prosecutor for two years and on the County Prosecutor's staff for two years before that. He was a five-foot-eight 170 pound high-energy achiever who had never prosecuted a murder case. There hadn't been that many homicide cases in Gogebic County during his years on staff. The only three murder cases had been handled successfully by the boss. His time had come and if there was a homicide to be charged in the Jameson matter, he was told it would be his to try.

Lehman had already read the four-page inspection report before he arrived at Wickerham's office.

"It's good to see you thinking outside the box on this case, Jesse. If you think this guy Dennison may be involved, give me a possible scenario that includes him."

"OK. Let's say he and the lady get into an argument Saturday night. Maybe she threatens to tell his wife about their affair. He gets pissed off and she gets the screaming meemies, and he slugs her or clubs her with something and she goes down dead. He disposes of the body somehow and plans to make it look like she wasn't even there when she disappeared. So, he drives the jeep to the shoulder on 45, flattens the tire to make it look like she was stranded and taken by who knows who. The fact that there's no print on the door handle also fits with that scenario, because he just wipes his prints clean."

"Not bad, except for two holes. How does he get back to the house after leaving the jeep on the road in the early hours, and how and where does he dispose of the body?"

"I see your point. I got the same answer to both. He had to have help. Someone had to follow him and drive him back to his Den. Also, he's not the kind of guy I would expect could handle taking a body somewhere and then disposing of it somehow. He would have to have had help with that as well."

"So, your scenario falls apart because there was no one else at the house when this presumed action took place."

"Not necessarily. He could have called for help."

"And who might that have been?"

"He's got a caretaker up here. Big, strong guy who seems slightly retarded. His name is Frank Wallensky. He lives on Crooked Lake Road, not far from Dennison's house."

"Now you're cookin', Jesse. If there's any truth to this, a tough interview with Wallensky might crack the case. Would you like me to do it?"

"No. I know Frank and I think I know how to deal with him. I'll set that up as soon as possible."

"By the way, did you do any blood search when you were inspecting the place?"

"Just a visual. The place is too big to even think about doing any chemical stuff. I guess you know that Dennison is a wealthy guy, with strong connections in Chicago and the state of Illinois. He's also popular up here, supports the economy and contributes to some local charities. We need to be careful with him."

"I understand all that, but it's not going to help him if your scenario or something like it turns out to be fact."

CHAPTER TWENTY-SIX

When Cal got home from a full day of guiding on Thursday, Emma was not there to greet him at the kitchen door. After depositing his walleye catch in the garage refrigerator, he entered the kitchen calling her name. No response. She was nowhere to be found on the ground floor. He started up the stairs again calling her name, this time with some urgency. As he reached the top of the stairs, he heard a faint call of his name coming from their bedroom area. She was not in the bedroom. He found Emma on the floor of the bathroom attached to their bedroom. She was naked, moaning and not moving. She explained she had slipped while trying to get out of the tub and had been lying on the bathroom floor for at least two hours in great pain, aggravated by any attempted movement.

Cal covered her shivering body with a blanket and placed a pillow beneath her head. He called 911. He then called Doc Hilliard who told him to have the ambulance take her directly to the hospital in Eagle River. He would call ahead to have them expect her. Cal unhitched his boat and followed the ambulance to Eagle River.

The MRI determined that Emma had suffered a crushing fracture of the head of the femur, which could only be corrected by hip replacement surgery, if she wished to avoid being wheelchair bound for the rest of her life. On the following day, Friday, she was transferred to the medical center in Minoqua, Wisconsin, where a highly qualified orthopedic staff could handle such surgery.

Cal wanted only the best for his Emma, but he was overwhelmed by what was involved. Several days in the hospital, ten days to two weeks in a rehab facility, and home nursing for a time to be determined. The cost would run into thousands of dollars beyond his insurance coverage, and probably thousands of dollars beyond his meager savings. That was not even figuring any number of possible complications the surgeon said could occur.

Minoqua was about forty-five miles from Watersmeet. Cal wanted to spend as much time as possible with Emma during those trying days. He decided not to book any guiding for days that were open in his calendar for the next thirty days. That would average about two days a week. Those days and other evenings he would be with her. There would be an obvious reduction in his income at a time when he would be facing huge expenses.

*   *   *

At its westernmost end, Main Street becomes Route 45 again as it makes a right turn and heads north. At that corner of Main Street and Route 45 is the Watersmeet Township's Sheriff's Office, headquarters for undersheriff Wickerham and Deputy Luke. On the tenth day of the reported disappearance of Allison Jameson, Frank Wallensky sat on a wooden chair at a table in a small, barren room, prepared to be interviewed by Deputy Wickerham. The court reporter was present and ready.

"This is Sheriff's Deputy Jesse Wickerham questioning Frank Wallensky on Tuesday, May 29, 1997. Now, Frank, you understand I'm going to ask you some questions about the disappearance of this girl, Allison Jameson?"

"I don't know anything about it."

"Well, that may be so, but you might be helpful just the same. How long have you been caretaker for Dennison's Den?"

"Ever since the place was built. I don't remember how many years."

"The cabin where you live is on Crooked Lake Road?"

"Yes, sir."

"How close is that to Dennison's Den?"

"Less than a ten-minute drive."

"When was the last time you were at Dennison's Den?"

"I don't remember."

Jesse got up to get himself a cup of coffee. Offered one to Frank, who declined.

"Were you there two weekends ago?"

"I don't know anything about it."

"About what?"

"About anything."

"Were you there two weekends ago?"

"I don't remember."

"When did you last see Allison Jameson?"

"I didn't see her."

"Did you ever see Allison Jameson?"

"I didn't see her."

"Ever?"

"I don't remember."

"Did Mr. Dennison ever talk to you about Allison?"

"I don't know anything about it."

"Did Mr. Dennison ever tell you to say you don't know anything about it?"

"I don't remember."

"Do you know that you can be in a lot of trouble if you don't tell me the truth?"

"I just don't know anything about it."

"OK. That's all I have for you today. You'll come back in if I need you, won't you?"

"Yes, sir, I will."

Jesse thought he'd hit the jackpot. Wallensky sounded prepped. There was still a need for hard evidence but, for sure, he felt he was on the right track. He looked forward to talking to Lehman after he read the transcript of Wallensky's statement.

* * *

Emma's surgery was performed without complication. Cal called Meg in Madison to tell her about her mom's misfortune, but successful surgery. Meg was graduating nursing school in a week and would return home to provide Emma with the needed nursing care for as long as it would take. Cal was spending sleepless nights worrying about how his bills were going to be paid. He had no one in Watersmeet to look to for financial aid. As a last resort, he decided to call Roy Dennison in Chicago.

"I know you're dealing with a lot of bad stuff, but I wanted you to know what's going on here with Emma. She had a fall last Thursday and busted up her hip real bad. She had surgery already, replaced her whole hip. She'll be out of commission for quite a while."

"Oh, God, that's awful. Poor Emma. Is she in a lot of pain?"

"She was suffering on the bathroom floor for a couple of hours until I got home. She's on drugs now and the pain seems to have settled down."

"Is there anything you need, anything I can do?"

"That's why I'm calling you. My insurance is going to fall short and I'm going to be wiped out moneywise. It hurts me to be asking for hand-outs, but maybe you could help some with the expenses."

"Don't say another word, friend, I'll take care of any medical expenses that exceed your insurance coverage. Send me the bills and I'll pay them directly. You just take care of your sweet wife."

Cal couldn't speak. He burst into tears and couldn't stop sobbing for several moments. After pulling himself together, he responded in faltering voice.

"Roy, I'll never forget this. You've just taken such a heavy load off my shoulders. I can't wait to tell Emma about your generosity. By the way, thought you might want to know that Jesse Wickerham had a talk with me about you and Allison."

"He mentioned that to me. What was he asking?"

"How you two were getting along. I just told him the truth, that you weren't talking to each other much on Saturday. That was the whole thing."

Dennison did not like the way Wickerham was broadening his investigation. He feared he had made mistakes he was not yet aware of that would be his undoing. He was mostly troubled by not knowing where she was buried and how good a job Frank did in selecting the spot and performing the burial.

CHAPTER TWENTY-SEVEN

The Ontonagon River flows from Lake Superior easterly and divides into several branches, some of which proceed in a southeasterly direction, completing their paths at the Cisco Chain of lakes. The river carries salmon and steelhead runs from Lake Superior and is known as one of the best brown trout fisheries in the UP. Fishing is particularly good in a stretch of river near Bond Falls and the Calderton Reservoir.

The Stapleton brothers, Billy and Bart, residents of Watersmeet, were avid and competent fly fishermen with a particular love for pursuing brown trout on the Ontonagon. Most weeks they spent Saturdays casting from shore or hip high in the water at a section of the river near Bond Falls. On Saturday, the last day of May, they drove north on Route 45 to the town of Paulding, about nine miles from Watersmeet, took a right turn on a one lane dirt and gravel road, and proceeded another half mile to a turn-around where they parked their vehicle. This left them about 100 yards to traverse through heavy woods to reach their favorite area of the river.

They proceeded along carefully, Billy behind Bart, with creels strapped around their waists. They carried their rods a little above the handle with the length of the rods trailing behind. When they reached near the halfway point to the river, Bart stopped suddenly, pointing to something he thought at first might be a snake.

"What the hell is that?" Billy asked.

Bart picked up one end of it and held it high.

"Looks like a dirty length of cloth or something," Billy said.

"Holy smokes!" Bart said after closer inspection of the long piece of material. "This looks like a belt for a bathrobe."

"What's the big deal about that?"

"Don't you remember the posters for the missing girl? They're still all over town. It said she was last seen in a white terry-cloth bathrobe. We gotta let the Sheriff know about this."

"How we going to do that?"

"I'll get the car and go back to Paulding. You stay here so we don't lose track of the location. I'll be back in fifteen or twenty minutes. Leave this thing right where we found it," Bart said.

Later at the scene, Deputy Luke photographed the area and the presumed robe belt, which he placed in an evidence bag. He tied a piece of yellow ribbon to a tree to mark the area where the belt was found. Wickerham then enlisted the Stapleton boys to assist in a search. The plan was for the four of them to line up ten yards apart to the left of the yellow ribbon and proceed slowly to the river, looking for items of clothing or any area of ground that appeared to have been shoveled or changed in any way. They would then inspect the river shore in the area. Finally, they would start back, again ten yards apart, but on the other side of where the ribbon was located.

It was on the way back from the river that Deputy Luke shouted out, "Over here! This don't look right."

Wickerham and the boys rushed over to check on Luke's find. There it was, in a small clearing guarded by a trio of black ash trees, a highly suspicious- looking four-foot by three-foot section of earth having a decidedly different texture of soil from the surrounding land. Jesse and Luke looked at each other, with eyes stretched open. This could be it.

"I'll go back to the car and get the shovel while you take pictures," Jesse said.

"Is there anything you need us for?" Billy asked, seemingly anxious to get on with hunting the brown trout.

"I need you to be around for a while to witness whatever we find here. By the way, you guys did great calling us on this. Might even get your names in the paper," Jesse said.

On his way back to the car, Jesse thought he needed to call Lehman and the coroner's office. Now would be premature. He figured he best wait to see what, if anything, he's got here. The forest was not easy to pass through. It was heavily wooded with white and red pines, wide-branched blue spruces, black ash trees, waste-high thick brush and small trees stunted in growth by mature neighbors blocking out the sunlight.

He gave Luke the shovel and asked him to dig carefully, so as not to damage anything of value below the surface. The soil was loose and easily moved. He dug only in a section of two square feet. In just a few minutes Luke put the shovel aside, dropped to his knees, and started clearing the loose soil with his hands.

"Jesus Christ, there it is!" Luke shouted. They all leaned in to see what was exposed in the two-foot-deep hole.

CHAPTER TWENTY-EIGHT

The coroner, Archie Bremer, his assistant and Otto Lehman drove in from Bessemer in an ambulance. Wickerham and Luke were joined by two other deputies from adjoining Iron County. Lehman had also arranged for a videographer to be present to record the entire activity for evidentiary purposes. The Iron County boys commenced the careful digging of the full dimensions of the disturbed ground. The others stood to the side in a semi-circle, leaning forward and peering into the deepening hole as the pungent smell of death wafted from the grave. The shoveling stopped to avoid damage when much of the corpse was still covered by loose dirt. The face was covered by a bath towel. Enough of the feminine feet with evidence of early decomposition, and portions of the white terry-cloth bathrobe not covered by the blanket, were exposed, making it obvious this would be the body of Allison Jameson.

Extricating the corpse from the grave without damaging it, and then through the dense forest to the ambulance, would be challenging. Running a gurney through the fifty yards of forest would not be possible. It was decided to extend the grave by three feet on each side. This would enable the deputies to step into the grave and work from that position.

Jesse and Luke took one side and the Iron County boys the

other. After entering the grave, they were able to place three eighteen-inch-wide bands side by side under the body. Then, standing on level ground, they lifted the bands and the body out of the hole and placed it on a canvas stretcher. The four deputies carried the stretcher slowly and carefully through the trees. Lehman and Bremer walked ahead of them, breaking branches and clearing the ground as much as possible. Half way to the road Luke yelled, "Hold it! God damn." A branch from a stunted buckthorn shrub had got inside his pants leg and scraped his calf, drawing blood and causing pain. Lehman held his corner of the stretcher while Luke removed the thorny branch. They continued to the road and placed the stretcher in the ambulance. Otto Lehman waved at Wickerham to join him in the middle of the road.

"Nice going, Jesse. Really good work. Looks like Mr. Dennison is going to have his hands full. I'd like to keep all this quiet and out of the press at least until Monday. I'll talk to Archie about that and you can cover it with the Iron County people. Archie will start his autopsy tonight, after he cleans her up. I want to meet with you Monday morning. Can you come to Bessemer?"

"Of course. What time?"

"See you at 9:00 a.m.?"

"Could you make it 10:00 a.m.? I've got the kids that found the bathrobe belt coming in to see me early."

"Sure, 10:00 a.m. it is, and you better have Luke clean his leg up. Those buckthorns can be nasty."

CHAPTER TWENTY-NINE

The weather on Sunday was sunny and mild, perfect for the VFW Club's Annual Spring BBQ, called for at 4:00 p.m. until whenever. All twelve members were expected with their wives, and those without wives were entitled to bring one guest. Children of members were also allowed, though not encouraged because a considerable amount of drinking was expected. Deputy Luke, a member, was not married. He persuaded Jesse to come to the BBQ as his guest.

The bar was open inside and there were three oversized coolers outside, packed with ice and dozens of cans and bottles of the club's favorite drinks. On the other side of the front lawn stood three large grills, side by side, getting ready to receive brats and burgers. In between, the lawn was sprinkled with four-seater card tables covered with red and white checkered plastic cloths. On the porch, the turntable owned by the club was playing all time country favorites of the forties and fifties. All in all, a very festive atmosphere.

Jesse and Luke arrived at 6:15 p.m., finding the party in full swing. They got their beers from one of the coolers and then took seats at a table occupied by Cal and Bert, who were halfway through their burgers.

"How long you guys been here?" Jesse asked.

"Hell, I fished Crooked all day. I just got here ten minutes ago and got started on a burger as quick as I could."

"Do any good on Crooked?" Luke asked.

"Damn right. Got my limit and one of them was near four pounds."

Jesse caught Luke's eyes as he made a sudden change of subject.

"Do you guys know Frank Wallensky?"

"I know Frank. He's been around town as long as I can remember. Kind of a weirdo. Big and strong, sorta dumb, and has a strange kinda look in his eyes, makes you feel like you don't want to get too close," Bert said.

"Has he ever been in trouble, far as you know?" Jesse asked.

"He hurt a couple of boys awhile back. They were making fun of him for some stupid stuff he said and he took offense. Put one of 'em in the hospital," Bert said.

"I remember that. The boys had it coming and Frank wasn't prosecuted," Jesse said.

"He's a real loner, has no friends I know of. Works for Dennison, taking care of his place. Anything new on that missing girl?" Cal asked.

"We've got a couple of clues we're following up on and should have some news this week," Jesse said.

"I hope that poor kid turns up in one piece," Cal said.

By 7:30 p.m. the party was getting too noisy for Wickerham. A couple of the wives were trying to fix him up with their girlfriends. He was not about to start dating. The whole idea of being with other women was offensive to him. There would only be one woman in his life and she was gone, wasted along with the life of a white tail buck. He prevailed on Luke to leave the party with him.

"I'd love to go right by Wallensky's cabin and confront him with our discovery yesterday. Seems like there's already a circumstantial case against Dennison, but Wallensky really holds the key. I better hold off at least until I meet with Lehman in the morning."

"I agree."

"The Stapleton boys are coming in early in the morning. I might need you. I'll get back from Bessemer near noon."

"I'll be in at 7:00 a.m."

In the morning, after giving Luke the task of getting the statements typed up and signed by the Stapleton brothers, Wickerham set out for Bessemer and his meeting with Otto Lehman. During the fifty-minute drive he kept recounting the points he wanted to raise with Lehman. Autopsy results, if available, especially cause of death, would help complete the story.

The receptionist told Wickerham that Mr. Lehman was finishing a conference with the coroner and would be with him shortly. Wickerham could tell Lehman was pleased about his meeting with Archie by his wide glowing smile as he greeted him. He ushered Jesse into his office and then, while clasping his hands and rubbing his palms together, broke the news.

"Archie isn't finished with his report, but he told me the cause of death was definitely a severe blow to the side of the head with a blunt object. One other important finding—this girl was about six weeks pregnant."

Jesse jumped off his chair, smashed a fist into an open hand

and said,

"Holy smokes! There's your motive, and Cal Cooley said they weren't talking to each other because of some personal issue."

"You said it. The case against Dennison is strong, even without the murder weapon. What juror is going to believe that this girl left the house in a bathrobe without her purse to make some purchases at the general store, and stark naked under the bathrobe at that. She was never in that jeep that night, and that explains the absence of her prints on the door handle."

"What possible defense could Dennison have?" Wickerham asked.

"They could argue that she was an eccentric girl and after a few glasses of wine was capable of almost anything or that after Dennison fell asleep, an intruder entered the house and kidnapped her. Both are unbelievable and without any supporting evidence. Finally, I suppose they could argue that she accidentally fell and hit her head. They couldn't make that argument without putting Dennison on the witness stand. No competent counsel could let him testify when he has already committed himself to being asleep and, therefore, doesn't know what happened. Beyond that, he would have to explain what happened to the blood and why and how the body got buried."

"Are you ready to file charges?"

"Not yet. I want to wait for the final autopsy report and take another stab at breaking Wallensky. I am going to start putting the charging documents together and you get to work on Wallensky."

"I got a call from Dennison yesterday. Surprised the hell out of me. He was wondering if he could be of help in the investigation if he came up here."

"What'd you tell him?"

"I said I'd think about it and try to give him a call back tomorrow. What do you think?"

"If I was ready to file charges I'd let him come up here tomorrow. That would save us the whole process of getting an interstate extradition. Trouble is we're not quite ready to charge and we have to come out with a statement to the press today about finding the body. Once Dennison gets that news, you can be sure he won't be in a hurry to return to the Upper Peninsula."

"Can't we delay the announcement and get him to come up here on the day we are charging?"

"We can't delay the announcement any more than we already have. The Governor wouldn't be happy to find out we held back this much as it is. Besides, that would probably cause them to claim entrapment and get us bogged down with that issue for months."

"Dennison also wanted to know if a reward offer would be a good idea. I told him it never hurts to offer rewards."

"Reward time has expired."

"Any thoughts on a good tack to take with Wallensky?" Wickerham asked.

"The *Watersmeet News* is distributed on Thursday. Make your appointment with him on Friday and bring a copy of the paper for him to look at. Then tell him we've got the goods on Dennison who told us about his involvement and go from there."

"Sounds good. I'll call you Friday after I meet with him."

CHAPTER THIRTY

Late Tuesday afternoon, the County Prosecutor issued the following statement to the *Watersmeet News* and other newspapers and television outlets in the Upper Peninsula:

> *On Saturday, May 31, 1997, the body of a young woman was discovered in a shallow grave in the woods near the town of Paulding. The body is presumed to be Allison Jameson, the Chicago attorney who has been missing since May18. Authorities located the site based on a call from Watersmeet residents Bart and Billy Stapleton, who came across an item of the victim's clothing near the gravesite. An autopsy is being conducted.*

The Wednesday night and Thursday morning editions of the *Chicago Tribune* carried the news release along with a review of the earlier stories referencing Roy Dennison.

On Thursday morning, Dennison was in the coffee shop of his hotel awaiting service of his coffee. As he opened the morning *Trib* his eyes moved quickly to the far-right column on the front page with the heading:

Lawyers' Body Found In Upper Peninsula

He felt his heart fall into his stomach. His growing sense of safety was shattered. Everything was about to fall down on him from every direction. Who should he call first? Clara, Dan, Jennifer, Wallensky? He called the office and told the receptionist to tell Jennifer he would not be in today. He was afraid to call Wallensky. Could there be a wiretap? He wouldn't know what to say to Clara. She wouldn't talk to him, anyway. It's time to call Clyde Fuller, he thought.

* * *

Jarvis and Fuller was the name of the firm. Jarvis died in 1991, leaving the criminal law practice to Clyde Fuller and his two associates. Fuller was noted for his defense of white-collar greed crimes such as fraud and embezzlement. Rarely was the firm involved in the defense of violent crimes. However, Dennison valued Fuller's smarts and strategic prowess and, in his present state of panic, looked forward to finally speaking truth to a confidant he could rely upon.

Fuller's painfully thin body, his craggy facial features and graying hair just above shoulder length were reminiscent of the character Fagin in the musical *Oliver*. His law offices were eerily quiet compared to the constant hustle and bustle of Rogers and Dennison. He and Roy sat at right angles to each other at one end of the conference table in Fuller's office. Dennison's anxiety was evident from the slight tremor of his left hand as it rested on the table and his faltering voice breaking the silence.

"I'm talking to you as my counsel, so all the rules of

confidentiality are in place."

"Absolutely."

"I know the articles in the paper make it look like I did something nefarious to this girl. It's not true."

Dennison proceeded to recount the facts in painful detail. He told Fuller everything, except he did not mention Allison's pregnancy.

"I assume you've already been interviewed by authorities up there?"

"Yes. The Sheriff's deputy in charge of the investigation took a court reporter statement from me."

"What did you tell him?"

"That I passed out from too much wine before she left to go to town."

"Jesus, Roy. Why didn't you just call and report the home accident?"

"I know. I was afraid there'd be a homicide investigation. I guess I wasn't thinking clearly."

"I'll check out what the penalty is in Michigan for failing to report a death and for intentionally hiding or burying an unreported death. Those appear to be your only two crimes, if you can prove it. Only your testimony could do that."

"Is there anything I should be doing now?"

"You just have to wait and see what the prosecutors in—what county is it?"

"Gogebic County."

"You just have to wait and see what they do. We don't know what they have or what the autopsy shows. They'll certainly do one. They may think they have enough to file murder or manslaughter charges. If they do, we'll have time to plan our response. They can't come here and arrest you. They'd have to start an interstate extradition process for you to be extradited to Gogebic County to stand trial. That all takes time."

"So, I just sit tight. Seems like I should be doing something."

"I'm sure you've got a lot of bases to cover, like Clara and Dan. I don't know how you're going to do it, but don't discuss the facts of the case or anything about your part in it. That will all be discoverable in time."

"Can you believe what I've done to myself?"

"I know you're in an impossible situation. I'll represent you here in Chicago, and I'll do research to find you the best representation in Michigan, if it comes to that."

After leaving Fuller's office, Dennison immediately called Dan and asked him to come to the coffee shop in the Mid-City Hotel as soon as he could break away. Twenty minutes later, Dan walked into the coffee shop and found Dennison seated at a booth in a corner formed by a wall and a picture window to the street.

"Thanks for coming right over. I'm sure you saw the *Trib* this morning."

"Of course I did. My God, what in the world happened with you and Allison?"

"I just came from a meeting with Clyde. He instructed me not to discuss the facts with anyone, including you. But, Dan, I swear to you by everything holy, I did not do anything to harm that girl."

"You leveled with Clyde, right?"

"Yes, I did. I told him everything."

"What did he think?"

"He said I should just wait to see what, if anything, the prosecutors in the UP decide to do. I'm ashamed to show my face in the office. I'd like to take a couple of weeks off, waiting to see what comes out of Michigan. Is that OK with you?"

"I understand how you feel, but we have to wrap up the United Supplies matter."

"You're right. I'll cover it with Marvell on the phone. He'll be able to close it with my guidance."

"Clients are going to start calling in about this. How should we handle it?" Rogers asked.

"Jesus, I don't know. I guess you can tell them I'm taking a leave of absence to deal with the issue, and I want them to be assured I am not in any way involved in the harm that came to that girl."

"That's how I'll deal with it. I'll try to hold things together. I'm afraid your indiscretion has created an existential threat to the firm. Sorry to say that to you, but I fear we're heading down a bleak road."

"If I had the courage, I'd blow my brains out. I'm so, so sorry."

CHAPTER THIRTY-ONE

On Friday morning, Frank Wallensky was again seated at headquarters and waiting for Deputy Wickerham to appear and start a second interview. This time, without a court reporter. Jesse walked into the room with a copy of the *Watersmeet News*.

"If you haven't seen it before, take a good look at it now." Jesse pushed the front page in front of Wallensky. "I want you to read every word of it."

"I already told you, I don't know anything about it," Wallensky said after slowly reading the article.

"It's time for truth telling, Frank. We already know that Dennison was involved and that he got you to help him. We know you didn't hurt this girl and that you only buried her. That won't get you in much trouble. But if you continue to lie about it, then you're going to end up as guilty as he is and pay the same price he's going to pay. It's all over, Frank. Tell the truth and save your soul."

"Did Mr. Dennison tell you that I helped him?"

"Yes, he did."

"Then I guess I can tell you the same."

"OK. Hold on, I'll be right back."

Wickerham returned momentarily with the court reporter.

"This is the statement of Frank Wallensky, taken on Thursday, June 5, 1997, as part of the investigation of the disappearance of

Allison Jameson. Frank, if you have something you want to tell us, go right ahead.

"He called me over and there she was, lying on the floor with her head bashed in. He said it was an accident."

Wallensky continued about the fingerprinting of the steering wheel, the burial and picking Dennison up at the jeep parked on Route 45. Wickerham told the reporter to transcribe the statement immediately and fax a copy to Otto Lehman in Bessemer.

"Jesse, you know you broke the law when you buried that girl and kept it a secret."

"I guess I know it wasn't right."

"I'll have to keep you here tonight. Luke or I will drive you to Bessemer in the morning. We'll see what the judge wants to do. He'll probably appoint you a public defender."

After he settled Frank into one of the two jail cells in the rear of the office, Jesse walked out the front door, took a deep breath of the crisp spring air and thought, *That son of a bitch, lying through his teeth. He killed that little girl. Goddamn it, thank you Frank Wallensky.*

CHAPTER THIRTY-TWO

Overcome by a sense of doom, Dennison spent the next several days mostly confined to his hotel room. Then there were those dreams, those bad, unspeakable dreams. The dozen different things he should have been attending to in his office seemed to be of little consequence. What he really wanted was to talk to Clara and hoped she would permit him to see his children. He wondered what the boys knew about his absence, and what they might have heard from other kids at school. Clyde said not to talk to anyone.

"Is it OK for me to talk to Clara about this?"

"What are you planning on saying?"

"The truth of what actually happened."

"There is such a thing as spousal immunity, where one spouse can refuse to testify where the other is facing a criminal trial regarding confidential communications. It can be a tricky issue and is not always sustained. The simple answer is don't tell her anything about what happened. You don't know what kind of charges may be coming or what your response will ultimately be. Keep all your options open by keeping your mouth closed."

"Couldn't I just tell her that I didn't do anything to harm Allison? Wouldn't that be my position with respect to any option?"

"She'll then ask you what happened and you'll refuse to say any more. How do you think that will sit with Clara? What will you have gained? I'll tell you. Nothing. If anything, you'll have aggravated the situation."

"All right. I won't call her. It's just that I've been hanging around this hotel room feeling alone and disconnected. I'm plenty scared about what's going to be coming at me. Would you like to have dinner with me?"

"Sorry, Roy. I'm tied up tonight."

"My God, Clyde, you're the only person I can talk to. How long will that last?"

"Until we find you a Michigan lawyer. I don't want to give you more to be depressed about, but I did say I would do a little Michigan law research. What you actually did, failing to inform law enforcement of a death with the purpose of concealing the fact or cause of the death, is a felony punishable by imprisonment for up to five years. That's the bad news. The good news is there's no death penalty in Michigan."

*   *   *

Otto Lehman was ready to put together his charges against Roy Dennison. The charges would consist of murder in the first degree, voluntary manslaughter and purposefully concealing the fact or cause of death of an individual. He was confident that the overwhelming circumstantial evidence would support probable cause for murder or voluntary manslaughter. The purposeful concealment case, a serious felony, was a slam dunk. Getting Dennison to appear and stand trial in Michigan was a separate issue. The state of Michigan does not have authority over a person present in another state. Assuming Dennison would not come to Michigan voluntarily, he would have to be arrested by Illinois law enforcement and extradited to Michigan.

The charging documents filed with the Circuit Court of Gogebic County in Bessemer contained the affidavit of Wickerham which included, as exhibits, the transcribed statements of Wallensky and Dennison, and Wickerham's own account of Cal Cooley's description of a personal issue between Dennison and the victim. Jesse's affidavit also described the condition of the body found in the shallow grave and attached the autopsy report highlighting the cause of death and the pregnancy of the victim.

Circuit Court Judge Matenson was satisfied there was probable cause for the charges and issued an out-of-state warrant for the arrest of Dennison. Following the dictates of the Extradition Act, the charging documents along with the arrest warrant and Judge Matenson's affidavit as to probable cause were sent to the Michigan Governor with the request that the Governor convey a demand to the Governor of Illinois for the return to Michigan of the charged person. The Michigan Governor was elated with the progress being made by the County Prosecutor toward the closure of this case and promptly forwarded all the documentation to the Governor of Illinois with his "demand" that Dennison be arrested and extradited to Gogebic County, Michigan.

Roy Dennison was a popular figure in the legal community of Chicago and the state of Illinois. He had met the Governor on numerous occasions and served with distinction for several years on the Governor's Commission on Economic Development. The Governor was shocked by the papers he received from his

Michigan counterpart. Due to Dennison's prominence, he did not want to act hastily in ordering an arrest warrant. Following the authority of the Extradition Act, he called upon the Cook County State's Attorney to review the papers, investigate the demand, and report back on the situation and circumstances of the person demanded and whether he ought to be surrendered.

* * *

It didn't take long for Clyde Fuller to hear about the pending extradition from his contacts at the state's attorney's office. He called Dennison and told him to come to his office immediately to discuss urgent developments. Dennison hurried to Fuller's office.

"The governor of the asylum state, being Illinois, rarely has the option of refusing the demand for extradition. That's certainly true where the charges are as serious as these. By turning this over to the state's attorney for investigation, the Governor is not expecting there to be a challenge to the extradition but, rather, as a courtesy, is giving you some time to determine your course of action. However, the statute requires he act on the demand before the expiration of thirty days."

"Jesus, Clyde, what are my options?"

"Number one, you can voluntarily turn yourself in and authorities will come and take you back to Gogebic County to stand trial. Number two, you can get in your car or get on a plane and run to whereever and hide, take on a new identity and hope never to be caught. In other words, become a fugitive. Finally, number three, you can sit tight, let the thirty days run and wait for the Illinois authorities to come arrest you and turn you over. Choose your poison—they all stink."

"Number one is best. Why not wait twenty-nine days, then turn myself in and avoid the circus of an arrest?"

"That's what I would do in your shoes. We could use that time to locate Michigan defense counsel and meet with him to discuss strategy and the extradition issue."

"I need to go back to the hotel, call Dan and bring him up to date. Call me when you have some advice on counsel."

Back at the hotel, Dennison called his partner. He told him about the charges and the fact that he had thirty days before he must turn himself in to Illinois authorities.

"Then what happens?" Dan asked.

"Then the Michigan people come here and take me back to the UP for trial."

"Wow! How are you holding up?"

"I think I'm in some kind of shock. I feel like crying, but tears aren't coming. Like I'm in a room with four walls all moving toward me, getting ready to crush the life out of me, and there's no way out."

"I'm going to call a meeting of all the juniors to discuss how this may affect the firm and the best way for us to handle it. Do you want to participate in that meeting?"

"I'll just go along with whatever comes out of it. The few days I have will be dedicated to finding representation by Michigan counsel and strategizing with him. Clyde is helping me on this."

"Is there anything I can do for you? Anything?"

"There is one thing you can do. I'm too ashamed to call

Clara. She probably wouldn't talk to me if I did. Please call her and tell her I have to go to Michigan to stand trial for the charges against me. But tell her that I have professed to you that I did no harm or injury to that girl—that I swear to God I am innocent of any charge that I harmed her."

"I'll do that, and let you know how the call and the meeting go. Meanwhile, call me whenever you need to talk or you feel that your walls are getting too close."

CHAPTER THIRTY-THREE

The Lehman and Cooley families were Watersmeet neighbors, living only three short blocks apart. Otto was four years older than Meg. They spent time together as friends until Otto went off to Northern Michigan University in Marquette. They started dating the summer following Otto's sophomore year.

Cal and Emma Cooley were not a particularly handsome couple. It was a wonder they had produced a child as beautiful and fetching as Meg. Otto fell head over heels in love with her. Their relationship grew in intensity and passion from summer to summer, through Otto's undergraduate and then his law school years at Cooley Law School (no relation), a division of Western Michigan University in Lansing. The winters were long and full of yearning for the couple, who had to be content with letters and phone calls. They remained true to each other through it all.

During the years Otto was away at school, Meg occupied herself with a number of jobs, including waitress, seamstress, receptionist for the dentist and, from time to time, assisting Emma with the fish cleaning. She saved money until she could pursue her goal, with some help from Cal, to become a registered nurse. The turning point came when Otto returned home after finishing law school and having taken the Michigan Bar examination. He picked Meg up and drove to their favorite scenic lookout to watch the sun set.

"I have some very good news to share with you. I've been accepted for a job in the County Prosecutor's office in Bessemer."

"That's marvelous, Otto. Just what you were hoping for."

"I start right after Labor Day. I'll be moving to Bessemer and living there. I don't have a ring to give you, but you'd make me the happiest man alive if you'd marry me and come with me. Otto pulled Meg to him and kissed her gently.

Meg gently interrupted the kiss saying sadly, "I don't know if I'm ready for that."

Surprised and hurt, Otto removed his arm from around Meg and asked,

"What's holding you back?"

"I want to make something of myself first. I see what happens to wives in the Upper Peninsula, and I don't want that to happen to me. Your mother, my mother, all of them, have babies and cook and clean for their men. I want more than that."

"Why can't you find that in Bessemer?"

"If there was a nursing school in Bessemer, I'd say 'I'm in, let's go'—but there isn't. Think about it, Otto, what would I be doing in Bessemer every day while you were busy at work? No college degree, no special skill, probably waitressing or cashier in a grocery store, waiting to bear kids, if I was lucky. No thanks. I've just got this one life and I intend to make something of it. I'm going to be attending Herzing University School of Nursing in Madison on a three-year program to become a registered nurse. Then we can see about marriage, if we still feel the way we do now."

Meg's matter-of-fact presentation irked Otto. Was this her way of calling it quits?

"OK, I understand. At least we have the rest of this summer to make some memories to carry us through the next three years. Maybe you could visit me in Bessemer during your breaks."

"Maybe. We'll see."

CHAPTER THIRTY-FOUR

Mark Travis was seated at his desk in the office he rented for the duration of a trial in Bay City, Michigan, waiting for the jury to come back with its verdict. He was defending a doctor charged with sexual assault of two female patients. The jury started deliberations the previous day and were sent home after three hours, ordered to return and continue their work this morning. Travis was cautiously optimistic, believing he had closed the deal in closing arguments. He was reliving some of those moments in his mind when he was startled by the trumpeting ring of his cell phone. He immediately thought it was the bailiff calling to advise that the jury was returning. He was wrong.

"My name is Clyde Fuller. I'm a lawyer in Chicago representing another Chicago lawyer who's been charged with some serious crimes in Gogebic County, Michigan."

"Is your client Roy Dennison?"

"Yes, that's right. I see you've been following the case."

"I pretty much keep on top of all the serious crimes making the newspapers in Michigan."

"I've done some research on you and like what I see. Think you might be interested in representing Mr. Dennison in an Upper Peninsula trial?"

"I might be. I'd have to meet him first and talk through some issues, including fees, because I am expensive."

"Fees will not be an issue, I assure you. The Governor of Illinois has given him thirty days before issuing an arrest warrant to extradite him to Michigan. We are now on day three. Where would you like to meet him?"

"Not in Michigan. I don't want to expose him to process here. Might as well be your office in Chicago. I'm waiting for a jury to return in Bay City. Shouldn't be long now. I'll be heading back to my office in Grand Rapids. Need a day or two there to catch up. Then I can come to Chicago. How about Friday? I'll drive in in the morning and should be able to make 1:00 p.m. How about 1:00 p.m."

"Excellent. 1:00 p.m. Friday at 100 North LaSalle Street, suite 1520."

During his three-hour drive to Chicago, Travis kept his mind churning over the facts alleged in the charges, especially the statement of Frank Wallensky. He presumed Dennison was going to tell him that her death was an accident, not caused by him. He had obtained copies of the documents, through sources, as he was most always able to do in Michigan.

They were waiting for him in the conference room when he arrived. Well-built and a shade under six foot tall, Travis was casually dressed in jeans and a lightweight leather jacket over an orange open-collar shirt.

"I see you gentlemen are dressed for business. You'll have to pardon me for wearing my driving clothes. Neither one of you look like defendants, but I'm guessing you're Roy Dennison."

Travis reached to shake Roy's hand.

Fuller identified himself, shook hands with Travis and they took seats at the table.

"Thanks for driving down today. Can I start by filling you in on the charges and where we stand?" Fuller said.

"I've read the charges and the supporting documents, and I assume it's your position that this was an accident. Before we get to all that, I want to get the question of fees out of the way. Is that OK with you?"

"Certainly," Fuller said, and Roy nodded.

"My rate is $500 an hour and $4,000 a day for time in court during trial or any extended hearing. If I'm retained, I'm charging for my time here in Mr. Fuller's office, but I will not charge for my travel time today. As far as costs are concerned, they are to be reimbursed separate from fees. I will incur costs as they are needed, but I will consult with you, Mr. Dennison, with regard to major costs, such as retention of expert witnesses, if required. If you agree, I will send you a retainer agreement setting out these terms."

"I'll go with Mr. Fuller's recommendation," Dennison said.

"I told you that fees would not be an issue," Fuller said.

"One more thing. It's best that we start with a retainer, so we won't have to be sending bills and checks back and forth. I suggest $50,000 and maybe a $10,000 cost retainer as well. Hearing no protest, we can now get down to business. Roy, and please call me Mark, tell me what happened the night Allison died." Travis opened a folder containing a legal-size pad of yellow lined paper and prepared to take notes.

Dennison started with the steak dinner and wine drinking, and carried the story through to his call to the Sheriff the following morning. He was true to the facts, except he said nothing about her pregnancy.

"Did you push her or touch her in any way before she fell? Any contact?"

"No. She was unsteady from the wine and as she turned she tripped on the carpet and went down."

"What was the personal issue you mentioned to Cooley earlier that day?"

"Nothing dramatic or unusual. She was a pretty religious girl. I knew that her relationship with me troubled her and from time to time her sense of guilt would cause her to shut down on me. We had very strong feelings for each other. By dinnertime Saturday night, all was well again."

"Why didn't you just call the Sheriff and report the accident, instead of constructing this elaborate set of lies? Your explanation better be good because your life may well depend upon its believability."

"My judgment was totally screwed up by the suddenness and horror of the situation. I made a terrible and stupid mistake. I knew there would be no sympathy for me, a married man here with this young girl. I feared an investigation and being charged with a homicide if Allison was found in this condition in my house. All of this raced through my mind in a matter of seconds, pushing me to a hasty and not well thought out decision. As soon as Frank took her away in a blanket, I knew I had made a horrendous mistake, but it was too late, much too late."

"It's believable. Only way to prove it, of course, is for you to testify. I generally don't have my clients testify, yet there are rare exceptions and this is one of them. It's a lot to ask a jury to swallow in view of the statement you gave the Sheriff. It's a classic 'were you lying then or are you lying now' situation. Did you know that she was pregnant?"

"I did not. She didn't mention it. I don't know that she knew. What are my chances with a jury in the UP?"

"You can't possibly walk away with no jail time, but you've got a decent chance to avoid the homicide charges. They have no weapon and no eye witness to challenge your account. The fact that the prosecutor added the deceased body felony suggests less than full confidence in their homicide charges. They want to be sure they get you for something. At the same time, by adding that charge they help us defeat the homicide charges, because it allows the jury to have the satisfaction of punishing you without nailing you for murder or manslaughter."

"So, success for me would be guilty on the lesser charge and not guilty on the others. What kind of jail time would that success bring me?"

"Michigan is a state that has indeterminate sentencing. That means defendants are usually sentenced to prison with a range of minimum and maximum years. Your lesser felony charge has a maximum term of five years, so you might expect your sentence to be two to five years. Early release is available where earned. After serving the minimum sentence, the Parole Board may release the defendant on parole if they are satisfied the prisoner no longer poses a risk to society. A defendant can be paroled at any time between the minimum and maximum dates."

"That means I'm probably jailed for a minimum of two years with the best-case scenario."

"Yes, but guilty on murder one is life imprisonment without parole."

That caused Dennison to wince and drop his head. Fuller entered the conversation, changing the subject.

"Any suggestions on the extradition issue?"

"Absolutely. Roy should turn himself in before any arrest warrant is issued. Don't wait until the last day. This will help in getting the UP court to let you out on bail, with or without ankle monitors. Can you handle a bond of $500,000 or $1,000,000? That would require a ten per cent premium," Travis said.

"Yes. What will happen after I turn myself in?"

"Cook County will hold you in the city jail until authorities come from Gogebic County to get you. You'll then sit in jail in Bessemer until I bail you out, if possible. If not possible, you'll stay in jail in Bessemer until the trial's over, and then we'll see where they want to send you."

The thought of being jailed for two years or a lifetime caused an emotional upheaval in Dennison. With elbows on the table, his face resting in both hands, and his head moving from side to side, he uttered some unintelligible mournful sounds. Clyde stepped behind Roy, put both hands on his shoulders in an effort to comfort him, but said nothing. There were no words to make this better.

*　*　*

Later that afternoon, while back in his hotel room, Dennison
called his partner.

"Have you had your meeting with the juniors yet?"

"Not yet. It's scheduled for tomorrow morning. How are you
holding up?"

"I have some additional information. I'm going to turn
myself in and stand trial up there. Clyde has connected me with
a top-notch Michigan trial lawyer who tells me the best result will
be at least two years in jail and the worst would be life without
parole. How do you like that future?"

"Ugh! Holy shit, this is unbelievable. When do you turn
yourself in?"

"In about three weeks. I'm going to use the time to start
raising cash. I'm going to sell enough stocks or bonds to have at
least $1,000,000 in my checking account. I'll tell you—I've been
thinking about getting on a plane and going somewhere far away
to get away from all of this. I can't do it. That would be the
end of my kids, Clara, you and everything else that made my life
worth living. I just have to see this through and hope for the best."

"Do you still want to avoid the meeting tomorrow?"

"Oh God! I can't go there. I'm going to call Jen and let her
know what's going on. She'll have to find herself another job.
Maybe you can help her with that. Have you talked to Clara yet?"

"Not yet. I decided not to do it on the phone. I'm going to
visit her one evening this week in Winnetka. You better give some
thought on how you want to treat your status with the firm."

"What do you mean?"

"Your continuing as a senior partner, under these circumstances, might not bode well for the viability of the firm."

"Don't tell me I'm losing your support. That's the last thing I need now. What happened to innocent until proven guilty?"

"I'm just trying to be realistic. You just told me you're going to be incarcerated between two years and the rest of your life. You don't want the whole ship to go down with you, do you? Besides, any felony conviction is going to cost you your law license."

"I hadn't even thought about that. I'm fucked from here to eternity. You'll have to buy out my interest in the firm. Have the CPA figure the value and then we can talk about it. We don't have much time. Jesus, my head is spinning."

This was new territory for Roy Dennison. Throughout his adult life he faced many crises, both professionally and socially. There were always options. Invariably, he would choose the right path, the one leading to a successful outcome. Here, there was only one way to go, and that was down. He had no control over his future or his dreams—a recurrent dream or nightmare which he could describe to no one. That sweet girl, wrapped in a white robe, rotting away in a dirt hole, with mites and beetles and worms eating and crawling about that beautiful face, a fetus faintly crying in her belly. *Oh, Lord, please stop the dreams.*

CHAPTER THIRTY-FIVE

The juniors met with Rogers in the morning. All the seats were occupied in the conference room with some standing against the wall. Three of the juniors were absent, having given notice the previous day of their withdrawal from the firm with plans to form their own. Associates and staff were excluded from the meeting. Rogers explained Dennison's dire circumstances and the fact that he would ultimately be required to withdraw from the firm.

"Do you have any questions?" Rogers asked.

"Is it possible the firm is going to be sued?" asked a junior.

"In the event of a civil action brought by Allison's family, the firm, meaning me, would provide legal representation for any juniors joined in the case. I didn't mean to suggest that such an action was imminent, but the potential is there."

"If we do get sued, would our individual assets be at risk?" asked another.

"Not likely. Mr. Dennison would be the first target and I would be next. You need not be concerned about that. May not be any lawsuit and if there is one, the likelihood is it would be settled without your involvement."

The light chatter in the room was replaced by silence and a pall of unease, interrupted by a question from another junior.

"Let's have the truth. It wasn't a business trip he took with

Allison. He was sexually harassing her. Isn't that the truth?"

Rogers raised his voice to quiet the rumblings of his audience.

"We're not going to be talking about that relationship here. The truth, whatever it is, will come out in the proceedings in the Upper Peninsula of Michigan. It's best not to be talking about the Dennison case. Any requests for information you receive from newspapers or other media should be directed to me. Now let's get back to servicing our clients."

Rogers wondered how many more juniors would withdraw from the firm in the coming days. He feared the days of Rogers and Dennison were numbered.

CHAPTER THIRTY-SIX

The house key was under the clay flower pot to the left of the front door. Meg let herself in. Cal was fishing and Emma's rehab would be over in two days. It was Meg's intention to attend to her mother while waiting for the results of her State Board examination. When she became registered and her mother was back to being independent, she would look for a permanent position, preferably at a hospital or clinic in Michigan or Wisconsin.

She had had little contact with Otto ever since she started nursing school. He was busy in Bessemer the next two summers, while she was at home or living with and tending to an aunt in Wausau who suffered from advanced Parkinson's disease. The separation had definitely cooled the relationship. Meg no longer contemplated a romantic future with Otto and expected they would just continue as friends.

Her father expected her today or tomorrow. She wanted to prepare a surprise dinner for him. There was very little in the fridge or the shelves to work with. She went out and shopped and had a modest dinner ready, expecting him home around 6:00 p.m. She began to worry when he was not home by 6:30 p.m. When 7:00 p.m. came and went and there was no Cal, she thought he might have gone directly from fishing to visit Emma in Minoqua. It seemed unlikely he would do that without first coming home and cleaning up. She called the rehab and learned he was not there. Next call, with increasing anxiousness, was to the Sheriff's office.

"Wickerham here."

"Hello Jesse, this is Meg Cooley. I just got home from nursing school and I'm looking for my dad. Any idea where he might be?"

"Oh my gosh, Meg, I didn't know you were home. If I did, I would have called you. Cal is at the hospital in Eagle River. Don't get all upset—he's going to be all right."

"What happened to him?"

"He was cranking his boat onto the trailer and I guess he got dizzy and kind of passed out. The folks he was with brought him to town and an ambulance took him to the Eagle River hospital. I was told he regained consciousness by the time he got to the ambulance. I haven't heard any more about it."

"Thanks, Jesse. I'm off to the hospital right now."

"Drive careful. Try not to worry too much. He's going to be OK."

Meg located Cal's attending physician when she arrived at the hospital.

"I'm Mr. Cooley's daughter and I'm a registered nurse. Please tell me his diagnosis and his current status."

'The tests disclose he's had a stroke. He's already receiving IV medication to dissolve the clot. That will continue through the night and we'll redo the tests in the morning. He's resting quietly. It's too early to know if there will be any residual."

"Would it be all right for me to see him?"

"Better if you were to wait until morning. It's best that he remains quiet."

"I understand. I'll come back in the morning."

Driving back to Watersmeet, Meg was reviewing some of the knowledge she had acquired regarding strokes. She knew that blood clot strokes, depending on their size, location and speed of treatment, can result in complete recovery. The same considerations can result in minor or major disabilities. She prayed this would not be the end of her dad's guiding career. If that were to happen, her own life would take a totally different direction than the one she had planned. As soon as she got to the house she called her brothers to give them the unhappy news.

In the morning, there was good news and bad news from the Eagle River hospital. Cal survived the night and his condition was now stable. The stroke, however, had left residuals. His right extremities, arm and leg, had suffered partial paralysis. Cal would be able to walk with a brace on his leg and the aid of a cane, but he would have little use of his right hand. His guiding days and even his fishing days were done. At age forty-six he had no way to earn a living. He would apply for Social Security Disability benefits. The amount he would receive would be based on the average of his lifetime earnings. Unfortunately, his guiding was strictly a cash business and for the past twenty-five years he had only reported about half his actual earnings. Cal and Emma, both seriously impaired within a two-week period, would be disabled and destitute.

Meg had to rededicate her life to the care and financial assistance of her parents. She would have to find work nearby, no further away than Eagle River, and would live in the house she grew up in.

Five days later, Cal and Emma were both back home. Meg assisted Cal in composing a letter to be sent to Cal's twenty-odd regular annual fishing clients, explaining his plight and regretting that he would no longer be able to service them. Meg typed the letter, had copies made and then let Cal dictate personal notes to those who were special to him. One such note was added to Dennison's letter.

> *Roy—sorry I won't be fishing with you anymore.*
> *I'll never forget your kindness and generosity.*
> *I know they're trying to give you a hard time*
> *up here. I don't believe you did anything to hurt*
> *her. Good luck and God's speed. Cal*

The catastrophe that befell Cal Cooley stunned Dennison. For a few moments he escaped the heavy cloud of doom that had been ever present since his first meeting with Mark Travis and was able to sympathize with another human being's suffering. He felt compelled to talk to Cal.

"Hello Cal. It's Roy. Just got your letter. How you doing? And Emma, how is she?"

"Jeez, Roy. Thanks for calling. We're really a mess. Thank goodness Meg is living with us now. Couldn't survive without her."

"Listen to me, Cal. I'll be on trial in Bessemer soon and will probably end up spending time in prison for not reporting

Allison's death. You're right, I didn't do anything to harm her. I swear to you that's the truth. I won't be in a position to receive or write checks on the excess medical bills for Emma and now you, but here's what I want to do. Give me the name of your bank and your account number and I will wire $100,000 to your account. Hopefully, that will take care of your bills and your living expenses for a good while."

"Are you serious? Why would you do that for me?"

"First of all, because I can. More importantly, because you're good people in need. Now, the bank and the account number."

"It's the Headwaters State Bank in Land O' Lakes. Account number 1465. I can't believe you're doing this. Don't know what words to say... grateful, I guess. Can't wait to tell Emma and Meg. God bless you, Roy."

CHAPTER THIRTY-SEVEN

Rogers pulled in the circular drive and parked next to the front door. Lily let him in and led him to the den, where he waited for Clara. The wall above the sofa was covered with photographs. Roy still appeared in several of them, probably not for long. How many happy hours he spent with Roy and Clara, sitting around the antique lion-pawed cocktail table, chatting, laughing and drinking. He had envied the life the Dennisons led, the children, the home, their shared love. Dan shook his head, thinking that life was over for Roy.

"Hello, Dan. Thanks for coming," Clara said, tying her hostess robe snuggly at the waist.

She really is a beautiful woman. I've always thought so, but I don't remember seeing such sadness around her eyes. Rogers took her hand and kissed her cheek.

"I promised Roy I'd check on you and he wanted me to deliver a message."

"What's the message?"

"No matter what you've read in the papers, he wants you to know that he did not physically harm that girl."

"And you believe that? He's been lying to me about her for over a year. Why the hell would I believe him now? Either way, it's not what he did to her that tortures me—it's what he's done to me."

As tears began falling down her cheeks, a wave of compassion came over Rogers. He reached out to Clara and drew her close, folding his arms around her as he said words intending to comfort.

"He's not a bad man. He's a good man who made a bad mistake."

Clara forcefully pushed her way out of his arms, stepped back and let loose a torrent of virulence.

"That's bullshit. He's a lying son-of-a-bitch, maybe even a murderer, who I want nothing to do with ever again. You can't imagine what my life is like now. I'm embarrassed to be out in public. I don't dare attend my board meetings. My friends stopped calling me. Martha, Lily and my kids are the only humans I've been talking to. I'm sorry for all this self-pity. I'm so glad you're here."

"Roy is in big trouble. He's going back to the UP to stand trial and says he will be incarcerated between two years and the rest of his life."

"The rest of his life sounds just about right. I'm going to divorce him. I have to lookout for my kids and myself. I don't know how all this is going to affect the finances."

"I'm going to buy out his interest in the firm, when we determine a value."

"One favor. Will you find a divorce attorney for me?"

"I'd rather not be put in the middle of this."

"Please. No one needs to know. I just need someone I can trust, who won't be bamboozled by my mogul husband."

"I'll see what I can come up with. But promise me, please, that my name will never be mentioned."

"I promise. I really need a friend now. Please be my friend." Clara leant in and kissed Dan on the cheek.

As he left Clara, Dan reflected on the stupidity of his partner to have put at risk all that was in that house to get his rocks off with a girl half his age.

CHAPTER THIRTY-EIGHT

The afternoon mail brought Mark Travis the retainer agreement signed by Dennison, along with the referenced checks. He had already started his preparations for the trial. He located a Travel Inn Motel one block from the Bessemer courthouse where Dennison could stay during the trial, if bail was available. He had begun research on Judge Clarence Matenson, who was sure to be presiding over the trial. The judge's early years in law were in general practice in Rhinelander, Wisconsin. He moved to the UP fifteen years ago, after a rancorous divorce which involved his wife's charges of physical abuse. His political republican leanings earned him a job in the County Prosecutor's office in Bessemer. After seven years of prosecuting misdemeanors and low-level felonies, he ran for Circuit Judge and was elected. He was repeatedly rated as fair regarding legal ability and temperament by the Gogebic County bar. Fair was in third place in the ratings behind excellent and good.

Travis was particularly interested in learning Judge Matenson's attitude with regard to bail in serious felonies. By calling around to local defense attorneys he surmised the judge favored bail for those who posed little risk of flight, but with constraints in serious matters. Limited capacity of the Bessemer County Jail and saving the county money were cited as additional reasons.

Travis called Dennison to confirm receipt of the contract and checks and for other reasons.

"You must be around day eight of your thirty days. I want you to plan on turning yourself in by day twenty-five or six, but not to the Cook County State's Attorney. I want you to drive to Bessemer and meet me so we can turn you in at the Sheriff's headquarters."

"Why so?"

"By voluntarily crossing state lines and submitting to the jurisdiction, we are laying the groundwork for a persuasive application for bail. We'll meet in the lobby of the Travel Inn, just a block from the courthouse. Call me and let me know the date and time you expect to be there. I'd bring enough clothes for a couple of weeks, including a couple of suits—make that slacks and conservative sport jackets."

"I'll point for the twenty-fifth and will call you with details," Dennison said.

*   *   *

Lehman was passing through Watersmeet early morning on his way to a litigators seminar in Iron Mountain. He stopped to visit Wickerham.

"I'm really psyched about this Dennison trial. Thinking about it all the time. Even started making notes for my opening," Lehman said.

"Sure. It's a big deal case. You're going to put that boy away for a long time."

"Wallensky and Cooley—they are my key witnesses. You

better keep a close eye on them. Don't want them leaving town or getting into trouble."

"No problem there. Cooley's crippled up and ain't going nowhere. The judge let Frank out on his own recognizance, pending his sentencing. He's delaying that until after the Dennison trial. Frank is still watching Dennison's place like nothing happened. I'll keep an eye on him."

"As soon as we get Dennison up here and the trial is scheduled, I'll get you subpoenas to serve on those boys."

"Be my pleasure."

"You got a big part in this thing, finding the body and all. We'll get together and work on your testimony when the time is right."

"Whenever you say."

Lehman moved on to the café for breakfast before the hour and a half drive to Iron Mountain. Approaching the café, he saw Meg Cooley seated alone by the window. Standing at her table, he cleared his throat to distract her from her book.

"Otto!"

"Hi, Meg! Didn't know you were home. School over?"

"Please, sit. School is over. I'm waiting for the results of my registration exam."

"Heard about your dad. What a bad break. Really sorry. Your mom, too. How are they managing?"

"They're not happy, and pretty helpless. Taking care of them is my job, for now. Haven't seen you or talked to you in quite a while. How's everything going?"

"You been reading about Dennison and the dead Chicago girl?"

"Sure. A little bit. Why?"

"That murder case is mine to try. My first big case will probably be the most publicized murder trial in the UP in our lifetime."

"What makes you think you can win?"

"What do you mean? The evidence is pretty strong."

"Dennison is not the kind of man that could do something like that."

"What do you know about Dennison?"

"I know that he's loving and kind, and generous beyond belief."

"Where's all this coming from?"

"He just deposited $100,000 in my dad's bank account, so my folks can live free of financial worries. Does that sound like a murderer to you?"

Otto looked away, shaking his head with disbelief.

"One thing got nothing to do with the other. Spreading money around doesn't change the fact that your dad is going to be a witness in my case."

"Witness to what?"

"Never you mind. Come to court during the trial and you'll find out."

"No need for you to get so curt."

"Are you going to eat?" Otto said.

"No, I'm done. Just about to leave when you came in."

CHAPTER THIRTY-NINE

Only twelve days until Dennison would be driving to the UP to surrender and possibly never have another day of freedom for the rest of his life. That thought produced a chill down his spine to the seat of his pants. His bank account was prepared to meet every contingency. He had not heard from Dan regarding the office meeting or his message to Clara. Sitting on his bed in his hotel room, he called Dan.

"I'm going to be surrendering to the Sheriff of Gogebic County on June 25, so I don't have much time. What's going on?"

"A lot. Two more juniors quit. I've had to lay off three associates and six staff. General Advertising Corp. has left us, abruptly. No conversation. I don't know how to stop this. Bound to get even worse when your trial starts."

"What does accounting say about a buyout price?"

"No way to value your interest or mine under these circumstances. Everything in flux. A month from now, the firm might be worth zilch. I'm thinking of telling the remaining juniors that if there is a civil damage suit, I will provide for their defense as long as they are still associated with the firm. Otherwise, they'll be on their own. What do you think?"

"Don't ask me. I'm in no shape to make decisions. What's happening in Philly?"

"Nothing yet, but they're plenty nervous. I can't fucking sleep at night."

"I know what you mean about sleep. Have you talked to Clara?"

"I went to see her and delivered your message."

"And?"

"She doesn't believe you and hopes you spend the rest of your life in prison. I don't blame her for being so bitter. Her life has been turned upside down."

"Do you believe me when I say I did not harm Allison?"

"I don't know what to believe."

Dennison hung up the phone, covered his face with his hands, uttered a loud guttural moan, and began to sob.

It was midday. Dennison had fallen into a light sleep and was jarred awake by his phone.

"Hi Mr. Dennison. It's Jerry in Eagle River, calling you about the jeep."

"Oh, yeah, Jerry. Right."

"Wickerham said my jeep will be tied up at least for a few months, so I found a used jeep I can pick up for $12,000. Does that sound OK?"

"Sure. That sounds OK Give me an address and I'll send you a check."

Feeling his face, unshaven for four days, he walked to the dresser and looked in the mirror. If he had a gun, he thought, he would end it right now. He had never looked so ugly, so undeserving of the good life, of his freedom. *Better make the best of it while I still have a few days.*

He shaved, showered, dressed and left the hotel room. He chose to walk on the sunny side of the street, feeling the warmth of the sun, observing every detail around him with purpose, as though seeing the everyday for the last time. He passed a woman walking with two young children while pushing a baby carriage, reminding him of his family. *Will I ever see them again? I will, if only once, to say goodbye.* He experienced a strange sense of envy of the crippled man at the corner, hopefully holding his cup out toward him. As he dropped a $10 bill in the cup, he thought, *better to be crippled and free.*

CHAPTER FORTY

"I'm going to be on the north shore on business early this evening. Thought I might stop by your place with some divorce lawyer information," Rogers said.

"That would be great. I'd love to see you. Can you come for dinner?" Clara asked.

"No, thank you. I'll be later than that. Maybe about 8:30 p.m."

He had no business on the north shore but wanted his visit with Clara to appear more casual than a special trip to the suburbs. He arrived at 9:00 p.m. The children had already been put to bed. Clara greeted him with a momentary hug, wearing an elegant hostess outfit. Dan breathed in her sweet perfume as his face brushed her ear. She had carefully made herself ready for his visit.

"Is your life any better than the last time I was here?"

"Actually, it's worse. I've been getting hate calls two or three times a day."

"From the same caller?"

"Oh, no. Some repeaters and a lot of different male voices. This morning I got a call from a woman who asked 'How does it feel to be married to a murderer?' That's about the mildest of them."

"Why don't you change the number?"

"That's a big hassle I'd like to avoid. I'll wait a few days, see if it improves."

Rogers had always admired Clara's appearance but had never thought of her as anything other than his partner's dutiful wife. Now, alone and needy, he found her attractive and desirable. His growing resentment of Roy made it easy to accommodate such thoughts.

"Do you have a lawyer recommendation for me?"

"I do. I thought you might be comfortable with a woman. I've got a good one for you. Alicia Binder. She's young, mid-thirties I think, developing a terrific reputation for high-quality representation of her clients."

"Sounds perfect for me."

"Here's her information. You take it from there."

"Can I offer you a glass of wine? I have some red in the kitchen."

"I could go for that."

They sat silently sipping their wine in the den, Rogers wondering what else they could talk about.

"How's the firm going without the boy wonder?"

"The firm is in trouble. Our client base has been disintegrating. Your husband really did a job on us. He's heading to the UP soon to face the music."

"You didn't deserve it and neither did I."

"We're both in the same leaking boat, the one Roy punched a hole in."

For the first time in years, Rogers imagined a meaningful relationship with a woman. It was three years ago that his lady friend of many years, actually fiancée for three months, ran away to take up with a ski instructor in Taos.

Rogers said goodbye with a half hug and kiss on the cheek. He was sure he felt Clara's body release into him as he hugged her.

*   *   *

The law office of Alicia Binder was modest in size and décor. It consisted of Alicia, one secretary and one paralegal. Clara Dennison approached the entrance with trepidation. Being married for so many years to a lawyer did not prepare her for dealing with a lawyer, one on one, on a business matter.

"You were recommended to me by a very close friend who prefers to remain anonymous."

"My guess is that friend is not a lawyer, because most lawyers would be interested in securing a referral fee. I'm aware of your husband's situation and assume that's why you're here. Please call me Alicia. May I call you Clara?"

"Of course. I've been told that he expects to be incarcerated in Michigan for a period of two years up to the rest of his life. I want to divorce him."

Alicia was not an attractive woman. Her slightly graying, unkempt hair and makeup-less thin-lipped face gave her a fifty-something look, rather than Rogers' suggestion that she was in her thirties.

Clara narrated the history of Roy's adulterous relationship with Allison, his lies and her expulsion of him from the home. After identifying the children and their ages, she responded to

Alicia's questions.

"Where is Roy living at the present time?"

"Downtown, in the Mid-City Hotel. I've been told that he will be going to the UP of Michigan later this month. Can I divorce him if he's in jail in Michigan?"

"Sure can. Ordinarily, one state doesn't have personal jurisdiction over a person in another state, but Illinois is one of the states with a long arm statute that would apply here. Illinois would have personal jurisdiction over a guy in jail in Michigan whose permanent residence has been and continues to be in Illinois. How resolute are you in your desire for a divorce? Do you need some time to think about it?"

"I need to disassociate myself from this man. Don't need any time to think about it."

"In that case, I recommend we file suit immediately and get him served with process while he's still in Chicago. That will eliminate any possible issue with regard to personal jurisdiction. Are you OK with that?"

"Absolutely."

"Grounds will be chronic adultery and mental cruelty."

"How do I pay for this?"

"You can give me $2,000 as a cost retainer. I will look to your husband for fees. If that doesn't work, I'll bill you."

Notwithstanding ten years of happy marriage, Clara knew from the moment she learned Roy had taken a woman with him to the UP that she would never share her bed with him again. There would be no forgiveness. That's just the way she was. She held him responsible for the death of that girl, whether by his hand or not. The turmoil in her life that followed the discovery of Allison's body made it impossible for her to continue the marriage. She would have to sever all connection to Roy and the community, take her children and get away.

CHAPTER FORTY-ONE

There were items Dennison wanted to recover from his office before leaving town, including a cash box, various documents, an expensive antique wall clock and photographs of his wife and children. Other valuable art pieces in the office belonged to the firm. He called Rogers, requested they meet in the office at 7:00 p.m., after everyone had left, and then possibly go to dinner together. Rogers agreed.

As he passed through the hotel lobby on his way to the front door, a man came up to him and asked, "Are you Roy Dennison?"

"Yes, I am."

The man handed him an envelope and said, "You've been served."

Dennison sat on a lobby chair and opened the envelope. Divorce papers. *Why would she do this so fucking fast?* He put the papers away and continued on to the office.

"I just got served with divorce papers. Can you believe it? No conversation. No discussion about the kids. Boom! Just like that."

"Sorry to hear that. Get your things together and we'll talk about it at dinner."

They went to Ditka's Steak House. It was the first time in a week that Dennison had eaten anywhere other than the hotel coffee shop.

"I never heard of this lawyer, Alicia Binder. You know anything about her?"

"Nope. I can check her out for you, if you like."

"Well, sure. She probably rushed Clara into this. Seasoned divorce lawyers wouldn't likely file so quickly. I don't have any time to deal with this. I'm going to ask Clyde to cover it for me, for now."

"What's your position going to be?"

"What do you mean?

"With regard to everything, the money, the kids."

"Jesus, I don't know. I'm going to be gone for a long time, maybe forever. I'll have to talk to Clyde. Maybe he can talk to this Binder woman and slow her down."

"What does your Michigan lawyer think your chances are of beating the murder and manslaughter charges?"

"He thinks their case is weak without a weapon or an eye witness, but who really knows? I could survive a two-year prison sentence, but I'm scared to death my life may be over."

"Whatever happens, you can count on me to keep an eye open for Clara and the kids."

"Thanks. It's good to know you feel that way, after all I've done to you. One more favor? I don't know where I'm going with this clock. I should have left it in the office. Will you take it home with you and maybe, God willing, I'll pick it up from you in about two years?"

"Be my pleasure. It's a beautiful clock."

* * *

Back in his hotel room, Dennison was recounting the evidence against him on the serious charges. He was upset when he initially read Wallensky's statement in the charging documents, outlining all the gruesome details of the cover-up. He now realized that once the body was found, naked but for a bathrobe, Wallensky's confession was essential. His hope was that Wallensky would remember when he first saw Allison on the floor, Dennison told him it was an accident. His impulse was to call Frank and remind him it was an accident and he must remember to say that. He quickly realized that would be a mistake.

He had to talk to Clara about this divorce business. It was getting late, after 10:00 p.m., but he called.

"Hello," she weakly answered.

"I hope I didn't wake you."

"No. I've been getting a lot of hate calls and at this hour, I thought this might have been one."

"What kind of hate calls?"

"What do you think? Your husband's a fucking murderer. That kind."

"Jesus. What's wrong with people?"

"That's very funny, coming from you."

"I was served with your divorce papers today and just had to call you."

"We have nothing to talk about. I hope you don't get the chair up there, or whatever they do. If you get away with it, good for you. Just stay out of my life."

"I'm leaving town next week. Don't know when I'll be back, if ever. I need to see the kids before I go, just to hug them and say goodbye. I also need to pick up a few things to take with me."

"OK You're entitled to that. We'll tell them you're going away on a long business trip. Best you come by right after their dinner so you can see them before they go to bed. Call me when you know what day you're coming."

"By the way, what's the big hurry for divorce?"

"It's simple. I don't want to be married to you anymore."

The call concluded, he sat on the bed and thought, *God, could I use a smoke*. He had been an inveterate chain smoker until a good friend died of lung cancer at age twenty-eight. If ever there was a time to start smoking again, this was it. Why not? What did he have to lose? He had visited his friend several times in his final days. Watching the fatal misery that disease imposed on someone he cared for compelled him to quit cold turkey ten years ago. He settled for a double shot of whiskey and turned in.

CHAPTER FORTY-TWO

A law clerk pulling a cart with documents stacked three feet high stepped up to the counter at the office of the Clerk of the Circuit Court of Cook County.

"Good morning. We're filing this lawsuit today. Sorry, here's the original and twenty-five copies because we have eighteen defendants."

The documents were piled on the counter as the clerk, frowning to display his annoyance, proceeded to time stamp each one. The plaintiff in the lawsuit was Albert Jameson, Administrator of the Estate of Allison Jameson, deceased. The defendants were Dennison, Rogers and sixteen junior partners. The complaint contained multiple counts, the basic claims being wrongful death and sexual harassment. Monetary damages were sought in the amount of $25,000,000.

All documents except the original were then carted one floor down to the office of the Sheriff of Cook County where summonses and complaints were issued to be served on each of the eighteen defendants. Within three days Rogers and half of the juniors were served. In two days, Dennison would be leaving for the UP. Rogers called him.

"Have you been served yet?" Rogers asked.

"No, but I'm sure they'll get me in Michigan, once they figure out where I'll be. I was at the house last night saying goodbye to the kids. Clara read about the case and she feared all our assets would be at risk. I calmed her down about it, but it is something to be concerned about."

"The juniors are running scared. No work getting done around here. I spoke to our liability insurance carrier this morning. He wants the summons and complaint and he will have attorneys appear in the case on behalf of all the defendants. Under our policy the insurance company is required to provide a defense, but the coverage will not protect us against judgments based on intentional torts," Rogers said.

"So, we're on the hook for any damages?"

"That seems to be the case. I'm going to ask Clyde to file an appearance as co-counsel, to make sure the insurance guys are doing their job."

"Most of these cases get settled somewhere along the way," Dennison said.

"The sooner the better. What are you doing about the divorce?"

"I spoke to Clyde. He had someone pick up the papers. He'll file his appearance in the case and said not to worry about it now. I'm going to call him after we're done."

"I'm afraid this lawsuit will end the firm. I expect more clients will start peeling away in the next few days. No way to stop it. As the clients leave, we'll have to cut lawyers and staff. Sixty days from now there'll be no Rogers and Dennison."

"Do you think it would help if I released a statement to the press to the effect that I was withdrawing from the firm, and the firm had nothing to do with my connection to Allison Jameson?

I'll be happy to do it."

"You shouldn't do anything without the knowledge of your Michigan lawyer, and you can bet he'd counsel you to make no statements. Probably wouldn't help, anyhow."

"I'm guessing that the value of my half of the firm is equal to half the bank account and half the receivables, less half the payables, just like yours. You know what? Keep my share for yourself, whatever it is. That's the least I owe you for crapping all over the great thing we had going."

"It's been a great ride. Sorry it had to end this way," Rogers said.

"I'm leaving in two days. I'll try to keep in touch."

First the divorce and now this lawsuit. Not a bad time to leave town. He called Clyde Fuller.

"I'm leaving town for the UP in two days. I suppose you read about the lawsuit."

"I did. I was getting ready to call you about it. How serious do you think it is?" asked Fuller.

"It's pretty damn serious. We have no insurance coverage on the damages."

"In that case, you better think about protecting the kids and Clara."

"What do you mean?"

"I know it takes time for these damage cases to reach trial or settlement, but you need to make sure Clara and the children are protected financially before there's a raid on your assets."

"How do we do that?"

"By promptly working out a property settlement with Clara,

including provisions for child support and getting it approved by a court. Before you leave, give me a list of estimated value of each category of your assets. I'll call Alicia and explain the importance of an early agreement and see if she is inclined to work something out."

"That's fine, but these will be ballpark estimates. I'll mail you the list tomorrow. "

"All right, buddy. Good luck in Michigan."

CHAPTER FORTY-THREE

For a small town, with a population of approximately 1800, Bessemer was a beehive of activity. It housed the headquarters of all the government offices of Gogebic County. The weekly *Herald* was a newspaper published in Bessemer until it closed down in 1970. After that, the primary written news absorbed by the citizens of Bessemer was the *Daily News* published in Ironwood. That paper came out five days a week and serviced both Gogebic and Ontonagon Counties. Ironwood was located just seven miles west of Bessemer.

Dennison was to meet Mark Travis at the Travel Inn at 3:00 p.m. He left Chicago at 7:00 a.m., driving the jeep he picked up in Winnetka when saying goodbye to the kids. He got Frank on the way so Frank could return the jeep and garage it at Dennison's Den for the duration. Mark was already at the Inn when he arrived.

"We're going to walk down to the Sheriff's office and surrender you. You don't do any talking unless I ask you to. You'll probably have to stay there overnight, until I have a chance to speak to the judge. I hope you brought a good book."

"Actually, I did."

It was a short block to the Sheriff's office. Dennison was despondent, thinking these might be the last steps he would ever take as a free man. His knees buckled as he approached the office. Travis understood the moment, as he placed his hand on Dennison's shoulder.

They stepped up to the counter, where a seated deputy raised his hand in greeting as he hung up the phone.

"What can I do for you boys?"

"We're here to voluntarily surrender Roy Dennison. This is Mr. Dennison. There is an open warrant for his arrest."

"You fellows take seats over there while I get the Sheriff."

Sheriff Hermanson appeared sporting a bushy white moustache, with his waist belt riding low, supporting a major protruding stomach.

"Congratulations on having the good judgment to come in voluntarily. Now, stand up and give me your hands so I can put these cuffs on."

"That's hardly necessary under these circumstances," Travis said.

"Just following protocol. You'll have to stay here until the judge says otherwise. Come this way." The Sheriff took Dennison by the arm and started to lead him away.

"Hold on a minute. I'd like to talk to my client before you take him."

"Come along with us. You can talk to him once we get him settled. I'll hold off processing him 'till your done with your talk."

They walked to the back of the office, then through two doors, entering the jail area consisting of four unoccupied cells. The cuffs were removed as Dennison and Travis entered one of the cells. Dennison flinched at the sound of the door clanging shut.

"Just shout out when you're finished, Mr. Lawyer. We'll hear you on the speaker."

The nine-by-six cell was a shade nicer than the ones Dennison was used to seeing in the movies. It had a cot, a sink, a toilet and a makeshift desk with a simple wooden chair. The floor was covered with a plain linoleum. There was a barred window high enough on the wall so you could only see the sky.

"I'll speak to the judge in the morning and see what can be done to bail you out of here. I'm holding a room for you at the Travel Inn. There'll be an arraignment, hopefully in just a few days from now, at which time you'll plead not guilty to all charges."

"But I am guilty of the lesser charge."

"Understood. We have to make sure the jury knows you acknowledge guilt of the lesser charge. If you plead guilty before we start the trial, the judge might exclude any reference to the lesser charge and the jury would never know you pled guilty to anything. We'll change the plea in the presence of the jury at some point during the trial. Is there anything I can get for you from your jeep?"

"My book and my toilet kit are in the small suitcase. Oh, and the charger for my cell phone. Maybe it'll work in Bessemer."

After Travis left and was on his way to set up his morning petition for bail, Sheriff Hermanson called Otto Lehman.

"I have a surprise for you," Hermanson said.

"I only like good surprises," Lehman said.

"I have Roy Dennison in custody. He just walked in here with his lawyer."

"That is a great surprise. Who's his lawyer?"

"He didn't say, and I didn't ask him."

"Thanks for the heads up. Trial's a lot closer now than I thought it would be."

The following morning in the courtroom of Judge Clarence Matenson, the clerk called out "State of Michigan versus Roy Dennison" Travis, Roy and Lehman stepped before the court.

"I've read your petition for bail. Never saw one quite like it before. Sounds like you're asking me to bail him out to the Travel Inn."

"Good morning, Your Honor. Mr. Dennison voluntarily left Illinois and came to Michigan to stand trial on these charges. He came for the trial with the intention of remaining for the trial. He obviously poses no flight risk. The county jail is unoccupied except for Mr. Dennison. To keep him there will require the activation of all personnel and procedures for one inmate. These costs to the county are unnecessary where the defendant is absolutely not a flight risk."

"What do you have to say, Mr. Lehman?" the Judge asked.

"Pretty rare to allow any bail for a man charged with murder one. What would the public think about a man charged with this grizzly murder walking free about town?"

"What do you say to that Mr. Travis?"

"Here's a solution, Judge. As a condition of his bail, require the defendant to be confined to his unit in the Travel Inn for the duration of the trial—same confinement as though he were in a jail cell. I'll also be staying at the Travel Inn during the trial and will be responsible for the defendant's compliance with your bail conditions."

"I see merit in your suggestion, counsel, with these added conditions. First, I will set bail at $300,000. Second, the defendant will wear an ankle monitor, and third, if he is detected leaving the Travel Inn, other than going to and from court on trial days in the company of a deputy, his bail will be immediately suspended, and he will be incarcerated. Is that agreed?"

"Mr. Dennison will comply with those restrictions and conditions."

"Mr. Lehman?"

"Most unusual, but the State can live with it."

"You gentlemen get together and draft an order for me."

"Your Honor, Mr. Dennison is ready to go to trial as soon as your schedule permits. We, therefore, request an early arraignment date."

"We can do the arraignment tomorrow morning, if that's all right with Mr. Lehman."

"No problem, Your Honor."

"How many days will this trial take?" the judge asked.

"The State's case would be nine or ten court days."

"No more than one or two days for the defense."

"OK, then. We'll start the trial two weeks from today. Does that give you enough time, Mr. Lehman?"

"Yes, sir. The State will be ready."

Judge Matenson invited the lawyers to join him in chambers.

"Have you fellows had any discussion about a possible plea? It would be nice if we could avoid a trial and spare this town all that excitement."

"Actually, I've discussed the matter with the County Prosecutor, but not yet with counsel," Lehman said.

"Why not talk about it now?" the Judge said.

"OK. The State is willing to drop the murder charge in exchange for a guilty plea to voluntary manslaughter and a fifteen-year sentence."

"Counsel?"

"I will recommend against that to my client. I believe conviction on murder one is highly unlikely, with no eye witness and no murder weapon. Fifteen years is the maximum penalty allowed for voluntary manslaughter. I will report the offer to my client, but it will be refused."

Dennison arranged for his bail bond and ankle monitor in the clerk's office and was escorted by a sheriff's deputy to the Travel Inn. Travis, having already checked him in, guided him to his room. Two beds and a single chair next to a small dresser supporting a thirty-two-inch television. It was a big improvement over the cell he occupied last night. Dennison was pleased, and started unpacking as Travis told him about the plea offer and his recommendation that it be declined. Dennison gasped at the thought of having to falsely admit to causing Allison's death.

"I couldn't do that" he said.

"No need to even think about it, unless they cut the years way down."

"Even then, I'm not going to confess to killing her."

"Look, Roy, suppose they said plead guilty to voluntary manslaughter and you can go home with no prison time. Would you be tempted?"

"That would make the decision a lot harder."

"Just remember, principles only go so far. They knew their opening offer wouldn't be acceptable. Let's wait and see if they have anything better."

"It would have to be close to no prison time for me to even consider pleading guilty to causing her death."

"Some prison time is coming, for sure, on the lesser charge."

"Right. When you're picking up groceries could you also get my book, toilet kit and charger from the Sheriff's office?"

"Sure. I have three rooms booked here. Yours, mine and the third is for one of my girls who will set up an office here before and during the trial. She'll also be your gofer while we're here in Bessemer. You probably didn't get much sleep last night. Why don't you take a nap and we'll talk about the arraignment later tonight?"

"That bed does look good to me. Thanks for everything, Mark. You did a hell of a job this morning."

At the arraignment, Dennison pled not guilty to all charges. Travis advised Lehman and the court that his client rejected the plea offer. He privately told Lehman not to bother with any offers that required his client to plead guilty to a homicide, unless it was an offer of less than a total of five years for all charges.

Lehman scoffed and said, "We got a trial."

CHAPTER FORTY-FOUR

Lehman had a clerk drive half way to Watersmeet to meet Wickerham and deliver the subpoenas to be served on Wallensky, Cooley and Bart Stapleton. He was busy outlining his direct examination of Archie Bremer and the other fact witnesses. He doubted Travis would opt to have Dennison testify, but he would have time later to outline that cross-examination, which he anticipated would be devastating.

He was confident he could make a compelling case for motive. Here was this forty-five-year-old prominent Chicago lawyer, married with three young children, imposing himself on an employee half his age. He impregnates her and the night her head gets bashed in follows a day they were not speaking to each other because of a "personal issue." Then he hides the body and lies about it. Lehman thought a UP jury would find such facts intolerable and would convict on one of the homicide charges.

Meg greeted Wickerham at the front door. "Hi Jesse," she said as she let him in.

"I'm here to see your dad. How's he doing?"

"He's pretty frustrated, hanging around the house most of the time. He'll be happy for the company. He's upstairs. I'll get him down here."

"Hi ya, Cal. Haven't seen you in a long while. Heard you been teaching fishing to kids at the church. That's really cool. The Dennison trial is coming up pretty soon. Otto Lehman told me to give you this." He handed Cal an envelope.

"What's this?"

"It's a subpoena for you to come testify at the trial."

"What has he got to testify about?" Meg asked.

"Well, I'm not sure, but probably about how those two were when they were fishing with you."

"Shit, Jesse, I'm not going to help Lehman put Mr. Dennison away."

"You have no choice. You got to obey the subpoena, else you'll be the one ending up in jail."

"If they want to put me in jail, so be it. I ain't gonna testify against Roy Dennison."

"I'll tell Otto how you feel about it."

"You can also tell Otto if he persists on harassing my father, he better keep a long distance away from me."

Just then, Emma hobbled from the kitchen into the living room.

"What's all the commotion about?"

"Jesse, here, wants Dad to go to Bessemer and testify against Roy Dennison."

"Are you nuts? No one in this house is going to lift a finger against that man. Roy Dennison is the kindest, most generous human being God ever created. Jesse Wickerham, take your nonsense and get out of here."

CHAPTER FORTY-FIVE

Three days after the arraignment, there was a knock on Dennison's door. A young lady introduced herself.

"I'm Vera Stemple. Mark Travis sent me. I just checked into the second unit down from you. Mark has the one in between. Just wanted you to know I'm here."

"Would you like to step in and visit for a while?"

"Thanks, but I've got some setting up to do, computer, printer etcetera. I'll stop back when I'm done and we can talk."

Roy was pleased he was going to have some company. He spent the days reading, watching television and making phone calls to Rogers and Travis. His cell phone worked in the Travel Inn. Living was similar to his days in the Mid-City Hotel and much better than it would have been in the town jail.

Vera returned an hour later.

"Mark wants me here to take care of your needs, food, drug store, whatever you need and can't get for yourself. Don't be shy to ask."

"Let's start with a fifth of Dewar's Scotch."

She smiled and made a note of it.

Vera with her short brown hair, was not beautiful, sort of plain-looking, but had a nicely formed body and a winning smile. He guessed her age to be in the thirty to thirty-five range.

"What will you be doing here, other than running errands for me?"

"Mark will be calling in or e-mailing work product for the trial for me to type. Stuff like direct and cross-examinations, voir dire questions for the prospective jury and court documents. I'm sure I'll be getting busy in the next couple of days."

"Why don't you find us some kind of dinner and then come back here to share it? Maybe we can find a good movie to watch together. I could use the company."

"Sounds like a reasonable thing to do. Got any preference for dinner?"

"Whatever you can find. I'm not fussy."

*　*　*

Rogers' prediction about the demise of Rogers and Dennison was coming to pass. More clients were jumping ship even before the trial began. While most of the juniors were staying on to take advantage of legal representation paid for by the firm, it was becoming obvious that the reduced fee intake would soon be insufficient to cover salaries and other overheads.

Marvell Jackson completed the United Supplies merger which was scheduled to close in a month. He had quietly been arranging to leave with two other juniors to start their own practice. His commitment to Roy to finish up United Supplies was the only thing holding up his departure.

The civil litigation was progressing. Ben Greenblatt had served notices to take the depositions of Dennison, Rogers,

Jackson and Cathy Riley. Dennison would assert his rights under the fifth amendment not to testify until his criminal case was over. Greenblatt would move forward preparing his case. He would have to decide whether to wait for Dennison or complete preparation of the case without his sworn testimony.

Rogers kept in contact with Dennison on a daily basis during the first week of his Travel Inn confinement. His interest in doing so diminished as the destruction of his law firm accelerated. A creeping bitterness transformed into a growing anger directed at Dennison for bringing on this calamity. His thoughts soon turned to Clara. *Poor girl, what she has to go through. She's scared, alone. I need to be there for her.* He arranged a date to pick her up and take her to dinner for the purpose, he said, of bringing her up to date on all things related to Dennison. In truth, he felt like a white knight coming to her aid. He enjoyed her company and believed she may have developed some feelings for him.

They went to dinner at the Don Roth Steakhouse in Wheeling, a Chicago suburb.

"This is so nice of you. I haven't been out for dinner in a long time," Clara said. She dressed elegantly for the occasion, wearing a hunter green satin evening dress and the chinchilla jacket Roy gave her for their tenth anniversary.

"I wanted to tell you what's going on with Roy and, frankly, I thought you would like to have some company. I could use some, myself."

He talked about Roy's bail situation, the trial starting in a week and the big damage lawsuit.

"Now, let's talk about you. Anything new on your divorce?"

"Yes. I was going to call you about it. My lawyer received a proposal, based on Roy's estimate of his total assets. He claims his assets, excluding the value of our home and any value of his interest in the law firm, is approximately $16,000,000. The offer is $8,000,000 plus the Winnetka home. He's also willing to contribute toward the children's education. What do you think?"

"Wow! That really happened fast. It sounds like a very generous offer. I can't vouch for his estimate of value, but it's probably not off more than two or three million. Even so, still a generous offer."

"I'm inclined to want to accept it and be done with the divorce stuff."

"Once the divorce and the property settlement are final, what do you plan to do?" Rogers asked.

"I want to leave the Chicago area. I'm miserable here."

"And go where?"

"San Diego or Scottsdale, I think."

"Does Alicia say you can take the kids out of this jurisdiction?"

"She would apply to the court for permission to do so and would expect no problem in view of Roy's likely extensive imprisonment."

"You know, Rogers and Dennison will be caput by the time you're able to leave town. Would you consider my joining you going west?"

"Daniel! I would have to get to know you better before I answered."

"Well then, let's get started with that."

CHAPTER FORTY-SIX

As the day of jury selection was drawing near, prosecutor Otto Lehman was losing some of his bravado to an insecure feeling that his homicide case was not as strong as he initially believed. Wickerham reported that Cal Cooley was refusing to testify. Without him, evidence of motive was weak, maybe nonexistent. Then there was no evidence of a weapon and no eye witness to contradict Dennison if he took the stand and testified to an accident. He was always surprised to have been given the prosecution of such a major murder case. He was beginning to suspect that the boss gave him the case because it was weak but had to be prosecuted because of political pressure—thereby protecting his own prosecutorial record.

He had always been concerned about the absence of a murder weapon. The more he thought about it, the more he believed he was being made the fall guy to protect his boss's political career. With the trial now imminent, he had convinced himself he would go down in flames if he didn't account for a weapon. He came to believe Wallensky must have disposed of the weapon as he did the body. That subject was not covered in the statements Wickerham took from Wallensky. Lehman called Wickerham and made a mistake, nearly as consequential and life changing as Dennison's.

"We have to account for the weapon," Lehman said.

"How do we do that?"

"You have to get it out of Wallensky. He must have got rid of it, whatever it was."

"What do you want me to do?"

"Go see Wallensky. Talk it out of him. You know he's half-witted. Remind him that he dropped it in the woods. A bat, a wrench, any object that could have done that damage."

"Christ, I'm not sure I can do that."

"Get tough with him, Jesse. If we want a homicide conviction, we better account for a weapon. That's all we need to sew this up."

"That doesn't seem right."

"Jesse, do you believe that Dennison killed this girl?"

"Yes, I do."

"And do you want to see him found guilty of that murder?"

"I sure do."

"Then, goddamn it, do what I'm telling you."

"OK, I'll try, but I don't like it."

That evening, Jesse paid a surprise visit to Frank at his cabin. The front door was open leading to one large room containing a sitting area, a bed and a kitchen against one wall. That was the only room, besides a bath room. The room was a mess with newspapers strewn about, dirty dishes filling the sink and garbage littering the counters. Frank was seated at a short-wave radio listening to music. There was no television set in the cabin.

"Hi Frank. You got some time for me? I need to talk to you about the night Roy called you and you went to the Den and found the Allison girl."

"Sure, deputy. Take a seat. What do you want to know?"

"You saw her on the ground with her head bashed in."

"Yep."

"There must have been a weapon there that did that to her, right?"

"Mr. Dennison said it was an accident."

"Forget about that. Did she look like she could have been hit on the head with something?"

"Could've been."

"Like some kind of a tool, a hammer or a wrench."

"Could've been."

"What did you do with the tool?"

"I didn't do anything with any tool."

"There must have been a tool there and you must have taken it with you when you took the body."

"I didn't take anything other than the body wrapped in a blanket."

"Frank, the people on the jury are going to think you are crazy if you say there was no weapon. There must have been a weapon. Do you want people to think you're crazy?"

"I ain't crazy, and I don't want no people thinking or saying that I'm crazy."

"Then you better say you took the hammer and threw it away somewhere in the woods."

"I threw it away somewhere in the woods?"

"That's right. Can you remember that?"

"I threw it away somewhere in the woods."

"What did you throw away?"

"A hammer."

"Where did you throw it?"

"Somewhere in the woods."

"It's important you remember to say that when Mr. Lehman asks you the question on the witness stand."

"I'll remember. I don't want anyone thinking I'm crazy, 'cause I ain't."

"Now, you gotta remember that me and Mr. Lehman only want you to tell the truth. If anyone asks you what we said, it was just that you tell the truth. Right?"

"I got it. You said tell the truth."

"And the truth is you threw the hammer somewhere in the woods. Correct?"

"Somewhere in the woods."

"I'll call you and give you a day's notice when you have to come to the courthouse in Bessemer. Nice seeing you, Frank."

"Same here. Thanks for coming."

Disgusted with himself, Wickerham had a premonition this was going to turn out badly.

CHAPTER FORTY-SEVEN

Mark Travis checked in the Travel Inn the day before jury selection was to begin. Looking for Vera, he entered Dennison's room unannounced and found them both sitting on the bed, Roy shirtless and Vera with her hair a mess and her blouse untucked.

"When I told you to tend to his needs, I didn't mean all of his needs. Tuck your blouse in and come with me. We've got some work to do."

With Vera at the computer keyboard, Travis began dictating a motion to limit the introduction of certain evidence or reference to the same during jury selection and opening statement.

"The State having informed the defense of its intention to offer into evidence all content of the autopsy report of Dr. Archie Bremer, defense moves to bar any reference to the pregnancy of Allison Jameson in the absence of any evidence that either she or the defendant had knowledge of such pregnancy on the grounds that the relevancy of such evidence would be outweighed by the prejudice it would cause."

The next morning, in chambers, Travis presented his motion.

"What do you say to that, Otto?" Judge Matenson said.

"I'm actually surprised that so experienced a trial lawyer as Mr. Travis would file so spurious a motion. I most certainly object."

"Otto is right on this one. Her pregnancy is a fact and

bears on the relationship between the defendant and the victim. Its relevancy is for you to deal with in your argument. Motion denied. Now let's get out there and start picking our jury."

One benefit of Dennison being out on bail was he could pick his clothes when in court, instead of what was provided by his jailors. He also avoided the indicia of guilt when jurors get peeks of cuffs being removed or put on a prisoner. Today, Travis had him dressed in slacks, a sport jacket and a plain open-collared shirt.

Jury selection filled the balance of the day and most of the next day. When twelve were approved by both sides, Judge Matenson took counsel into his chambers.

"What do you say we waive alternates and agree to go with a minimum of ten. That will expedite things."

"The State agrees."

"No. I don't want this case submitted with less than twelve jurors. Let's pick four alternates, so we avoid any chance of a mistrial," Travis said.

"OK I'll let them go home now and we'll finish up the jury in the morning. Opening statements in the afternoon."

Lehman would not allow Cal Cooley's refusal to comply with the subpoena stand.

"I'll get an order for you to pick him up and bring him to the courthouse tomorrow, so I can talk to him at the lunch break before opening statements. That son-of-a-bitch gives us motive. He's got to testify."

The following morning, Wickerham and Deputy Luke went to the house on Catalpa Street, showed Meg the court order, apologized, and said they had no choice but to bring Cal to Bessemer.

"Why don't you just leave this poor man alone? He's not going to testify against Mr. Dennison, no matter what."

"Mr. Lehman's going to put him in jail if he doesn't take the stand. He's not foolin'."

Cal came slowly down the stairs, having heard Meg's raised voice.

"Dad, they're here to take you to the courthouse. They have a court order for you to appear."

"I'll go peacefully, but I ain't gonna testify."

"You can give Mr. Lehman a message from me. You can tell him to drop dead," Meg said.

The deputies brought Cal to the courthouse and had him wait for Lehman in one of the lawyer conference rooms. Lehman came to the room after the alternates were selected and the noon break was on.

"I've known you for a long time and I know you're a law-abiding, God-fearing man, who always wants to do the right thing," Lehman said.

"The right thing for me is not to testify against Roy Dennison."

"The right thing for you and anyone is to tell the truth. I need you to tell the truth just the way you told it to Jesse Wickerham. Your time on the stand will be very short. Need only confirm that Dennison told you they weren't talking because they had a personal problem. That's all of it."

"I won't do it. If you put me on the stand, I'll deny it, and on cross examination I'll do everything I can to destroy any case you got. So, here I am, responding to your subpoena. You decide what you want to do."

Lehman leaves the room and finds Wickerham.

"I can't use him. Put him on a bench outside the courtroom and let him figure out how he's going to get home," Lehman said.

"I got a message for you from Meg Cooley, if you want to hear it."

"What's that?"

"She said you should drop dead."

* * *

The jury was composed of six men and six women. They all had heard or read something about the case but insisted they could be fair and decide the case only on the evidence presented. Half of them had heard of Roy Dennison before this case, although not in any negative or especially positive way.

Before opening statements, Lehman had an objection to present out of the presence of the jury.

"I object to any reference during the defense's opening to the girl's death being an accident in the absence of any evidence supporting such an assertion."

"Mr. Travis, is there going to be any evidence of this being an accident?" Judge Matenson asked.

"Indeed, there will be Your Honor. Mr. Dennison will provide such testimony."

"In that case, the objection is overruled."

CHAPTER FORTY-EIGHT

The *Daily News* headline, *Chicago Lawyer in Bessemer to Stand Trial For Murder*, captured the interest of the community. People came from Ironwood, Wakefield and Watersmeet with the hope of getting a seat to witness some of the trial. The courtroom had a seating capacity of eighty. Every seat was taken for the opening statements. A line had formed in the corridor of folks waiting to be allowed in. Very few gave up their seats once they gained them. It would be like this every day of the trial.

Lehman guided his witnesses Bart Stapleton and Cathy Riley through their stories with no objections by Travis. Travis waived cross-examination. Lehman's next witness was Wickerham. He testified in detail about locating and removing the body. He identified the authenticity of various photographs taken at the scene, which the court allowed in evidence instead of the video of the same events. He also testified regarding the forensic report on the jeep. Several jurors leaned forward as Wickerham related his conversation with the defendant, all of which was total fabrication. Then came the questions that caused Travis to rise and interrupt.

"Did you come to know that earlier on the day she disappeared Allison and the defendant were fishing with the guide, Cal Cooley?"

"Yes."

"Did you speak to Cal Cooley about that day?"

"Your Honor, may we approach the bench?" Travis asked.

The attorneys leaned in toward the judge and spoke in whispers.

"I fear that Mr. Lehman is about to elicit rank hearsay testimony from this witness, which will necessitate a mistrial or reversible error."

"You wouldn't be doing that, would you, Mr. Lehman?"

"Your Honor, Cal Cooley is crippled from a stroke, lives in Watersmeet and can't make it to court."

"That doesn't make it any less hearsay. The fact is Mr. Lehman caused Cooley to be served with a subpoena and had him brought to the courthouse earlier in this trial so he could converse with him. Mr. Lehman is getting careless with the truth."

"Otto, what's going on here? Is that true?"

"I apologize, Judge. I misspoke."

"All right. Drop the subject and get on to your next question."

On the fifth day of the trial Archie Bremer took the stand. Lehman led him through his background and experience leading to his job as coroner of Gogebic County. He repeated the care taken in recovering the body from the gravesite. Before getting into the detail of the autopsy he identified color photographs depicting the bloody gash to Allison's head, with closeups showing the depth of the wound and particles of skull bone. After detailing the autopsy findings, with particular emphasis on the pregnancy, Lehman put the following question.

"Do you have an opinion, based upon a reasonable degree of medical certainty, whether the wound depicted in these photographs could have been caused by someone striking Allison Jameson with a hammer?"

"Objection, Your Honor. May I be heard?" Travis said.

"This is a good time to take a ten-minute break. Bailiff, take the jury, and counsel— in chambers."

"What's your objection, counsel?"

"As far as I know or have been told by Mr. Lehman, there is no evidence regarding a hammer or any other kind of weapon. Talking about some nonexistent hammer is highly prejudicial."

"Have you been withholding anything?"

"No, Judge. We have new evidence, discovered on the eve of trial, as to the existence of a hammer."

"That's news to me. Where did this new evidence come from?" Travis asked.

"I'd rather not say at this time."

"I'd rather you did say," Judge Matenson said.

"Disclosed to Jesse Wickerham by Frank Wallensky in a recent interview."

"I can't believe you've got yourself involved in these kinds of shenanigans. Judge, Frank Wallensky is deeply flawed intellectually, you might say retarded. He can be talked into saying or doing almost anything. Witness what he did at the request of my client."

"That may be so, but you'll have to take care of that in cross or in your argument. On the representation of counsel that he will be coming forward with evidence on the existence of a hammer, I will overrule your objection and allow the question."

Day six was Frank Wallensky day. With Lehman's prompting, he appeared wearing a clean white shirt and his Sunday church suit. Lehman carefully took him through all the facts that appeared in his second court reporter statement. He did not ask him about any conversation he had with Dennison when he came to the Den that night, so "accident" was not mentioned.

"Now, Frank, you took something from the Den and put it somewhere in the woods?"

"Objection to leading question."

"Sustained. Don't lead the witness."

"We know you buried the girl's body in the woods. Did you also put anything else somewhere in the woods?"

"Objection. Still leading."

"I'll let him answer."

"You can go ahead and answer that question," Lehman said.

"Somewhere in the woods," Frank said.

"What did you put somewhere in the woods?"

"A hammer."

"You took the hammer with you from the Den?"

"Objection. He's leading the witness."

"Sustained. Counsel, stop leading the witness."

"Where did you get the hammer?"

"I don't remember."

"Who did you first talk to about the hammer?"

"Jesse."

"Jesse Wickerham?"

"Yes."

"What did Jesse tell you when you mentioned the hammer?"

"He said to tell the truth."

"And what is the truth?"

"Somewhere in the woods."

"Was there blood on the hammer?"

"I don't remember."

"Why did you drop the hammer somewhere in the woods?"

"I don't know."

Afraid to press any further, Lehman stopped right there.

"Your Honor, may we have a side bar?" Travis said.

The attorneys moved to the side of the judge opposite the jury box, out of range of the jury's hearing.

"I move to strike any of this testimony relating to a hammer and request the court to instruct the jury to disregard all references to a hammer."

"I must say the testimony sounds nonsensical. I'm not sure that it proves anything. Are you intending to cross examine this witness?"

"I certainly will if you don't grant my motion."

"Then let's proceed with the cross-examination. You can renew your motion, if necessary, when you're done."

The lawyers returned to their seats.

"You may cross examine the witness, Mr. Travis."

Travis slowly walked across the full length of the jury box toward the witness. As he passed, he exchanged eye contact with as many jurors as were willing to do so.

"When you went to Mr. Dennison's home that night and saw the lady on the floor, did Mr. Dennison say anything about what happened?"

"He said it was an accident."

"Objection to that, Judge, it's self-serving."

"Overruled. Counsel, you opened the door in your direct examination."

"Did he tell you what kind of an accident?"

"Same objection."

"Same ruling. You may answer."

"He said she tripped and hit her head on the ledge of the fireplace."

"Mr. Lehman asked you about a lot of things from the transcript of Deputy Wickerham's interview. Did you also tell Deputy Wickerham in that interview that Mr. Dennison said it was an accident."

"I think I did."

"Was her head on the floor next to the marble ledge of the fireplace?"

"Yes sir."

"Was there a lot of blood on the ledge of the fireplace?"

"There sure was a lot of blood."

"Did Mr. Dennison give you anything to take with you when you left with the body of Miss Jameson?"

"No sir."

"In your recent meeting with Deputy Wickerham, who mentioned the word hammer first, Deputy Wickerham or you?"

"Jesse did."

"And who mentioned the words 'somewhere in the woods' first, Jesse or you?"

"Jesse did."

"Did Jesse tell you to say the words 'somewhere in the woods' when you testify in court?"

"Objection! He's leading the witness."

"Mr. Lehman, this is cross-examination. He can lead, and I want to hear this answer."

"Did Jesse tell you to say the words somewhere in the woods when you testify in court?"

"Yes sir. He said that was the truth and people would think I was crazy if I didn't say it, and I ain't crazy."

"That's all. Thank you, Mr. Wallensky."

"Any redirect, Mr. Lehman?"

"No sir."

"Ladies and gentlemen, I'm letting you go home a little early today. Just remember, no discussion with anyone about this case and we will see you in the morning. Lawyers, please follow me."

The judge removed his robe and told the court reporter she would not be needed. Travis and Lehman sat facing a scowling Judge Matenson.

"I hope you didn't have anything to do with this. If you did, you're in for a heap of trouble."

"I told Wickerham to visit Wallensky and see what he could find out about a weapon. I didn't tell him to plant any ideas in his head," Lehman said.

"I'll grant you a mistrial, if that's what you want."

"Thank you, but I'm not interested in a mistrial," Travis said.

"I'll grant your motion to strike all references to a hammer in Wickerham's testimony."

"That motion is withdrawn, your Honor. I'm satisfied with

the record as it is."

"I understand. When this case is over and the jury is discharged, I want you, Wickerham and a court reporter in my chambers. I want to find out how this subornation of perjury came about."

"Yes sir," a distraught Lehman said.

Otto wanted to call Wickerham back on the stand in the morning to assert it was Wallensky who first mentioned the hammer and its disposition somewhere in the woods. Wickerham refused, saying he wasn't going to lie under oath. At that point, Otto rested the State's case.

The State's homicide case had gone so poorly Travis was tempted not to put any case on. He finally concluded that the record had to contain Dennison's statement that Allison's death was the result of an accidental fall.

"Counsel, are you ready to proceed?"

"Yes, Your Honor. First, Mr. Dennison would like to change his plea to guilty to the charge of purposefully concealing the fact or cause of death of Allison Jameson. He continues to plead not guilty to the charges that he caused her death. Defense will ask Mr. Dennison to take the stand."

He testified about his relationship with Allison, the fondness they had for each other and the wine drinking on the fatal night. He identified photographs of the Den's living room, fireplace and close-ups of the marble ledge and the shag rug. He then described the accident that caused her death.

"Mr. Dennison, you heard the direct testimony of Frank Wallensky regarding what you and he did to make it appear that Allison died somewhere other than in your home on

Crooked Lake?"

"Yes sir, I did."

"Was all of that testimony true?"

"Yes sir, it was."

"When Allison fell and hit her head on the marble ledge, you had the choice of calling the authorities and reporting her death or embarking on this complex chain of lies to establish that she died somewhere else. Why did you choose the chain of lies?"

Following the prep instructions of his counsel, Dennison turned in his chair to face the jury, making eye contact with those who would return eye contact as he spoke.

"My judgment was totally messed up by the suddenness and horror of the situation. When I checked and found no pulse, I panicked. I made a terrible and stupid mistake. I knew there would be no sympathy for me here with this young woman. I feared an investigation and being charged with a homicide if Allison was found in my house in this condition. All of this raced through my mind in a matter of seconds. I made a hasty and not well thought out decision. As soon as Frank took her away, I knew I had made a horrendous mistake, but it was too late, too late."

"Did you know, according to the autopsy report, that Allison was six weeks pregnant?"

"I did not, and I don't even think she did."

"Objection!"

"I'll let it stand." Judge Matenson said.

"Did you and Allison argue the night before this happened?"

"Absolutely not."

"Did you give anything to Frank to take with him when he

took Allison away?"

"No."

"You heard references to a hammer in Wallensky's testimony?"

"Yes, I heard that."

"Was there a hammer in your living room that night?"

"Of course not."

"Did you strike this girl that you loved?"

"Oh my God, no."

"Your witness."

Lehman could do little with Dennison on cross since he readily admitted to all the lies he had constructed. Other than establishing Allison's occasional pouting and moodiness about being with a married man and showing Dennison to be a liar by the contents of the court reporter statement taken by Wickerham, the twenty-minute cross was ineffective.

At the close of all the evidence, Travis moved for the dismissal of the homicide charges on the grounds there was insufficient evidence to support guilt beyond a reasonable doubt.

"I see there is some merit to your motion, but I will reserve ruling on it until after the jury returns its verdict."

During closing arguments, Lehman contended the claim of accident was laughable, that it was ludicrous to believe Dennison made this all up to avoid an investigation, and that common sense required finding the defendant's actions were designed to hide a homicide.

Travis excoriated the State and Mr. Lehman for attempting to concoct a story about a mysterious hammer and doing so by inducing a mentally challenged man to perjure himself. No motive, no eye witness, no weapon. The State's case was replete with reasonable doubt.

Waiting for juries to return their verdicts is always torturous for defendants and their counsel. Life or death, freedom or imprisonment, you can cut the tension with a knife. Dennison's optimism reached a peak with the cross examination of Wallensky. Still, his life was in the balance. Travis had cautioned him you can never really tell what a jury is going to do. So, he sat alone with his counsel in the courtroom and nervously waited.

They didn't have to wait long. The bailiff went to answer a rap on the jury room door. They had reached their verdict in only one hour of deliberation. Waiting for Lehman to return and for the Judge to take the bench, Travis put his hand on Roy's shoulder.

"My feeling is a one-hour deliberation in this case is a good sign."

"Hope to God your feeling is right."

The judge, Roy and the attorneys stood as the jury returned to their seats. The foreman gave the verdict form to the clerk, who passed it on to the judge. Roy closed his eyes as the judge began to speak.

"As to the charge of murder one—not guilty. As to the charge of voluntary manslaughter—not guilty."

Roy covered his face with his hands and fell back into his seat, as Judge Matenson thanked the jury for their service and discharged them. He then rose with tears flowing and took the breadth out of Travis with a grateful bear hug.

His life was not over.

CHAPTER FORTY-NINE

Judge Matenson scheduled sentencing for one week and allowed Dennison to remain out on bail until then. He didn't request a presentence investigation other than criminal record, if there was one.

Vera and Travis came to Dennison's room that night for a party of sorts. They finished what was left of Dennison's second bottle of Scotch and dined on quarter pounders and fries from a nearby McDonalds. Vera had been coming to Dennison's room occasionally at night to spend some time with him, charitably recognizing he would soon be deprived of such opportunities—and because she enjoyed the sex.

Travis and Vera were leaving in the morning, after Vera did some shopping to stock Dennison with enough food to cover him for the week. Travis would return for the sentencing.

"What are you thinking my sentence will be?"

"Hard to say. The maximum would be two to five years. I'm going to ask him for probation. That won't happen. You're going to have to spend some time in prison."

"Where will they send me?"

"I'm confident it will be a minimum-security prison. Parnall is in Jackson, pretty close to Grand Rapids. That would be a good place for you. Close enough for Chicago folks to visit. I'll ask the judge for Parnall."

*　*　*

Dennison was anxious to break the news to Rogers and Clyde Fuller that his life was far from over. The shroud having lifted on his future, he felt energized and anxious to be brought up to date on the status of things.

"Not guilty on the homicide charges!" Dennison said.

"Congratulations. How much time on the other?" Rogers asked.

"Don't know yet. Sentencing is next week. Haven't heard from you in a while. What's new with the firm?"

"We lost General Plastics and Jensen Container, and four more juniors are gone. They're starting to feel it in Philly now. Won't be long before I close the office. Fortunately, there's only three months left on our lease."

"Have you kept in touch with Clara? Are she and the kids OK?"

"I talk to her from time to time and everything is fine."

"I may be serving my time in a facility near Grand Rapids. If so, maybe you'll drive up sometime for a visit."

"For sure. Let me know the details."

Rogers didn't sound that excited about his news. He couldn't blame him, seeing the way he messed up his career. He'd try Clyde next.

"The trial is over. Only took the jury one hour to come up with not guilty on the homicide charges."

"That's terrific. So happy for you," Clyde said.

"Mark did a great job, and you did a great job in finding him. Tell me about the civil case."

"Greenblatt will start taking depositions next week. I met the insurance company lawyers. They seem to know what they're doing, but I'll keep an eye on them."

"And the divorce?"

"Alicia recommended the deal to Clara and it looks like she's going to take it."

"She's really going through with it. Do you think she might reconsider if she knew I wasn't going away for life?"

"I don't think so. Thought I ought to tell you, she's been seeing a lot of Dan."

"How so?"

"Well, I understand he's been out to the house just about every other night."

"I just talked to him and he didn't say anything about it."

"I can understand that. Pretty awkward subject."

"I don't think I like that idea one single bit. Jesus Christ."

"Don't get all upset. Might not be anything to it. Maybe he's advising her on the divorce."

"I'm going to call Clara and find out what's going on."

"OK, but be cool."

He found it hard to believe that Dan would be making a play for Clara. *What would he want to do with three kids? Maybe it's just for the sex. He could have waited a little longer, given her a chance to recognize she'd be better with me than being alone. All these things are happening and I can't do a fucking thing about them.* He called Clara.

"Hi Clara. Are you and the kids OK?"

"We're fine. What's happening with your trial?"

"It's over. Not guilty on the homicide charges. I pled guilty to the less serious charge."

"What does that mean?"

"Probably a stint in prison for a year or so. Won't know for a week."

"So, I guess congratulations are in order."

"I don't know about that. I've been thinking about you and the kids every day. Miss you all terribly."

"That's nice, and I'm happy you'll still have a life to look forward to, but it won't be with me. I've agreed to the divorce terms you offered."

"So, that's that."

"That's that."

"I've heard you've been spending some time with Dan."

"Dan has been wonderful. He knows what I've been going through, and he's restored some sense of normalcy to my life."

"Is there something serious between you two?"

"I'm very fond of him. We're really just getting to know each other."

"Jesus, Clara, are you sleeping with him?"

"What kind of question is that? It's none of your goddamn business."

"The hell it isn't. I'm entitled to know if my wife is sleeping with my partner."

"You're not entitled to shit." She hung up.

Dennison turned the light out, laid back on his pillow, closed his eyes and thought, *I wish Vera was here.*

CHAPTER FIFTY

The week went by slowly for Dennison. He watched television, did a little reading and tried to sleep as many hours as possible each night. Travis checked in the night before sentencing morning. As they walked to the courthouse, Travis cautioned his client.

"The judge will probably ask you if you have anything to say before he announces his sentence. You can say nothing or you can simply thank him for the fairness with which he conducted the trial. That's it. Nothing about sentencing."

"I got it."

Judge Matenson took the bench in an empty courtroom.

"Counsel. Do you have anything you would like to say at the outset?"

"Your Honor, I would like to urge you to consider no jail time for Mr. Dennison and, instead, a period of probation and community service. Mr. Dennison has no criminal record and the likely suspension of his license to practice law would seem to be adequate punishment for this offense."

"Mr. Dennison, do you have anything you would like to say before I sentence you?"

"Only to thank you for the manner in which you conducted this trial."

"You may think the offense to which you pled guilty is not a big deal, but your conduct had consequences that should not and cannot be ignored. It caused unnecessary and extended grief to the family and friends of this poor girl. It caused the State and county to conduct an expensive investigation necessitated by your lies and then pursue a murder trial, again because of your lies. The statute in question provides for a maximum prison sentence of five years and a maximum fine of $10,000. I believe that prison time is required. I sentence you to a term of eighteen to twenty-four months and a fine of $10,000. I'll see counsel in chambers to discuss the location of Mr. Dennison's imprisonment."

Dennison had maintained an unrealistic hope for probation, while being conditioned by Travis to realistically expect to serve two years in prison. He viewed eighteen months as a six-month bonus—nothing to be sneezed at.

"I'll have a parole hearing scheduled immediately after you complete eighteen months. I'm confident you'll be released at that time."

* * *

His prison term at Parnall Correctional Facility commenced on October 15, 1997. Parnall was a minimum-security prison housing near 1500 males aged eighteen on up. While there were no violent crime inmates at Parnall, it did have a Violence Prevention Program to assist with anger management. There were many angry people at Parnall. Prisoners were required to work, unless prohibited for health reasons. Many different jobs were offered, most involving trades or manual labor. Dennison quickly assumed a lead role as a counselor in the law section of the library.

The facility was composed of five residential buildings on forty-five acres, security provided by a double chain link fence with sensor alarms and cameras around the perimeter.

His cellmate for most of his first year was John Baker, owner of a small business in Detroit, imprisoned for cheating the State on sales taxes and cheating his employees by withholding and pocketing excessive amounts from salaries. Baker had a good sense of humor and an easy and frequent laugh, which helped keep Dennison's spirits up. Unfortunately, Baker was released about halfway through Roy's minimum sentence. Dennison had no cellmate the balance of his time.

Cell phones were considered contraband and not allowed in the Michigan prison system. Prison phones were readily available to Dennison since he was able to set up a prepaid calling account for that purpose. The stream of news he received from Clyde Fuller was deflating and depressing.

"Thought you should know the divorce decree was finalized by the court yesterday."

Just one week later.

"I hesitate to tell you this, but it's no secret and I guess you'd want to know. Dan moved into the Winnetka house right after the divorce was done."

A month after that.

"Dan, Clara and the kids are planning to move to San Diego after the first of the year. We were in court yesterday on their motion for an order from the court permitting the kids to be taken out of the jurisdiction."

"How can they do that? Don't I have father's rights?"

"I objected on your behalf. The court allowed them to go and said you had enough money to fly there and see them any time you want."

"I'd like to fucking kill both of them."

"Clara told me at the hearing that they plan to marry after they get to California. Sorry to be piling on, but your law license was suspended with the right to apply for reinstatement after three years."

"Fuck the law license. I'm done with that. How can Rogers go to California? What about the firm?"

"What's left of the firm, at least in Chicago, will be gone by then. The doors will be shut."

How much can one man take? When I get out of this fucking hell hole there'll be no life to return to.

* * *

After Baker left, Dennison was alone and falling into a dark place. It had been almost a month since he last spoke to Clyde. He had no one else, or did he? He called Cal Cooley.

"Hey, Roy, great to hear from you. How's it going in the pokey? How long you got to go?"

"Another nine or ten months. How are you and Emma?"

"We do a lot of sitting around, but we're OK. Meg is still living with us and she's a great help. I still drive a little—just short trips around town."

"What's new in the UP?"

"A lot you'd be interested in. There was talk about a criminal prosecution of your friend, Otto Lehman, for suborning perjury or knowingly putting on perjured testimony. Instead, he bought his freedom by resigning, forfeiting his pension and surrendering his law license. Don't see or hear much about him anymore. Wickerham was suspended from his job as deputy for sixty days without pay. Pretty much a clean sweep."

"Well deserved punishment, I'd say. I'm feeling pretty down and just wanted to hear a familiar voice. My love to Emma and Meg. Gotta go now."

Dennison took his hankie out and wiped tears from his face. He was crying a lot these days, often with good reason, sometimes without reason he could identify.

Helping inmates with their legal issues in the library was his only saving grace. Sometimes he helped with their pro se appeals. One semi-lunatic, known only as "Rags" to Dennison, was repeatedly in and out of the law library, arguing to no avail for Dennison to help him with a nonsensical appeal to the US Supreme Court. He turned him down at least three times and finally told Rags to stop bothering him with his crazy legal theories. Rags was also in and out of anger management, as he was quick to turn rejection or perceived threats into tantrums or raging rants.

On the Fourth of July, Dennison and a dozen inmates were in the library discussing the Declaration of Independence, when Rags raced into the room behind Dennison in a frenzy and slammed a full four inches of the blade of a knife deep into the base of his right shoulder. Dennison screamed out in excruciating pain, the knife having pierced and disrupted the brachial plexus, a network of nerves controlling the right shoulder, arm and hand.

Two days in the infirmary were followed by two weeks of daily physical therapy. Dennison was told to use the arm and hand as much as possible. His residual was severe. He had limited use of the hand and arm and couldn't raise his elbow up to shoulder height. He couldn't use his right hand to comb his hair, brush his teeth, write or clean himself in the bathroom. Eating with his right hand was difficult. The strength was gone. He spent the balance of his time at Parnall adjusting to being left-handed.

Dennison had become immersed in self-pity. Added to his nightmares of Allison in the grave were dreams of Clara and Dan, luxuriating with his money and enjoying his children. In these, Rob was continually referring to Dan as "Daddy". *When do the punishments stop for my one sin?*

CHAPTER FIFTY-ONE

The nerves did not regenerate, as the doctor said they might. Roy's right arm and hand were pretty much useless, permanently. He lost interest in and gave up his library job. He was not required to work any job due to his physical disability. That meant long hours alone in his cell every day. Fearing an inability to defend himself from attack, he took no advantage of the prison's liberal policy allowing inmates to intermingle outdoors or use recreational facilities. He stayed away from people.

Dennison's bitterness, anger and paranoia rendered him a shell of his former self. All his confidence and self-possession were gone. The remaining months of his imprisonment were marked by aging, weight and hair loss and thoughts mired in self-pity.

When Clyde called him in October of 1998, he was shocked to hear the weakness and hesitation in Dennison's voice.

"I spoke to Mark Travis this morning. He said he's starting to work on scheduling a parole hearing in April, as soon as your minimum sentence has been served."

"That's good. Where will I go?"

"You'll go wherever you want. Do you want me to set up an apartment for you in the city?"

"I don't know. It's still a long way off."

"Negotiations have been going on in Greenblatt's case. The

plaintiffs' proposal is $12,000,000. The insurance lawyers say that's just a starter, but they're asking whether you and Dan want to make a counter."

"I don't even know what I have."

"I can tell you that. Besides the Den, the boats, the Alfa Romeo and the plane, you've got about $5,500,000 still invested in the market and about $475,000 in the bank."

"What happened to all my money?"

"I've been taking care of your expenses, just like you told me. A thousand dollars a month to Frank Wallensky and whatever else he needs to keep the place up. Another $40,000 to Travis, in addition to his original retainer. I've been writing checks to myself once in a while, when the hours build up. I saw you sent $100,000 to Cal Cooley. Don't forget, Clara got $8,000,000 in the divorce settlement."

"What does Rogers want to do?"

"He and Clara have pretty substantial combined assets. He's waiting on you. He says he'll match you on it."

"What do you think I should do?"

"I think you'd like to get this over before you're released. If a trial went badly, you could be wiped out. Maybe you should offer to contribute $2,000,000 to a settlement."

"That bastard should pay twice as much as me. I'm always the one that gets fucked. Go ahead, make that offer."

"Good decision. How are things going there? You don't sound so good."

"Some goddamn nut fucking stabbed me through my right armpit. Made my right arm and hand useless."

"Holy shit! I thought you were at a minimum-security place. That's awful."

"It's unbearable. Try wiping your ass with your left hand. I need to get out of here before I totally lose my mind."

"I'll let Travis know what's going on with you. Meanwhile, hang in there. You're more than two-thirds of the way done."

"That parole thing better work. I won't be able to make it through any added time."

"By the way, I forgot to tell you, Clara took her Acura to the West Coast. She had your jeep and the Alfa Romeo stored in a private garage and I've been paying for that every month. I'll report back to you on negotiations."

Two weeks later, Clyde called again.

"Greenblatt has come down to $8,000,000. The insurance guys think a deal could be made at $6,000,000. Unfortunately, the stock market just took a twenty per cent dive. The brokers are undecided whether it's going to recover, stay flat or drop another twenty per cent."

"Even the stock market is fucking me. Better sell me out before I lose everything."

"Are you sure?"

"Goddamn right I'm sure."

"I'll start working on it as soon as we hang up. What about the $6,000,000?"

"I'll contribute $3,000,000, but that's it. Any more than that, I'd have to sell the Den. That miserable bastard, Rogers, ought to pay the whole thing. That son-of-a-bitch is sitting there on the beach with his fucking money and half of mine."

"I spoke to Dan the other day. He and Clara sold most of their market holdings last month and put the money in CDs. He either knew something or got some good advice."

"Some guys find a shelter in every storm. I just get drenched and sink deeper and deeper in shit. Sorry, I'm starting to cry. Happens to me a lot these days."

"I'll keep in touch." Fuller said.

CHAPTER FIFTY-TWO

Dennison had not shaved for three weeks. His sleep was constantly interrupted by dreams of Allison turning into nightmares. Dreams of Clara sleeping with Rogers, dreams of Wickerham chasing him to oblivion. Sometimes, a pleasant dream, being on a boat on Crooked Lake with Cal Cooley.

There were people from the outside world coming to see inmates on visiting days. Dennison had been at Parnall over a year and had not had a single visitor. What did that say about how the world cared for him? Who should have visited him? Clyde, maybe. For God's sake, Travis's office was just an hour and a half away in Grand Rapids. Who else?

He located Marvell Jackson's phone number through Chicago information.

"Is that you, Marvell?"

"Yes, it is. Who's calling?"

"Roy Dennison, from Parnall Correctional Facility in Jackson, Michigan."

"Wow! Surprised to hear from you."

"Are you still practicing law?"

"Yeah. I joined up with two other juniors and we started our own firm."

"That's nice."

"What can I do for you, Mr. Dennison?"

"Just felt like talking. Been here about a year and never had a visitor. Thought maybe you'd like to come up on a Sunday and visit with me. I could tell you about my trial and you could tell me about how the firm wound down. I've been alone here a lot and could use some company. I hear it's only about a two hour drive from the city."

There was an awkward silence for about ten seconds.

"I'm sure I could do that. Maybe the Sunday after next. Would that be OK?"

"That would be great. I'll look forward to it very much."

The weather accommodated outdoor visiting in a park-like area within the double fenced confines of Parnall. The trees still showed some autumn color, the remaining oak and maple leaves fluttering to the ground with the slightest breeze. Dennison shaved his beard for the occasion of the visit. Marvell was astonished by Dennison's appearance. The weight loss, balding and discolored puffiness below the eyes were signs of extended physical and emotional deprivation. Dennison did not respond to Marvell's offer of a handshake.

"Can't use my right hand hardly at all since my accident."

"What kind of accident?"

"Some asshole stabbed me in the back."

"Oh my God. How terrible."

"I wanted to tell you I was found not guilty of the homicide charges. I swear, it's true I did nothing to harm Allison."

"I followed it all in the papers. I believe you. I always did.

And I wanted to thank you for attempting to protect me against Wickerham when he was suspecting me."

Dennison told Marvell about the dishonesty of the prosecutor in the trial and how it backfired against the State. He bragged about his unique bail situation and how his lawyer inadvertently provided him with a sex partner during the trial. Marvell said, "Sounds like it would make a great movie."

"Did you and your wife go back to the UP in summer like you planned?"

"No. I kind of lost my taste for it."

"Did the United Supply deal ever get done?"

"Was about the last thing I worked on. We finished it up shortly before we closed the doors."

"How's the rest of your life coming along?"

"Actually, Louanna and I are doing great. We're expecting our first baby in about three months. When are you getting out of here?"

"My lawyer says the earliest would be in April. Did you know that Rogers ran away with my wife and kids?"

"I heard there was something going on there, but didn't know that. Must be really hard to take."

"I keep thinking of ways I might take vengeance on that man. He's taken them all to California, and with a lot of my money."

"You don't want to be thinking that way. By the way, I heard the damage case may be settling for $6,000,000."

"Oh, really? There goes the rest of my money."

"Please tell me if there's anything I can do for you in the city."

"You did everything you could by coming to see me today. I

wish you the best of luck with your firm, with Louanna and with the baby. Thanks for making the trip and drive safe going home."

Watching Marvell crossing the park toward the car lot, he couldn't help but envy him. A young, happily married man starting a legal enterprise with his friends. That was him and Dan twenty-two years ago, beginning their journey to stardom in Chicago's legal community. His daydream ended abruptly, remembering why he now hated that man. *That son-of-a-bitch took over my life. He's the husband of my wife, the father of my children and the manager of half my money.*

Marvell was right. The case did settle. Clyde managed to sell all of Dennison's securities over a period of three weeks as the market continued to slip downward. Three million dollars went into the settlement kitty and the balance to Dennison's bank account.

Dennison received a call from Travis advising that a parole hearing was scheduled for Wednesday, April 19, 1999, two days after the completion of his minimum term.

CHAPTER FIFTY-THREE

To maintain his sanity during his imprisonment, Dennison decided to read with a purpose. He took the opportunity to educate himself regarding subjects of interest to him. The library contained books about nature, trees, fishing. He read what he could find, some of them twice. While perusing the shelves, he came across two books on the subject of domestic violence and abused women. As an homage to the memory of Allison and her mother, he read both books and was moved by the desperation and paralysis women endured at the hands of depraved, maniacal men, a subject about which he previously knew little. Allison's mother was one of many who succumbed to suicide to avoid the incessant physical abuse and emotional terror. Poor Allison, he thought, a nine -year-old witnessing all that and then finding her mother dead.

As April drew near, Dennison became apprehensive about the upcoming parole hearing. There was no guarantee that he would be released. One week before the hearing, Travis called him to talk about what he should expect from the Parole Board and to give advice on how to conduct himself at the hearing.

"Sorry I haven't been out to see you before this, but I've been busy as hell with one trial after another. I heard about the stabbing and I'm glad you never did anything to retaliate. Your record is clean. Should be no trouble getting you released."

"I'm happy to hear you say that. I've been very worried about what will happen."

"The board is made up of decent people. I know the chairman well and he puts a lot of stock in my comments and opinions. There is one woman on the board, Grace Merrens, who gets a little sticky sometimes."

"What does that mean?"

"She'll search the record to find something that causes her to hesitate. I think she just likes to put a little fear in the inmate before she ultimately goes along with the chairman."

"How sweet."

"Your job is to answer all questions politely. Try not to be offended by anything that might be said. You'll be asked what living arrangements you've made in the event you are released. How will you answer that?"

"I have a home in Michigan's Upper Peninsula. The weather will be breaking about that time. I thought I would go there, enjoy the beautiful country while I decide what I want to do with my life."

"That answer should satisfy. Well, that's it. I'll see you on the 19th."

The Parole Board had a dedicated hearing room at Parnall. Dennison and his lawyer sat at one end of the conference table. The chairman was at the other end and three board members sat on each side of the table.

The hearing went well with the chairman complimenting Dennison on the clean record he had as an inmate. Travis stated his opinion that Dennison had the intelligence and moral integrity to make substantial contributions to society throughout the rest of his life. Grace Merrens interrupted at that point.

"Speaking of moral integrity, Mr. Dennison, do you think the not guilty verdict on the homicide charges resulted from your innocence or more likely from the incompetence of the prosecutor?"

"I'd say it was a combination of the two. I was innocent and the prosecutor was worse than incompetent. He was criminal."

The hearing adjourned with the chairman making the usual comment that the board would consider the request for parole and would render its decision within twenty-four hours. Later that same day, Dennison received a phone call from Travis.

"The board has granted your parole. Your release date is May 1. Congratulations. You'll only be required to check in with your parole officer by phone once a month for three months, starting June 1. That's the shortest parole I ever heard of in Michigan."

"Thanks, Mark. I can't believe I'm going to be fucking free. Sorry, I can't hold back the tears. Thank you, thank you."

Soon he would be away from these concrete walls and free of the constant anxiety that had consumed him ever since the night Allison died. A new anxiety was about to take hold. How would he lead his new life?

He called Clyde with the news and asked him to pick him up at Parnall on May 1 and drive on up to the Den. He could stay overnight and head home the following morning. Clyde agreed.

"Don't forget to bring my checkbook and ledger covering the past year and a half."

CHAPTER FIFTY-FOUR

It would be dark when they got to the Den, but he didn't care. The drive to the UP had always been an arduous endeavor. That's why he bought a plane and learned to fly. This was different. Clyde did all the driving while Roy relished every moment. With windows open and classical music playing on the radio, he absorbed the countryside as never before. The vast farm acreage with new growth just beginning to appear and the trees awakening from winter with new branches and green buds sprouting, signifying the arrival of spring. The world was still beautiful, more beautiful than he had ever realized.

"Farmhouse after farmhouse, herd after herd. I don't remember ever seeing so many cows," Roy said.

Not surprising, with Wisconsin having near 7,000 registered farms holding about 1 million cows, producing 2 billion pounds of milk per month. That's why it's called America's Dairyland.

"You think they have any dairy farms in the UP? I don't remember seeing many cows up there," Roy said.

"I'm pretty sure they do, but nothing like Wisconsin."

"Maybe I'll check that out as a possible business to get into."

"Oh, yeah. I can just see that. Roy Dennison, farmer."

"You never know."

Halfway up, they stopped at a drive-in for a sandwich and

coke. He called Frank and told him he was on his way to the Den and asked him to make sure the fridge was cleared out and cleaned up and there were no obstructions like trees down on the dirt road leading to the house.

They arrived at the Den at around 10:00 p.m. and found Frank's truck parked in front of the house. The same truck that carried Allison, wrapped in a blanket, to her final resting place. Roy carried a bag of groceries to the front door which was ajar.

"Frank, you in here?"

Dennison walked into the living room and found Frank seated on the fireplace ledge.

"What are you still doing here?"

"I was waiting for you, 'cause we need to talk."

"This is Clyde Fuller, my Chicago lawyer. Meet my good friend, Frank Wallensky, caretaker of Dennison's Den. What do you want to talk about?"

"I was in jail for forty-five days for helping you out with that girl."

"I didn't know that. I'm sorry you had to go through that. I know how it feels to be in jail. It's not good."

"You broke your promise to me."

"What promise was that?"

"You promised me I would get a big bonus if I said I didn't know anything about it, and that's what I said until Jesse told me you already told them everything that happened. You forgot all about my bonus."

"With all that was going on, I guess I did. It's not too late for that. You just sit there. I'll be right back." Dennison sat at the kitchen table with the checkbook Clyde brought along and came back with a $10,000 check for Frank.

"Thank you, sir. Let me know when you want the boats out of dry dock or anything else I can do for you. Oh, I can pick you up tomorrow and take you back to my place so you can get your jeep. Goodnight, sir, and you too, Mr. Fuller."

Frank had thoughtfully filled the wood space with logs and tinder. Dennison started a fire. He and Clyde sat down with brandies. Did he ever miss these glorious moments, these opportunities to think in comfort and luxury. Dennison opened his checkbook and ledger to see exactly where he stood financially. The cash balance in his account was $1,765,000. That, plus the Den and its boats, a jeep, the Alfa Romeo and a Piper Cub plane were his total assets. He scratched his balding head and crunched his eyes, dismayed by the evaporation of his $20,000,000 wealth in just two years. He was curious what Clyde had taken for himself during his time at Parnall. It added up to $185,000. Seemed high to Dennison.

"What the hell did you do to earn $185,000?"

"Jesus, Roy. I've got time sheets to support all of it. I handled the divorce for you and sat through the civil case until it was settled, researched the Michigan law and found you a top-notch criminal trial lawyer. You can add to that umpteen telephone calls keeping you up to date on Clara, Dan and the kids. I really resent your suggesting I over charged for anything."

"Sorry, sorry. Prison made me a little paranoid. Suspicious about most everyone and everything. I know you've been terrific for me. I don't need to see your time records. We're good. OK?"

"Of course. This has been a long day. I'm going to turn in

and get an early start in the morning."

Dennison poured himself another brandy, put his feet up on the hassock, and thought, *So, what am I going to do with the rest of my life?*

* * *

Dennison slept late and awoke to an overcast day. Clyde was already gone. He left a note next to the Keurig machine.

Happy you're free. Keep your head up.
I'm just a phone call away. Anything I can do,
I will. Clyde

Clyde was a good guy. Roy felt bad about challenging his honesty. He hoped Clyde realized it was a product of his incarceration and not a rational suspicion.

Roy stretched for ten minutes, had coffee and toast and set out to spend the morning walking along and through the woods, feeling and smelling the intermittent drizzles of rain. The sky partially cleared in the afternoon. He went down to the lake and sat on the wooden bench located at the end of the forty-five-foot permanent dock.

There was a slight silent ripple on the lake. Dennison was marveling at the natural beauty of the scene and enjoying the quiet when he heard the wailing call of the prehistoric loon. He searched the lake and spotted the black and white creature near the closest island. The loon was alone, wailed again, reminding

Dennison of his own loneliness. The difference was the loon's calls would soon cause it to be joined by its life partner.

There, on the dock, the euphoria Dennison had been experiencing since his release began fading away as the bitterness and anger worked up during months of isolation crept back into his psyche. He contemplated the disastrous consequences that flowed from his one mistake of infidelity, a mistake made by many if not most men, some repeatedly, with no apparent consequences. The unfairness of his situation was stifling. The more he dwelt on it, the darker his thoughts became. He walked back up to the house, downed a couple of shots of whiskey and laid on the couch. What next? He decided he needed some company.

"Hello, Cal. It's Roy. I'm at the Den. Got out of prison yesterday."

"Great to hear your voice. You're a free man again. Must feel awfully good."

"How about you coming to the Den tomorrow for lunch and some catching up?"

"I aint driving distances these days because of the stroke. Meg would take me, but she works on Fridays. How about Saturday?"

"Saturday is fine. Be sure to come before noon so we can have lunch and have a lot of time to talk. Bring Emma, if you like."

It stormed on Friday evening. One of those mighty Northwoods squalls with high winds, hard driving rain and thunder blasts that seemed to rock the house. The sound and smell of mother nature venting her power somehow comforted him. He watched and listened, sitting on the screened-in porch with all lights off. It was totally dark. He closed his eyes as he felt a drizzle of water across his face from the gusty wind driving rain through the screen. A lightning bolt suddenly lit the sky. For a brief moment the lake, the island and the far shore could be seen as though it was daylight. The light was followed immediately by a blast of thunder so powerful and loud it must have occurred directly above the house. It had been so long since he had felt any weather he relished every moment of the storm.

Saturday was the perfect calm after, sunny with light jacket temperature. Cal and Meg arrived at 11:00 a.m. Emma didn't come along, needing to prepare for a neighbor guest coming for dinner. The last time Roy saw Meg she was still in her teens. Now, at twenty-seven she was a beautiful young woman and a fully certified registered nurse. They visited briefly in the living room. Roy suggested that he and Cal go down to the dock to converse while Meg put lunch together. He pointed out all the makings for cold cut sandwiches and soft drinks.

"Set the table in the breakfast room and give us a yell when you're ready."

Cal was struggling some, walking the stairs to the dock.

"Is that limp part of what that stroke did to you?"

"Sure is. I have to wear a brace on my right leg." Cal stopped, held onto the wooden railing and lifted his pants leg to display the brace.

"We don't have to go down to the dock. Let's go back to the porch."

"No way. I haven't been close to that lake in a long time. I'm looking forward to sitting on the dock. I can handle it. Walked with a cane for a year and eventually got rid of it."

Roy walked closely behind Cal, ready to grab him with his left hand should he have any trouble with the steps. They sat on the bench on the dock.

"Did you hear any of that storm last night?" Roy asked.

"Did I ever. One of my pines got burned by lightning—a streak of black running a good way down the trunk. Probably do in that tree in time."

"As I remember, you were never very fond of those storms."

"Hated them. That thunder would chase them walleye down into the deepest water. If I was ever going to be close to shut out it would be the couple of days after one of them storms."

"You and I have developed a misery in common," Dennison said.

"What's that?"

"A fucked-up right arm and hand. I didn't tell you. I got stabbed through my right armpit by a crazy inmate and the nerve damage was pretty bad."

"What made the guy do something like that?"

"He was pissed because I wouldn't take his idiot case to the Supreme Court. The arm never got better. I see you have the same situation."

"Yep. I've learned to do pretty much everything with the left hand."

"I'm still learning. We have something else in common," Roy said.

"Tell me."

"We both lost our careers at an early age—you, because of a

physical disability and me, due to disbarment."

"You mean you can't practice law anymore?"

"Not for at least three years, but I don't think I'll be interested in reinstating. I'm glad you're here, my friend. Do you mind if I dump on you?"

"Not at all. What's the problem?"

"I have so much anger in me sometimes I can't fucking see straight."

"What're you so angry about?"

"Just about everybody I know. My wife, my ex-partner, that asshole Otto Lehman and his deputy Wickerham. Trouble is there's nothing I can do about any of it. Can't get it out. Oh, I suppose I could get on a plane to San Diego and go shoot Clara and Rogers, but then my kids wouldn't have a mother."

"Whoa! Hold your horses. You gotta start thinking about today and tomorrow and forget all that crap from the past. You can't keep on with all that stuff. You think you're in trouble now? Why, you just keep dwelling on being angry and hating and you'll end up in the loony bin."

"I can't forget that shit."

"Roy, look at where we are. Look at this lake, at your house up on that bluff. Look at that eagle soaring up near them clouds. You're in heaven, buddy. Try to remember that."

Roy looked up at his house and at the soaring eagle and shook his head.

"I just can't believe how bad things have gone for me. I don't think I deserved it. I'm not a bad man, Cal. Everything I had is gone. I know you've been dealt a bad hand in life, and I don't mean that as a joke. You had your life's work taken away from you in your forties. How have you handled the anger flowing from that?" Roy asked.

"I always considered my life's work to be a blessing I could bring to other people, showing them how to appreciate the pleasures of the outdoors. Catching fish may have been the object, but giving the experience was the purpose. Giving is the cure all of bitterness and anger. So, I just continued giving to the extent of my capabilities."

"How are you doing that?"

"I help serve lunches or dinners at the church mission twice a week, and once a week I give a class on fishing to interested kids in the fifth to eighth grades. Giving is a wonderful thing. It continues to make my life worthwhile. You have a lot to give, Roy. Concentrate on that and you'll be a happy man again."

"I've lost all my connections to life. No idea where to go or what to do."

"You're still connected to me and to the UP. Sometimes things have a way of happening out of the blue, unexpected and when you need help most. Like you calling me up and putting $100,000 in my bank account. You'll see. Things will fall into place for you."

"Lunch is ready!" Meg shouted from above.

At the table, Meg stood to offer a toast.

"Here's to Mr. Dennison. Great to have him back in the UP. Prayers for a healthy, happy life."

"Thank you, thank you, but please, not so formal. Roy will do nicely."

Later that afternoon, as they were getting ready to leave, Cal and Roy shook right hands, aided by their lefts.

"Give some thought to what we talked about," Cal said.

"I promise I will, and Meg, come back again soon. Bring Cal with you if he has nothing else to do."

Meg smiled and ran to Dennison, gave him a hug and kiss on the cheek, and thanked him for his generosity in saving her parents' financial lives.

CHAPTER FIFTY-FIVE

In the morning Roy sat at his kitchen table with coffee, a pen and a pad of paper. As an attorney, one of his problem-solving processes was to set forth his options on paper and list the pros and cons of each. The first question he addressed was *where should I live?* His listed options were Chicago, San Diego and the UP. The pros for Chicago were the presence of friends like Clyde and staying close to the legal community in case he decided to reinstate his license in three years. The one and deciding con was the likelihood he would be looked upon by the many who knew him as a pariah, an ex-con who may very well have killed that girl, notwithstanding the verdict.

The pros for San Diego were easy. Being close to his children, at least as close as Clara would agree to. The weather and year-round golf were plusses. The cons were having to deal with the two people who abandoned him and who he had grown to despise. Also, he knew no one in San Diego. He couldn't bear the thought of having to negotiate with Dan or Clara on a daily basis to be with his kids.

Then there was the UP. He had this lovely home and beautiful country. He had friends in the Cooley family. The community was very familiar with the details of his trial and generally accepted that he was not guilty of the serious charges.

He could stay in the UP for three years and then decide if he wanted to return to Illinois and reinstate his license. Opinions on him might soften in three years, as might his hatred of Mr. and Mrs. Rogers. Reuniting with the children could wait for three years. There were no cons with respect to the UP. No hurry to go to Chicago or San Diego. He would stay in the UP, for now.

The next question was *what shall I do in the UP?* One option was to live in retirement. His money would last his lifetime here. Still, he was too young to retire. He had always lived an active life. He could only take so much relaxation. He could dedicate himself to charitable causes, though not motivated by any special cause. He could do something for lung cancer as an homage to his friend, but charity would be a parttime thing for him, not a career.

He could start a business. That struck him as the best idea. After discarding a number of possibilities, including purchasing property and starting a dairy farm, he tentatively settled on converting the Den to a luxury fishing resort. The Den would not require much renovation. He would hire a kitchen staff to prepare gourmet breakfasts and dinners and buy a fleet of fishing boats with high-powered motors. The guides in the area would flock to work for him. Advertising in national resort and fishing publications would produce business from all across the country. He would pick up customers at the Eagle River airport. Maybe he could find a job for Cal.

* * *

May passed into June. The woods were in full bloom with their multiple shades of green. The mallards and their trail of ducklings were swimming around and under the docks. The loon was united with his mate, who was continually occupied with protecting her two eggs in a nest at the water's edge. The bald eagles had constructed their aerie in the tallest pine on the island. The guides were working the bays for bass and the drop-offs for walleyes. Dennison was yet to take his first steps toward initiating his new business. Something was holding him back.

His dreams were less about Allison, and more about Clara and Dan, wrapped in each others arms in sunny San Diego, living it up on his money—Dan, playing father to his children. That bastard had taken everything from him, all at a time he could do nothing about it. His bitterness and anger seemed to paralyze him from moving forward.

While monitoring a couple of burgers on the BBQ, he remembered what Cal said about bitterness. *Giving is the cure of all bitterness and anger.*

That night Dennison dreamt of Allison and her mother's suicidal escape from an abusive husband. He saw Allison, nine years old, sitting at her dead mother's bedside, holding her cold hand and crying. He awoke from the dream in the middle of the night and began thinking of the books he had read in prison about domestic violence. His thoughts turned again to Cal's advice regarding the healing effects of giving. Suddenly, it came to him, the answer to how he would live the restof his life.

He could hardly wait until morning to get started.

CHAPTER FIFTY-SIX

Dennison's research disclosed the existence of only one facility in the Upper Peninsula serving the needs of female survivors of domestic violence. The Harbor House, located in Marquette and serving Marquette and Alger Counties, was initiated in 1973. Nothing from Gogebic County west to Bessemer, Ironwood and Lake Superior. The isolation and alcoholism of the UP made it fertile ground for domestic violence. How many women were suffering in silence with nowhere to go?

The first step would be to create a tax-exempt status for a charitable corporation. He had done this several times during his practice. Making the application did not require a law license. It did require naming the corporation. It would be most appropriate to name it after Allison's mother, but he didn't know her name and was not about to call the Senator. Would people think it strange if he named it after Allison? *What if they do? That's the least I can do to keep her name and memory alive.* He named it The Allison Jameson House.

After funding the corporation with a $50,000 contribution, he contacted The Harbor House to find out who the architect was for their most recent expansion. In the days that followed, he scheduled a meeting at the Den with the architect, and promotional meetings with newspaper editors in Bessemer,

Ironwood and Watersmeet. He prepared and filed numerous applications for grants to the state of Michigan and to the federal government. Cal was right. He was giving and it felt really good.

In late June the architect had begun supervising the reconfiguration of the interior of the Den to provide more bedrooms and the construction of a two-story free-standing addition that would provide ten more two-resident rooms, a parlor and a large bathroom, including three shower stalls and an equal number of toilet rooms. Labor was contributed from the Watersmeet Township community for the forest clearing necessitated for the addition.

Dennison called Clyde Fuller to bring him up to date and to ask a favor.

"I'm turning my house on Crooked Lake into a refuge for victims of domestic violence, calling it The Allison Jameson House. I would like you to locate a PR guy or a press agent to get the story in the papers. Give him my number for more information and I'll be happy to pay for his services."

"I can do that. Are you coming back to the city?"

"Not for a long time. Maybe never."

"Well, I'll be damned. That's a beautiful thing you're doing. You're sounding a lot better than the last time we talked."

"I am better. Getting better all the time."

*   *   *

Dennison invited Cal and Meg to come to the property for a Fourth of July BBQ. This time he insisted they bring Emma along. The Cooleys learned about his plans for the house from the Watersmeet News. The weather was perfect as they gathered together in the small patio area just outside the screened-in porch.

"I take it you've heard about what's going on here. It's quiet today, but generally there's a big racket with workmen moving in and out."

"I think it's wonderful what you're doing with the Den," Meg said.

"You guys are here to celebrate the holiday with me, and for another reason. I have to start thinking about staffing The Allison Jameson House. Are you interested in hearing about this?"

"Of course we are," Cal said.

"I'm going to start with Meg. I know you have some kind of clinic job right now, but I would like you to be the primary medical person in this new facility. It would be a full-time job and I'm sure you would be earning more than you do now."

With her eyes wide open and her mouth agape, Meg gave him a look like she thought he had gone mad.

"Thank you, but I'm sorry. I couldn't do that. I don't know anything about how to run something like that. I appreciate the suggestion, but I'm afraid not."

"Hold on. I spoke to the administrator of The Harbor House, a similar facility in Marquette, and she agreed to have you visit with her medical director for a weekend, to learn what there is to know about that job. All I ask is that you take advantage of that offer and then decide whether you can handle the job."

"That sounds like a reasonable plan," Cal said.

"I'm going to be the administrator of The Allison Jameson

House. You'd be working daily and closely with me. I have no doubt we would get it right together. Tell me you'll give it a try."

"Wow! You make it sound possible. I'll agree to go to Marquette, and then we'll see."

"Marvelous. Now, Emma, it's your turn. I know you're no longer in the fish cleaning business, so you must have some time on your hands. I have a job for you. I want you to be in charge of the kitchen in the House. Not alone, because you'll have help. I don't expect you to be doing the cooking for dozens of people, unless you decide you want to be involved with that. No, you would be in charge of planning, buying and supervising kitchen staff. I can see from the expression on your face I have terrified you. You'll meet with the head of kitchen at The Harbor House at the same time Meg is there. It's all arranged. You'll go there together."

"No, no, no. I couldn't do that. My experience has been cooking for one man, not buying food for a house full of abused women."

"I don't expect a commitment now. Let me know what you think after your weekend in Marquette. If you still feel you can't do it, that's fine. I'll understand."

"It would be a nice trip for you and Meg to spend some time together. I say you should both go," Cal said.

"I'll go to Marquette with Meg, but don't you count on me."

"We'll all get together after your visit to The Harbor House and see where we stand."

The Harbor House was almost always at full capacity, causing it to frequently turn down referrals or put people on a waiting list. The administrator was pleased that another facility would be opening in the other half of the UP and anxious to help in any way possible. Emma came home from Marquette with menus, reading materials on nutrition and lists of suppliers of everything needed to operate a kitchen in such a facility.

With a better understanding of what she should expect as the nurse in charge and learning that Doc Hilliard would be spending half a day a week at the house to see patients, Meg was ready to take on the job. Working closely with Roy on a daily basis was the real closer. She admired him greatly, first for his generosity to her parents, and now for the gift of his beloved Den as a refuge for women fleeing physically and emotionally abusive husbands. The physical attraction that seemed to grow each time she was in his presence was also an unspoken factor.

Meg and Cal joined forces to persuade Emma to give it a try. She would have time to study and learn more about the job, since the house would not be open until sometime in the fall. Even then, they would start with a small group of residents and Emma could adapt, as would the entire staff, as the resident population grew.

CHAPTER FIFTY-SEVEN

Shortly after his release from Parnall, Dennison called Mike Travis and requested a transcript of his testimony at the trial. When he received the transcript, he mailed it to Clara with the following note:

> *Dear Clara—This is a transcript of my testimony under oath at the trial. I wanted you to know the truth and this is the truth. Somewhere along the way the kids are bound to hear rumors about their father and his possible misdeeds. When the children are old enough to understand, I would appreciate it if you would allow them to read my testimony. Current photographs of the kids would be appreciated.   Thanks, Roy*

Still seated with pen in hand, he composed a letter to Senator Jameson, informing him of the memorial he was establishing for both his granddaughter and his daughter in the form of The Allison Jameson House, a refuge for the victims of domestic abuse. He couldn't think of anything else to add that would sound right, so he just ended with "Respectfully, Roy Dennison." He received no response to either letter.

*   *   *

As construction of the addition and reconfiguration of the main house neared completion, Meg was busy arranging and supplying the clinic room with essentials. Roy marveled at her energy and the joy with which she approached every task. He found it difficult to take his eyes off her whenever she was nearby, which was very often. He smiled as he watched her flick back a curl of strawberry blonde hair that was continually falling to the top of her left eye. Her Hollywood-white teeth were always visible through the half smile that was on display most of the time.

Dennison had not been with a woman for over two years, except for his adventures with Vera. He could not deny the feelings Meg stirred in him. He was tempted to test the waters with Meg, but he hesitated. Had she not been the daughter of Cal and Emma, he would have made his interest known days ago. He didn't want to offend and didn't know how they would feel about their daughter being pursued by a man twenty years her senior, and an ex-con at that.

He found Meg sitting in front of the television set in the great room, dabbing a hankie at her tear-filled eyes.

"What's the matter, Meg?"

"I just turned on the news and heard that John Kennedy Jr. was killed in a plane crash off the coast of Martha's Vineyard. His wife, Carolyn, also died. It's just awful."

"So young and so much to live for."

Dennison had put a few pounds back on. He was looking healthier and stronger every day. He had preserved the kitchen and an unused servant's bedroom adjacent to the kitchen as his living quarters during the construction work. He didn't want to spend the rest of his life living in a room in The Allison Jameson House. Instead, he decided to have a log home constructed on the bluff on the opposite side of the house from the new addition. He drew the simple floor plan himself—two bedrooms, a full bath and shower, a great room and a large kitchen, including a deck facing the lake. His architect recommended a log home construction company that finished the job in thirty days. Dennison had an idea for another log home on the property. He asked Meg to bring Cal with her tomorrow so they could talk.

Roy and Cal went to the bench at the end of the dock.

"I've got a proposition I want you to hear and take home to discuss with Emma and Meg."

"Let's hear it."

"I want to build a log home for you guys, set in off the dirt road leading to the Den—a two-bedroom home with plenty of room, at no cost to you. I want you to sell your house and move in to the log home as your permanent home. The convenience is compelling, with Meg and Emma coming daily to the House. And there's more. I want you to serve as an assistant to Frank in maintenance and security, a paying job. You'll all be working at the House and living nearby. What do you think?"

"I don't understand where all this is coming from. What did I ever do for you to justify such kindness?"

"I need you guys and I want to make it comfortable for you. Besides, I might never have contemplated The Allison Jameson House if it wasn't for your inspiration. Take it home. I hope you'll all go for it."

"What about the proceeds from the sale of the house, if we go ahead?"

"That's yours. I want no part of it."

"How you going to handle all this stuff financially?"

"No need to worry about that. I'm selling my Alfa Romeo and the Piper-Cub. Part of those proceeds will pay for your home. There is something personal I'd like to talk to you about."

"I'm listening."

"Meg and I have become good friends. She's a wonderful girl and beautiful as well. You wouldn't believe me if I said I wasn't attracted to her. But I know my place. I'm quite a bit older than Meg. I would understand if you preferred that I kept that relationship on a purely friendship level."

"Roy, it would be my fondest wish for my daughter to find a life with a man of your character and intelligence. You've paid the price for your mistake. Only question—is it something Meg wants?"

"I don't know the answer to that, but I'm going to find out. Thanks, Cal. Glad to get that out of the way."

* * *

The Cooley family agreed to accept Dennison's offer. Clearing the forest for construction of the Cooley log home was underway. The home was due to be built and ready for occupancy by mid-October. The Allison Jameson House was scheduled to open its doors for business on November 1. Applicant interviews for employees and residents started being set up in September. Most residents would be referred by social agencies, law enforcement or overflow from Harbor House. State and federal grants and private donations were being received, putting the house on a sound financial footing. Everything was moving smoothly according to schedule, except Roy's Meg Cooley project.

His approach to Meg was awkward and not very romantic. Having known her since she was a teenager and he was near forty, he didn't know quite how to approach her. She seemed to enjoy his company, but that was just her nature. She was joyful with everyone. He feared the age differential would be insurmountable and wasn't sure how he could handle her rejection.

Finally, before the dinner hour, he invited her for a tour of his new log home. Afterwards, they sat on rockers on the deck facing the lake. Fall came late that year. The lake was still encircled by the glorious colors of autumn. Sitting quietly, breathing in the crisp October air, they looked at each other and smiled, silently sharing nature's bounty before them.

"You've done a great job setting up your clinic. I've watched you closely and I'm confident the medical department will be in good hands. Doc Hilliard will respond to emergency calls and will spend time at the house answering residents' questions and covering things that might be beyond your level of expertise. Now, on a personal note, I'm sure you know I've grown very fond of you these past couple of months. I've been wondering if you…"

"Wait, Roy, my father told me about the conversation you had about me. I understand you have feelings for me, and I have feelings for you. I always have. You're kind, generous, smart and," as she smiled, "pretty good-looking. Still, this is all so new. I don't think we should be distracted from the job at hand. Right now, all our energy should be devoted to the house and getting it successfully off the ground. Let's continue as friends and work together for the next three months to get the house off to a good start and see how we go from there."

"I don't know how, but I'm willing to try."

"Oh, Roy, forgive me. I don't mean to be cruel, but I have doubts."

"What kind of doubts?"

"I know what you risked to be unfaithful to your wife. You have far less to risk now. You've demonstrated the capacity to be unfaithful. I couldn't bear that happening to me."

"I promise I'm not that same man anymore, not physically or morally. I love you, Meg. If you'll have me, I'll cherish you forever."

"I believe you, but please, give me more time."

Meg Cooley did love Roy Dennison. She loved and admired hm for his many qualities and for his good soul. She always did but was not preoccupied thinking about him in a sexual way. In her pragmatic way, she approached Roy's urgings realistically, considering all factors that might lead to the success or failure of the relationship. She chose not to mention it to Roy, but the age difference did concern her. Meg had always wanted children, at least one. Roy had been through all of that with three of his own. She didn't know if he would want to start another family at his age. The disclosure of their feelings being so recent, that subject had not yet come up.

Approaching her twenty-eighth birthday, she was beginning to hear her biological clock ticking. The reality was she was fortunate to have Roy wanting her. Living on Crooked Lake and working in a house where her father and Frank Wallensky were the only other males, made the prospects for an alternative partner slim to nonexistent. She knew all this, yet she believed that no marriage was better than a bad one, and so she was compelled by her nature to do her due diligence. *I'll talk to him about children at the first opportunity. I know I would make him a good wife.*

CHAPTER FIFTY-EIGHT

The first four residents, referred by Harbor House, checked in to the house on November 1. The staff, besides the Cooley family and Frank Wallensky, included two housekeeper-waitresses, two licensed practical nurses, a receptionist, a cook and a kitchen assistant. Staff would grow commensurate with the population of the house. By December 1, the resident population reached nineteen, more than half the thirty-six total capacity. Staff had increased by one additional LPN and a recently graduated and licensed psychologist, Lucy Devonshire. A laundry company came from Bessemer once a week to pick up and return sheets and towels.

To celebrate the first successful month of operations, Roy hosted a BBQ dinner at his log home, with the Cooley family and Lucy Devonshire as his guests. There had been a four-inch snowfall earlier in the day. The mid-twenties temperature didn't discourage Roy from BBQing on his deck. Everyone had their choice of hamburgers or fillets. By 9:00 p.m. Cal, Emma and Lucy were ready to call it a night. Roy asked Meg to stay for a while to cover some things for the coming week. He assured Cal he would accompany Meg home when they were done.

Roy added a couple of logs to the fading fire and waved to Meg to come sit next to him on the sofa.

"There's something I need to discuss with you before I

respond to your proposal," she said.

"Of course. Go ahead."

"I desperately want to be a mother, have my own kids, at least one, maybe two. How do you feel about that?"

Roy moved closer to her on the sofa. He took her hand and kissed it.

"How do I feel? I feel ecstatic. You will be the most wonderful mother."

Meg kissed him and rose from the sofa, spinning like a ballerina.

"Do you dance?" Meg asked.

"Do I what?"

"Dance."

"Not for a long time."

Meg went to the radio and turned on some music. She waived to Roy to come dance with her. He put his left arm around her waist and held her left hand in his right, with their intertwined hands resting down alongside his thigh. In this awkward position there was little dancing, but a lot of holding and swaying. With her head on his shoulder, she whispered, "I don't want to wait either."

"Stay with me tonight," he whispered back.

"I will."

The Cooley log home was quiet when Meg walked in at 6:30 a.m. She went to her parents' bedroom and found them in bed, just awakening for the start of the day.

"I spent the night with Roy," she sheepishly said with a lowered head.

Before Cal or Emma could respond in any way, Meg raised up and proudly proclaimed, "We're getting married a week from Sunday." Cal got out of bed as quickly as he could to give his daughter a tight hug. Meg laid down next to her mother whose eyes filled with tears as she held her daughter close.

"That's wonderful, darling. I'm so happy for you—but you're not giving us much time to plan the wedding."

CHAPTER FIFTY-NINE

Roy invited Judge Matenson and his wife to come Sunday for a tour of the house and for the judge to perform a marriage ceremony. The judge expressed delight for the invitation and said they would be there, provided the winter storm expected on Friday or Saturday did not make road travel from Bessemer to Watersmeet too hazardous. Roy also invited both Clyde Fuller and Mark Travis to come see the house and attend the wedding. Travis couldn't make it. Fuller said he would make every effort to be there. Meg called her brothers, who she hadn't seen in ages. They promised to attend.

The weather cooperated. Six inches of snow fell on Friday. Sunny Saturday and Sunday, with temperatures hovering around thirty-two degrees, provided some thaw, rendering the roads manageable. The Matensons arrived, as did Clyde Fuller and the Cooley brothers.

The wedding took place in the great room of the house, with most of the residents in attendance. Meg's older brother, just met by Roy for the first time, served as Roy's best man. Lucy Devonshire was Meg's maid of honor. Roy wore khaki pants with an untucked long-sleeved white shirt. Meg, at a loss to find something appropriate, wore her recently laundered registered nurse dress.

After the ceremony and a brief reception of wine, cheese, chips and pretzels, Meg went home to pack her things for moving in to Roy's home. At the same time, Roy escorted Clyde Fuller to see the home Roy had built for himself. They sat in Roy's great room with glasses of wine they carried from the reception.

"You've really done something to be proud of here. Think you'll ever get back to the city?"

"Not if I can avoid it. You can't imagine what this experience has done for me. Money means nothing to me, other than what is needed to take care of this house and its' residents. Meg feels the same way. We are totally in sync in every aspect of our lives. Her mom and dad, my new in-laws, are salt of the earth. You've met these folks. You know what I mean."

"I thought you might want to know that Dan and Clara are planning to come to Chicago after the first of the year."

"Really? Why?"

"Dan has a couple of real estate investments he's closing out and his presence is required. Clara is coming along to visit friends she hasn't seen in some time."

"Are they bringing the children?"

"I haven't heard, but I'll let you know when I find out."

"That would be the one thing that would bring me back to the city—to see those kids. I don't talk about them much, but I sure do miss them. I wonder if they ever think about me. Will you stay for one of the dinners that Emma cooks up for the house?"

"No, thanks. I'm going to head back to Mandy's. Maybe pick up a burger at the café. I want to hit the hay early so I can be on the road by 6:00 a.m. Your Meg is a beautiful girl. I wish you all the happiness in the world."

"Thanks, Clyde. Be sure to let me know about the kids."

"I will. So long, buddy."

*   *   *

The success of The Allison Jameson House elicited increasing grants from government agencies and major corporate donations. By Christmas, the house was near capacity. Staff was increased by a chef and a baker in the kitchen and two waiters. Emma ambled around the kitchen with a cane, periodically resting in a chair at the desk where she conducted her business. She had given up the little cooking she did and all her energy was dedicated to buying and managing the kitchen staff.

Meg's work in the clinic was rewarding, but emotionally draining. The women she tended to freely spoke of the horrendous physical and emotional abuse they absorbed from their volcanic spouses. Some of these men were imprisoned for their brutality, giving their wives the opportunity to escape to a safe place. Other women found the courage to leave although threatened with harm by men who vowed to find them and bring them back. The house recognized the potential for such intrusions. Frank and Cal were instructed that one of them should be attending the front door, which was kept locked, and turn away any unexpected male visitor who could not establish his bona fides. Any indication of resistance or controversy would cause an immediate call to the Sheriff's office.

The house could not accommodate children. Sadly, residents would be separated from their children until circumstances permitted them to leave the House and resume independent living. In the interim, children would be placed with other family members or otherwise cared for by divisions of the Michigan Department of Health and Human Services.

Roy and Meg most often had their dinner at the house with the residents. Occasionally, they would make dinner for themselves and eat in the kitchen of their home. That's when Meg would talk non-stop about the women she had seen that day—about the fear, desperation and ego destruction. The stories of near suicide to get away from the abuse.

"God, this was such a wonderful thing you did with your Den. I'm so proud to be a part of it and to be your wife."

"I've never told you this because I don't like bringing up Allison in conversation with you, but The Allison Jameson House is not actually a memorial to Allison. It was inspired by the fate of Allison's mother, who I never knew. Allison told me her father was terribly abusive. She actually left home to live with her grandparents when she was just a child after her mother was driven to suicide because of the emotional and physical abuse she endured from her alcoholic husband. That's where the whole idea came from. It was your dad and his outlook on life that made the idea become a reality."

Except for one time, Roy never spoke to Meg about his children. In answer to her question some time ago, he said he had two boys and a girl, the oldest being near ten. He changed the subject so abruptly, she didn't bring it up again. He also avoided conversation about his former wife. He denied any trouble sleeping, but she knew better. His twisting, turning and mumbling almost nightly portended issues he kept to himself. Meg hoped, in time, he would share his secret thoughts with her.

CHAPTER SIXTY

On New Year's Day, Roy received a call from Clyde Fuller.

"Happy new year, my friend," Clyde said.

"Same to you. What do you hear from the happy Rogers?"

"They're planning on coming here January 10 for a week. They're bringing the children with them. If you're considering coming here to see the kids, I suggest you call Clara and make those arrangements in advance. I have her phone number, if you want it."

Roy took the number and thanked Clyde for being a good friend.

It was still too early to call San Diego—7:00 a.m. in California. He waited until 1:00 p.m. UP time and then placed his call.

"Hi Clara! It's your ex-husband calling."

"Where are you calling from?"

"From the UP. That's where I live now."

"Clyde told me about your project about three months ago and said you probably would be in the UP for good. How's it going?"

"It's going great. Our house for survivors of domestic abuse is thriving, and I recently got married."

"Really? Who's the lucky girl?"

"You won't believe this. I married Cal Cooley's daughter."

"I didn't know he had one. Congratulations."

"I understand you're going to be spending a week in Chicago starting ten days from now."

"Got that from Clyde, did you? Well, that's right."

"And you're bringing the kids with you?"

"That's the plan."

The conversation seemed so civil Roy was gaining confidence that his intention to see his children would go off without a hitch.

"I'd like to make an arrangement to come to Chicago and spend an afternoon with the children. You just tell me the day, time and place and I'll be there."

"I don't think that's a very good idea."

"What do you mean, 'not a good idea'? What's wrong with it?"

"It would be too confusing for them."

"Confusing? What's confusing about a visit with their father?"

"You don't understand."

"Explain it to me."

"They're so young. You've been gone a long time. They're used to you not being around."

"That's bullshit. What's going on here?"

"The kids asked me about you incessantly, especially Rob. Talking about a long business trip over and over was unsustainable. They were too young to understand what happened to us, so I finally told them you went to heaven."

"What! Jesus Christ, Clara, who gave you the right to eliminate me? Does Dan know you did that?"

"Dan doesn't know. I figured you were going to spend the rest of your life in the UP and might never see the kids again. I had to tell them something to stop all the questions."

"Well, the kids will be happy to know that Daddy has returned from heaven. Are you going to tell them or shall I?"

"You can't do that now. If you must, wait until they're older, maybe in three or four years."

"Have you lost your mind? Put Dan on the phone."

"I don't want you to talk to him. Please, Roy."

"Don't 'please Roy' me. Put him on the phone."

"He's watching a football game. I'll get him."

Clara called Dan to the phone and went to her bedroom to listen in on an extension.

"Hello, Roy? Been a long time. How's life in the UP?"

"Did you know that your wife told my kids their father went to heaven?"

"She didn't? (aside)—Clara, come over here." Clara put down her phone and hurried to Dan's side.

"Did you tell the kids Roy went to heaven? She's nodding yes. I can't believe it. I swear, Roy, I had nothing to do with it."

"Will you see to it that she corrects that situation? I expect to see the children when you're in Chicago."

"I'll do my best and let you know where it stands before we come to the city."

Dennison thought, *The goddamn nerve of that woman.*

* * *

Winter was setting in to the UP. Roy had never come north during the winter months. Snowmobiling and ice fishing were not his things. Realizing he didn't have appropriate wardrobe for the season, he headed for Bessemer with a list of necessities provided by Meg. While in town he stopped by the courthouse to say hello to Judge Matenson. The judge was happy he dropped by.

"I was thinking of calling you to give you a heads up on a rumor I've been hearing."

"What kind of rumor, Judge?"

"I had lunch with the County Prosecutor last week. He told me his office still believes you killed that girl. They've been playing with the idea of charging you for the death of the unborn fetus—the theory being the fetus still had life in it when you buried Allison and ended the life of the fetus."

"Jesus, Judge. They're talking about a six-week-old fetus. It couldn't survive with Allison being dead."

"Precisely how I responded to that idea. I'm familiar with the applicable Michigan statute, which provides for a charge of manslaughter against the killing of an unborn 'quick child' as a result of any wrongful act resulting in the death of the mother. That statute is not applicable because 'quick child' is defined to mean a fetus developed to such a stage that it moves within the womb of the mother. Furthermore, it has already been determined that no act on your part caused the death of Allison Jameson."

"I sure do appreciate your giving that analysis to those guys."

"I really shouldn't be getting so involved, but since he brought it up at lunch I felt justified in putting a damper on the whole idea. He said there was an amendment to the statute that would include a six-week-old fetus. I responded that any such case would be decided under the law as it existed at the time of the event. I hope that's the end of it. Thought you'd like to know."

"Again, Judge, thanks for your concern and your kindness."

"It looks like that office is looking for some way to nail you, so you better mind your p's and q's."

CHAPTER SIXTY-ONE

The Mental Health Department of the UP Health System Hospital in Marquette, Michigan, focused on the treatment of the full range of mental illnesses, including that malady commonly referred to as a nervous breakdown. That's how his parents described Otto Lehman's condition when asked by neighbors and friends.

Seated in their idling Chevy in front of the hospital, waiting for their son to emerge after seven weeks of psychiatric care, the Lehmans were cautiously optimistic that Otto would have regained his old self. He came through the door with a male nurse at his side, stopped briefly to take a deep breath of the crisp January air and proceeded to the car. Mom had taken a back seat so Otto could sit next to his father on the two-hour drive to their home in Watersmeet.

Otto's reputation was so sullied by his misconduct in the Dennison trial that he was unable to find a position with any law firm throughout the UP. He tried hard but unsuccessfully from Ironwood in the west to Marquette in the east. With no income and limited savings, after a few months he had to give up his Bessemer apartment and return to Watersmeet to live with his parents. Shortly after his return, he learned that the ethics committee of the Michigan State Bar Association had undertaken an investigation to determine whether his license to practice law in Michigan should be suspended.

Lehman had been absorbed in self-pity during his fruitless search for a job. Taking on a hermit-like existence in the family home along with the prospect of imminent disbarment plunged him into a state of acute depression. He was still communicating and taking meals with his parents. He slept abnormally long hours and spent his awake hours staring at whatever happened to be on TV. The medication prescribed by Doc Hilliard, intended to improve Otto's mood, had minimal effect.

After several months of despondency, Otto suddenly stopped talking—not only stopped communicating, but was non-responsive to communication or direction. He was taken to the Eagle River Hospital where it was suspected that he had fallen into a catatonic state, where one is non-responsive while otherwise awake. He was immediately ambulanced to the hospital in Marquette for appropriate psychiatric care.

Sedative treatment administered intravenously was initiated but didn't work for Otto. After two weeks of increasing doses of tranquilizers, the physician in charge met with Otto's parents.

"Sedative treatment has not been successful. We've reached maximum dosage and have discontinued that approach. Otto's catatonia continues. We must do whatever we can to reverse it. The next and best treatment is ECT."

"What's that?" Mr. Lehman asked.

"ECT stands for electro convulsive therapy. It's commonly referred to as 'shock treatment'. That probably startles you because that term conjures up Hollywood-inspired images of torture. It's nothing like that. The patient is under anesthesia and feels no pain."

The treatment was authorized by Otto's parents. He received the jolts twice a week for two weeks, at which time the catatonia resolved and he was again speaking with his parents and hospital personnel. His depression, however, was still evident. Now in charge of his own treatment decisions, he authorized continuation of ECT to see if that would put an end to his depression. After another week of ECT he phoned his folks to tell them it was like he had just awakened from a long bad dream. He felt terrific and couldn't wait to get out of the hospital and get after life again.

The psychiatrist leading Otto's case spoke to him about his insistence on being discharged.

"I know you're anxious to get out of here, but I'm not ready to discharge you. You need some fortification to avoid slipping back into depression. I want you to remain in the hospital to receive one-on-one psycho-therapy three times a week and participate daily in a support group of other patients newly emerged from depressive states." That regimen continued for another two weeks, leading to his discharge and a hopeful return to a normal life.

The only negative consequence of the ECT was a spotty memory loss which the doctor said would be temporary and should resolve in a matter of weeks. Included in the few subjects of his memory loss was the unpleasant ending of his relationship with Meg Cooley. In fact, an intended revival of his romance with Meg was a prominent subject in his therapy sessions—the therapist taking advantage of the positive vibes emanating from Otto at each mention of her name. Encouraged to pursue happiness with Meg, Otto left the hospital with that pursuit his highest priority.

The morning after his discharge he awoke well rested and eager to begin his efforts to reaffirm the love of Meg Cooley. After preparing his own breakfast of juice, coffee and toast, he set out for the house on Catalpa Street. A middle-aged woman he had never seen before appeared in response to the chimes. Through the screen door she said, "Can I help you?"

"Is Meg Cooley here?"

"Sorry. The Cooleys don't live here anymore. We moved in about six weeks ago."

Otto was speechless for a few moments, trying to imagine what tragedy must have befallen the Cooley family for them to have sold the family home.

"Do you know what happened to them or where they are?"

"Sorry. Don't have any information on them."

A sense of desperation crept into Otto's psyche. He hurried back to the Chevy and took off for the Sheriff's office. If anyone would know, Wickerham would. Jesse was sitting at his desk, busy with the morning paper work, when Otto burst into the office. Jesse was not about to hide his contempt for the former prosecutor.

"I see they let you out of the asylum. Probably a mistake."

"Jesse, where did the Cooleys go?"

"They live in a cabin on Dennison's property."

"What? Is Meg there too?"

"Sure is. What you want her for?"

"I need to see her, to speak to her. Thanks for the info."

Relieved to hear that the Cooleys, especially Meg, were OK and in the area, he was puzzled by the fact they were living on Dennison's property. What was that all about? He had to find out, and now. He drove down Crooked Lake Road, turned onto Dennison's dirt road, which was now smooth asphalt, and stopped when he saw a new log cabin set in from the road. He knew it was Cooley's cabin because Cal's truck was parked there. There was no answer to his rapping on the door. He drove on to the house and went to the front door, finding it locked. He rang the bell and pounded on the door. As he was pounding, Frank Wallensky arrived and opened the door.

"What the hell are you doing here?" Frank asked.

"I'm looking for Meg Cooley. Is she here?"

"Yeah, she's here. What business you got with her?"

"I've been away for a couple of months and I need to talk to her."

"She's busy with her clinic hours now, so you'll have to call and make an appointment to see her."

Roy came to the door to see if Frank needed any assistance. He was startled to see Otto Lehman standing there.

"What in the world are you doing here?"

"I'm looking for Meg. It's important that I speak with her."

"She has nothing to talk to you about. Just take off."

"Whatever exists between Meg and me is none of your business."

"Oh, yes, it is. Anything to do with Meg is my business. She's my wife."

"No, that's not possible."

"Of course it is. A lot has happened since you've been away."

Otto was stunned into silence, quickly followed by a surge of anger that reddened his face and pinched his shoulders in toward his neck.

"Fuck you, Dennison. You murdered that girl. I know it and you know it. Someday, you'll pay."

Frank made a move toward Lehman, but Dennison held him back.

"Leave here Otto, before you get yourself into a whole heap of trouble."

Returning to his car, Otto continued shouting obscenities while he appeared to be crying. Roy put a hand on Frank's shoulder and said, "This boy is sick."

Otto, utterly confused and bereft of reason, drove north without destination to the end of Route 45 at the shore of Lake Superior. He cut the engine, dropped his forehead on the steering wheel and tried to organize his thoughts on what he had just learned. *Married to Dennison. My God, how could she?* He felt abandoned by Meg. Her submission to another crushed the hopes he had nurtured the last few weeks in the hospital. His love turned to hatred. *This was Dennison's choice of vengeance for my prosecution. I despise that man. This will not stand without retaliation.* Feeling comforted by his resolve to seek justice, he raised up and viewed the first twenty yards of the lake frozen hard.

A chill went through his body as he started the engine.

* * *

Roy was ready to turn in at 10:00 p.m. so he could hit the road for Chicago by 5:00 a.m. Meg was not going with him, having decided it would be best for the children to have this first, short visit be by Daddy alone. Dan called and explained how

Clara handled Roy's resurrection for the kids.

"She thought you must have gone to heaven because they hadn't heard from you for such a long time. She said she was mistaken, that you called and said you wanted to see them while they're in Chicago."

"That wasn't so hard," Roy said.

"Only the boys are coming. Jessica is just getting over a mild pneumonia and the doctor recommends against her flying and going into a winter climate. She'll be spending the week with Clara's folks. They moved out here several weeks ago to be near the children."

"I'll have to catch up with Jessica on the next visit. I expect to arrive around noon and spend the rest of the day with the boys—lunch and dinner and have them back to your hotel before 9:00 p.m."

"That's the deal. Call when you get here and I'll bring them down."

"Come down alone so we can talk before you deliver the boys."

* * *

Roy left for Chicago early as planned. Later that morning, Cal was walking the grounds when he saw something move in the trees. Could've been a deer or some other creature. He moved closer to the edge of the forest. Nothing moving. The sound of a vehicle engine starting up caused him to take a couple of steps to his right, giving him a view of the road. He saw what looked like a Chevy a hundred yards from him, leaving the property. There had not been any recent visitor to the house. *Someone just made a wrong turn onto the house's private road*, he thought. Nevertheless, he would make a note of it in his daily log.

Roy instituted the log, requiring Frank and Cal to enter any problems or interesting events occurring during the course of each day. Most days the logs were blank or had entries of "no problems".

*   *   *

Otto Lehman called The Allison Jameson House and asked to speak to Meg.

"Hello Meg. It's your old boyfriend, Otto."

"Otto? Why are you calling me?"

"Why shouldn't I be calling you? Don't you remember? We almost got married."

Familiar with Otto's confinement to a mental ward, Meg cautiously continued the conversation.

"That was a long time ago. I'm sure you know I'm married now."

"Yes, I know—to that murderer, Roy Dennison. How could you do that to me? I thought you loved me."

"I cared for you once. Those feelings ended for good with your treatment of my dad in your prosecution of Roy."

"I don't know what you're talking about. You were going to get your RN certification and then come live with me in Bessemer. You and Roy are punishing me for doing my job as a prosecutor. It's not fair and it's not right. I won't stand for that."

He seemed detached from reality. She didn't know if he escaped from the mental ward or was prematurely discharged.

"So, you live with him in that log cabin?"

"Of course."

"Do you sleep in the same bed with him?"

"Otto! What kind of a question is that? I'm married to a good man and I love him very much."

"Better be careful he doesn't bludgeon you to death someday."

She was frightened by the increasing volume, tension and irrationality of his words. She hoped to calm him down with a suggestion.

"Maybe the three of us should get together and straighten everything out. How does that sound to you?"

"Sounds like a bunch of bullshit. The damage is done, and I'll never forgive you for breaking my heart. As far as your husband is concerned, he can go to hell."

CHAPTER SIXTY-TWO

Roy started out his seven-hour drive thinking what he might say or do to Dan Rogers to even their lopsided score. It wasn't long before his mind began to wander back to the beginnings with Dan.

He stayed in Cambridge for a week following law school graduation. His student-teacher relationship with Dan had been a highlight of the last three years. Dennison greatly respected Dan's mastery of corporate and securities law, and his innovative thinking about corporate organization. He was complimented and intrigued by Dan's invitation to join him for dinner at an upscale restaurant to discuss matters of some importance.

While enjoying their martinis, Rogers outlined his thinking.

"I want to start a law practice. I'm tired of teaching. Time to put some of my ideas into action."

"That's exciting news. How do you start a law practice?"

"I have confided in a few of my former students who are rising in importance in their large New York firms. They suggest I stay out of New York. The competition is too tough for a start-up. Instead, open up in another large city, one where their firms don't have satellite offices, so they can refer business to help get off the ground."

"That makes a lot of sense. Have you decided where you're going to locate?"

"I'm thinking about Chicago, and that's why you're here. Roy, I have a proposition for you. What would you think about being a founding partner of Rogers and Dennison?"

Dennison smiled as he recalled his shock at receiving such a proposal. He was in Wisconsin now, just three miles south of Antigo. It was a dry, overcast morning. Perfect day for driving.

Until the dinner with Dan, Dennison had two options for starting his career. One was to join his father's small real estate and property tax adjustment firm in Chicago. The other, was to accept one of two offers he had received from large New York firms, with generous starting salaries.

"Why Chicago? Why me? How would that work?"

"Chicago is a great business town. Several large Wall Street firms don't have satellites there and process their Chicago business through local firms. Most importantly, you're the best spieler and promoter of positions I've come across in all my years of teaching, and you're loaded with Chicago contacts."

Initially, Dennison did not take the proposed partnership seriously. He was not about to forego his opportunities in New York to take on such a wild flyer. Rogers persisted. He said they would start out as equal partners and would contribute equal financial contributions to set up the law office.

"I know we could make it work. Sleep on it and call me tomorrow. I'm heading for Chicago with or without you. Together, we could build our own little dynamo."

He had forgotten how confident Dan was that he could create a successful law firm from scratch. He did sleep on it. The idea of being Dan's partner, equal partner, in such an adventure had appeal. He was the beneficiary of a trust his father had started for him when he entered high school. The principal of the trust exceeded $200,000. He could participate financially. He ultimately decided to throw in with Dan, feeling secure that if it wasn't working out after two years, he would always have the backstop of his father's law firm.

It was 10:00 a.m. and he was approaching Milwaukee. His reminiscence brought him an illuminating realization, an epiphany of sorts. Rogers and Dennison was totally Dan's creation. The idea he dreamt of for years proved to be successful beyond expectation. Dennison was a beneficiary of its success, but it was Dan's baby grown into manhood. *What a crushing blow to Dan to have it all wiped away at its peak by my self-absorbed act,* thought Roy. *It's a miracle he supported me as long as he did.* During the remaining hour of his drive, Dennison's thoughts of vengeance turned to acceptance and understanding, with respect to both Dan and Clara.

Dennison pulled up to the Drake Hotel at 11:30 a.m. He checked in to the room he reserved for overnight, then went to the bar and called Dan to meet him there.

Roy made an effort to shake hands with Dan by supporting his right forearm with his left hand.

"Clyde told me about your injury. I see you haven't fully recovered yet."

"Never will. We haven't talked much since . . ."

"I thought about calling you, but it seemed so awkward."

"All I thought about was you, sitting on the beach or at the pool, with my wife, my kids and my money—full of anger and plotting how someday I could get even."

"The thing with Clara was not what you think. I didn't set out to steal her from you. My God, you were the one who asked me to look out for her. My initial interest in Clara was compassion, not romance."

"Getting ready to make this trip, I was trying to think of a way I could settle the score with you for having stolen Clara from me. But on the drive up I began to realize that was a fantasy, that Clara was done with me for good before you started up with her. As a matter of fact, in spite of a lot of pain getting there, I wouldn't trade my current life for my pre-Allison life, even if that were possible."

"It's really good to hear that. As far as the kids are concerned, you'll see they refer to me as Uncle Dan. They know you are their father and I would never attempt anything to change that."

"I'm happy to hear that. Actually, perhaps you would help me with a project I have in mind."

"Sure, if I can. What's that?"

"I always promised the boys I would take them up north for fishing when they got older. This summer Rob will be closing in on eleven and Ben nine. It's time for me to come through on that promise. I want all three of them for two weeks this summer. I'll pick them up at the airport in Chicago and deliver them to the airport at trip's end."

"What would you like me to do?"

"Simple. Urge Clara to agree to it."

"I'll do better than that. She's been pleading to go on a

ten-day Alaska cruise. I'll sell her on that being the perfect time to do it."

"Sounds good. Now get those boys down here. I'll be in the lobby."

Roy did all he could to keep from falling as Rob rushed into his arms screaming "Dad, Dad." Ben trailed slowly behind, seemingly unsure of who this man was, but soon silently rested the side of his head against Roy's waist.

"Wow! You guys have really grown up since I last saw you. Let me have a good look at you." Tears filled his eyes as he gazed at the boys he had not seen for two years.

Lunch was followed by a trip to the Lincoln Park Zoo. Most of the animals were inside that time of the year. The highlight was the Lion House. They were there at feeding time, where the lions' hungry roars echoed against the walls and caused the boys to move closer to their father. At 4:00 p.m. they took a cab to a nearby theater and saw the animated Disney film "*Dinosaur*."

After the movie, which had the boys frozen to their seats, they went to R.J. Grunts in Lincoln Park for dinner, known for its comfort food classics. Roy drew the boys out about their experiences at school, favorite teacher, least favorite teacher, volume and nature of homework, grades and after school sports. Rob, as usual, did most of the talking. He actually asked Roy why they had not heard from him for such a long time—such a long time that their mother thought he had gone to heaven. Roy explained he was extremely busy with business matters in the UP, and he wanted to give them a chance to get used to their new life in San Diego and their new relationship with Uncle Dan.

After dinner, they went back to the hotel and found a quiet spot in the lobby to continue their conversation.

"Remember my promise to take you on a fishing trip up north when you got older?"

"I sure do," Rob said."

"Well, I'm going to ask Mom to let you spend two weeks with me in the Upper Peninsula this summer."

"Yeah!" Rob shouted.

"What do you think of that, Ben?"

"Good."

"If Mom or Uncle Dan ask you about it, be sure to tell them you want to go."

"Will we go on a boat and fish?" Rob asked.

"From a boat and from the dock. There'll be swimming and speed boat rides. You'll have great fun. I'm going to call Uncle Dan to come down and get you now. Give me a hug and a kiss, guys. I won't be seeing you until the summer."

Both boys responded with hugs and kisses. Rob thanked him for coming to visit and said "I'm happy you're not in heaven."

After Dan took the boys away, Roy went into the bar for a double Grand Marnier in preparation for an early retirement and an early morning start for home. He sat on the bed and called Meg. He told her the visit was a big success, the kids were wonderful, he missed her and would be home tomorrow by mid-afternoon, at which time he'd fill her in on the details.

My kids with me in the UP. Roy felt he was on the cusp of having the best of everything.

CHAPTER SIXTY-THREE

The first major snowstorm of the winter started at about 3:00 a.m. By noon, eight inches of snow had fallen in the UP with no let-up expected until the evening hours. At 2:00 p.m. driving conditions in northern Wisconsin were hazardous with reports that it was going to get worse. Roy pulled into a motel where he would stay the night and resume his trip home when the sun rose. He left a message for Meg explaining his plan and said he'd be home tomorrow by noon. He'd stop somewhere and call her if he was delayed.

The sun shone bright in a cloudless sky the morning after the storm.

His four-wheel drive jeep enabled Roy to make it home by noon. Meg and the residents were having lunch in the early shift when he arrived, so he went directly to his office. He checked for phone calls while he was away and then glanced at yesterday's log. Noting Cal's entry about what looked like a Chevy, he recalled that Otto drove a Chevy and wondered whether it could have been Otto snooping around the property.

He stood when Meg walked in to receive her kiss and hug. Being separated for just one day reminded him of just how much he loved this girl.

"You're looking especially beautiful to me today. Next time I go anywhere, you're coming with."

"I'm so glad you're home. I must tell you about the call I got yesterday."

"Let's hear it."

"It was from Otto."

"Oh. What did he want?"

"I don't know what he wanted. He was angry—angry that I married you instead of him. He was angry at you as well. Threatening, really."

"What kind of threat?

"I can't recall exactly. He said he'd never forgive me and wouldn't stand for what you and I did to him. He didn't seem to remember that he and I had ended any remaining friendship we had at the time of your trial when he was abusing Dad."

"Otto has problems. I didn't tell you, the day before I left for the city he came to the front door asking to see you. Frank and I turned him away. As he left he was swearing, accusing me again of being a murderer."

"Do you think he could be dangerous?"

"You're the medical person. What do you think?"

"If he's psychotic, there's no telling what he might do—to himself or someone else. If he's just manic-depressive, that's something else. Whatever, he probably could use some therapy or medication."

"I'll tell Frank and Cal to keep an eye out for him."

"I have better news to tell you. Sweetheart, I'm pregnant."

"That's wonderful news. How do you know?"

"I did one of those tests and it was positive. I spoke to Doc

Hilliard while you were away. He's scheduling me for visits once a month, just to see that everything is going smoothly."

Roy put his good arm around Meg and held her close, whispering in her ear, "You are going to be a marvelous mother."

Roy told Meg about his visit and the plan to have the kids come north for two weeks in the summer. He had more concern about Otto than he let on to Meg. After she left to get ready for her afternoon clinic hours, he called Jesse Wickerham.

"Jesse, this is Roy. I'm calling to give you a heads up on Otto Lehman. He's been harassing Meg and me as well, with threats about getting even for being the cause of all his problems. He scared Meg with a phone call while I was out of town. He also might have been prowling around the property. I know he's just out of the mental ward and may be unpredictable."

"What do you expect me to do?"

"It's a small town. Just pay attention. Maybe you could speak to him, calm him down or speak to his parents to find out how he's doing. Maybe he needs to see the doctor again."

"I understand. I'll watch out for him."

"Thanks. Enough time has gone by, so you and I should be OK. I'm willing to forget the past and move forward. What do you think?"

"If you can forgive my being misguided by Lehman, then I think we should be OK."

CHAPTER SIXTY-FOUR

It was a hard winter, as most were in the UP. Snow drifts, accentuated by the plow, had narrowed the road to the house to one undersized lane, with only one turn-around carved out of the snow at the driveway to the Cooley cabin. The thaw began early, with temperatures reaching forty degrees a couple of days in mid-March. From the time of the first heavy storm in January to early March, 120 inches of snow had fallen, keeping the residents confined indoors, except for the few hearty soles who enjoyed romping in the snow in frigid temperatures. Roy and Meg realized they needed to be better prepared to occupy the women through the dreary winters. They would try to find an activities person to get on board in advance of next winter.

Emma had lost some ground over the winter, advancing from a cane to a walker, and spending more time in her cabin than in the house. Cal, on the other hand, was gaining in energy and agility. With little resistance from Frank, he had become the primary security person, confident in giving Frank directions. Roy heard nothing about Otto Lehman since his call to Deputy Wickerham.

* * *

The winter had been hard on the Lehman family. Father and son spending so much time together in the home was a recipe for chaos. Ludwig, Otto's father, was intoxicated with alcohol much of the time. He had always been a strict father, expecting obedience and respect from his son. Ludwig had no problem with Otto's depression, other than disappointment at his inability to cope, because he could simply be ignored. This post-hospital Otto could not be ignored. His anger was loud and went in many directions, mostly against those he determined had caused him to lose his job, his law license, the love of his life, and his sanity. When sober, Ludwig tried to urge him to forget the grievances of the past and think ahead to a better life. When drunk, which was more often the case, he would engage Otto in nonsensical arguments, sometimes leading to physical contact. His mother was a frightened soul, hiding in her bedroom whenever the arguments occurred.

One day in late February Deputy Wickerham was driving past the Lehman home when he saw Otto shoveling snow from the walkway between the house and the garage. He pulled over, opened his window and called Otto over.

"Better take it easy with that shovel. Don't want to overdo it."

Otto jammed the shovel into a snow drift, removed the muffler from around his mouth and leaned into Jesse's open window.

"Helps me get my mind off some shit. What's up?"

"I heard about your phone call to Meg Dennison. You said some stuff that scared her. What's that all about?"

"I was upset when I found out she married Dennison. She went and married a fucking murderer instead of me."

"You gotta get over that. She had the right to marry whoever she wanted. Don't you go doing anything stupid. You hear?"

"You know he murdered that girl, right?"

"Jury said no. Case closed."

"Bullshit. That fucking Cal Cooley refused to testify—refused to give us the motive we needed, and then you refused to back me up."

"No point in rehashing all that. Just be sure you behave yourself and don't cause anybody any trouble."

"Yeah. Sure. I get it. Just suck it up."

*   *   *

At 2:00 a.m. Cal was in his kitchen brewing a cup of tea for Emma, who was having trouble sleeping with an upset stomach. He heard sounds which caused him to move to his front window. There was a car with no headlights going round the turn-around. The half-moon reflecting off the remaining white snow provided Cal with some visibility. The car, which looked like the Chevy he had seen earlier, stopped on the asphalt facing Crooked Lake Road. The driver exited wearing a hooded sweatshirt and was walking toward the house carrying some kind of container. Cal immediately called Roy, the only other man on the property. Awakened by the first ring, Roy took the call quickly, hoping not to disturb Meg.

"Roy, it's Cal. There's some guy with a hood on walking down the road toward the house. He came out of that same Chevy. He's carrying some kind of container and obviously looking to cause trouble. I wouldn't be surprised if it's Otto."

"Thanks, Cal. You stay put. I'll handle it."

Roy didn't bother with shoes or any clothes other than the pajama bottoms he was wearing. He grabbed a flashlight and a pipe wrench and went to his front window. He saw the figure walking toward the house on the road. When forty yards from the house, he veered to his right and was walking across the slush-covered ground between the house and Roy's cabin. When he was within twenty yards of the cabin, Roy stepped out on the porch, turned his flashlight on the man and shouted—

"Otto, if you come any closer, I'm going to use this pipe wrench. Wickerham is already on his way, so you better get the hell out of here now."

Otto turned and started running toward the asphalt. He dropped the container as he ran down the road to his car. Cal watched his retreat. When the Chevy took off and disappeared he turned the porch light on and called Roy.

"What the hell was he doing?" Cal asked.

"Not sure. Thank goodness you were awake and saw him. I'll call Jesse in the morning. Go back to sleep."

Cal returned to the kitchen and Emma's tea.

In the morning, Roy recovered the container—a full two-gallon gasoline can. He called Wickerham and related the early morning events, identifying the figure as Otto.

"You've got to do something about this before something really bad happens. Maybe arrest him and charge him with attempted arson. Meg and I could have been burned up in a fire if Cal hadn't spotted him."

"I understand. Otto's got some loose wires. I'll talk to the County Prosecutor's office to see if they think there's enough for a charge. I'll get over to his folks place later today, tell them what happened, and urge them to get Otto some care."

"If you think that's enough."

"I don't know what else I can do at this point."

CHAPTER SIXTY-FIVE

April was a strange month in the UP. It was no longer winter, but not yet spring. Thawing snow and ice in mid-forties afternoon temperatures created slush and puddles of water everywhere making boots a requisite for foot travel. There was too much ice on the lakes for boats to go out and the ice was too thin to allow for ice fishing. The dimensions of open water on Crooked Lake were widening every day. It wouldn't be long before you would see catch and release guides exploring the lake for spots holding fish in preparation for the season's opening in May. There were no buds on the trees and the first robin had not yet been spotted, so Michiganders knew they were still subject to a winter resurgence.

Its first winter presented food challenges for the house. Emma was delighted that the Sysco Food Company had resumed deliveries to the UP in mid-March. Service had been suspended for thirty days due to weather and road conditions. During that suspension, Frank and Emma made weekly trips to Bessemer to purchase food. Frank would carry Emma from the jeep to a supermarket cart and back to the jeep when shopping was done.

The house was always at or near capacity, the average stay of residents being four to six weeks. Those who stayed longer seemed to fare better finding a place in society than those who impatiently cut their stay short. Roy and Meg were busy with their respective labors of love. All things considered, all was well at The Allison Jameson House.

Not so at the Lehman house. Otto and Ludwig were constantly at each other's throats. At one point Otto threatened his father with a baseball bat.

Ludwig wrestled his son to the floor and started choking him, until his screaming wife, Mary, grabbed hold of his hair with both hands and yanked with all her might. Ludwig rose up howling with pain, threw her to the floor, and stumbled out of the house. Fearing for her own life and desperate to get away from the two crazed men, she moved out and went to stay with her sister several houses down the street. In a moment of sobriety, Ludwig gave his son three days to find another place to live.

* * *

Dennison was opening the afternoon mail, when he noticed a letter bearing the return address of Senator Albert Jameson. He stared at the envelope and tried to imagine what kind of problem awaited him inside. His contemplation was interrupted by a call from Jesse Wickerham.

"Hello there, Mr. Dennison. Have you heard the news?"

"I guess not. What's the news?"

"You won't have to worry about Otto Lehman anymore."

"Why is that?"

"He shot and killed his father and then shot himself. He's dead."

"Wow! I knew he wasn't well, but this is something else. What about his mother?"

"She wasn't there. Deputy Luke is at their home. He responded to the 'shots heard' call. I'm just pulling up to the house. Archie and the state police are on their way. Knew you'd want to know. I'm cutting out."

Gruesome news, yet Dennison felt no sympathy for Otto. He went looking for Meg. She was busy with residents in her clinic, so he went to find Cal. He needed to share the news with someone. He found Cal at the front door.

"I just heard that Otto Lehman is dead. Killed his father and then shot himself."

"Oh my God. No, no—in little Watersmeet. How do you feel about that?"

"You know how I felt about Otto. He wasn't a good man, and then he became a sick man. I won't miss him—that's for sure. How about you?"

"I had nothing against him, except he was prosecuting you and trying to get me to help him. I never wished him dead. As for Ludwig—hard to see any man dead at the hands of his son."

Roy went back to his office and his mail. He opened Senator Jameson's letter.

> *Mr. Roy Dennison:*
>
> *I am enclosing herewith a check in the amount of $1,000,000, payable to The Allison Jameson House. This contribution is actually a return of a portion of the money you contributed to me in the lawsuit. Your acceptance of this money will constitute your agreement to name your recently constructed*

addition the MILDRED JAMESON ANNEX. Mildred
was Allison's mother and my daughter. I will expect you to send
me a photograph of a prominent sign attached to the building
displaying that name.
Senator Albert Jameson

Meg entered the office. "Lucy said you were looking for me."

"I want you to read this letter, but first I have some news. Otto Lehman is dead."

"What? What happened?"

"Shot his father and then shot himself. Both dead. Wickerham just called with the news."

"That's horrible. What about Mary?"

"Who's Mary?"

"Otto's mother."

"I guess she's OK. She wasn't there."

"That poor woman. Can you imagine? Losing your family like that. She's such a fragile soul. She'll never survive this," said Meg.

"They shouldn't have let Otto out. He was a sick man, a bomb ready to explode. Thank God he exploded at home and not in this house."

"Watersmeet won't get over this for a long time, if ever. I've been concerned about his anger and apprehensive it could erupt at any time. As terrible as this is, it does bring me a sense of relief. Should I feel bad about that?" asked Meg.

"Of course not. I feel the same way."

Roy embraced Meg with his good arm and kissed her forehead. He seated her in his desk chair and placed the Senator's letter in front of her.

"Now, read this."

Meg read each word, mouthing the words until her mouth formed a wide smile.

"This is marvelous. What a wonderful thing for the Senator to do."

"I agree. There's no forgiveness that comes with this contribution. You can tell that from the tone. That's OK. I don't expect it and don't deserve it."

"You do deserve it but I agree you shouldn't expect it from him. I'll find a sign maker in Bessemer and you respond immediately with thanks and acceptance of his terms."

CHAPTER SIXTY-SIX

It was May 1, the one-year anniversary of his release from Parnall. Dennison had accomplished a great deal in that past year. The house was operating at full capacity with additional staff, including another registered nurse being trained to share clinic responsibilities, as Meg's first baby was expected to arrive in about six months.

Dan Rogers called to announce tentative plans for the boys to visit the UP the first two weeks of August. Jessica was given the option to go to the UP or join her mother and Uncle Dan on the Alaska cruise. She chose the cruise.

Dennison received an unexpected call from Arnold Bender, Chairman of the Gogebic County Board of Commissioners.

"Congratulations on your Allison Jameson House project. You're filling a desperate need for the community."

"Thank you for that. Nice of you to call."

"Am I correct in assuming you are now a permanent resident of Gogebic County?"

"Yes, sir, you are correct."

"Good. I've been looking into your background a bit and see you were not only a successful attorney, but also served on the Illinois Governor's Economic Development Commission."

"You're correct on that as well. What can I do for you, Mr.

Bender?"

"I have to fill a vacancy on the Gogebic County Planning Commission and would like you to take that spot."

"Thank you for thinking of me. What kind of time commitment is involved?"

"Monthly meetings at the Gogebic County Court House in Bessemer, and whatever work flows from those meetings. You'd be working with others to plan for the economic development of the county. I'm sure your input would be of great value."

"I'm sure flattered you'd think of me."

"You understand there's no monetary compensation for the position. Your reward is knowing you're giving of your time and expertise to improve the economy and the lives of the residents of the community."

"I'm tempted to accept your offer right now, still I think I should confer with my wife before giving you a final answer."

"Since you show interest, I'll clear my suggestion with the Commission, so we're ready to go when you are. Thank you in advance for your participation."

Dennison knew Meg would be all for the idea. Clearing it with her was just a matter of showing her proper respect. As he left the house and headed for his cabin, he thought, *Just like Cal said, giving is a wonderful thing. It helps make life worthwhile.*

* * *

By mid-May, the snow, ice and slush were gone. Spring was well underway. The lake was sprinkled with boats participating in opening day fishing. Roy asked Frank to get the boats out of dry dock. Residents were walking the asphalt road, lounging on the porch and patio, and sitting on the dock. Good news was Rob and Ben would be visiting the UP August 1—14.

Roy and Meg had attended the funeral of the Lehmans, held in the small Lutheran church in Watersmeet. The preacher spoke a few words about the tragic circumstances of the Lehmans' deaths..When the preacher reminded those in attendance of how steadfast and devoted a wife and mother she was, Mary dropped her face into her hands and began alternately sobbing and crying out her grief. Meg rose, whispered to Roy "I have to", and went to sit next to Mary. She had known Mary since she was a preschooler and had become close to her when her friendship with Otto blossomed. She put her arm around her and kissed her forehead. She stayed like that until the service was over.

On the way home, Meg had not yet recovered from the emotions ignited by the service.

"Mary's going to need some help surviving all of this. Is there something we can do?" Meg asked.

"Do you have something in mind?"

"I'm not sure. She's going to need some activity to occupy her interest and make her life worth living."

"Man, do I ever understand what you're saying. Does she drive a car?"

"Yes, I'm sure she does. Why do you ask?"

"Maybe you can figure out some way we can use her at the house?"

"I'm glad you said it before I did."

*   *   *

One morning, two of the residents were returning from a walk down the asphalt road. As they were approaching the Cooley turn-around a mature male black bear trotted out from behind the Cooley cabin onto the road. He stopped there, facing the women, no more than twenty yards from them. The women, though fearing for their lives, followed instructions in their admission orientation, and stood motionless while screaming at the top of their lungs. The bear took two steps toward them, then stopped and uttered a low-level growl. Frank was at the front door of the house and saw what was happening. He ran to the kitchen, grabbed two fry pans and raced down the road screaming and slamming the pans together, making a racket that caused the bear to leap off the road and disappear into the woods. The adventure made for great story telling at the afternoon meal.

CHAPTER SIXTY-SEVEN

Roy received Rob and Ben at O'hare, stayed overnight in a motel near Lake Geneva, and arrived at the house with them in time for dinner on August 2. They stayed in the second bedroom in Roy's cabin. On the ride up, Roy explained that Meg was his wife and they'd notice she has a big tummy because she's due to have a baby pretty soon. "That baby will be your half-brother or half-sister." The boys showed interest in Meg's condition and were excited to feel the baby moving.

This was promised to be a fishing trip for the boys, and so it was. Every day, except the day it stormed, Roy and Cal took them out on the pontoon at 10:00 a.m. for two hours. Roy operated the boat and Cal did the fishing instruction. Their education started with still fishing with live bait, mainly worms. It took a while before they were comfortable with handling the worms and piercing the barb of the hook all the way through. They learned how the spin casting reel worked. Roy marveled at the patience of Cal in dealing with the distractions and fidgeting common in boys their age. They took to Cal. Bonding was evident on the first day.

The boys grew to love Auntie Meg, as they called her. They imitated their father in treating her delicate condition with kindness and care.

By the last day of fishing the boys, especially Rob, had advanced to casting artificial lures toward the shoreline with some degree of accuracy and competence. They pulled in several bass, two being keeper size. Many pictures were taken to take home and show Mom. After lunch they went for speed boat rides on the Chris-Craft and spent the remaining hour before dinner on their own, fishing off the dock.

On the morning of the 13th Roy and the boys were ready to head back to Chicago. After one more touch of Meg's tummy and a kiss on her cheek, and a left-handed handshake with Cal, they were on their way.

After a night in the airport hotel, they arrived at the gate at noon. Roy looked proudly at his seasoned travelers, each toting their own backpack.

"This was a great trip. Next summer, again, for some serious fishing," Roy said.

"I loved casting for the bass. That's what I want to do," Rob said.

"What about you, Ben? What was your favorite?"

"I like fishing from the dock."

"We'll do it all next summer. Cal will be ready for you, and so will your half-sister or half-brother. Kisses and hugs and off you go. Mom and Uncle Dan will be waiting for you when you land." The airline agent took one in each hand and guided them to the plane.

* * *

The Dennisons' baby girl arrived on time. They officially named her Calma as a tribute to Meg's parents, fully intending her to be called Callie throughout her life. Meg had been active in her duties at the house until two weeks before delivery, when the seven and a half pounds of Calma began to take a toll.

The boys summertime trips to the UP continued for the next four years. At age fifteen, Rob had become an accomplished junior golfer, committed in the spring and summer of 2005 to competing in junior tournaments throughout southern California. That ended his trips to the UP and, unfortunately, Ben's as well. Rob wrote to his father, explaining why he and Ben would not be coming north in the summer, and added the following:

> *This past year I've had access to the internet and learned a bit about your history in the UP and the trial. I asked Mom about it and she gave me a transcript of your testimony. I want you to know I believe this whole thing was an accident. Let me know if you would like me to talk to Ben about it and give him the transcript. I now have my own mobile phone. 618-432-8737. I love you—Rob*

Roy promptly called Rob, thanked him for his understanding and told him to share the information with Ben. That night he proudly read Rob's letter to Meg.

"That's some maturity for a fifteen-year-old," Meg said.

* * *

In 2006, Roy and Meg were ready for a vacation. They planned a late summer, early fall trip to Yosemite National Park and then down to San Diego where they would attend Rob's graduation from high school. Emma was tasked with minding five-year-old Callie in their absence.

They flew to Yosemite and two days later rented a car and drove the 400 miles to San Diego. During the drive, Roy sensed Meg's atypical quietness portended something troubling her.

"Why so quiet?"

"Just wondering how you feel about seeing Clara after all these years."

Roy's thoughts had been centered on seeing his kids, especially Jessica.

"Haven't given Clara hardly any thought. I'd bet she's kept herself together pretty good. Clara always took pains to keep herself neat and trim. You know, with the hair, the nails, even the toenails."

"Nothing like me, huh?"

"That's for sure. Thank God, you're nothing like that. Sweetheart, I love you just the way you are—precious and natural."

"I'm a little nervous that I'm not going to be dressed properly."

"Don't worry about that. No need for us to be fancy. You'll be just fine."

* * *

The Rogers and Dennisons were seated apart in the assembly hall at the graduation ceremony. They didn't see each other until they met in the corridor outside the hall, waiting for Rob to appear. Roy introduced Meg to Clara and Dan. They engaged in awkward small talk until thankfully interrupted by Ben and Jessica coming toward them through the crowd. Ben arrived first. "Hey, slugger, how's my boy?" He kissed his Dad and Meg. "You've grown some in two years. You're just as tall as Meg."

Roy saw ten-year-old Jessica for the first time since she was a toddler. As he moved to greet her, she drew back with eyes down, no recognition, seemingly intimidated by this tall stranger with a scar under his eye.

"Jessica, darling, this is your Daddy," Clara said.

Dennison was sad to see his own daughter cower to avoid contact with him. How could he have gone more than eight years without seeing this beautiful child? Was it a simple case of out of sight, out of mind? Or was it something more—a character flaw, indifference, maybe selfishness? *I better make something of this*, he thought, *I don't know when I'll ever see her again.*

"Jessica, I've missed you so much."

Encouraged by her mother, Jessica took his hand. As he walked her toward a quieter place where they could sit and talk, Jessica turned and looked apprehensively at her mother, who was nodding her head up and down.

"Sweetheart, I remember when you were born, just a baby and then when you first started to walk. You were beautiful then and even more beautiful now. I've been away ever since then, far up north. I should've made trips to see you, but I didn't, and that was my mistake. I'm asking you to forgive me for that mistake. Could you do that?"

"I forgive you. What's wrong with your arm?"

"Had an accident and it doesn't work very well anymore. Thank you for asking."

"I had an accident with my arm once, but it got all better."

"Can I ask you for one more favor?"

"Sure."

"Can I give you a little hug and a kiss on your cheek?"

"OK."

As Jessica submitted to Roy's kiss, Rob came by, still in his graduation gown.

"Hey, Dad, great to see you."

"Congratulations, buddy. Proud of you. What are your plans for college?"

"I got a partial golf scholarship to the University of San Diego. I could stay at home it's so close, but I don't want to. The campus is beautiful and I'll be staying in a dorm."

"Sounds good. Are we ever going to fish together again?"

"Maybe. I hope so. Next summer I'll be playing in some national junior tournaments that will likely take me into the Midwest. Maybe we can work something out."

"Let me know your tournament schedule. I'd love to follow you on the golf course, if that's possible."

"It's possible. There may be a tournament in Michigan."

"Any idea what you want to do when you're done with school?"

"First, I want to see how far I can go with golf. Will I be good enough to make a living at it? We'll see."

CHAPTER SIXTY-EIGHT

The Rogers' home was located in Rancho Santa Fe, a swanky neighborhood just east of Del Mar, a twenty-minute drive from the Dennisons' hotel in San Diego proper. The home was lavish with a large pool encircled by patio. Rob was off to a graduation party with friends. Ben and Jessica were changing for the pool. Dan took Meg for a tour of the house. Roy and Clara sat at an umbrella table by the pool with their cocktails.

"You've got a great-looking place here, and you're looking pretty good yourself," Roy said.

"Sorry, I can't say the same for you. You look like shit."

"What a thing to say—even if it's true."

"Your wifey looks a little young for you. What is there, a thirty-year difference?"

"Actually, twenty. You still angry about us?"

"Not us—you. So angry I could spit every time I think about how you shattered my life, my heart. I'll never forget it and I'll never forgive you."

Roy stood and moved close to Clara's chair. He hovered over her.

"I don't need your forgiveness. I've already forgiven myself. That's what you need to do. It's not good for you to live with all this hate and anger. Believe me, I know what it can do to you."

"Does she ever ask you about Allison? Does she believe you?"

"You know what? I'll wait until the kids come out so I can say goodbye. We'll leave then and head back to our hotel. This is no good."

Nasty as she was, Roy empathized with Carla. She couldn't help herself. She hadn't found the blessing of forgiveness, and maybe she never would.

* * *

On their early morning flight to Chicago, where his jeep was waiting in the long-term parking lot, Roy was reflecting on their visit to San Diego.

"The kids are good. Did you notice how good-looking Ben is becoming?"

"Yes. He's a handsome boy."

"Got a lot of Clara in him. Seems like she's done a damn good job raising them."

"You should be very proud."

"Proud of them, not of myself. I feel like I abandoned my daughter. How could I have let that happen?"

"Circumstances. The last ten years of your life have been full of restricting circumstances and limited options. You've done the best you could. Little Jessica also had options. Don't beat yourself up over it. You'll see her again and again. I'll see to that."

"If you say you will, I know you will."

"Do you think Clara will ever get over her anger?"

"Probably not. It's not in her nature to let things go—c'est la vie."

It was an exhausting travel day. They sat quietly listening to classical music during the last two hours of their seven-hour drive, following their four-hour flight. It was a few minutes before 9:00 p.m. when they arrived at the lake. Meg went directly to their cabin while Roy went to check in at the house. Lucy Devonshire was standing on the porch as Meg approached.

"Oh, Meg! Something awful. Cal had another stroke yesterday. He's in a coma in Minocqua. Emma is there with him and she's been with him since it happened. I've been with Callie since Emma left."

Roy heard Lucy's report as he was entering the cabin.

"Come on Meg, let's go."

Meg ran to check on Callie and found her fast asleep. She and Roy then headed for the door.

"Where are you going?" asked Lucy.

"To be with Emma," Roy said.

"It's too late—wait until morning," but they were gone.

Meg was sobbing as they undertook the one-hour drive to the Minocqua Medical Center.

"I can't stand the thought of Mom being there alone with Dad in an unconscious state all this time."

"Hopefully, his coma will be temporary. Maybe he'll be out of it by the time we get there."

"Please, God, let it be so."

It was not so.

Arriving at the center, they went directly to Cal's ICU room. He was unconscious with tubes coming out of his face. Emma was asleep in her chair, undisturbed by the periodic hum of the breathing machinery. The ICU nurse explained that Cal was still in a coma. They met outside the room with the doctor on duty in ICU.

"Are you next of kin?"

"I'm his son-in-law. That's his daughter, Meg."

"Mr. Cooley had massive intracranial bleeding. I'm sorry, but the prognosis is not good. He may not survive. If he does, it will be with profound residuals."

Meg felt like she was going to pass out and headed for a seat.

"What does 'profound residuals' mean?" Roy asked.

"Any one or more of being unable to walk, think, speak, see, hear, control his bladder or bowel. Not good, I'm afraid."

"Do you expect him to come out of this coma at some point?" Roy asked.

"Unfortunately, there's no way to know if or when that might happen."

Roy took a seat on the small sofa next to Meg. The doctor followed him and stood before them.

"Mr. Cooley is on a ventilator. He needs assistance with his breathing. I'm glad you're here. His wife has been inconsolable ever since they arrived. I have not given her the report I just gave to you. I gave her a second tranquilizer a couple of hours ago. She's been asleep since then. I'll let you explain how dire the situation is, unless you want me to."

"We'll handle that," Roy said.

"I recommend you take her home. We'll call you when there's any change."

They returned to the ICU room. Meg went to the bedside, took Cal's limp hand in hers and quietly said, "I love you Dad. Please come back to us." She then joined Roy at Emma's side. They gently woke her, saying it was time to go home.

"Oh Meg—Meg. He's still unconscious. What am I going to do without him?"

"He's resting quietly. It's time for us to go home. We'll come back soon."

Emma slept in the back seat the whole ride home. When they arrived at the property, they went directly to their cabin. Lucy was waiting for them.

"How's he doing?"

"No change. Prognosis is not good," Roy said quietly.

They insisted Emma stay with them. She resisted only mildly and fell asleep on the couch in the living room, where she remained all night. Roy and Meg were wiped out at the end of the longest day of their lives.

The phone rang at 5:30 a.m. Roy was in a light sleep and answered after the first ring.

"This is the ICU nurse at the center. I'm sorry to report that Mr. Cooley passed about forty minutes ago. He never awoke from his coma. His passing was peaceful. Please call to advise as to arrangements for the body."

There was no need to wake Meg or Emma with the news at this hour. He let them sleep as they needed the rest. Wouldn't make any difference. The news had him wide awake. He made himself a coffee and began to research the UP for funeral parlors. As he contemplated the future of this family without Cal, he thought, *Passing this way saved Emma and Meg from having to make a life-ending decision.*

Sitting with coffee and toast at the kitchen table, the news having been shared and wept over, Emma revealed Cal's preference after death.

"We never talked much about dying. He didn't have any will. He told me more than once he didn't want there to be any fussin'. He wanted to be cremated and wanted his ashes spread around Crooked Lake."

"Then that's what we'll do. Agreed?" Roy asked. Both women agreed. "With your permission, I'll call Jefferson and make arrangements. Meg, why don't you and Emma compose an obituary for the *Watersmeet News.*"

* * *

At 7:00 a.m. on a cool morning in early October, before any boats were stirring up the lake, Roy, Meg, Emma and Frank walked down the steps to the dock. Roy led the way, carrying an ornate plastic container. Meg followed him and then came Frank, carefully walking the steep stairs with Emma in his arms. The lake was calm with a morning haze still suspended several feet above the water's surface. They heard the lonesome wail of the loon in the distance as they boarded the pontoon and went out on the lake with Cal. They each took a turn distributing his ashes at three spots on the lake which Roy recalled were among Cal's favorites. As they watched the last of the ashes slowly descend, Meg said, "Goodbye, Daddy." After several moments of contemplative silence, Frank said,

"I'm gonna miss him. He was always nice to me."

"I'll bet them walleyes are the only ones happy he's gone. He used to decimate them," Emma said with a smile.

CHAPTER SIXTY-NINE

Emma moved all her things out of her cabin and into Roy's, becoming roommates with Callie in the second bedroom. Roy had a plan for more construction in the spring. He would add a third bedroom and second bathroom to his cabin. He also planned to add a four-bedroom, two-bathroom extension to the Cooleys' cabin, making space for eight more residents.

The Dennisons welcomed the new year with the news of Meg's second pregnancy. This time they decided to learn the baby's sex in advance. In early March, an ultrasound performed in Eagle River reported a boy was coming, prematurely named Roy Jr.

* * *

The construction projects commenced in late April and were completed by mid-July. Roy distributed a flyer throughout the house, announcing a memorial service for Cal would be held at the turn-around on Sunday, October 15, at 4:00 p.m.

It was a warm, sunny fall day as people began to gather at the turn-around. By 4:00 p.m. most of the residents were there, along with Meg and Emma, who now used a wheelchair when she was away from the house or cabin. Also present were Lucy Devonshire, Mary Lehman, who had become the activities lady, deputies Wickerham and Luke and eighty-eight-year-old Bert Clinton, who had retired and closed his bait stand at the end of the last season.Roy had Meg sitting on the cabin's porch. She was in full bloom, ready and anxious to welcome Roy Jr. to the world at any moment. The turn-around was full with people spilling out onto the asphalt.

Roy ascended the two steps to the porch and started the proceedings.

"Thank you all for being here for Cal. We all loved him. What about that Jesse?" Roy shouted out to Wickerham who was standing back near the asphalt.

"He was an OK guy in my book," Jesse shouted back.

"None of us would be here today if it wasn't for the inspiration of Cal Cooley. It was his philosophy of life that lifted me out of a deep, dark hole and led to the creation of this house. My personal debt to Cal is immeasurable. In a sense, I asked his permission to marry his daughter. He granted that request, thank God, and any request I ever made of him. He loved this house and all the people in it. Most of all, he loved his Emma and his Meg. He was taken from us much, much too soon. To remind us always of his contribution to the success of The Allison Jameson House, we make this dedication."

Roy then climbed a short ladder and nailed a sign above the steps to the porch which read *CAL COOLEY CABIN.*

* * *

In August of 2007, after celebrating Roy Jr.'s one year birthday party, Roy and Meg were on their way to Traverse City to follow Rob's play in a national junior tournament at Suttons Bay Golf Course.

EPILOGUE

Roy Dennison reached his seventy-second birthday in 2021. He took the steps to the dock more slowly and carefully than he used to. Walking along the dock toward his bench, he still peered into the deepening water to see what new underwater mysteries may have appeared since yesterday.

As a member of the Gogebic County Planning Commission, Dennison was largely responsible for establishing the Gogebic County airport, now featuring daily flights to Chicago and Minneapolis. Meg was on her way there now with the kids and their mates, having completed their two-week summer vacation to the UP.

Rob, still single, would be returning to Palm Springs where he was assistant pro at a posh country club, having never got close to qualifying for the PGA Tour. Ben was married to a lovely girl, Clarice. No children yet but trying. Jessica, now age twenty-five, married to Aaron Fielder, a West Hollywood stock broker, was four months into her first pregnancy. In the past fifteen years the kids or combinations of them had come to the UP six times. Meg had fulfilled her promise to Roy by making sure he and Jessica kept in regular contact

Poor Emma died of a heart attack four years previously. She was cremated and her ashes spread in the same locations on the lake as Cal's. Once Emma was gone, Roy and Meg felt they were free to travel. They hired a professional administrator for the house., and the clinic was run by a young doctor in-house after Doc Hilliard passed away.

Roy purchased a Lincoln Continental for their travels throughout the country the full year of 2020. Callie was attending the University of Wisconsin in Madison most of that year, while Roy Jr. remained at home under the watchful eyes of Mary Lehman as he attended Watersmeet Township High School. Before these road trips, Meg had been nowhere other than San Diego. They started out to Niagara Falls, then through New England, from Maine to Massachusetts, down the East Coast to Savannah, the Carolinas, all the way to Naples, Florida and then New Orleans. They worked their way as far west as the Grand Canyon before starting for home, going through Chicago, where they stopped for a while to visit Clyde, and in Grand Rapids to have lunch with Mark Travis. Then home to the UP.

Sitting on his bench, lighting up a cigar, a habit he picked up in New Orleans, Roy's thoughts turned to the past and all he had gone through, and to Clara. He was sure that Clara's pre-occupation with hate and anger contributed to causing her early onset dementia. *Dan must really have his hands full with that,* he thought.

It was warm for late August. A gentle breeze was coming off the lake. Roy could hear the chatter of fishermen anchored off the island. Canada geese were beginning to gather and form order in the distance. The faint sound of their honking was a reminder that fall was approaching.

He turned when he heard someone on the steps. It was Meg.

He watched her glide down the steps with a big smile on her face. She seemed happy to be coming to be with him. He was happy too.

ABOUT THE AUTHOR

P.M. Berk is the pseudonym for the author, living in Itasca, Illinois with his wife, Nancy. He is a retired trial lawyer who started writing fiction during a covid isolation. His next novel to be published is *The Last of the Clevengers* — the story of a lawyer whose impotency controlled and almost destroyed his life.

Made in the USA
Monee, IL
11 February 2023

27586810R00197